# FEMINIST

# ♀FATALE

# FEMINIST

## ♀FATALE

Voices from the
"Twentysomething" Generation
Explore the Future of the
"Women's Movement"

*by Paula Kamen*

DONALD I. FINE, INC.
NEW YORK

Library of Congress Cataloging-in-Publication Data
Kamen, Paula.
Feminist fatale / Paula Kamen.
p.      cm.
ISBN 1-55611-256-4—ISBN 1-55611-257-2 (pbk.)
1. Feminism—United States.   I. Title.
HQ1421.K25   1991
305.42′0973—dc20          90-56063
CIP

Manufactured in the United States of America

10   9   8   7   6   5   4   3   2   1

Designed by Irving Perkins Associates

Grateful acknowledgment is made for permission to reprint excerpts from the
following copyrighted works.

*Feminist Theory: From Margin to Center* by Bell Hooks. Copyright 1984.
By permission of South End Press.

*The Sisterhood* by Marcia Cohen. Copyright 1988. By permission
of Simon and Schuster.

"Diving into the Wreck" from *The Fact of A Doorframe: Poems Selected Old and New
1950 to 1984* by Adrienne Rich, are reprinted with the permission of the author and
the publisher, W.W. Norton & Company, Inc. Copyright © 1984 by Adrienne Rich.
Copyright © 1975, 1978 by W.W. Norton & Company, Inc. Copyright © 1981 by
Adrienne Rich.

"Feminism: Still Hazy After All These Years" by Felicia Kornbluh. Copyright 1991.
Reprinted with permission of *Tikkun,* a bimonthly Jewish critique of politics,
culture and society based in Oakland, California.

# Acknowledgments

Thanks most of all to Steve Rhodes, for being a voice of conscience, criticism and feminist mentorship since Day One at Allen Hall. Abundant thanks to my agent Laura Gross and Norman Solomon for your confidence and guidance and making this book possible. Great thanks also to editor Lisa Eskow for your enthusiasm and insight.

Thanks to the following people who gave me eyes and ears and contacts across the country, including: Farnaz Fatemi of the Santa Cruz bureau, Mary Servatius of the Chicago bureau, Mary Dowd of the San Francisco bureau, Anna Minkov of the Cincinnati bureau, Carla Pommert-Cherry of the Texas bureau and Jenny Kauss of the kingpin Danville, Illinois bureau. Also thanks to Nadia Moritz, Tammy Gouldstone, Fatima Cortez, Virginia Volker, Julie Spencer Robinson, Florence Parry Heide, Chris Heide, Patricia Solomon, Bridget Johnson, Laura Tarantini, Rachel Stoll, Dawn at Gateway, Chrills, Adrienne Kneeland and Chris, the Grande Prairie Library reference staff, Kristen Walsh, professor Jo Thomas, all of the people at non-profits I bothered for statistics, the makers of Eight O'Clock Bean; Rebecca and Michael Kamen; and my parents.

And thanks to the generous sponsors who granted me deluxe futon or sofa use during my travels: Anna, Steve, Karen, Kathy, Rachel, Laura, Jenny, Dan, Paula, Ann, Farnaz, Eric, Liesel and Becky.

# Contents

the Night   ♀   Pro-Choice   ♀   Youth Groups   ♀
Oral History   ♀   A Chasm

**STUDENT ORGANIZING**   ♀   Abortion-Rights Activists   ♀
NARAL: Building Coalitions   ♀   Students Organizing
Students   ♀   Other National Campus Networks   ♀
Acquaintance Rape Battles   ♀   Men Stopping Rape
♀   More Mainstream   ♀   **OFF-CAMPUS ACTIVISM**   ♀
Conferences As Barometers   ♀   NOW   ♀   Young
Women's Groups   ♀   Direct Action   ♀   Fighting
Poverty   ♀   Labor Organizing   ♀   **WOMEN OF COLOR**   ♀
Activism Through Art   ♀   Three Seeds Planted   ♀
**CAREER ACTIVISM**

*There is a ladder.*
*The ladder is always there*
*hanging innocently*
*close to the side of the schooner.*
*We know what it is for,*
*we who have used it.*
*Otherwise*
*it's a piece of maritime floss*
*some sundry equipment.*

—ADRIENNE RICH
*"Diving into the Wreck"*
(1972)

# No Stigmas Attached

IN THE EARLY 1970s, feminists rallied under the self-assured slogan "Sisterhood Is Powerful." Nearly twenty years later, as I contemplated my generation—the twentysomething generation of young women—I found myself wondering if sisterhood was even possible.

While I was in college at the University of Illinois, it struck me that instead of "sisterhood," the word that more accurately summed up the condition of young women and feminism was "isolation." I quickly learned that taking a stand on anything even remotely construed as a women's issue aroused strange and strong suspicions.

As a columnist for the *Daily Illini* student newspaper, I found myself addressing feminist-oriented concerns, partly because they were not being covered by other columnists on the opinions page. These "women's issues" that were being labeled "fringe" topics—violence against women, reproductive rights, sexism—were the same ones that people across campus were debating and personally confronting in their lives.

I thought I could escape the feminist stigma by buffering these columns with other topics, but still, by the time my second "women's" column appeared in the fall of 1988, I was branded. People I met began to treat me like a radical separatist Marxist; a co-columnist labeled me "feminist fatale." A friend alerted me that when she mentioned my name in conversation to her fellow engineering majors they recoiled in horror and asked, "Isn't she a *feminist?*" Others asked why I suddenly hated men so much. Even when I retreated home for the

1

holidays, certain folks in my neighborhood cautioned that I was jeopardizing my future by scaring off potential male suitors.

Although at the time I myself was struggling to overcome many of the stereotypes of feminism, I wondered why and how this stigma had become so powerful. I didn't know if I was alone in confronting doubts about speaking out on "women's" issues. Were people at other schools experiencing the same backlash? I wondered if other young feminists were connecting with each other on a larger scale and, if so, how I could learn from them.

Looking beyond my vast Big Ten campus in the middle of east central Illinois cornfields, I found no answers. There was no public dialogue—by, for or about young feminists; during our "coming of age" years from 1980 to 1990, young feminists didn't seem to exist.

Since then, my feminist consciousness has grown, as has my bewilderment at the apparent absence of a vocal young feminist voice. Unable to define us simply, some outsiders have recently referred to my age group as "the new lost generation"; but regarding the women's movement, we seem to be more like "the missing generation." Young feminists have been remarkably unchronicled and, as a result, misunderstood—along with the general age group of twentysomethings, who have all quietly assumed adulthood in the shadow of the older, more demographically correct Baby Boomers.

Other young women I have interviewed for this book felt as if they were hunting for four-leaf clovers in the wilderness during their own searches for answers in newspapers, popular books, scholarly research and texts. Young feminist voices as authors in debate have been scarce. We have only served as serious laboratory subjects for a handful of older sociologists.

Part of the reason young feminists have gone unrecognized for so long by others is that we have been dismissed along with the rest of the women's movement. The mainstream media has declared the movement either dead on arrival or unnecessary in this "postfeminist" age. Also, feminist magazines and newspapers have hardly touched upon the issue of passing the torch to the next generation. As older feminists grapple with their identity crisis, younger feminists suffer from a lack of one.

Even at the grandiose NOW (National Organization for Women) march for abortion rights in April 1989, there was only one young speaker on the program during the three-and-a-half-hour final rally. She was finally granted the microphone two hours after the rally began, after all the celebrities and politicians and older feminists had spoken and most reporters had left to meet deadlines. It was an ironic outcome, considering the purpose of the day was to address a topic that more directly affects young women—who composed a great number of those attending the march—than any other age group.

Even younger women who have been vocal addressing a variety of political issues through the Reagan-Bush era suddenly seem to shy away from strongly making their voices heard as *women*. The staunchest feminist activists have admitted to me some initial fear of speaking up because of lack of confidence and fear of disapproval.

Perhaps we have ourselves begun to believe we have no authority to speak. We have too much credibility to risk sounding naive among those more streetwise and sophisticated feminists. Even at a breakthrough regional conference I attended in 1990 for and by East Coast young feminists, older women were the dominant speakers and young women had scarce time to debate.

During the time I spent researching and conducting interviews for this book, I found that despite the lack of popular dialogue, women and men of all ages are becoming increasingly politically active and aware of feminism, and they are asking these questions: Who are we, and how do we fit into this unfinished, misunderstood and graying movement? What are our perceptions and special needs and approaches and politics and prejudices and loyalties and distortions and connections to others?

Finding answers to these questions is an urgent first step in planning for the future of the women's movement and safeguarding past progress. After all, young people are the single greatest natural resource of the women's movement. It's time to step forward and talk to each other. Then we can reevaluate and redefine feminism as a force to unite us, rather than a source of suspicion and divisiveness.

On the surface, the need for a dialogue between and about young feminists may not seem necessary, as some I interviewed have said. In the interviews I conducted, as well as in polls by publications such as *Time* magazine and the *New York Times,* young women have shown they support the feminist political agenda, appreciate the strides made by the women's movement and know instinctively that men and women are entitled to the same opportunities. Since 1989 young feminist activists have been awakened and galvanized by threats to abortion rights.

Other action by young feminist activists—most of it not taking the visible form of protests—is steadily increasing: working within older women's organizations, educating and lobbying from campuses, mobilizing communities at a grass-roots level and taking the lead in other progressive struggles, including environmental and antiracism work.

But something vital and fundamental is missing for many people with an interest in feminism: good old-fashioned consciousness-raising. Older women forget that we are generally missing that key element that fueled the older generation twenty years ago, both informally and formally, around kitchen tables and in organized coalitions. I have read accounts from the Sixties and Seventies exalting this phenomenon and its power. Women rhapsodize about how they learned to ask new questions about themselves, built self-esteem and a sense of entitlement to opportunity, gave names to their common experiences and discovered that they were not alone. Consciousness-raising was a foundation for change from that point on. This new exhilaration spurred a revolution in attitudes, a lot of rage and a rush in political action.

"It makes you very sensitive—raw, even—this consciousness," said Robin Morgan in her now classic anthology *Sisterhood Is Powerful*. "Everything, from the verbal assault on the street, to a 'well-meant' sexist joke your husband tells, to the lower pay you get at work (for doing the same job a man would be paid more for), to television commercials, to rock-song lyrics, to the pink or blue blanket they put on your infant in the hospital nursery."

For our generation now, consciousness-raising could revive us spiritually, emotionally and politically. It might also provide urgent relief from a pervasive and profound sense of isolation. For better and for worse, we have been raised on the tenets of the American Dream and its rigid ideology of self-reliance and individualism. As a result, any problems we face, we blame on our own inadequacies. Seeking outside support translates into admitting weakness. I witnessed this line of thinking during my interviews for this book. I interviewed one woman who was battered by her husband and said she didn't go for help because she thought that was what all marriages were like; a single mother explained that she didn't seek emotional support from peers because it made her seem unable to make it on her own. Consciousness-raising can remind us all that we are not alone; others go through similar experiences.

At the same time, the process also reveals important differences that have to be recognized in order for the movement to succeed, such as the special needs and perceptions of the various racial groups who help constitute the movement. Without this struggle, without looking at ourselves and those around us, without relieving our isolation, we fail to exploit our greatest potential for power: organizing.

Young women—who are the single mothers (composing one-third of single women eighteen to thirty-four); the ones trying to pay for child care while making minimum wage at Hardee's; the ones being assaulted in the streets and in their homes; the ones being paid 30 percent less than their male peers at all levels; the ones being stripped of their most fundamental reproductive freedoms—deserve and need a collective voice. If we just look to each other for support, we can have an influence on politics, what happens in the media, in our family realms, on the places in which we work.

While exploring the meaning of feminism, we are also creating the potential for change by examining what we stand for. Taking women seriously becomes one more factor, one more value guiding our decisions. This transforms the passive thoughts of believing in equality to actually doing something about it, even if only in the most individual and routine ways.

Too often, members of the older generation expect us to cruise on autopilot and organize to build upon their progress without ever going through the basic training of consciousness-raising. They forget their long, often deliberate process of self- and social discovery and how crucial it was in motivating their actions. We can't undergo personal and political transformations just by existing or picking up a textbook about past injustices. We need to talk to others and challenge ourselves introspectively too.

We also can't wait until we get older and our bad experiences radicalize us, as some prominent feminists, such as Gloria Steinem, have reasoned. Just having problems doesn't bestow the tools to confront them. It's better to be prepared with self-esteem, knowledge of resources and networks, and a sense of strength to fight back. Furthermore, the great majority of people I've interviewed don't need to wait to discover conflicts related to sexism. All of us—even the college students at the most elite of schools—aren't as sheltered as we look.

Once the process of self-discovery is complete, consciousness-raising can be utilized to shed light on feminist history, which fuels action and reasserts the true meaning and purpose of the movement. The past is vital not only to the present, but also to the future. We need knowledge to pass on to our daughters and sons so that they can enforce the rights that already have been won.

In the past, feminists have made the mistake of ignoring this key factor and, as a result, every generation has had to start almost from scratch.

In her book *Feminist Theory: The Intellectual Traditions of American Feminism,* historian Josephine Donovan writes: "One of the sad conclusions I have reached in writing this book is that feminists have reinvented the wheel a number of times. While the theories developed in the late Sixties and early Seventies came as a kind of revelation to many of us at the time, it has since become clear, as we have learned about earlier feminist movements, that there was little really new in what these 'radicals' had to say. Much of it had been said repeatedly, over a century before. The eclipse of feminist theory must not happen again."

But even though women's studies is now a thriving and burgeoning tradition, this knowledge can't be confined to the academic realm—it also has to be perpetuated and find a home in the civilian world. Feminism can't go the way of Marxism, which seems to be celebrated within university walls by those living securely with tenure, but then mocked as irrelevant anywhere else where people punch a clock or break a sweat for a dollar. Feminism too has to be seen as more than a type of perspective for academic social critique.

Some might dismiss consciousness-raising as unimportant because there are young feminist activists already out there who don't seem hindered by the lack of it. But I've talked to these women and men in vibrant activist communities and struggling nonprofit groups who are laboring alone. They are tired and could use some support.

But, as with other issues, change doesn't stop when the drawbridge to opportunity officially opens: Sharks still inhabit apparently calm waters. As activists of my generation have constantly stressed, legislation doesn't automatically translate into liberation. Wages are still often skewed, the laws aren't always enforceable, and many workplace structures—still frozen in time from 1952—are unaccommodating for women's special needs and experiences.

Paraphrasing a famous feminist quote, one Rutgers University student aptly summed up the path for the future: "Now that some women have fought for a bigger slice of the pie, it's time to change the recipe."

That means learning to look at feminism in terms beyond access to certain careers, a prevalent perception of my generation. That means exploring and changing attitudes to value all women's work—at home as well as in the office, outside the executive suite. That means looking carefully at choice, and who still does not have enough of it. That means seeing beyond one's own experience to make connections to types of oppression blocking other women's paths, such as classism, racism, and homophobia.

This lack of consciousness-raising is revealed by a powerful force repelling this generation from feminism: its stigma. The twisted, all-too-common logic about feminists goes like this: If you stand up for women, you must hate men. Therefore, you must be angry. Thus, you must be ugly and can't get a man anyway. Hence, you must be a dyke.

The older generation also doesn't seem to recognize the special threat of the feminist stigma to people of our age group. True, other women through the years have shunned the label. But with a lack of consciousness-raising, without a sense of history and without personal exposure to feminism's initial momentum, *the stereotypes are all we know.*

Under these conditions, the feminist stigma is powerful and self-perpetuating. It blocks people from raising their consciousness, discovering the fundamentals behind feminism and taking a stand. In a way, the stigma acts like barbed wire around the real issues, the real problems, the real history and the real connections. If you dare move in the direction of feminism, you get ensnared and cut up.

This image of feminism as a radical ideology is also threatening because it radicalizes the issues themselves. It marginalizes and discourages discussion on even the most basic of problems, such as child care and women's health—which are considered bread-and-butter topics in the rest of the industrialized world. As women in America still aren't taken seriously, neither are so-called women's issues.

I know the stigma's effects firsthand. The reactions my *Daily Illini* column received surprised me because I never considered myself a radical. I laid out the issues in calm, unsensational terms, telling both sides of the story, without rage or rhetoric or crying wolf or thought-policing. Instead of quoting opinions of campus "radicals," I made sure to cite more seemingly trustworthy types, such as student leaders and administrators. Statistics and studies took the place of raw emotions or testimonials.

Sure, during that time at the tail end of the Reagan years on that campus, my four housemates and I were considered to be living on the fringe of that conservative business- and engineering-dominated, land-grant, all-American school. But, even in our cooperative rented house, we certainly weren't radicals. Our most nonconformist, subversive acts were probably listening to public radio, supporting Democratic candidates and letting a grade slip to B–.

I was not raised by dreaming hippies or a pack of wild feminists. My formative years were defined by an unusually nondysfunctional, traditional family structure in strip mall–laden south suburban Chicago. My mom stayed home with us and my dad, a business professor, voted for George Bush.

Even when I switched my beat at the college paper from the opinions page to the city desk, I could not escape the feminist stigma. I remember one afternoon when a new reporter and I were racing to the scene of a bank robbery. My editor had heard a vague message on the police scanner and sent us to find out about an unknown robber who stole an undisclosed amount of money at an uncertain time, and we had to quickly get the story into lucid, inverted-pyramid form. As I was driving and frantically flipping through the phone book to find the map in the middle to locate the bank's unfamiliar street, I noticed peripherally two eyes almost grazing my face with their intensity.

"Are you a . . . *radical* feminist???" asked the other reporter.

I looked over and saw that she was examining me as if I were some curious, exotic specimen, like a wildebeest at the zoo.

"No, no. I wouldn't go so far as to describe myself as a *radical*. I'm actually quite moderate in my views."

"Well, I decided I really don't believe in any of that stuff. I'm not a feminist."

"Oh."

"I mean, I'm easygoing, laid-back. I don't care if you call it a 'fire fighter' or a 'fireman.' Or a 'chairman' instead of 'chairwoman.' What's the big deal anyway?"

I wanted to tell her that feminism instilled more in people than an obsession to monitor others' language. But how could I describe all the values behind those words and explain that, in any case, the words themselves weren't the central issue. Her comments bothered me because I couldn't easily dismiss them. She was no freak or ignoramus just spouting an off-the-wall view I had never heard before. She was describing that pervasive and unappealing image of feminists that many—including myself—were observing day-to-day.

Perhaps all of us, both the nonfeminists and feminists, can begin explaining ourselves with a dialogue. By talking to each other, we can dismantle the stereotypes and trek beyond boundaries that seem to define us. Also, by examining and taking apart the feminist stigma, we can learn from it.

What does the feminist stigma reveal about the faults of the organized women's movement—both real and imagined?

This book is a confrontation of the stigma and the images behind it. Meanwhile, perhaps the process of reading about others' views and experiences can spark some consciousness-raising of our own. Maybe, among feminists and nonfeminists alike, it can arouse some questions, such as those I myself recently started to ask.


BEFORE a few years ago, like many of my generation, I had vague images in my head—from the media and hearing people talk—of lunatic, testosterone-crazed lesbians burning their confining underthings in garbage-can bonfires. They were wearing something masculine and practical, like flannel lumberjack shirts. Toughskins jeans from Sears—the kind we had to wear when we were little—and, of course, combat boots.

But, at the age of nineteen, while nervous about exposing my overwhelming ignorance, I took the risk and actually talked with a bona-fide feminist. Her name was Susan. She was a young, approachable activist, only twenty-four, a guest-in-residence at my dorm. My roommate Anna coerced me into going to her small-group discussion session. Tired of giving other lectures around campus all day, Susan surprised us and said she would just answer our questions.

So, I started for the first time to voice my doubts and ask some really elementary questions: What is feminism? Why are feminists so angry? How do feminists think men and women are different?

Curious to know more, I asked to interview Susan for a profile. What was supposed to be a half-hour interview turned into a two-hour argument. Every question was a struggle. Susan would answer me with something I perceived as utterly radical and insane, and then she would defend herself until I understood what she was talking about.

When I simply asked her to describe the typical feminist or rank the most important feminist issue, she said that the whole idea of feminism wasn't to have a typical feminist—you were supposed to make the choices best for you. Besides protesting traditionally male "linear thought," she did not think according to "hierarchal schemes." All right. Fair enough. Whatever.

More startling, she pointed out how feminist criticism can shed new light on old problems. She had written a play about anorexia, which I had never perceived as a woman's issue, although most of the victims are females who are literally killing themselves to assume the socially desired figure of an anemic sixth grader. (I then remembered a girl from my high school gym class who suddenly died from anorexia when her body didn't have enough defenses to fight off a bout of flu. She had months earlier revealed to me a sad, lyrical poem she had written in her notebook about sand castles crumbling, slowly, irrevocably—and I hounded her to submit it to our literary magazine. No one but she realized she was dying.)

Susan demystified feminism. She honestly and openly confronted criticism and transformed "the feminist" from something angry, academic and removed to someone relevant. From that dialogue I also learned that feminism could mean more than just getting white men's jobs. Susan put it in the perspective of a basic set of values that could be applied on a larger scale: from the most routine parts of life to global politics.

In my December 1986 story, she gave her definition: "My thesis is that we live in a 'masculinist' society—a society that in the public view always reveres these 'masculine' tendencies above the female tendencies so that we make decisions based on profit, expediency and aggressiveness—and lack of importance of individual needs, human needs."

Hmm, a little crazy, a little radical, even a little socialist-sounding, but still worth pondering, I thought.

While still wary of these "feminists," I read a few more books when they happened to end up in my path: an oversized *The Decade of Woman: A Ms. Book,* summing up the Seventies with masses of pictures and accompanying timeline, bought at the student Illini Union used-book sale for one dollar; a hardcover edition of Susan Brownmiller's *Femininity,* a study of women's roles as defined by society that I found on sale in the triple-clearance rack at Crown Books in the mall.

To learn with more direction, I chose a women's-studies-oriented class, "Women in the Literary Imagination," to fill my English requirement. But something was missing. The readings were good, but they were just so depressing. Our main subject matter was white women with stifled ambitions who killed themselves. We read ghastly stories of girls trapped by their own sexuality written by Joyce Carol Oates. There was Sylvia Plath's chilling *The Bell Jar.* I recall the story "To Room 19" by Doris Lessing about the "perfect" mother, who was really going crazy keeping up that veneer and committed suicide in the end:

"She was quite content lying there, listening to the faint soft hiss of the gas that poured into the room, into her lungs, into her brain, as she drifted off into the dark river."

Was this how feminists were supposed to feel? I walked home every day from class in the ever-present spring-semester rain feeling like drifting off into that dark river myself.

But I did become more curious to learn and gained some tools for analysis. With more independent reading, I gained a new vocabulary and could now engage in witty repartee with the most erudite of women's-studies scholars. Name it. I knew them all: *patriarchy, ecofeminist, misogynist, objectify, empower, phallocentric* and (while rare, my personal all-time favorite) *phallocratic.*

A year later, during my senior year, I saw a unique chance to learn about the relevance of feminism and test theory against reality with reporting. I decided to tackle the issue of acquaintance rape in my *Illini* column.

At first, discussing rape sounded like something to resist like the plague; the problem was obvious and I didn't want to seem too sensitive or paranoid about it. Besides, I was sure that everyone would think that I hated and feared men. This would be the kiss of death to all facets of my social life because I had no official boyfriend at the time to convey the proper heterosexual credentials to the reading public. Maybe I should tackle something safe, I thought, like cafeteria food, the old college writer's standby.

But I started researching and found that the beginning of the year is when the threat of rape is greatest, and the target group of victims is freshmen. At this time, for many, their guard is most down as they are first experiencing the joys of escaping totalitarian parents and experimenting with newfound freedom. That may include attending fraternity parties, the staple of campus social life, where no outside authorities are present and alcohol flows like the milk and honey described in biblical Canaan.

I checked to find some source of education for freshmen about acquaintance rape, but came up empty-handed. The student-orientation programs only lasted a few hours and barely included enough time for registration. But what alarmed me most were the students' attitudes toward rape, which were, in a sense, perpetuating the crime. I remember hearing some guys on my floor freshman year engaged in a serious intellectual debate laying out the circumstances that justify rape. One opined that a woman is making an implicit promise to have sex when she goes up the stairs to a guy's room with him at a party, even if he tells her they are just going to see his new stereo. Others—from small towns and a big city, who did not appear at all menacing or violent—readily agreed.

I wrote the column and for a few queasy days, I was terrified that I was wrong. Would I wake up that morning when it was in print and realize that the feminists had brainwashed me?

But I soon learned a strange lesson that contradicted all that I believed: I could make a difference. Feminists and activists of all types call it "being empowered," a feeling that has driven women's organizing. Feminism was more than just picking apart problems and holding a "pity party" for yourself (as one woman I interviewed put it); it was gaining the strength to do something about it.

I soon bumped into a high school associate on the Quad who told me that her friends in Sigma Nu fraternity "thought the article was really interesting, and they never knew girls felt that way." The vice chancellor asked me for permission to hand out the article to new students.

Educating myself about the prevalence of this violence and the cultural myths perpetuating it made me notice more and more things—all of which I didn't want to see. Images of rape and abuse of women were all around us, even in my favorite movies from long ago. In *Animal House,* I saw the scene where the hero, with the comical counsel of a debating angel and devil on his shoulders, was contemplating having sex with a teenage girl who had just passed out on the floor. Earlier to me, instead of rape, it was just a case of pragmatically seizing the opportunity.

Then, for the God-knows-what time, I saw *Gone With the Wind.* In one scene, in a fit of alcohol-induced frenzy, Rhett grabs Scarlett and carries her upstairs kicking and punching. The next morning, we see her nestled in her room, humming gaily to herself, looking more chipper and satisfied than even the most victorious of Yankees. Earlier to me, that had not been rape, it was romantic seduction.

Instantly I felt betrayed. Now even this classic escapist movie was offensive. Rhett Butler, the prototypical debonair leading man, was committing a first-degree sexual assault, as defined by Illinois state statutes.

I wondered: Why hadn't I ever seen this before? Why were so many people I knew suddenly coming out of the woodwork and telling me about their experiences, or those of their friends, of being assaulted?

Another emerging, major issue for many, abortion rights, also prompted some inquiry. In April of 1989, along with thousands of other college students, I attended the abortion-rights march in Washington, D.C., covering it with another *Daily Illini* reporter. During the rally, we finessed our way into the VIP tent and interviewed some vibrant feminist leaders. They and the marchers conveyed a new sense of this issue as connected to many others and also placed it in the larger historical context of women controlling their own destinies.

I took a break for a few months from writing about "women's issues," but then was summoned back by a call from some people at the campus ARC, Abortion Rights Coalition. They asked me to investigate complaints about a new bogus abortion clinic, run by anti-abortion church forces, that was intimidating students. I didn't respond right away because I didn't see much of a problem. I knew that these counseling centers were also providing much-needed alternatives to abortion, and, besides, this is a free country.

Still I went with an ARC member to an appointment (posing as her supportive, nurturing friend) to investigate the situation for myself. I was shocked. After not stating the center's mission or point of view, the counselor read us passages from the Bible for fifteen minutes that documented how abortion was sin. She then gave us completely false medical data, stating that the odds were likely that after an abortion, you would become infertile, experience fatal complications or be tortured until the end of eternity with unquenchable guilt. These "facts" were all documented in a pamphlet I picked up on my way out and used in my story.

I found out that similar centers, while not all so misleading about their stance, were proliferating across the country and were as numerous as abortion clinics. They mainly attracted clients by advertising free pregnancy tests in any medium possible—even in our college newspaper and in fliers on the Quad and classroom bulletin boards. While at worst students I talked to ended up with some unexpected fright, the threat was more serious to poor and uneducated young teens, who might not be able to as easily distinguish the advice as being slanted from a particular perspective.

After the story was published, the anti-abortion forces called me through finals week. They were distracting, but flattered me with the news that they had devoted a special prayer to me at their last meeting to save my soul.

While the writing I did that year was the most rewarding I had ever done, it made me wonder why it was so difficult to speak out. If all this was so urgent, why weren't more people enraged? I wondered if I was too sensitive or paranoid. Perhaps this was one of those naive stages of youthful idealism one quickly outgrew. It was all like a summer romance I thought would end in inconvenience when I returned to the sober world awaiting me.

After graduation, I decided to avoid feminist topics and once again lead a normal, nonthreatening and docile life. But while working as a free-lance writer in November of 1989, I decided at the last minute to take a train to a national feminist conference for young women in Washington, D.C. For me the weekend was undeniably powerful. Its significance was to give young feminists, often working in isolation, a chance to just meet each other. Those with budding curiosity in the feminist movement were challenged to learn more with new questions, and even seasoned activists were invigorated.

Also at that conference, I saw how endless the questions about feminism are, and I realized that my struggles to understand it and various types of oppression were just beginning. Heated disputes at the end of the conference erupted over a gap in consciousness about race. Black women were tired of educating the whites to recognize racism as an issue and challenged our stereotypes of each other. They demanded that more homework be done before we dared meet together again.

In writing this book, the challenge of questioning my own assumptions about others and myself continued to emerge with every person I met. I kept finding another string with others connected, as if I were pulling an endless handkerchief from a magician's hat. As soon as I thought I had a grasp, I realized I had to work harder just to keep up. This knowledge has come from people who never before thought about feminism, as well as experienced, visionary activists.

The wide variety of groups of women I met across the country supporting and learning from each other demonstrated that sisterhood is indeed powerful. This intangible yet undeniably electric force hung heavy in the air at the pioneering Women's Center at Medgar Evers College in Brooklyn, in the stately dining hall at Mount Holyoke College for women in Massachusetts, among a tireless group organizing for tenant rights in inner-city Chicago housing projects and in a small gathering of women filmmakers in a Los Angeles apartment.

Writing this book has been a journey from isolation with feminism, both personally and geographically. In tracking down people my age, I traveled from Kenosha, Wisconsin (a factory town in which I had been working as a city reporter), across America, by trains, planes, buses and my father's Oldsmobile. I have found subjects mainly through shameless, ceaseless, heavy-duty networking with friends, acquaintances of friends, sisters of neighbors of friends of friends, social service agencies, college campuses, technical schools, community colleges and whomever I happened to be sitting next to on a given day on the bus. The interviews ranged from a majority of one-on-one encounters to a talk with a group of five sisters, a classroom of high school seniors, an entire women's-studies discussion session and a crowd of people marching in a rally. I interviewed about 80 percent in person and the rest by phone.

The 236 people I interviewed included 103 in the core group of nonactivists, seventy-four activists and twenty-eight "feminists," who were most often quoted specifically in relation to their attendance of a women's college or their enrollment in women's-studies classes. Also included were thirty-one older people, who were both activist and nonactivist. I talked with both men and women of different classes, races, religions and sexual orientations, from urban and rural parts of the country.[1]

My sample group was defined as the twentysomethings, the Baby Busters, those individualists behind the Baby Boomers. They are people who generally fall in the age group between eighteen and thirty, born between 1960 and 1972.

In the selection of people interviewed, the form of this book reflects the future direction of the women's movement. Essential are the voices of women of color and low-income women. "Of color" means non-

[1]People of color, a total of forty-three interviewed, made up 18 percent of the complete sample, including: 15 percent of the nonactivists in the core group, 23 percent of the activists, 15 percent of the feminists sought out in specific feminist settings for quotes in later chapters, 15 percent of the male sample and 26 percent of the older people. (I did not usually label people according to their race, except when relevant to the context of the quote.)

Of the core group of 103 people, five stated they were lesbian, bisexual or gay; two in the feminist group and three activists said they were lesbians. This was 4 percent of the sample (although in actuality the percentage is probably much higher, since I didn't ask anyone outright about their sexual orientation unless they brought it up or it was obvious from the setting; three people from the nonactivist core group were contacted at "20something," a gay and lesbian social group in New York.)

Also, of the sixty non-full-time students in the core group of 103 people, 27 percent were working blue-collar jobs or training for them. However, the number was probably higher because this is not an easily definable category (for example, several sales clerks, managers and business representatives who did not need a college degree were considered white collar). In the core sample, forty-three full-time college students, mostly interviewed in groups, came from a wide variety of backgrounds.

white or minority. This word, recently entering the mainstream from activist communities, defines people according to their own identities, not their relationship with white people. It also unites people of all cultures across the world who constitute a majority of the globe's population. I have tried to make a real, genuine inclusion, not a token one, as many I approached had told me they feared. As well as including their voices, I have made an effort to include their issues. Their opinions have been and are still vital to forming a philosophy for the future. Like young women in general, all those viewing life from the margin usually provide the most penetrating criticism.

The authors with the most undeniable influence on my generation, who have also influenced my understanding of feminism through this book, are women of color. Throughout my interviews, feminists of all races, both male and female, freely quoted from and voiced their deepest respect for Oberlin College professor and feminist theorist Bell Hooks and poet Audre Lorde, both African American. They also frequently cited the anthology: *This Bridge Called My Back*, edited by Gloria Anzaldua and Cherrie Moraga, both Latinas.

I also interviewed young men to reflect another voice that must be heard. The reason is simple. Women just can't do it alone. We need their hard work to make change on all levels, from the mundane tasks of sharing housework to taking responsibility for their children in support payments to taking women seriously at promotion time.

No one is denying it. Men are an integral and vital part of many women's lives. Men are our friends, our companions, our fathers, our brothers, our sons, the ones who tend to get us pregnant, those we often shamelessly spill our guts to. By creating a dialogue together, we can learn to better respect each other.

Besides, as readers, they too need to be challenged to examine their perceptions. Why should women transform only half of society's attitudes while the other half remains stuck in time, halting the movement like a stubborn weight grounding the other end of a seesaw.

For too long, feminist books have read as if only women existed on the planet. But young feminists I interviewed don't desire a matriarchy or a patriarchy. The stated goal is not to create an all-women's Amazon society and decide to split. Even Wonder Woman from the comic strips found that world too stifling.

I have also interviewed some older women for realistic reasons. I talked to veteran activists (including both low-key grass-roots and stellar media figures), housewives, working women, people with careers and a few respected opinion-makers from the national press. They can provide criticism and comparison of us and create a sense of history, which my generation is sadly lacking.

A dialogue between the generations is also essential for the future to bridge the chasm between us. Both older self-declared feminists and nonfeminists offer strength and experience to build upon and consider. But I am careful not to quote them too heavily—as with the men—or let them draw the major conclusions. We young women need a chance to define ourselves.

As readers, I hope that older women derive some use from our dialogue, that they see what we are talking about. Then they can look beyond the stereotypes, learn to take chances on us for leadership and recognize the awesome potential of young women to bring relief to some beleaguered troops.

Meeting many of the more famous feminists was a strange and somewhat frightening experience because of their historical significance. I felt like the protagonists of *Bill and Ted's Excellent Adventure,* who went back in time for their history project to bring back famous figures from the past.

Researching this book involved a long process of disrupting my own stereotypes. It's a powerful thing, talking to someone with a perspective that challenges the one you have never questioned, whose world may be close, but still removed from yours. This covers a wide variety of people, from the single mother in the housing project you pass on the expressway to the Ivy League graduate in the next suburb who seemed to go directly from kindergarten to prep school.

Also startling, I learned about people I had been close to—but never met. I had an introspective conversation with five women in a sorority house living on Greek Row at my former university, in a part of town I had avoided at all costs. The Latina woman who worked as a bartender in a Chicago train station lounge, which I had passed by countless times, also enlightened me. She was able to most widely explain the social impact of popular music figures, better than those scholars quoted in my clip files.

I broke through the surface of conversation with people I did not know, as well as those whom I thought I knew pretty well. I interviewed my old college housemates and realized we had never discussed feminism (I learned that one wanted to be a priest when she was young!) My younger brother, who has repeatedly teased me for my writing and whose knowledge of societal trends I thought was limited to Aerosmith videos or late-night movies on Cinemax, gave me one of the most insightful analyses on role models.

In processing all these conversations, I did not act like a sociologist. I will state up front that I am no scientist and this research is far from empirical. I have no doctorate in postadolescent political development from Wellesley or Barnard or any other major feminist bastion and have used others' hard-earned statistics to back up my research.

But that is no apology. For this project, I embraced the most important goal of a reporter: to tell a story and construct the best possible human picture of what is going on, using some facts for mortar.

This is done by providing close-ups of different personalities and a collage of the influences that form human opinions: others' voices, personal experiences, excerpts from the popular media, feminist writing and everyday observations.

I also do not have the pretense to be able to speak for everyone and describe an entire, amorphous generation. No one could do that, not even with a lifetime of interviews or one's consciousness raised to high heaven. Instead, I have waded into the waters and found a wave, a tidal one, in fact, that represents the feeling of one part of the larger sea that encompasses us all.

I also differ from scientists, and most other journalists, for that matter, in injecting myself into my research. This story of my generation and the women's movement is undeniably being told from my personal perspective. I have made sure to do this without distorting or masking the voices that I report or directing their conversation to fit into my predetermined scheme. I started all the interviews with a loose set of questions and let the subjects' concerns and experiences determine the territories to be covered.

Though I express my opinions while telling the story, my goal isn't to convert anyone. I'm no feminist missionary on a crusade to reform the backward and apolitical. No feminist group is financing me or advertising me, and all propaganda will be checked at the door. My only agenda is to get readers to ask some new questions.

That is the most essential, and powerful, way to start.

# PART ONE

# BASIC PERCEPTIONS

*Chapter One*

# Connections to the "F" Word

I ASKED THEM, and they answered, with some slight variations:

"What do you associate with the word "feminist"?

"I imagine: bra-burning, hairy-legged, amazon, castrating, militant-almost-antifeminine, communist, Marxist, separatist, female skinheads, female supremacists, he-woman types, bunch-a-lesbians, you-know-dykes, man-haters, man-bashers, wanting-men's-jobs, want-to-dominate-men, want-to-be-men, wear-short-hair-to-look-unattractive, bizarre-chicks-running-around-doing-kooky-things, i-am-woman-hear-me-roar, uptight, angry, white-middle-class radicals."

This condensed reply includes nearly every description given by the core group of 103 nonactivists interviewed. This feminist image, while indeed rooted in both distortions and reality, is also a stereotype—a solid, rigid, often impenetrable one. Ironically, while the original purpose of feminism was to dismantle stereotypes, those aligned with the philosophy have themselves become most rigidly defined.

But while many felt some understandable resistance to feminism's nasty image, not all those interviewed were completely negative in their responses. Even those who fiercely denied that they were feminists or never before heard the word voiced strong support for women's rights in general. Most said they appreciated the women's movement and believed in what they described as its most basic goals and principles.

What was generally missing in their thinking was a sense of connection and commitment to feminism itself. Most didn't identify with feminism or want to be associated with it on a personal or political level. The great irony is that although feminism has generally made a tremendous difference in the perceptions and opportunities in many of these people's lives, it is something that they almost universally shun.

This chapter explores the conflict between perceived ideology and actual issues, examining the implications of looking past the stereotype and making a commitment to feminism.

## Feminism 101

While in my interviews the term "feminist" usually carried a negative connotation, some of the people I questioned did have positive associations with the term. When it wasn't being defined according to a particular type of person, feminism was commonly perceived as meaning one thing: equality.

"Feminism is a belief that we should all have the same rights and that what you do with those rights is up to you," said Lisa Scheeler, eighteen, a first-year student at American University in Washington, D.C., who was raised in Princeton, New Jersey.

"Feminism, to me, is the theory underlying the idea that women are equal to men, and therefore women deserve the same respect, chances and pay that men do," said Steve Klein, twenty-five, a math teacher at Napa High School in northern California.

Many defined feminism in terms of relationships.

"I think it's just equal partnership," said Marita Vasquez, twenty-six, a bartender from Richton Park, Illinois, who, like most, said she wasn't a feminist because of the term's extremist associations. "I'm not going to come home and cook dinner just because my man wants me to," she continued. "That's why I have Dave, because he isn't like that. . . . I bring money into this household the way he does, and we are going to share everything equally."

"The equality of men and women, certainly in the workplace and the home," said Sarah Edmunds, twenty-eight, a television-commercial producer in New York City, who also said she is not a feminist.

Some went beyond equal rights, responsibilities and opportunities to embrace the essence of womanhood:

Nancy Harris, twenty-three, an assistant manager of a women's clothing store in Matteson, Illinois, said it means being considered an "equal and taking pride in yourself as a woman."

A classic women's-studies text, *Women's Realities, Women's Choices: An Introduction to Women's Studies,* basically says that feminism means taking women seriously:

"Feminism has been defined in various ways, but it is agreed that it encompasses a set of beliefs, values and attitudes centered on the high valuation of women as human beings. Women are not valued for attributes imposed on us by others, but for those that exist in and are chosen by women ourselves."

Considering both these definitions—equality and valuing what is female—feminist writer Barbara Ehrenreich makes a valuable synthesis in her book *The Worst Years of Our Lives:* "The original idea of feminism as I first encountered it, in about 1969, was twofold: that nothing short of equality will do and that in a society marred by injustice and cruelty, equality will never be good enough."

One small women's-studies class I interviewed at the venerable Mount Holyoke College in South Hadley, Massachusetts fully reflected the wide range of positive perceptions. After a discussion about women's colleges, they volunteered to take a minute on their way out to give their definitions:

They talked about *identity:* "Feminism is knowing who you are as a woman," stated Tracey DeVaux, a sophomore. "You must identify your own oppression and educate yourself and others about it." *Autonomy:* "Feminism is the ability to make choices. To define who you are, not to have someone tell you who you are. Of course, there is more," said Elizabeth Zimmerman, a senior. *Political inclusion:* "I believe feminism to be a woman's ability to identify her position in society with respect to sexism, racism and classism. She also has an idea of how to confront the respective barriers she faces with respect to the above oppressive categories," said Diane Greenfield, a senior. *Freedom:* "Feminism is the struggle to keep choices open to women and the struggle against the oppression of all people," said Kimberly Cate, also a senior.

This discussion reflects the definitions made by a diverse array of feminist writers and scholars. But academics have also further clarified the various approaches that feminists utilize to bring about change. Some measure feminism according to its degrees of "radicalness." A common type is liberal feminism, which advocates reform of existing social and political institutions with roots in equality efforts of Nineteenth Century suffragettes. Liberal feminists identify areas of inequality, such as discrimination in the law, equal pay for equal work and abortion rights. The definition of a radical feminist seems to vary greatly from author to author, but many seem to share a belief in change at the root, whether of attitudes or political systems. This form of feminism, which emerged in the Sixties left movements, can be directed primarily against sexism and connected to a myriad of other oppressions.

Another way to classify feminism is as cultural or political. Those in the first category seem to elicit change through personal channels. This can be expressed through alternative lifestyles, such as in feminist approaches to medicine, music, religion, politics or art. Cultural feminists act at the most intimate personal level to explore identity or at a broader international level to feel bonds with women from different countries. The cultural component also suggests that feminism would still be relevant even if discrimination against women halted. The definitions together go beyond women securing rights equal to men's. To transform society, cultural feminists stress valuing women's differences and traditional approaches to life. This pride would never be obsolete.

While the cultural feminists often celebrate women's differences, the political feminists emphasize male-female similarities in their efforts to secure rights equal to men's. Political feminists tend to look outward to changing the system through economic, legal and electoral reform, such as in voting for a certain candidate or making laws for equal pay.

A highly simplified comparison that illustrates the two varying focuses can be seen in the environmental movement. Cultural environmentalists may live an ecologically pure lifestyle, setting up compost piles, washing clothes in biodegradable soap and eating low on the food chain to help discourage deforestation of land. Political environmentalists may push for reform in laws regulating disposal of organic waste or chemicals in soap or importation of beef raised on former rain-forest land.

Men have also created three separate movements that have been compared to or viewed as related to feminism. The first type, which is relevant to this book and is least controversial, employs a feminist political analysis and discusses sexism and men's roles in addressing "women's issues." For example, the men's antirape and antibattering movements address socialized attitudes of dominance and aggression.

The next two will not be discussed in this book because they are not based on feminism. Of these, a type that has been recently popularized is a spiritual and cultural men's movement to get in touch with their inner, primitive male selves. A leader is poet Robert Bly, who has led retreats into the woods to summon this lost spirit, which he calls "Iron John." Others are working in the category of "men's rights," such as in securing child custody or monitoring funding for women's groups, and often work against feminist interests.

In all these feminist classifications, the theories are easier to define than the concrete actions of individuals. Each person takes a unique route, often overlapping into other categories, to achieve the goal of equality and self-realization for women.

## Sexism: Is it the System, Or Is it Just Me?

Feminists of all schools generally address the issue of sexism, or discrimination based on gender. Almost everyone I interviewed agreed that sexism exists and is not a figment of the imagination.

According to A *Feminist Dictionary,* sexism is defined as "Behavior, policy, language or other action of men or women which expresses the institutionalized, systematic, comprehensive or consistent view that women are inferior."

Oberlin College professor Bell Hooks, who speaks widely on issues of sex, race and class, streamlines the definition of feminism as "a movement to end sexism and sexist oppression." This makes feminism accessible to men in not naming women as the victims, leaves it to individuals to devise the strategy best for their own level of awareness and links it to other struggles against oppression.

While most women interviewed have not felt personally discriminated against by sexism, a majority felt touched by it in some way.

One common complaint was not being taken seriously academically. Nancy Hybert, twenty-nine, a corporate research analyst in Chicago, said her high school advisor resisted her academic requests. "My father was always high on taking a lot of math and science: 'I want you to be able to function on your own and support yourself and be independent.' One of my advisors was quoted as saying in response, 'Let her take the English because she is just going to marry someone anyhow.' "

Surprisingly, a large number said that they first perceived inequities at an early age while playing sports. As children, they saw they weren't allowed to play on certain teams and when older in high school and college, they noticed other discrepancies.

Suzanne Hiernaux, twenty-four, a systems analyst from Cincinnati who played soccer from fifth grade through college, said this was a common gripe. She noticed male teams generated more money while also receiving more funding. "And the coverage of it. If you just watch the news. You get the women's blurbs: 'And the women, undefeated now for two seasons. . . . ' You don't want to hear about them unless they win the national title." Now she sees sexism in sports continuing with a corecreational team at work. The team has the rule that a woman has to touch the ball before a goal can be scored to assure that the men will let the females in on the action.

But most interviewed expressed confusion and helplessness at detecting sexism, which they suspect as a subtle undercurrent in both professional and personal relationships. While antidiscrimination laws have fought sexism in the past, no one has figured out a way to legislate attitudes.

Lisa Krohn, twenty-six, a New York industrial designer, described this feeling of confusion. "If I'm in a room with five male designers and there's a project everyone wants, and I'm of equal or better credentials and experience and track record than any of the men involved, and I don't get the project, I can explain that many ways.

[Sexism has] definitely come into my head. I definitely feel I have been excluded from 'boys' clubs,' from school to professional situations. But I would be reluctant to whine about it, because I haven't yet felt it could help to face that reality head-on. It seems like such a powerful psychological undertone, that to point it out and get upset about it is like spinning your wheels. You almost have to consider it an obstacle, like when it rains on the day of your picnic. You're going to have your picnic no matter what, no one can stop you, but you sure wish it wouldn't rain. But then again, just like the rain, what can you really do about it? Sometimes it seems inevitable, sometimes it seems ubiquitous. It is pervasive, and it is insurmountable. The only choice is to ignore it and try to plug away."

Some are also confused as to how to confront more blatant displays, such as harassment, a frequent complaint. Stephanie Boatley, twenty-one, who works at a supermarket in Arlington, Texas, said she had trouble dealing with disparaging comments she regularly received from one Navy officer.

"The way he harassed me was when I bent over, he'd say, 'Hmm, oh, the things I could do to you.' I told him he was totally out of place. I told him I was going to file a report. He said it's a joke. It's the excuse they always use: a joke."

Men from all walks of life—from the construction site to the corporate office carrel—were equally quick to recognize sexism as a reality. They said while men's treatment of women has improved in the workplace and home, they observed problems in their own attitudes and those expressed by others behind closed doors.

"I see it at work," said Todd Boots, twenty-four, a carpenter from Chicago Ridge, Illinois. "The guys talk about their wives. They say things they would never say to their wives' face. Jokes. Calling her a bitch. 'Oh, that stupid bitch.' One guy is always talking about how stupid his wife is. She does this or she does that."

"I think a lot of men have retained all their same attitudes and haven't really changed at all or been affected very much by the women's movement, so I wouldn't necessarily say if it's been bad or good," said Greg Beaubien, twenty-seven, a corporate public relations writer in Chicago. "They might have had to swallow their pride and deal with certain threats from women after the Baby Boom kind of slid off and more women came back into the workplace."

The central difference in the sexes in perceiving sexism was how seriously they took it. In general, women were more concerned about its effects than men and saw it as the root of large problems. Buttressing these findings is an unpublished 1988 and 1989 study of attitudes toward sexual harassment, homophobia and sexism by the sociology department of Grinnell College in Grinnell, Iowa. After surveying half the student enrollment—659 people—researchers concluded that female students there were more likely to see sexism at the root of sexual harassment, were significantly more likely to have been victims themselves of sexual harassment and see it as a problem. Almost half the female students and fewer than one-fifth of the male students disagreed with the idea that sexual harassment is rare at their college. Women were also more likely to define questionable actions as sexual harassment and to refuse to blame harassment on the victim.

## Not Over Yet

Nearly everyone implied that the battles for women's equality couldn't be won by listing issues that concern them. When I asked them to name issues women need to rally for in the 1990s, most came up with at least two and almost all named at least one. The strongest feelings were undeniably for the struggles to fight violence against women, secure abortion rights and achieve equal pay for equal work. Next were child care and health needs, especially for single mothers, and racism's effects on women. The family was a major issue throughout conversations that called for more tolerance of women's choices and a higher valuation and more support for motherhood.

Other polls confirm the younger generation's continued interest in women's advancement, such as a *New York Times* survey conducted in June of 1989. When asked if the United States continues to need a strong women's movement to push for changes that benefit women, 67 percent of the 1,025 women questioned and 51 percent of the 472 men said yes. Within this group, 71 percent of the respondents aged nineteen through twenty-nine supported an active women's movement.

Black women in particular seem to be more aware of the need for improvement. In the *New York Times* survey, 18 percent of black women polled cited the need for good jobs that pay a good wage as the most important problem facing women, while only 9 percent of white women had the same response.

## So, Do You Consider Yourself a "You-Know-What"?

Despite the aforementioned interest, identification or association with feminism was far weaker than support for its goals. About 10 percent of those I interviewed said they had no idea what the word meant or couldn't define it; 46 percent said they were not feminists; 13 percent said they "weren't feminists, but . . ."; 13 percent said they "are feminists, but . . ."; and 18 percent said "yes."[1]

The feedback from my interviews corresponds directly with the results of a poll reported in the September 1989 issue of *In View,* a magazine for women in college. The article reported that in a poll of 514 female undergraduates asked about the social gains made by women over the past twenty-five years 90 percent agreed that men and women should earn equal pay for equal work; 93 percent said that women want equality with men; 84 percent agreed that women should have access to birth control, regardless of age or marital status; 90 percent believed that sexism still exists, citing examples of persistent discrimination in the workplace, the political arena and the home.

Still, only 16 percent of the women polled said they were definitely feminists. And one-third definitely did *not* consider themselves feminists.

## A Privileged Thing

As stated, many I interviewed did not identify with feminism because they did not know how to define the term. I have to clarify that I recognize the word "feminist" is a privileged term and is perceived as such. It is something for people who have the time and inclination to intellectualize their lives and usually are exposed to some kind of academic discourse. (Almost all of the people who answered "yes" or "yes, but" in response to the question "Are you a feminist?" were from middle-class backgrounds or were anticipating professional careers.)

Also, women from all walks of life make connections to each other without having labeled them feminists. They may never think about it or have greater concerns. "I think for the majority of women, it's important," said Julie Spencer Robinson, twenty-eight, a development specialist at the Equity Institute in Amherst, Massachusetts, which

[1]The men I spoke with overwhelmingly fit the "no" category, with eighteen giving that answer, two responding "no, but . . . ," four answering "yes," one answering "yes, but" and one not familiar with the term.

helps companies diversify. "It may not be the first thing, and it may not be the second or third thing, but it's on their list and near the top. And they don't identify themselves as 'an organizer around women's issues' or 'a women's activist.' It's 'I'm a secretary and I have two kids.' It's not important that they aren't identifying themselves as feminists because they *do* identify themselves as women."

The people who were most unfamiliar with the term feminism were those outside the classification of white middle class. However, slightly more women of color proportionately identified themselves as feminists.

Nancy Harris, who is black, said that personal experiences with racism have made her more sensitive to understanding sexism. "[Racism] makes you more aware of other problems people might face," she said.

But many activists of color said that the word is out of the realm of their cultures and is an alien term.

Hortencia Velez and her friend Susana Vasquez, both 20, explained to me their own perceptions of the word feminist. Velez is the co-founder of the feminist Latina group "La Fuerza" at the University of Illinois. While their backgrounds contrast dramatically, they both felt the same influence from their ethnic heritage. Velez is from a high-crime Mexican neighborhood on the South Side of Chicago ("For me, it was just a challenge to go to school and come home alive"). Vasquez went to high school in a predominantly white suburb.

"If you look up in a Spanish/American dictionary the word feminism, it wouldn't exist," said Vasquez.

"When I was in high school or grammar school, I would say this or that isn't fair. I have to do all the chores and all these dishes and the guys don't have to do anything," said Velez. "There was never a word for it. It was more like: Shut up and do it. You can refuse and get slapped. My dad would always tell me I was a rebel. In Spanish, it would sound different: *rebelde.* I would say, 'Dad, I am not being rebellious. I'm just standing up for my own rights, and it isn't fair.' "

In Brooklyn, Safiya Bandele, forty-seven, the director of the Center for Women's Development at Medgar Evers College in Brooklyn, which is 95 percent black, said this is a word she does not use with her students in a women's-studies class she teaches infrequently (whenever funding is available).

"Feminism as a word never comes up. We talk about life experiences and the reality of being a woman of color. Through the readings and lectures and speakers, we connect that reality. We talk about what we need to be healthy and empowered human beings in the world."

"Do you bring up this word yourself?" I asked.

"I don't think so. I wouldn't run from it. But language is very important, and that word is sort of out of the mainstream of our language."

"What do you mean by that?"

"It has the general connotation that white equals feminism."

"Do you use a word to describe it?"

"What's the point? The point is to believe in women's rights. That's the way we talk about it. For example, we don't use the word 'client.' A lot of people use client in social-service agencies. People say how do you get away from using the word client? We use six words instead of client. We would rather use those six words than to use words like client so laden with the baggage of hierarchy, judgment and all of that. We say 'women who participate in our program.' Or 'program participants.' Because a 'client' sets up a different medium. We're not professionals in women's services with clients. We're all women on a continuum, and some have more information than others and we all learn from each other."

Obviously, by the strong assertions of these women, it is clear that you don't have to call yourself a feminist to be a fighter for the principles behind it. But regardless of any gap of exposure or association, the idea of "feminist" and the way in which people identify with it is still a valuable concept to explore for its potential and present use.

To further explore basic and common perceptions, I turned to someplace close to home that I knew represented the heartbeat of mainstream America.

## The Heartbeats in the Heartlands

We were sitting in a small and cozy room decorated with paddles and pictures in the Phi Mu house on fraternity row on the west side of the University of Illinois campus in Champaign.

I quickly learned these sorority members' strict definition of feminist, which was shared by about half of the other respondents: going out of your way to be a man, and meanwhile losing touch with all that is traditionally female. I looked at the five young women seated on the two beds in the room.

"My first question: Do you consider yourself a feminist?"

"No."

"No."

"No."

"No."

"No."

They all stopped, laughed a little and started to explain.

"We don't care," said Meiko Ogura, twenty. "Well, like, feminists, what exactly is a feminist? I want your definition."

"I believe in equal rights," said Betsy Lowery, twenty.

"But I wouldn't go out and draft myself," said Ogura. "You know what I mean? I probably wouldn't if I didn't have to.

"I enjoy the privileges. If it comes down to me doing the same as them, maybe, but not all the time."

"With what?" I asked.

"Like sure, I want the same opportunities for jobs and stuff and privileges," said Ogura. "But like with the draft, you know how guys are supposed to do things. I don't want to do the same things."

"I wouldn't want to go out and do construction work," said Lowery. "I think it's a man's job. I don't think there's anything wrong with women doing it, but I wouldn't go out and prove that I could do it.

"I don't think there's anything wrong with women staying home, at least for a couple of years. I'm not saying it's for everybody. I'm not saying it's for me. But I don't think everyone should have a career. But raising kids and working seven hours a day, not everyone can handle it," said Deborah Hann, twenty.

"I don't want to find myself in the middle of Kuwait. I think of myself as exempt from that kind of thing. It might be kind of two-sided, but I want the job opportunities, or at least to think that I do, that I don't have to stay and be a housewife all the time. Then again, I'm not going to be the first to go off and be Joe Marine either," said Suzanne Mayer, twenty.

"I don't want men and women to do the same thing. We're not used to the idea," said Shannon McCormack, twenty. "It hasn't been established for very long. We weren't able to do the same things until, what, twenty years ago. It was a gradual process. And with some of these things, we're just not used to the concept of it. It will take time."

Outside the campus, others interviewed drove home these same points in detail.

First, many people explained that they are not feminists because they prefer the female way of life, not the male one.

"Feminists are women who want the same role-taking as a man. . . . When I get married, I know I'll take on my boyfriend's name, and a lot of these women feel they don't want to. They want to be known as their own identity," said Denise Herdrich, twenty-three, a secretary from McHenry, Illinois. "I think it's a bunch of bull. I can't see getting married to someone and not taking on his name because it's always been that way. And a lot of times, these women are like why doesn't he take on my name? That question was brought up to me and I thought it was interesting. But since day one, when women and men have gotten married, that's how it's been."

Many added that it is inconsistent or hypocritical to call themselves feminists while wanting the privileges that go with being a woman. The main privilege most were not willing to sacrifice was having the door opened for them.

Second, with feminism's focus on careers, many without professional ambitions do not see it as relating to them and furthermore view it as antimotherhood. "I think it's something more for businesswomen to discuss who get together at work," said Patrice Calvi, twenty-nine, a homemaker, hairstylist and mother of three from suburban Chicago.

"I don't feel I'm a militant feminist and have to dress up in the suit and go to corporate America and compete with men," said Resa Hare, twenty-six, a teacher from Granada Hills, California.

Third, others said feminists deny what is feminine, and fourth, they associate feminists with lesbians. "I think women are feminine, and some of those people who are feminists with the short haircuts and no boobs or anything, it's not relating to most women who are full-figured and who do have a sexual curiosity about them and want to know more about how it's supposed to be," said Marita Vasquez. "I also wonder if they're dykes or not."

Like Vasquez, many in the above categories thought feminism did to gender what communism theoretically does to class: wipe out any distinctions.

Fifth, they think feminists hate men or think that women should be superior to them. "I used to consider myself a real full-fledged feminist. Not anymore. I believe more in equality. I don't think men should rule or women should rule. I think it should just be equal," said Heather Macdonald, nineteen, a freshman at the University of Maryland, College Park.

Sixth, others didn't see the struggle for women's rights as relevant to them. "I don't feel I've ever been discriminated against, so I don't think it's that big of an issue. Some of these women totally live and die for feminism. I've never been a part of any women's groups. I don't need to. It has just all come to me the way I thought it's supposed to," said Renee Boots, twenty-three, a homemaker from Chicago Ridge, Illinois.

Seventh and eighth, they said feminists are petty and confrontational. My sister's friend Bridget Johnson, twenty, the president of the sorority house at which I did the above interview, said she isn't a feminist because of her approach. She has been outspoken about providing education concerning acquaintance rape in the Greek system, but explained "I go out of my way for certain things like date rape, setting up programs about date rape, but I wouldn't go out of my way and go into a fraternity and say, "Okay. You guys are assholes." I look at it more as education, setting up programs," she said.

Ninth, others said they are not activist enough about the feminist cause. "You ask me if I'm a feminist? Right offhand, I would probably say no. Like I say I believe in women's rights and I hope women will be able to acquire more of these rights. But I'm not out promoting anything—but I'm not against them getting these rights. I'm in the middle," said Arthur McAdams, twenty-nine, a lab technician from Birmingham, Alabama.

Tenth, they say that feminism isn't on the top of their list of concerns or they don't follow the philosophy religiously. "On really important issues, I share their beliefs," said Simone Cooper, twenty-nine, a New York free-lance publicist from North Carolina, as well as a member of the National Abortion Rights Action League. "But not all the way to the core, because then you can take it too far."

## The "Yes, But" (and "No, But") Thing

Other women who answered yes or no wanted to separate themselves from the negative images the term represents.

"To say you're a feminist is a dirty word. I really don't like to say this out loud because I don't want people to associate me with the hard-ass people from the Sixties who are offended when the man opens the door," said Karen, twenty-four, a former law student in New York City between jobs, who did not want her last name used.

"I guess I would say, if I had to answer yes or no, I would probably answer yes. It would be one of those 'yes, but' things. It would be because people think of feminism in the more radical way or ERA type of way," said Amy Strassler, twenty-four, a graduate student in business at Columbia University.

"What do you mean?"

"The idea that people might have of feminism is that women are sick and tired of being second and want to be first and want to be treated exactly the same way that men are treated. I think it's nice that men and women are treated somewhat differently. But in the end, I would want the same opportunities that men would have, so I would say yes."

Even the black female rap star Queen Latifah (a.k.a. Dana Owens), twenty-two, whose classic song "Ladies First" is embraced by feminist intellectuals and other women as a source of confidence, was quoted with this view in a syndicated *New York Times* article. "I have a fear of feminism. To me, feminists were usually white women who hated men. A lot seemed to be gay. They were always fightin'. I didn't want to be that. The media showed them that way, [and the image has]never gone away. I don't want to be classified with them." (However, she was quoted in that same article as later changing her mind after meeting some real "feminists" at a university event.)

## The "Progressives" Agree

Some people who don't necessarily identify themselves as feminists are a testament to the effectiveness of the movement. It is something so widely accepted and common that it is taken for granted. This is true for many living in environments both hostile to and embracing of feminism.

For this reason, young women don't often see the urgency in making the connection to feminism.

"It's hard for me to tell because I've never gone out in the work world. College is really a very sheltered environment," said Rachel Spector, twenty-three, a graduate student at Northwestern University in Evanston, Illinois, who also attended Washington University in St. Louis. "It's kind of like you aren't treated equal, but you have a false sense you are. I feel as though I come from a generation where you are told you can do whatever you want to do. . . . I never looked at the world and felt that my options were limited, although they very much might be."

Even at Grinnell College, a liberal arts enclave that one student described as "more liberal than liberal," where the issue of sexism is openly and commonly discussed, many did not extend their politics to feminism. In the 1988 and 1989 attitudes survey, while 84.2 percent of the women agreed that they support equal rights for women, only 60.8 percent agreed that they considered themselves feminists. While 66.5 of the men said they strongly supported equal rights for women, only 32 percent indicated they considered themselves feminists.

In some "progressive" environments, women told me they don't identify themselves as feminists because it is such a basic part of the culture that everyone takes it for granted. There, femininism is more a part of a multicultural, progressive focus to fight all types of discrimination and value people's differences. These "politically correct" areas mainly seemed to be concentrated in the Northeast and West Coast (especially the Bay Area) and in pockets on campuses throughout the country.

Three women at Columbia University in New York City explained this phenomenon.

"In the Northeast, in New York, [femininism] is such a big thing. Everyone is aware. Men are aware. It's sort of this isolated haven," said Rachel Stoll, twenty.

"It's cool," said Beth Berkowitz, twenty. "It's a part of being politically correct to think that way."

Theodora Langbaum, twenty-one, said: "I think it's a pretty aware school."

"With some aggressive women—and I say that positively," said Stoll.

"It's like going to 'Take Back the Night' [a rally against sexual violence], being aware of these kinds of issues, being aware of not being homophobic, of racial issues," Berkowitz said. "They all sort of go together as part of what you're supposed to be."

One man agreed. "Just about every woman I know who I am close with who doesn't call herself a feminist does so only because of a slight semantic issue," said David Tepper, twenty-one, a Columbia University student.

Others—including many activists—voiced opposition with the identification for the sake of taking on any label. They observe that making distinctions can cause tensions. "I'm saying I'm proud to be a woman. I find incredible strength in women. I love women. But I don't want to further the walls that exist between women and men," said Amanda Dodds, eighteen, a freshman at Ohio University in Athens and an environmental activist. "A lot of times I see the feminist movement doing just that."

Kristen Walsh, twenty-three, a student at the University of Florida-Gainesville, said she finds any label limiting. "I don't like to call myself a feminist because it's a label, and I don't like labels. And I don't want people to think that's who I am. I don't like any label. I don't think that environmentalist is a bad label, but I don't want it either. It creates a stereotype. It means: 'You think this.'"

One of the most dedicated women's-rights activists I met, labor leader Donene Williams, twenty-seven, of Cambridge, Massachusetts, also does not call herself a feminist.

I visited her in her union's cramped basement office and asked her about her organizing. She is the president of the almost completely female local of Harvard University clerical workers, the largest private local of the mammoth American Federation of State, County and Municipal Employees (AFSCME), which is a model for other universities organizing throughout the country. In 1988, she was part of a large negotiating team that helped achieve a 32-percent increase in pay over a three-year term, including child-care allowances and other benefits.

Her fear is that the feminist label will marginalize "women's issues" in labor, which she considers top priority. "If someone asked me before, do you consider yourself a feminist or a trade unionist, I'd say trade unionist. The values I consider important are trade union values, making the most progress for the most people possible, helping those people who need help, caring about their issues."

"Isn't that also feminist?" I asked.

"I don't consider [feminism] a bad thing. I just have never identified with that. I think the idea of—I don't want to describe it in a way that [implies] I think being a feminist is wrong—the idea of women's groups within organized labor, well I think women's issues should be on the *main* agenda of organized labor. I don't think it should be on a separate agenda."

She later added, "I'm doing as much as anyone who calls herself a feminist to improve working conditions for women. But if someone says I'm not in solidarity because I don't call myself a feminist, they would be wrong."

Others say that dealing with labels can be personally distracting from what is really important. "It's a pity we spend so much time and effort making the rules for the game and fighting over the rules of the game, instead of playing the game. Because women have been excluded from the game for so long, and now that they're finally having a chance, it would be nice to get on with it. For their sake and for everyone's sake," said Lisa Krohn.

Lisa Harris, twenty, a student at Rutgers University in New Brunswick, New Jersey, said she also can't afford to get consumed in the rules of the game. As an African-American woman with sights set high for a future political office, she said thinking too much about her identity could become consuming.

"It's the same with race, and I don't want to get caught in that. I have friends who look at everything as coming from a racist point of view, and I don't want to do that. 'Why are there only two black guys in the film, or why is it always the black guy getting killed first?' I don't want to go to a movie and think that. It's just something that I see, especially with a really good friend of mine. She's so angry and I don't see that. I don't want to be so angry that I couldn't do anything because I was mad all the time."

Like others, Harris said that although she finds feminist analysis relevant to her life, being stigmatized by the label could be professionally hazardous.

"I don't want to be titled a feminist. I never want to be titled a feminist. It holds you back. If someone is not going to talk to me because they think I'm a feminist, yes, he's a jerk, but at the same time I don't want to be closed off from that person."

Lisa Harris also said she doesn't like the word because it sounds radical. Others who have reason to look out for their image also fear the consequences. Even some feminist organizations don't call themselves feminist. One of the most dramatic illustrations of this came during a conversation in Washington, D.C., with Vanessa Kirsch, twenty-five, an assistant to a political pollster. She is chairperson and co-founder of one of the most advanced, vibrant and dynamic young feminist groups in the country, the Women's Information Network. Shortly after WIN was begun in 1989, the group attracted more than 600 members with professional networking and extensive programming to promote progressive candidates and women's issues.

"WIN is, all of our philosophies are feminist; it's a feminist organization," Kirsch said. "But there is some kind of fear of being associated with it. I think part of it is that these women are politically active and they want professional results, and although they respect all the older generation has gone through, they see the need for further progress and don't want to be separated. They want to be mainstream. They want to make changes in the mainstream.

"In looking at women's groups, I as a young woman feel they have made huge leaps and bounds, but they have alienated themselves and have been overlooked on important issues. I mean, we watched Souter get nominated with no question, and the women's groups were out vocally, but they were just put aside."

Men who professed feminist beliefs gave similar answers, but a few also had philosophical conflicts about calling themselves feminists. Some men said this would be pretentious in taking over a woman's domain. An alternative was to call themselves "pro-feminist."

"It would insult the women I'd be working for to say I know their issues enough to speak out for them. It makes no sense. Really, I don't see my role in that," said Mike Brooks, twenty-five, an engineer from River Forest, Illinois.

## Alternative Words

Like others, Lisa Krohn had other suggestions for words to replace feminism to avoid divisions and being stigmatized.

"Feminism should be called humanism," she said. "You can't aggrandize women just because they have been the underdogs. You have to look at the whole society and try to get it back in balance. Feminist, womanist, anything that focuses on women is a big drag. It's just like the whole society has been so focused on men so long—"

Her friend Guy added, "—that they want to tip the balance the other way."

"It's reactionary," Krohn said.

Simone Cooper said she also prefers a more neutral word to separate herself from more radical views associated with feminism.

"I would describe myself more as an egalitarian because feminist, in my mind, in a lot of respects has a negative connotation. Feminism in its purest form is what I believe in: equal rights for women—politically, socially, economically. But some elements in 'feminism' bother me," said Cooper. "I think feminism should be about choice, and lot of women berate women who stay at home. I think that work is just as important and people have to do what makes them happy."

## Womanist

Another term that is more woman-centered preferred by several feminist women of color is "womanist." Tiffany Ferguson, twenty, a student at the University of Illinois, explained to me why she and others named their new support group for black women "the Womanist Circle." She and Velez, co-founder of La Fuerza, organized their groups in the university's YWCA.

" 'Womanist' comes from Alice Walker's book, *In Search of our*

*Mothers' Gardens,"* said Ferguson. "She coined a phrase and defined it as coming from black culture, with the connection of black women going around acting womanish, meaning acting like in control, actually taking charge, asking questions, wanting to know. That translated to womanist. There is a line where she defines what a womanist is, in defining womanhood, actually not only for black women but for all women of color: 'Womanist is to Feminist as purple is to lavender.' "

Ferguson, who also calls herself a feminist, explained that the word helps convey the solidarity of women of color and relieves apprehensions of being stigmatized and cut off from their communities, which may harbor mistrust of the feminist label. It also is a statement of autonomy from the mainstream feminist movement, which she said has excluded women of color and has not addressed their issues.

"We are different. Our experiences are different. I do experience sexism differently from white women. There are commonalities, certainly. But the cultural differences are so great that I should, or black women should, feel free to say 'I'm a womanist' if that's what they feel comfortable with. I think it's just as politically viable as calling themselves feminists, if not more so. By calling yourself a womanist, not only have you aligned yourself with feminism and being woman-centered, but you have also aligned yourself with other sisters of color across the globe."

## The Chilling Factor

A central reason many people avoid the term feminist is because any label hurts. The feminist title confines people into neat little packages, denying other dimensions to their personalities and obscuring other concerns.

For many, especially with issues not confronting them directly or not deemed critical for life to go on, the stigma will be a factor in inhibiting personal inquiry or public action.

The danger of the stigma is strongest to the majority of women and men not entrenched in activist communities or equipped with support networks. Who would want to risk isolation, risk being branded radical, by co-workers, community, friends or boyfriends?

In the past few years, and in particular while writing this book, I've witnessed how fear of the feminist label chills speech for many.

On many campuses to which I traveled, taking women's studies is an embarrassment, a weakness, something to hide. Hortencia Velez said some women's boyfriends are suspicious when they join her support group. Other women of color have noticed the special pressures they face in their communities to not make divisions by becoming feminists.

At a pro-choice meeting in Chicago, an activist said she has trouble getting friends to join the fight because they don't want to be called feminists. A city clerk said that she decided not to go to her union representatives to ask for a leave of absence after a pregnancy because the men in charge would not take her seriously.

Sarah Turoff, twenty-three, who worked at a bank in downtown Chicago, recently explained that women didn't feel comfortable arguing for more of a family-friendly environment, although she recognizes that employers are more and more realizing the need for such benefits.

"It's not the type of thing the single individual feels comfortable bringing up. I have very strong beliefs on the subject, but I would have been looked at in a bad light if I had started saying this stuff because they think that you're radical. Even though everyone believes it. To be the one to bring it up makes you radical."

This fear of branding can also act on a political level. At a conference for East Coast feminists, one young woman asked Republican Holly Cork, twenty-three, South Carolina's youngest state House representative, to share her feelings about the Equal Rights Amendment.

"I haven't had to take a position on ERA yet," said Cork. "I would probably say I support it. However, that's a really volatile issue. For me, one of the really hard things I have to deal with is trying to be the so-called good Republican and not appear like a radical feminist. For me, it's really hard to draw the line right there."

## The Branding

The word feminist often has nothing to do with being labeled. Just by broaching the topic of women's rights, no matter how extreme one's stand is, it's easy to get labeled.

Because the feminist label is considered as radical, many women who dare to venture to use it report a swift backlash. This phenomenon is not new. Writing back in 1913, journalist Rebecca West observed: "I myself have never been able to find out precisely what feminism is: I only know that people call me a feminist whenever I express sentiments that differentiate me from a doormat."

A more modern writer, Gloria Steinem, detailed scenes of the inescapable and widespread backlash against her for her role as a feminist spokesperson in her 1983 book *Outrageous Acts and Everyday Rebellions:*

—Opening a mass-mailed Christmas letter from a cousin and his wife with the misfortune of having the same last name as mine, and between the news of their fishing trip and other retirement activities, discovering an announcement they had formally disowned me. . . .

—Watching (mass murderer) Richard Speck explain on television that not all the women he had murdered were like "Gloria Steinem. . . ."

—Seeing displayed on newsstands all over New York a *Screw* magazine centerfold of a woman with my face and glasses. . . .

For young women across the country in the 1990s, speaking up about everyday matters and subtle sexism carries the threat of retribution.

"When a woman speaks out on any issue involving sexism or women, she gets singled out as [being] a woman having feminist feelings, or as 'the Feminist.' And it's done in a way that she's disqualified. She becomes the radical spokesperson for the group. It's a way of saying that person is crazy, and it happens all the time," said Andrea Rose Askowitz, twenty-two, an organizer affiliated with the New York City–based Students Organizing Students, an activist group devoted to protecting reproductive rights at campuses throughout the country.

She recalled learning about this phenomenon while attending the University of Pennsylvania in 1990.

"A perfect situation is I'm sitting in a classroom, and I say there is sexist language going on here, and then that this one man is controlling the class. And if I keep saying things like this—it doesn't take very long, maybe two times—then this is what will happen. The teacher will say, 'Andrea, how do you feel about this?' And just by saying that, by making me the voice of feminism in the classroom, he makes it seem like it isn't common, which it is."

This phenomenon was reported to me by women across the country in work and social situations. In some areas, a statement that would seem tame in other places could take on extremist proportions. Bonnie Bieze-Adrian, twenty-five, who works for an insurance company in suburban Chicago, told me her last name, which she recently hyphenated after marriage, is a constant source of jokes from men in her office.

Carla Pommert-Cherry, twenty-eight, said she took on this label within a group of friends in her service fraternity at the University of Virginia in Charlottesville when she was an undergraduate. At the fraternity's national convention, she was part of a group trying to change the words to the national song that referred to the "men of Alpha Phi Omega" and the use of "brother" to describe a member of the organization.

From that time on, she was treated differently in subtle ways. When inducted as the first female member of the organization's "stud core," a tongue-in-cheek honorary group, she was presented with a framed picture of the *Playboy* playmate of the year.

"At another meeting we had these bumper stickers, slogans for different brothers, and would say, 'Which brother is this?' They would hold up this made-up bumper sticker and we had to figure out who it was for. It wasn't for each brother in the chapter, but just for the ones who stood out for any reason. The one they held up for me was 'I Wear the Pants in My Family' and everyone knew it was for me.

"I don't mean to imply that it was done in a malicious way, because it wasn't. It was very playful and I felt those people cared about me and they weren't trying to make me feel bad about who I was, but it did make me stand out from other people, which was fine. I guess I did stand out from them," Pommert-Cherry said. "I never considered myself to be a radical person in any way, so it was kind of an eye-opening experience. These people think I'm radical even though I don't think so."

## Let Sleeping Movements Lie?

By these conversations, it might appear that feminism is just a lot of trouble. It creates needless tensions, divisions, misunderstandings, brandings.

Then why don't we just call it an era and go home? Forget about it. We accept its principles anyway and appreciate its past, so why bother?

Let sleeping movements lie.

But some have pointed out that for anyone concerned with women's rights, feminism is still worthwhile to consider, no matter what the connotations. They say it has value for its political, social and cultural power to critique and transform. And a commitment to feminism keeps people's guards up to preserve past progress and make future gains.

"There is a danger in being complacent, [in thinking] we have won the revolution because we can be doctors and lawyers, forgetting that feminist revolution is supposed to be about all women and really all people," Barbara Ehrenreich told me in an interview for this book.

Feminism is a base for action to accomplish any real change. This can happen individually, or, to really make a difference, on a collective level. It provides a link from one woman to the next, often working, caring or learning in isolation.

This solidarity or sisterhood (to use an old-fashioned term) is one of the most fundamental and meaningful visions of feminism. Without it, it's basically every woman for herself.

Feminism helps form a vision broader than one's own experiences to make a stand for other women, some with different backgrounds, with different pressures, with different priorities. While many problems, such as sexual violence and abortion rights, cross all lines, other problems (lack of health care, housing, poverty) are confined to those with the least resources to fight back.

To stop and discount feminism now is to accept the status quo, which isn't bad for some, but is indeed quite horrible for many. The effect is the same as climbing a ladder to a certain point and kicking it away. The general population is standing on a precipice higher than where their mothers began, but is abandoning the possibility of step-ping back on the ladder and making further ascent. Casting away the tools for making progress leaves one unarmed to fight to preserve past gains and forces one back down a few notches.

Other reasons to continue the feminist fight are cultural and intel-lectual. Feminism provides a set of questions with which we examine identity. It can encourage the most basic, routine introspection. These questions can extend to a wider social critique, providing tools to ex-amine literature, history, politics, leadership, religion, medicine and much more.

With a personal understanding of sexism, people also become more sensitive to other political struggles. It is a channel for politicizing or educating women, who make up half the population, to the meaning of oppression.

## Feminist: Connection or Commitment?

To create change or form insights around feminism, activists voice the need for some kind of personal connection. This might be anything from a concern to a commitment, whether personal or political. They say it doesn't matter if the term "feminist" is articulated.

This is different from saying one wants certain rights, such as equal pay for equal work, or appreciating the movement, or recognizing that sexism still exists. It's a commitment to the whole program, to women, not just one little limited bit of rights.

"I don't think it's just terminology. It's not just saying the name. It's saying I'm part of this. I can identify with this fight; this fight is my fight," said Marilyn Gerber Freid, feminist author, professor and direc-tor of the Civil Liberties Program at Hampshire College in Amherst, Massachusetts.

"Oftentimes when people say I'm not a feminist, it's a code word for saying I'm not a lesbian. I think it's important for people to be able to say I believe in these things. I do think all these things are important and I'm going to fight for them."

By no means does everyone have the obligation to make this com-mitment. People interviewed gave very reasonable answers for not making it, including much greater priorities and interests elsewhere. Sometimes it is a question of personality.

This answer given by one twenty-six-year-old woman struggling in her field summed up the difference:

"If you're going to get into a field you want to, and you'll be able to prove yourself, you're basically doing it for yourself. I'm not out to fight anyone's war. I'll fight my own war. I'm in a company with two female executives, lower management executives. If I want to do that, the opportunity is there."

But even on a small, personal level, there is a power in that identification. Being a feminist doesn't necessarily mean being someone who is willing to make feminism foremost and dedicate her life to it and start a union, operate a domestic violence shelter or run for public office. But in making any kind of commitment, taking women seriously becomes one more factor, one more value guiding decisions.

Identifying values can even be useful on the political level during election season to judge if a candidate is serving one's interests. A person may believe in empowering poor women, but never takes that belief into account when voting for someone who cuts social programs.

Several people interviewed told me how they act on their beliefs in everyday lives. Sarah Edmunds said that she tries to find female voice-overs, which many say lack authority to sell a product. Eric Shang, twenty-three, a high school teacher in Vallejo, California, makes sure to teach landmark events of the women's movement with other lessons in his history class.

Mark Halperin, twenty-five, a television network news reporter in Washington, D.C., and a self-proclaimed feminist, said he acts on his values in everyday life by getting women exposure on screen. "Television is not really complicated, but if you have a picture of something, you can say much, much more than a thousand words."

He gave an example of choosing a female expert on chemical weapons who was just as, but not more, qualified as male counterparts. "In some ways, I'd rather both men and women not get involved in the military, but as long as I have a job with that responsibility, I will get a woman icon out there that shatters people's normal perceptions of who they will be seeing talk about chemical weapons."

One difference between commitment and no commitment is social consciousness. This is what happens when one takes on that little, scary "ist."

The dynamics of this process of building social consciousness compares to the recent movement to raise the public's awareness about the environment. Before all the tremendous media attention with Earth Day in 1990, there didn't seem to be a problem with people's attitudes about the environment; just about any person polled agreed that pollution was bad and that it still existed and that the environmental movement of the past had been beneficial. But after seeing the images of the burdened landfills flashed repeatedly on television and the issue explored with concrete statistics and urgency, something changed. People identified what they believed in and made a commitment to improving the environment. More people personally made the connections of realizing their power for change and the consequences of their behavior on the earth. This had not been as obvious before and was thus taken for granted.

Like others, I expressed the commitment in an individual way. I began to go out of my way to recycle and buy different products. I now am going further to question some root values of our society that got us in this mess to begin with. While I do not articulate the word, I have done what really counts: I have taken a stand for the environment and have made some connections. What is needed is a similar sense of urgency and personal commitment to feminism.

## Use of the F-Word

Like "environmentalist," the word "feminist" signifies making a conscious stand for a set of principles.

But since the word is not required in making the commitment to feminism, some might question the use of it. More than with "environmentalist," "feminist" may seem unnecessary because of its stigma.

A natural response is to change the word "feminist" to a word with fewer stigmas attached. But inevitably the same thing will happen to that magical word. Part of the radical connotation of feminism is not due to the word, but to the action. The act of a woman standing up for herself is radical, whether she calls herself a feminist or not. For example, the father of Hortencia Velez called her a rebel when she stood up to him. This word *rebelde* carried the same insult as if he had said "feminist."

"You'll find that in any culture, people who think about change are outcasts," said Luke Garrott, twenty-three, a graduate student at the University of Florida, Gainesville. "People are set in their ways, and when others come in to change them, they're outcasts."

"Feminism" goes further than the more neutral words "humanism," "egalitarian," "nongenderist." It acknowledges a specific body of work and tradition for political, cultural and social analysis.

Farnaz Fatemi, twenty-two, a teaching assistant specializing in women's studies at the University of California-Santa Cruz, told me that her students prefer this word to include men, and gave her argument for preserving "feminist."

"We're not going to go anywhere if we keep calling it other things," she said, "because [a different name] changes what is behind it. The whole idea is that women have systematically not been treated equal. And when you go away from 'feminism,' you aren't acknowledging all the things that feminism has said in its theories. There's a lot behind it. There's a reason for that body of thought." She also said that discarding the word implies that all the battles are won and that we no longer need this theoretical base for women to get together.

Also, as the women's movement has demonstrated, there's a power in naming something. Pay equity, sexism, acquaintance rape. These labels helped define, articulate and legitimize issues.

On a level of principles, the word feminist also demonstrates integrity. It conveys that someone is willing to stand for what they believe in. Ken Kurson, twenty-three, a Chicago musician, gave this argument after a female friend gave a "yes, but" answer:

"Why are you allowing other people's judgments so much credence? If someone asks me what religion I am, I would say, 'I'm a Jew.' I wouldn't say, but I'm really generous. I don't cheat people. They can think whatever they want. I don't care whatever stigma they attach to that. There's no problem with it. If someone wants to think that if you're a feminist, then you're out there beating up men, then so what."

By using the F-word or making a feminist statement, feminism is introduced more into the mainstream and is de-radicalized. The first time the words "Ms." or "chairperson" were proposed, they sounded too awkward to work. But they do.

"I think the best way to deal with it is to keep saying things every time you can," said Andrea Rose Askowitz. "Don't let things get by. If the man in the restaurant says, 'Hey, baby, can I take your order,' you say, 'That's no way to deal with someone. That's no way to treat a customer.' And if more and more women start doing that, then it won't be that freak one woman anymore.

"So I don't think we should come off our crusade. We shouldn't bow down and stop having everyday rebellions, like Gloria Steinem says. But we should get more women to speak out, and we shouldn't be afraid of being labeled the one radical voice. Because that's okay. It's not okay because it disqualifies the person, but it's okay because people are still hearing it. And the more that someone hears something that sounds radical at first, [the more] they get used to it."

In making that commitment, feminists also feel relief from isolation by identifying with the movement as a whole. People are not alone in their work or concerns; they are joining a community.

Fatemi told me why she had attended a rally the previous night: "At least you know there are others who feel the same way you do sometimes. We're all involved in this together, and that's nice to know. That why I go to those things—you need to feel that. I know things are happening, and I definitely don't want to do it by myself."

Yet this issue of using the word is problematic. No one should be obligated to use it. After all, different people have more to risk. Some are in privileged situations in which it will bring acceptance, not alienation. It is not essential for change to take place.

"In a way it's intellectualizing because I think that the feeling of knowing you're conquering something, you're changing something yourself, doesn't need to have a name to have it happen," Fatemi said. "I think that's important. There is a danger in coming to the university and saying I'm enlightened because I know the names for it and you don't."

BY examining the conflicting perceptions young women and men have of feminism, a reevaluation is being sought. Such dialogue can reveal the stereotypes, along with the real needs and values. It can test to see how the feminist philosophy and women's movement have succeeded and failed to accommodate them.

Armed with this self-knowledge, young people can take command. Instead of rejecting feminism as unyielding and rigid, they can shape it themselves, make it flexible, permeable, malleable, to suit their own values and goals. There is potential to tailor it without sacrificing its original integrity.

The rigid definition of feminism in the first paragraph of this chapter just doesn't work. In all my interviews with feminists both novice and veteran, I can honestly say that I really didn't meet anyone who fits this description. Actually, I would be terrified if I did.

The term "feminist" can divide and repel. But the concept also has the potential to unite young people. And after all, wasn't that the whole point to begin with?

♀ PART TWO

# THE ROOTS OF OUR PERCEPTIONS

# Chapter Two

# Distortions and Exposures

WHEN ASKED TO describe a "feminist," most people interviewed had no trouble responding. The challenge was explaining the sources of these images.

Part of the confusion was rooted in stereotypes. Trying to explain one's perceptions about feminism is often like entering a hall of mirrors; you have to look hard to detect the true image.

The challenge is greater for the twentysomething generation, which has a limited history of and personal contact with feminism and the women's movement. With this lack of exposure, they rely more on stereotypes to explain and fill in the gaps.

Tracing one's experience with feminism helps distinguish the distortions. This process involves investigating media and personal exposure, the most common influences named, as well as addressing the issue of the lack of a young feminist voice. It also helps explain the connections and commitments being made to feminism and this generation's general reluctance to examine it beyond a surface level.

# THE STEREOTYPES

## Man-Bashers

A lingering, built-in mechanism for chilling feminist speech is its association with man-haters. Some think that one who speaks up for herself or for other women must have something against men or be unable to attract them.

This image is particularly threatening to heterosexual young women. They are at a stage in life when men seem crucial for forming basic identities and for being socially accepted.

They may also fear jeopardizing their future by scaring men off; this is a time in life when many lasting relationships are formed. Others are financially or emotionally dependent on men and don't want to make waves.

And the sad truth is that many men really are repelled by feminist associations. The men I interviewed were far more apt to describe feminists as man-haters than the women.

The worry of turning off men with feminist assertions is often greater off a college campus, where people socialize more in groups. Leaving the college community is like stepping right onto Noah's Ark; suddenly the couple becomes the focal point of all social life and emotional support.

I talked with Gilit Abraham, twenty-three, who said she knows the consequences of speaking up as a feminist. Abraham, who is working as a bartender to put herself through graduate school, expresses frustration at leaving her undergraduate progressive community. She is now living in a Chicago suburb where feminist views are considered alien.

"Probably, by the way my social life is going, which is nonexistent, there is always that worry," she said. "Am I going to meet people, people I'm interested in and want to spend time with? And a certain aspect of that is meeting guys. I am interested in having a family in the future and spending my life with people, with one person in particular, if I can find that."

She explained the conflict of acting like a feminist. "It's always a toss-up. Well, if I do this, which is more of an expression of myself, am I going to be able to find that person? It might be a slight turn-off for people."

She hesitated for a moment. "But then I have to accept that that type of person who would be turned off wouldn't be the type I would want anyway."

## Homophobia

Another undeniable smokescreen blocking exploration of feminism is homophobia.

At first, those interviewed hardly ever cited it as an influence. But then as interviews progressed and people became more honest, the word "lesbians" began to enter the conversation.

Sarah Edmunds said she sees lesbian rights as a central feminist issue that she doesn't feel personally affects her. She said she got this impression from a lesbian relative who is a feminist. "I think the women who were most active, who were the most aggressive-type feminists, a lot of it was associated with homosexuality and not women's rights. And that's not something that everyone necessarily wants to be associated with."

The image of feminists as lesbians is so strong that any feminist institution, even a women's college, becomes "suspect."

"My parents were pressuring me to transfer," said Jennifer Callahan, twenty-six, a teacher in New York City, who attended Smith College in Northampton, Massachusetts, and then Brown University in Providence. "And I think it's because they were afraid I would become a lesbian if I stayed."

One woman said this fear of being labeled a lesbian was a factor in her quitting the feminist action group at her conservative Ohio university. "Later the organization became more militant and the women who were leaders were lesbian separatists and didn't want anything to do with men. That's when I left the organization. It had a bad reputation."

This fear is not confined to women. One male antirape activist told me in a conversation after our interview that many people think he must be gay if he is standing up for women.

The societal condemnation of lesbians is so strong that it discourages many from "coming out" as feminists. Lisa, twenty-six, a law student from Los Angeles who is a lesbian and did not want her last name used, said she has felt this pressure.

"The difference from twenty years ago is more tolerance of lesbians with more openness in society, but acceptance is still far from a common reality," she said. "What is different is that people do talk about it and people who feel comfortable enough are public about their homosexuality, but it's not any more accepted than it ever was, and I don't think it ever will be. It is still seen as deviant behavior; it is still seen as personal choice, which I don't believe it necessarily is."

To overcome the pressure, people who take feminist stands face a great personal challenge. To feel strong enough, they must confront their own homophobia and fears. The goal is to be secure enough about their identities or have enough of a support system to risk being labeled.

Homophobia can be explained by many sources, including religious indoctrination and pressure from peers. But it is also perpetuated because of lesbians' invisibility. For example, there are few images of gay men in the media, even fewer of lesbian women.

In television, a great number of recurring gay characters are male. Kristin Schwartz, the director of public affairs for the New York chapter of the Gay and Lesbian Alliance Against Defamation, lists as examples ABC's "Hooperman" and "Thirtysomething" and CBS's "Doctor, Doctor." She says on talk shows gay males are frequently invited to give both gay and lesbian perspectives. I have only found a handful of newspaper articles mentioning lesbians from the past three years.

People naturally associate lesbians with feminism because historically lesbians have taken vital leadership roles in the women's movement and other struggles for peace and justice. This is true on college campuses, in the community and in current scholarship. Some of the most influential contemporary feminist theorists, including Adrienne Rich and Audre Lorde, write about how being lesbian has politicized them and enriched their lives.

Feminist groups now actively work for lesbian rights. Although initially leaders of NOW, such as Betty Friedan, spoke of "a lavender menace," NOW has since made lesbian rights a part of its platform.

Like other oppressed people, lesbians are also generally more sensitive and open to feminism, which addresses the oppression of women. Lesbians know firsthand that many roles women take on are not based on women's choices and are consigned to us by the system.

For some, feminism means living a more woman-identified life. This can translate to many parts of one's existence, from literature to personal relationships. To some feminists, lesbianism is a broad term that deals with attitudes, and doesn't necessarily encompass sexual relations. Rich defines it in a spectrum of intensity women feel for each other, starting with basic emotional bonding.

The real source of any automatic lesbian label is a societal fear of feminism and its effects. It is a powerful and simple mechanism to keep women from asserting themselves and from stepping out of line. This reminds me of when I was little and watched boys in my class playing together on the blacktop. When one didn't cooperate, they would call him a "girl," a "sissy." People also control women's behavior when they deviate from the accepted role of keeping quiet by calling them "lesbians" or "feminists." In this culture, questioning someone's sexuality means pulling their strings.

## THE MEDIA

People's stereotypes are frequently derived from the most common source of feminist contact: the media. This is the origin of one of the most unarguably notorious, enduring and pervasive feminist images: bra-burning.

For an explanation, I went right to the source, a key eyewitness on the scene, Robin Morgan, a veteran feminist activist and author, now editor in chief of *Ms.* magazine. Morgan engineered a protest of the Miss America Pageant in 1968 in Atlantic City, where this event was first widely alleged to have taken place.

"We never burned bras," she said, remarking that this is a common question reporters ask her. "What we did was we had this huge trash can that people decorated and that we called a freedom trash can. We threw bras into it along with steno pads and diapers and torture high heels and girdles and dishcloths and symbols of women's oppression, but we never burned them."

She explained bra-burning's origin in the press, which covered the protest widely. The Miss America protest was a major media event that first exposed millions of Americans to the women's movement. (In the *New York Times* alone, it received ten times the press attention as the pageant.)

"I think it was the invention of a headline writer of the *New York Post*," said Morgan. "At that point, men were burning draft cards, so he made up this headline that said: 'First men burned draft cards and now women are burning bras?' And the media took off and ran with it.

"I think something like five to seven years later a group of women, I believe in Chicago, finally made an honest media out of the media and actually did burn a bra on the shores of Lake Michigan, but that was way after the fact."

While this action looks extremist to people in the early Nineties, it was tame in the context of that era.

"The bra-burning came out of the Vietnam War," said Vivian Gornick, forty-seven, who wrote about radical feminists in the *Village Voice* in that period. "Those were the years that radicalized America. People were in SDS [Students for a Democratic Society, a New Left antiwar group]. People were burning alive across the world. Burning a bra wasn't that much."

Along with the bra-burners and others of the antiwar era, feminists in general have become historic media caricatures. They join the ranks of the hippies romping around in the mud in yet another "Let's remember Woodstock" special, or the airheads hawking albums on a cable "Freedom Rock" commercial. The greatest use for this cast of characters seems to be as a theme for a frat party, not a trigger of social consciousness.

The impact of television on Americans' frame of reference is enormous. According to the authors of *Unreliable Sources,* a 1990 guide to detecting media bias nationwide, in a twenty-four-hour period, an American home has a TV on for an average of nearly seven hours, with individual viewing averaging thirty-one hours a week. By age sixteen, the typical American has already witnessed 300,000 commercials. The sole source of news for most Americans comes from TV.

Television has been a particularly powerful influence on the younger generation—as a babysitter, long-time companion and lifeline to the outside world. According to *Time* magazine, 43 percent of 602 eighteen- to twenty-nine-year-old Americans polled in 1990 said they spent more time watching television than they did with their parents. They were suckled by "Sesame Street"; taught about right and wrong from "Brady Bunch" episodes after school; versed in civics by "Schoolhouse Rock" cartoons on Saturday mornings; schooled about sex (and taken on an odyssey of its possible variations) by Phil Donahue; and influenced in forming cultural tastes by music videos. MTV News, just like the newspapers, has played a major part in defining the twentysomething generation's notion of current events.

## Isn't It Dead Yet?

From day one, while supporting certain isolated feminist principles, the press has helped to ridicule feminism.

In the late 1960s, when the popular women's movement was emerging from other civil rights struggles, the media distorted it by covering the most sensational actions of radical groups. This included the Miss America pageant protesters, a street theater group hexing Wall Street and denouncing capitalism and pickets in front of the New York City marriage license bureau, protesting marriage because it enslaved women. Often these activists were acting in extreme reaction to traditional roles imposed on them and this coverage created an aura for feminism as antifamily or antitradition.

Ignored were the less sensational, but no less audacious forces of women slowly and inextricably forging change on a grass-roots level across the country.

"A growing number of women in government, unions, education, law—NOW members as well as those in other formal organizations, new and old—were battling discriminatory regulations in every walk of life," writes Marcia Cohen in her chronicle of the early movement, *The Sisterhood.*

"This was the 'scut work' of the movement, the hard, unglamorous, day-to-day work, the picketing in freezing weather when nary a reporter showed, the organizing that led that year to 7,500 charges of sex discrimination filed with the EEOC (federal Equal Employment Opportunity Commission). Try submitting a major ten-page proposal for a state constitutional change to the media dolts, some activists moaned, and the press would totally ignore it. But let some deranged soul scream obscenities and they'd cover it as 'women's lib.' "

"Ironically, the media myth in the late Sixties was 'This will never get off the ground,' " Robin Morgan said. "Then consistently, at least once a year thereafter, *Time* magazine would run a story saying, 'Okay, now the women's movement is dead. Surely it's dead. Isn't it dead yet?' It's always been wishful thinking. Then they came up with the term 'postfeminist.' It's hilarious. They have been prematurely and erroneously predicting our death for the last twenty years."

*Time,* which competently chronicled the women's movement's progress in a special issue in 1990, was a formidable critic in the 1970s. Marcia Cohen reports that an issue in 1970 offering readers "A Second Look" at women's lib failed to mention the grass-roots advances, instead presenting "a ridiculous sampling of nearly every opposing diatribe (and there were plenty to choose from) that had appeared in the press in the past few months. Dead center on the page was a grotesque and ludicrous drawing of a grim, balloon-breasted woman idiotically attired in leather sandals and a lacy, infantile pinafore that rode a foot above her knees," Cohen describes, assuming the caricature was of Kate Millett, author of *Sexual Politics,* a bible for feminists. "She was waving aloft in one ridiculous militant, upstretched arm a formidably capacious brassiere."

The media also dismissed as a failure the first concerted national feminist event, a strike for equality in August 1970, with demonstrations planned in more than two dozen cities. "Despite the fact that women shut down Fifth Avenue, *Newsweek* emphasized that 'lib supporters came up short' in getting women out in the streets, explaining that 'women's lib' was a badly splintered movement," reports Susan J. Douglas, in an article about coverage of the event in a September 1990 issue of *In These Times.*

By this time, the pattern of coverage of feminist demonstrations was for the reporter to give some sound bites to rally speakers and then get the other side by interviewing hostile onlookers or "go out of his way to visit a supermarket to interview regular women," Douglas writes.

Douglas cites as an example CBS's report the day of the strike from a shopping area in Chicago quoting "regular people" as saying: women are already "paid very well"; "I'm totally against it. I don't know what women's libbers want to be liberated from."

"One of the effects of this kind of juxtaposition, in which women with complaints were shown only in highly charged, dramatic, public demonstrations, and women without complaints were seen in more tranquil, everyday settings, was that women shoppers opposed to the movement appeared more thoughtful, rational and persuasive than their feminist counterparts. The visual positioning of them, in places such as supermarket parking lots, makes these women seem much more connected to and in touch with the real fabric of everyday life," writes Douglas.

Joining a large chorus of others, in January 1971, an *Esquire* writer called the current battle for women's rights "phony," "ludicrous," and "a hair-raising emotional orgy of hatred . . . ," reports Marcia Cohen, further quoting the *Esquire* piece as saying, "These are not normal women. I think they are freaks . . . incapable of coming to terms with their own natures as females . . . neurotic, inadequate women . . . appallingly selfish."

Early on, the image of the feminist as out of touch and strident was sealed and fixed. But enough women seemed to hear the message of these radicals to carry on the movement for decades.

"It is not surprising," writes Douglas, "given such coverage, which was for many Americans their only initial exposure to the women's movement, that feminism became a dirty word and that the Equal Rights Amendment ultimately failed. But it is also testimony to the power of women's real lived experience that, despite such coverage, support for certain of the movement's goals continued to increase every year, especially among working women."

## Same Story

Through the formative years of the next generation and into the present, the media treatment of feminists has been less sensational. But in subtle ways, the same dynamics have still always been at work.

They have also worked their way into mainstream forms of entertainment.

One student I interviewed pointed out the hairy-legged feminist character from Berke Breathed's "Bloom County" comic strip, which ran through the 1980s. One man said his neutral image of feminists came from the "Maud" television sitcom of the 1970s. A woman mentioned folksinger Joan Baez and another pointed out "Cagney and Lacey" from the 1980s.

An image on the edge of my consciousness has been the Ellen James Society, a radical separatist group portrayed in the satirical 1982 movie "The World According to Garp," based on the John Irving novel. It featured a sect whose members cut out their tongues as testament to a girl who was raped and mutilated; for safety, they flocked around Garp's mother, a radical feminist guru. While many women writers have portrayed feminists in different lights, these few images in popular culture are what stand out.

## Bashing the Next Generation

Perhaps the most powerful and constant influence in perceptions, the news media, has damaged the credibility of feminists of the next generation. In spring of 1990, the actions of young feminists were ridiculed and distorted in two highly publicized stories on both coasts.

The first was the Barbara Bush/Wellesley College fiasco, which started when 150 women from the school protested Bush's selection as a commencement speaker, because it was based solely on the man to whom she happened to be married. Also that May, students at Mills, an elite women's college in Oakland, California, closed down their campus for two weeks in protest after administrators announced plans to make the school coed in order to attract more students.

"Much of the media response to these stands has been so condescendingly sexist it is genuinely astonishing. 'Those sweet, silly young things, why look at them stamp their cute little feet and get upset; oogums, woogums,' " writes syndicated *Dallas Times Herald* columnist Molly Ivins in a May 21, 1990, article.

Some condemnation resulted in a misunderstanding of what the women were fighting for, which was the historic purpose of women's colleges. In the Wellesley controversy, the women were dismissed as antifamily, although the petition and a reply by one of the protesters made it clear they were not condemning Mrs. Bush for her chosen role as wife and mother.

"Barbara Bush was selected because of her husband's accomplishments and notoriety, not . . . her own," writes petition co-author Peggy Reid in a May 16, 1990, *New York Times* piece. "So it is not the validity of her choices in life that we are calling into question but rather the fact that we are honoring not Barbara Bush, but Mrs. George Bush."

Commentators and those quoted by the media defended Mrs. Bush, who was canonized throughout the whole ordeal as a hapless victim of these single-minded careerists, as pointed out by Barbara Ehrenreich in an interview.

A headline for a report on the reaction in *USA Today* read: "Wellesley 150 question first lady's choices." In that article, *Boston Globe* columnist Mike Barnicle was quoted as calling Wellesley students "unshaved feminists" who "after their parents are soaked for $80,000 in tuition, will go on to glorious and independent lives writing best sellers, conquering Wall Street, winning the Indianapolis 500 . . ."

Even the president himself got in on the action defending Mrs. Bush's life decisions: "I think that these young women can have a lot to learn from Barbara Bush and from her unselfishness and from her advocacy and being a good mother and a lot of other things," he was quoted as saying in the *New York Times*.

This criticism furthered the stereotype that feminism is antifamily. "The notion that the women's movement denigrates women who choose the traditional roles of wife and mother is errant nonsense," Molly Ivins writes. "I do not claim that no feminist has ever spoken disparagingly of those roles and their limitations. I do claim that the media have seized upon and overplayed those instances to an extent that it is a journalistic crime."

*Boston Globe* columnist Ellen Goodman, who had previously backed the choice of the First Lady as speaker, came out with a follow-up column recognizing that the media was perpetuating the image of a war between homemakers and careerists. "The Wellesley story fit the most popular scenario of social change: See these young (uppity) women trashing the older (virtuous) women. More to the point, it reinforced our favorite image that this is a fight (dare I say 'cat fight') between the CEO and the mommy, the woman at the office and at home."

Some knowledge of the history of women's colleges can help explain the young women's stance. The existence of such an institution makes a deliberate (and, indeed, radical) statement to teach women to form identities of their own. In such an environment, women are to be judged on their own merits, not by their relation to men or as "the coed." In this light, the endorsement of a speaker because of her association to a powerful man seems hypocritical, as the protesters rightfully pointed out.

While the Wellesley women were simply denounced, the Mills women were made to look like rabid man-haters, again affirming another feminist stereotype. The press also perpetuated the image of feminists as hysterics by focusing mainly on the women's initial episode of crying (when they first heard the announcement) and not the subsequent two weeks of cautious and expert organizing that resulted in the decision being reversed.

"I do not exaggerate. Some of the commentary has even been written in baby talk. Television keeps replaying the footage of the Mills girls weeping upon hearing they would have to go to school with what some commentators archly refer to as 'nasty, smelly boys.'" Ivins notes.

*Chicago Tribune* columnist Mike Royko illustrates this treatment of the "young hysterics" in a column headlined "Man, oh man, let's all loosen up a little bit": "The way they carried on, one might have thought that the administrators had said: 'We are going to admit large, hairy, naked hulks who drool, communicate by grunting and eat with their fingers.'"

While major papers on the West Coast and the *New York Times* thoroughly covered the subsequent events, many smaller papers received only the Associated Press photos of the crying scene, which they ran with little follow-up or explanation (such as was done at the small daily paper in Wisconsin for which I wrote). The broadcast media, based on three-second sound bites, also wasn't able to cover the situation in depth. On WNBC-TV in New York City, the anchors were laughing at the end of a report about the women's reaction, and a male said he felt as if he were being attacked.

Two participants in the protest said that they were portrayed with suspicion for living without men—and being happy. Angela Gibney, twenty, said that a common term used to describe their school was "cloister," while all-male institutions were termed "male strongholds."

"You can pick up all types of stuff from the media," she said. "For instance, you would never say men are sheltered or men are naive or men are virgins or gays because they want to live together."

She and the leader of the protest, Silja Talvi, twenty, told me members of the press personally voiced their suspicions, accusing the women on the campus of being lesbians for daring to prefer a single-sex learning environment.

While both women stressed that they did not see "lesbian" as an insult, and appreciated their campus as a generally tolerant refuge, the constant accusations from the media seemed like harassment.

I was surprised reporters were that hostile.

"They specifically asked you if you were lesbians?" I asked.

"Oh, definitely," said Gibney.

"Lots of people," said Talvi.

"Oh, lots!" Gibney echoed. "If you don't want to live with men, you must be lesbians!"

"Reporters?" I said.

"Sure!" both answered.

" 'Did something happen to you?' they'd ask," said Gibney. " 'Is that why you're a lesbian?' "

At the time, the press was also comparing the school to an all-male golf club and the Virginia Military Institute, both of which were being pressured to allow women to join.

"If males can't go to Mills, even the wimpy sort who would probably apply, why should I support the right of females to attend VMI?" Mike Royko asked in his column.

"If men were being constantly suppressed and oppressed and ignored and told they were not anything, there would definitely be a need for a man's college," Gibney said.

But none of the older people making the opinions stopped to recognize the real story emerging from both these defiant incidents: the next generation of feminists had arrived.

"I was asked at some point by some radio station or TV station to come on and talk about the Wellesley thing, and I said 'No, why don't you ask the students to come?'" said Barbara Ehrenreich. "That's ridiculous, that no one was saying here they are. They're grown up. Let's listen to them. It was really ageism to invite a forty-eight-year-old woman with no connection with any of these campuses to comment before asking these women themselves."

These two highly publicized feminist acts made an impact on young women watching. Julianna Sikes, seventeen, of Dixon, California, told me about the significance of the Mills protest for her when she heard media reports at her home near Oakland.

"For me, it was the first time I had ever seen women totally making a change for themselves and it showed me that women uniting together can make a change for their benefit. I agreed so much with their position, and it seemed everyone else didn't. My dad said Mills did 'this and this' and this is what is wrong with an all-women's college, and I totally didn't see it that way. I was really impressed."

## Broadcast News

As members of a generation not famous for being news readers, most people I interviewed reported that the most penetrating images come from an alternate source: TV talk shows.

"TV, that's where I got it," said homemaker Patrice Calvi. "You see all these he-woman types, keeping their hair short, even looking like a man. They have suits on. They can't even wear dresses. Women are fed up, jumping up, and taking men down with them."

"TV. Just from the talk shows. Oprah, Donahue is what we got. Shows like that. They were on at lunchtime, and I would watch once in a while," said Jason Skidmore, twenty-one, a student at the University of Maryland, referring to the years when he was stationed overseas at the school's military base. "They are pushy about it, and a lot of times a man will say something and [women] are not listening to what he's saying. They are taking into account he's male."

Together, Oprah and Phil have informed the minds of a generation about feminism. The images that many have come away with are portraits of man-bashers, especially from shows mentioning the word 'feminist' in their theme.

## Perceiving the "Radical" as Spokesperson

But it is difficult to tell which negative images of "feminists" reflect the actual behavior of a guest on a talk show, or merely viewers' perceptions of her. The one definite conclusion is that exposure to feminist thinkers is limited. As a result, the public is missing a "mainstream" feminist voice, and feminists seem like a fringe group when they finally do appear.

Those feminists in the spotlight, who are often the extremists, also seem to define the complete feminist view. The public is not exposed to enough of a variety to see that feminists represent a spectrum of ideas.

A perfect example is the May 11, 1990, episode of ABC-TV's "Nightline," the most highbrow of talk shows, which, incidentally, is notorious for not booking women guests. A study by Fairness and Accuracy in Reporting in New York reported in 1989 revealed that only 10.3 percent of the guests on "Nightline" were female, and of the twenty most frequent guests, none were women. Entitled "Entertainment or Bad Taste," the program in question featured a debate about the uproar surrounding the booking by "Saturday Night Live" of notorious comic Andrew Dice Clay, whose first two albums, featuring sexist and racist epithets, have sold more than 700,000 copies.

Inspired by the subsequent boycott of the show by one cast member, Nora Dunn, and musical guest Sinead O'Connor, "Nightline" decided to debate "whether well-known people who use this kind of language do so to reflect society's ills, or contribute to them," according to the show's promotional voice-over. Announced were the guest debaters: executive producer of "Saturday Night Live" Lorne Michaels and feminist psychologist Phyllis Chesler of City University of New York.

It seemed that finally Clay was going to get his just deserts. This feminist was going to explain the difference between humor and hatred and finally shed light on the other side of the argument. Hold all calls.

Host Chris Wallace asked Chesler if people were misjudging Clay's radicalism as they had Lenny Bruce's in the Fifties.

CHESLER: No, this is really cut-rate Lenny Bruce, and there's no re-
deeming social value that I'm able to pick up. I'm worried [about
an] atmosphere that allows gang rape and date rape and that rape
on the pool table with the onlookers cheering it on that took place
in New Bedford, Massachusetts. I am worried—

WALLACE: But wait a minute, we're talking about Andrew Dice Clay
and comedy.

CHESLER: —No, no, I am worried—see, this sort of comedy cashes in
on an atmosphere that is increasingly intimidating to women. And
let me congratulate the two women who refused to perform with
him because what they're telling other women is: "You don't have
to stay on the date and take it if you're beginning to feel uncomfortable. If it makes you feel bad, if it makes you feel scared, you
can walk off. You don't have to stay on the date."

Then, with a few verbal volleys, Chesler and Michaels cut each other
off back and forth.

In this particular case, certain factors were at work to make "the
feminist" look extremist. First, the format made it impossible to make
a complex point. Chesler had two-second sound bites to map out the
ways in which the media is not harmless. When she tried to explain
herself, she was heckled or cut off.

Perhaps she failed to effectively tailor her criticisms to this medium.
The connection between Clay and a rape on a pool table was based on
too much advanced sexual-violence theory to be made in such an ab-
breviated spot. The comparison seemed insulting to viewers, who came
away with an image of men as mindless savages, ready to rape women
at the slightest provocation.

Unfortunately, since Chesler, a radical feminist, was chosen as the
sole female guest, many perceived her as representing a mainstream
feminist view. A better representative might have been a female come-
dian, such as protesting SNL cast member Nora Dunn, who would
have provided a more balanced and accessible explanation of why Clay
clashed with her values.

Other extreme feminists have become spokespeople, so to speak,
because they are guaranteed to make interesting copy. The December
17, 1989, issue of the *Chicago Sun-Times* ran an Associated Press story
headlined "Mistletoe banned as risky to women," which included the

explanation that "a psychology instructor had filed a grievance saying she believed it encourages sexual harassment." Also appearing in the *Sun-Times,* syndicated columnist Suzanne Fields, in a May 15, 1990, column, lambasted "certain feminists" who "need a funny-bone transplant, and right away" because of the National Organization for Women's proclaimed boycott over an *Esquire* spoof, "Your Wife: An Owner's Manual."

"Boycott? Whoever would have imagined Molly Yard with a subscription to *Esquire* in the first place?" Fields asks.

Feminism's "radical" image is by no means to be blamed on NOW or the other feminists named here. In activist circles, NOW is often criticized for being too liberal and moderate. Also, if the organization tried to act according to what is considered "moderate," it would never challenge anything or make improvements in women's lives. Then it would blend in with every other mainstream political group (and perhaps be mistaken for one of the two major electoral parties). A characteristic of an "out" group is having to choose its battles so as not to tarnish the image of those associated with it. An example is someone cautioning a black or Jewish person not to be loud because his or her behavior reflects on others.

But regardless of these principles, members of NOW next made the news and reinforced the "fringe" feminist stereotype that year as extremists with their strong rejection of Justice David Souter for the Supreme Court. A Washington round-up on September 26, 1990, by the syndicated Scripps Howard News Service reports NOW's reaction to Souter's likely approval: "National Organization for Women, joined by other abortion rights groups, will stage a 'do or die' rally Tuesday wearing red-and-white 'Stop Souter' buttons. NOW will proclaim that 'women will die' if Souter goes to the high court."

Without providing a space for NOW to explain their justifiable fear of abortion rights being lost, the article portrays America's largest national feminist organization as equating Justice Souter with a crazed killer.

These more sensational actions have an influence on how people view feminism. When NOW talks, they are most likely to be listened to because of their established status. They are acceptable to the press as white and middle class. Reporters also seek them out when they need a quick quote representing a feminist viewpoint because of this recognition.

But selective media coverage is often devastating in terms of image projected. The other ongoing grass-roots work of the hundreds of NOW chapters nationwide, and its thousands of members as a lobbying force and advocate for women, has been obscured.

The answer isn't to stop putting radical feminists on the air or in print and to replace or supplement them with "moderates." To show a wider spectrum of perspectives, news shows such as "Nightline" and opinions pages should feature more feminists in situations in which traditional "women's issues" are not in the spotlight, as suggested by Fairness and Accuracy in Reporting. For example, during coverage of the Persian Gulf War, feminists and peace activists Barbara Ehrenreich and Robin Morgan would have made interesting commentators on CNN, along with the fleet of retired military brass. When the budget is passed and money gets doled out for social programs, more feminist analysts would also be useful to determine how half the population would be affected.

## Women's Issues: The Second Sex

While coverage of "women's issues" has greatly improved in moving up from the feature to the news pages, the press still generally considers women as the second sex.

With this treatment, feminist issues themselves also take on a marginal quality. "The incurable tendency of the media to trivialize and marginalize women's issues—to treat real issues of discrimination and empowerment as though it all came down to who is going to open doors for whom—is just as strong now as it was at the time of the first women's marches twenty-five years ago," writes columnist Molly Ivins.

Washington Post columnist Judy Mann, an outspoken media critic, describes the recent impact on newspaper sales because of editors' slowness to address changing interests and advance women to positions as decision-makers.

"The results were predictable: Daily newspapers have lost a quarter of their women readers. The conventional wisdom in the industry is that women readers don't have the time to read newspapers anymore. That's nonsense; women's magazines are among the fastest-growing segment of the magazine industry. We make time for what is relevant," she writes in her book, *Mann for All Seasons.*

Absence of coverage of the major issues is also an indication that editors do not see these issues as important to men and women. In a speech given during the fall of 1990, Mann pointed out sparse coverage of the Family and Medical Leave Act that Bush vetoed in the summer of 1990:

"I can guarantee you," Mann was quoted by the *Chicago Tribune* as saying, "that Wimbledon [tennis] got more coverage in your newspaper . . . than the Family Medical Leave Act did."

The family in general is a fringe issue. Newspapers rarely devote a word to "child care and the lack of it, which is a daily wrenching reality," Mann writes. She also points out that papers neglect to cover the daily struggles of men and women to balance responsibilities at work and at home.

In covering the next generation, the media also continues to focus on the choices women supposedly have of a career or family, when both are necessary for most. "The whole issue of the next wave of feminism has gotten bogged down in a whole lot of media stereotypes and clichés at this point," Barbara Ehrenreich told me. " 'If the first generation wanted careers, does the second want families too?' It very narrowly focuses on sort of the most elite women who talk about careers as opposed to jobs."

Those women's issues that do receive play generally relate to the upper-middle or upper class, with the concerns of working-class women and women of color neglected. For example, in discussing women's responsibilities at home, the focus has been a "second shift" of housework, or men not doing their fair share. The media seldom goes further to discuss the dilemmas of single mothers, a large part of the population, facing myriad more wrenching issues.

The difference in issues among the classes is that those concerning poor women more often involve social policy, such as child care or health care. This means making the government accountable. More self-reliant, affluent women simply buy these essential services.

Sociologist Ruth Sidel, author of *On Her Own,* a study of young women's expectations in the Nineties, says this focus follows the general trend of the media pretending that the entire nation is upper middle class. The show "Roseanne," which premiered in the late Eighties, stood out because it alone portrayed a more typical American family living from paycheck to paycheck and not working in such white-collar fields as corporate management, medicine or law.

When I interviewed her, Sidel, who also authored the landmark book on the feminization of poverty, *Women and Children Last,* explained why the upper-middle-class image is so appealing for attracting an audience.

"That's what makes people buy clothes, that's what makes people buy makeup, what makes people buy kitchen equipment and all the things we buy—briefcases and dress-for-success suits and all the rest. So they focus on those aspects of society that are going to sell the most products and denigrate and ignore largely everybody else in society."

In the past decade, the press also has been short on analyzing violence against women, although safety is one of the most pressing concerns women have. In a December 4, 1989, *Time* cover story on the women's movement, rape was cited in a poll as being among the three top issues "very important to women." Yet the story did not explore this issue.

Especially ignored for years has been acquaintance rape. While this is one of the central issues on college campuses across the country, it has been ignored by the media. A 1988 survey of college women showed that one in four reported being a victim of rape or attempted rape. Only recently has it been covered with sensitivity and depth, with some of the factors behind it explained, such as in a December 1990 article in *McCall's* and a December 17, 1990, *People* story focusing on men's efforts.

## Quota of One

Feminism is also relegated to the fringe by a lack of feminist commentators in editorial sections of publications. Few mainstream feminist voices are on call to balance the extremist ones making the news.

For this section, which demands voices of authority, editors demonstrate how seriously they take women with their appointments. Here, actions speak louder than words, with a usual "quota of one" taking effect (as termed by *New York Times* columnist Anna Quindlen).

"Two editors in the last month of midsized daily papers have said to me—without a sense of self-consciousness—I really wish I could run your column, but I already run Ellen Goodman. It never occurred to them they were running Buckley and Safire and Buchanan and Rosenthal and Baker and Wicker and Tony Lewis," Quindlen said in an interview.

"It never occurred to them that there was something peculiar in thinking you can only have one woman. If you said to them, 'Don't you understand what blatant tokenism that is?' the wheels would start to turn very slowly. But when they said it, they just didn't get it."

Her comments were echoed by *San Francisco Examiner* columnist Stephanie Salter, who described a limit of feminist voices.

"We used to have Ellen Goodman, but when they—which is the typical way that newspapers think—they gave me a column on the op-ed page, their thinking was 'Well, now we have our own local feminist, so why do we need Ellen Goodman?' Of course, that was idiotic. *The Chronicle* [the *Examiner*'s competitor] immediately picked her up because they aren't fools and she is a terrific spokeswoman. We have other women columnists, but they're kind of very political like Mary McGrory or tend toward a lot of soft, warm fuzzy stuff. And so, I think I'm the main columnist people can count on to say, 'Oh, that's sexist.' "

But she stressed that feminist voices aren't alike, just like the conservative male columnists or others don't always have the same angle.

"Anna Quindlen's take, Ellen Goodman's take and my take are not going to be identical, any more than Mike Royko or Calvin Trillin or any guy. 'They write about the same damn thing, what's the difference?' " she said. "It's okay to write about the same damn thing if it's missiles or the Bush administration. Not that we don't write about the Bush administration. I know I do, Anna does, Goodman does. We're still seen as an oddity."

Yet, she said she senses more editors willing to take a risk and address more women's issues on the opinions pages in response to dwindling readership.

"It's still not considered politically mainstream thought, but I contend it is. A lot of it is simply semantics. If you turn down the volume and don't look at the word [feminist] but you do look at the actions, young and old alike, there's a lot of them."

Still, when many pundits use the word "feminist," it is a synonym for "radical feminists," which works to group all feminists into a monolithic clump. I grew up reading my hometown paper, the *Chicago Tribune,* which has this attitude toward feminists as well as an enduring paucity of feminist commentators. In his January 21, 1990, article, "Feminism, Children and the Assault on Motherhood," columnist Stephen Chapman referred to "the feminist attempts to devalue motherhood," without recognizing that the majority of his female audience likely hold feminist beliefs.

## PERSONAL EXPOSURE

If not from the press, many people's exposure to real, live feminists was at their college campuses. And much of this was also narrow.

"That's when you see everyone stand up for everybody's rights. You don't see too many kids in high school protesting about the CIA. Everyone feels safe to voice their opinions when they're in school, but I haven't seen that when I'm not in school," said Chris Jackiw, twenty-four, an auditor from Chicago.

He said after being in the workplace a year, the discussion of feminist issues is minimal. "I don't think I've really seen anybody avidly feminist. The only thing I have heard anyone complain about was a woman at work whined about how she shouldn't have to do her husband's laundry. That's about the biggest feminist issue I have heard."

As in the national media, the most visible people are the radical feminists. Sometimes more extreme groups seem to be enforcers of "politically correct" behavior. The impression they convey in trying to confront more subtle manifestations of sexism—jokes, language, etc.— is of intolerance and pettiness.

"College is where you become more aware of the issues, and therefore you become more aware of comments that are sexist or something like that, but I really hate the overboard thing," said Resa Hare, who attended UCLA, where her impressions of feminists were made.

"There was a case recently [where] some guy at a dormitory stuck a note under a door to a girl student that said, 'How many men does it take to do the dishes?' and the answer was: 'None, because men don't do dishes.' And she's filing suit against this guy."

Apparent hypersensitive behavior offends both feminists and nonfeminists alike. Two Cincinnati women I met separately—one who considers herself a feminist and another who doesn't—said they were turned off by the same feminist group at their conservative private university in Ohio.

One, who didn't want her name used, said the visibility of the group she joined made it difficult for her to become active on campus.

"I did a couple of sit-ins for women's safety and stuff like that. I thought it was really important because there wasn't much of a women's voice on campus.

She said the group also drifted from the issues she considered important. "I can remember when all the people got together and we were talking about why we were there, and it always got boiled down to a couple of issues—if you should call a woman a girl or a woman or hold the door open for a woman. It always came down to these two things. It was really weird."

Jodie Jones, twenty-three, a computer consultant who said she is not a feminist, was turned off seeing her campus feminist group fight battles she thought did not represent her concerns. What sticks in her mind was a campaign to use inclusive or nonsexist language in the school song and a protest of a campus beauty pageant.

"I think they vandalized. It's no way to accomplish things. They didn't do things in a productive manner. They did them in a way that makes people on campus look down on women and say, 'These stupid women, what are they doing?' They didn't cause any real change. It was some women's organization you wouldn't want to be associated with because the thinking on campus was so anti that group because of the way they handled things."

A reason for such confrontational tactics is that asking nicely doesn't often spur change. A visible demonstration that made national news was graffiti on stalls at bathrooms of Brown University during the fall of 1990. According to press reports, it was a last resort to push the university to improve its handling of rape cases. Across the country, campus activists are frustrated in not being able to get administrators to respond to the issue and take it seriously, and militant methods are often effective.

Men expressed the most negative responses to the feminist groups on their campuses. Even those at "progressive" schools seemed confused.

During an interview in their dorm floor lounge, four men at Columbia University in New York, who expressed strong support for women's issues, started to discuss some feminist actions that confounded them.

"We saw the posters for the new women's spirituality group, and they go and perform rituals together," said Justin Lundgren, twenty-one, a senior from Cincinnati. "We saw that and thought it was weird. It seemed like an excuse for women—and I think it's great, women getting together, and supporting each other and bonding and whatever —but it just seems weird because men probably have it in other groups that are male, but not for the sake of being male. Like a football team you could say is a spiritual group and there's bonding."

"But you would never get the guys to saying it's a spiritual group," said David Tepper, who is from Champaign, Illinois.

They discussed a similar effect in women's-studies classes and Lundgren sought feedback on another puzzle.

"There's this health group on campus, and I was talking to my friend Catherine about it and she was telling me about it. It was sort of like do your own gynecology, and all the women in the group check each other out, and that just weirded me out."

They laughed.

"You have a room of thirty women and they all strip down and go to it," Lundgren said.

"That's really weird," agreed Tepper.

"I thought that was weird," Lundgren said, "but it's not the same for men."

"We've got group proctology," Tepper joked. "That can't be done. Group proctology and lacrosse. Nope. Hmm. Hmm."

"The fact is that men's anatomy is much more simple. You can see everything and it's not as complicated," Lundgren reasoned.

"Gynecology is something for the patriarchy. You need a degree to practice it. It's a setup by the patriarchy," explained Tepper.

"Someone is in charge and instructs the women," Lundgren said. "It hits me on different levels. To me, touching bodies and everything,

it's pretty much homosexual. I can't imagine. It's a great image,"
Lundgren said.

But despite the joking, they were understanding of the group. "It
makes sense, like Lamaze for childbirth," said Kevin O'Connor,
twenty.

Lundgren reflected, "This is an experience I'll never be a part of. It's
very mysterious. It's not a part of my reality. It's intriguing and it's
scary, sort of."

"I think it's important. A lot of people have a mysterious view of
their own body," O'Connor said. "It's gaining control. Like a relative
had breast cancer and she went to the doctor and he gave her a mastec-
tomy when she didn't really need one. She really wasn't in control. She
didn't know what was going on with her own body. I think it's a really
good attempt to get to know your own body.

"It is a little threatening," he added.

Lundgren was still introspective. "Women are taking power, I don't
know. I wonder if I feel this way because my sex is losing power.

"There has got to be a little jealousy that women feel so much more
comfortable with their own bodies that they can actually do this [and]
that it is conceivable women can do this and it's inconceivable that
there can be a men's group doing it," O'Connor said.

Many men seemed comfortable, if somewhat confused, while observing feminists at a distance. Other men were annoyed when they came
too close. Greg Beaubien said he felt tension with more radical feminists in his English classes at the University of Illinois-Chicago.

"I took a lot of classes with a lot of bookish people who really never
got out into the world much and cloistered themselves away reading
books all the time. Within that context, a lot of the professors and a lot
of the students were feminist women and a lot of them, if I even sat
down next to them, would regard me with distaste. It was extremely
divisive, and they didn't make any effort to conceal the fact that they
hated men.

"The word misogyny—there's no equivalent word for women who
hate men, other than feminism. I know that's not what feminism
means, but that's as close as I can get."

Like the others, he was turned off by what he saw as a conformist
way of thinking, which he said contradicts what feminism is supposed
to stand for.

"It's like punk rockers who become punks because they want to rebel against conformity, but yet within their own group, they become just as conformist, where only certain mohawk haircuts or black leather jackets are considered cool."

Many men express confusion over how to deal with self-avowed feminists in daily life. Frank Capasso, twenty-three, a mechanic from McHenry, Illinois, said he has been unfairly castigated for showing some common courtesy. "I have never met [a feminist] who wasn't nasty in one way or another," he said.

He recounted two episodes at parties where he opened the door for some women. "In both cases, they were like: 'Thank you, I can do this for myself.'"

## A Limited Education:
## Joan of Arc and the Marshall Plan

Feminists also seem out of the mainstream because people of this generation are missing education about the movement. Without a serious mention in the classroom, the women's movement, which has affected the lives of everyone present, seems like a fringe concern.

The principles that underlie the women's movement and the motivations behind it have been lost to the twentysomething generation along with all other history past the Marshall Plan and World War II. Few interviewed said they remembered learning in high school about the transforming political conditions in the Sixties—including the civil rights and antiwar movements—that led to the women's movement.

"It's a black hole in our lives," said Paula Barksdale, twenty-five, who grew up in Boston and is now a corporate manager in St. Louis.

Because of a lack of time, most high school history lessons of those interviewed ended before that period. Lisa Scheeler described a common pattern of the last lessons taught. "We dealt with global policy, U.S. foreign policy, and that gave us insight on the wars: World War I, World War II, Korea. We didn't go as far as Vietnam. We only had one semester; we did a lot with the Marshall Plan, and stuff like that."

Asked about women's history, people only knew women who took on traditional male roles, such as Catherine the Great or Joan of Arc. A few mentioned famous figures such as Harriet Tubman, who helped 300 blacks escape slavery in the South in the mid-nineteenth century, or Susan B. Anthony, who helped lead the fight for women's suffrage.

But a new phenomenon of education has emerged in the past de-
cad[...] [...] to introduce women and men to their lost
hist[...] the idea emerged in the late Sixties,
wh[...] has now become an institution.

[...] ited to that 59 percent of the twenty-
son[...] s college, and to the much lower pro-
por[...] or can afford to take a nonvocation-
ally-minded class. Also, men have been an overwhelming minority in most classes. In the five I visited across the country, they usually made up about 10 percent of the class.

Yet the recent emergence of this scholarship has created a unique contrast in education among the Baby Busters. As these classes become more established and legitimized, the younger people in the age range, primarily those under twenty-three, have the greatest access to and interest in them.

The oldest twentysomethings, over twenty-eight, have a distant memory of the actual women's movement from the Seventies. While some parts are hazy and they did not share the same communities as the older generation, they remember the social consciousness and can explain some of its excitement and tumult.

This means that the people in the middle, those twenty-four to twenty-eight, are feeling a strange gap of education and personal exposure that makes the women's movement seem particularly detached from their lives.

## THE MISSING LINK:
## A YOUNG FEMINIST VOICE

Most authors have to work hard to limit their bibliographies. In re-searching the next generation of feminists, I had to make an especially vigorous effort just to locate one.

While visible feminist voices in general are scarce, the next genera-tion seems to be missing them almost entirely. They have not had the chance to define themselves or an agenda concerning the issues they care about.

One result of a lack of voice is the overall message that no one is carrying on the torch. This generation associates feminism with the radicals from the Sixties, not with themselves. The feminists feel isolated and the "uninitiated" do not generally see an available route for becoming active.

Julie Spencer Robinson, who worked at a women's public-interest organization in Washington, D.C. said she has noticed this void in the media and in older women's organizations.

"I surveyed ten years of literature for articles about young women and feminism. The *Readers' Guide to Periodical Literature,* the *Los Angeles Times, New York Times, Chicago Tribune* and alternative press index, from 1979 to 1988. There were a handful. It was worse than my worst nightmare. And all I would do was flip to the sections on feminism, young women, women's liberation, and there would be at the most a handful of articles."

I did my own hunt, and at first only came up with a half dozen stories from 1985 to 1990. But I knew there had to be more. I decided to turn this challenge over to an expert: a bona fide graduate student— one in women's studies no less—Farnaz Fatemi. I first asked her about her findings in scholarly research. She showed me abstracts or summaries from three dissertations that were vaguely related.

"I went through at least ten years of dissertations," Fatemi said. "You would expect that from 1980 on in women's studies, a lot of women were doing a lot of work. There wasn't anything close to young women and feminism."

"There is very little written about young women, and in what little there is, young women are spoken for. Other women are saying this is what they care about—reproductive rights or whatever else," Spencer Robinson pointed out, stressing that young women alone can effectively direct their futures because of their strikingly different world views and experiences.

"We're talking about a group of women who formed their political consciousness during the Reagan era," she explained. "We don't know anything else. I vaguely remember Carter. The first election I could vote in was the one Reagan won in a landslide, and that is true for the rest of the generation."

Young people also may define "women's issues" differently according to a changing world. "You can bet it will go beyond reproductive rights or reproductive freedoms," Spencer Robinson said. "It will go to equality, to equal pay for equal worth to comparable worth. It's going to include housing and the environment and it's going to include economic justice and all those things, because that's what we care about. And because these are the times we live in. It's very different from the Sixties."

Without this voice, young women have been isolated by proclamations of "postfeminism" by the media or a general popular decree that feminism is no longer needed.

"I just don't think that gets us anywhere to say, 'Oh you're not doing anything.' I think it would get us much further to say: 'Look at what young women are doing. Let's try to identify it, see what they're doing and hold it up for everyone to see and get energized.' Instead we get de-energized."

## Missing a Spotlight

The lack of young feminist leaders was made apparent by the responses of those I interviewed. Only a minority were able to name a feminist figure, and those named were mainly older women.

"All I can think of is the face. The woman with the gray hair and glasses," said Stephanie Boatley.

The only recognizable figure for the minority of people who answered was Gloria Steinem, founder of *Ms.* magazine, which began publication in 1972. But few knew quite what she did. Two people told me they thought she was a former Playboy bunny, while, in fact, in the early Sixties she had gone undercover as one for an exposé.

Even those with a strong sense of connection to feminism and current events didn't feel influenced by feminist leaders. Those they could recognize seemed to be of a different generation. Michelle Traupmann, twenty-three, a tutor in San Diego, had a fairly representative response.

"I don't really know, unfortunately. I listen to National Public Radio every day, but I'm not a real newspaper person. Let's think, leader of the women's movement. You know, there aren't any really, and I'm sort of embarrassed to say that. But there aren't. I'm not political enough to say, oh, whoever is so wonderful. There are a lot of women who I admire and think they're wonderful but they certainly haven't influenced me per se. I can't think of anyone specific."

I asked her if she had heard of Gloria Steinem, the old standby.

"Oh, sure, and I think she's great. But I wouldn't say I have been influenced by her. She influenced the older generation much more strongly. Part of the reason I know about her is my mom thought she was so great."

Other leading feminists were hardly recognized, including Molly Yard, president of the largest national women's organization, the National Organization for Women (NOW), whose term ended in 1991. Those few that recognized her considered her too abrasive and out of their age range. Yard, who has provided a half-century of leadership in the feminist, civil rights and trade union movements, is known for her strong, thunderous approach (which many admire) and was a personal friend of Eleanor Roosevelt.

Also seldom recognized or named was Betty Friedan, a NOW founder who helped spark the women's movement with her ground-breaking book, *The Feminine Mystique.*

"[Friedan] was great for what she did at that time, but I don't know if I could apply her activism and her wants to make a difference in my life. Things were different back then, I guess. She grew up in a very conservative, traditional era, and just that makes her kind of different," said Ann Bittinger, nineteen, of Central City, Nebraska, who in 1990 co-founded a chapter of the National Organization for Women at American University.

As far as the slighly less well-known figures, forget it. I asked my friend Michelle if she had ever heard of Germaine Greer, the author of *The Female Eunuch,* who shocked the country with a philosophical account of socially warped female sexuality.

She replied: "Do you mean Germaine Jackson?"

Only in instances when feminist leaders had spoken on campuses did young women seem to identify with them. An example is Andrea Rose Askowitz, who refers to Betty Friedan as "Betty" ("Betty was at Columbia yesterday," Andrea told me).

"Molly Yard, she's getting a lot of flak, but she came to [University of Pennsylvania] twice," said Askowitz, who graduated from that school in 1990. "We're small, we're a small group of activist people, and she really appreciates us. She's always talking about students."

## Yuppie-Centric Media

One reason younger feminists are also not apt to get coverage is because of a yuppie-centric media. Because of its size, the generation of Baby Boomers has defined every era by its own life stages. The Sixties were the age of youth, the Seventies of swinging disco singles, and the Eighties of sedate family life. Don't be surprised if the Nineties becomes the mid-life crisis decade, and the first ten years of the next century, the age of retirement.

In general, the media, which is largely run by Baby Boomers, misses its opportunities to spotlight young leaders. Instead, it tends to direct the spotlight to older and established activists. At the largest gathering of student environmentalists in history in October of 1990, the media mainly focused on the "star" names speaking. During a speech, Helen Denham, an organizer for the Student Environmental Action Coalition's "Catalyst" conference, which attracted more than 3,000 people, discussed a new challenge to see beyond the ways in which the media describes young people's role.

"I was coordinating national media for this conference," said Denham. "Every phone call I took had to do with Robert Redford, Ralph Nader or Helen Caldicott (speakers at the conference). The media is creating a standard for us. We are not setting our own standard and have to start."

## A More Subtle Enemy

But young feminists often aren't seen or heard in the media because of the nature of their work. A central difference between young feminists of the Nineties and those of the Sixties is visibility. One factor is that the nature of the battles against sexism being fought every day is less public and dramatic in nature and thus attracts less media spot-news coverage. Instead of a breaking story about a demonstration, reporters are faced with a pervasive, constantly evolving phenomenon without clear who-what-why-where-and-when angles.

"In the Sixties and Seventies, the women's movement made really visible changes. They struck down laws and rules and regulations, and colleges couldn't prohibit women anymore—those real visible things in public. Because women's interactions with men are so constant, complex and comprehensive, there are way more changes to be made," Julie Spencer Robinson said.

"We're definitely making changes as women now, but they aren't as visible: They're in our relationships with our co-workers, with our colleagues, with our families, with our bosses, our fathers or brothers or husbands or lovers. It doesn't get a headline. It's not like 'Julie's father stops using sexist language.'

"That doesn't get a headline, but that's a major change in a person's life, in one man's life, and that's happening all over the country because of women like me, who I believe are all over the country."

With feminism more adapted to the mainstream, many activists don't take on the same dramatic and defiant anti-establishment character as those in the Sixties. Elisa McBride, twenty-four, student organizer for the National Abortion Rights Action League in Washington, D.C. said students from all walks of life, men and women, whether in sororities or activist communities, are approaching her to get involved in pro-choice issues.

She sees a distinct change in the shape of feminist organizing from the year 1988 at her alma mater, Carleton College in Northfield, Minnesota. She said the feminist community, which before was set apart from the rest of the population, is not as visible now as its ideas and presence have seeped into the mainstream.

"That's what the women's movement always said would happen," McBride said. "Enough women are going to get angry because of the issues they have to deal with just because they're women.

"And that's really, really a positive thing, and it's really really important for the women's movement to be recognized and respect this thing that's happened with young women, and not just say this is not feminism as we have always defined feminism. Or they say 'girl' instead of 'woman' so they can't really be feminist. No, let's take women where they are. Let's respect the fact that they are getting active on this issue and go on from there."

# A Missing Vehicle

Along with the voice of young women being absent from older people's media, it also has been missing from their own. The result is the lack of a forum to build consciousness and associate feminism with the mainstream during the formative reading years. This has been true during the Eighties and in the present.

"I think that there is a lack of something pulling [young] women together like Gloria Steinem and *Ms.* did before," said Jane Pratt, twenty-eight, the editor of *Sassy,* a magazine for teens aged fourteen to nineteen.

*Ms.* has been a unique institution for the women's movement that provided a connection between women. Pratt herself remembers being initiated into feminism as a little girl reading children's stories from a special section of *Ms.* magazine, which her mother kept in their house in stacks. Since Pratt was hired to head *Sassy* magazine when it began in 1988, she and her staff have injected it with a unique feminist personality.

Pratt pointed out that while many magazines have "a proper political stance," fashion and men are inherently the dominant focuses. Politically focused articles are rare. Strong editorial positions on important issues are rarer.

"With most women's magazines, if you take the ratio of what they're covering, a very small percentage of it is either political in nature or deals with something other than men, makeup or clothes or cooking," Pratt said.

Issues specifically vital to young women have been barely or not consistently covered. In July of 1990, the Supreme Court sent out shock waves to young women by upholding parental-consent laws for abortion, providing key ammunition for antichoice forces to chip away at the 1973 *Roe v. Wade* decision. This ruling made young women a political football by backing the laws being enforced in thirteen states and clearing the way for a flood of others on the books or about to be added. While statistics say that more than half of young people naturally consult their parents before having an abortion, the threat is to the lives of others who fail to get parental or court permission and resort to illegal and unsafe abortions.

This issue has been at the forefront in politicizing legions of women in high schools and college campuses and launching them into activist roles, but magazines for young women have barely touched it. Even general-interest magazines such as *Time, People* and *Newsweek* covered this issue in 1990. While others may have followed the next year, besides *Ms.*, only one young women's magazine, *Seventeen,* was listed in the magazine reference guide as addressing it in 1989 (with a short side story).

In general, the magazines for twentysomething women cover issues directly relating to its largely white middle class over-eighteen audience. They rarely include coverage of working-class or poor women's issues, such as child-support enforcement, housing, public-aid reform or lack of prenatal care. Like the articles on beauty, the issues covered rarely involve a social consciousness. Instead of focusing on society, they mainly concentrate on the self.

Young women's magazines also fail to regularly profile or give sufficient voice to the ample number of new, young, articulate and visionary feminist leaders across the country. When they do appear, they are featured in lists of the top ten college women or top ten women of the year. These blurbs allow just enough space to include credentials. More often the people profiled in depth are models or television or film stars.

While the young women's magazines sometimes espouse feminist principles and often feature outstanding articles on certain "women's issues," the messages they give are often contradictory. Much of this is subtle, such as in the images constantly used of perfect women, which set up impossible standards for readers. Other magazines are almost schizophrenic. The February 1991 issue of *Cosmopolitan* includes two outstanding articles on acquaintance rape and making corporate employees more accountable to women. But other advice regularly given, such as how to manipulate people, namely men, seems to contradict the positive messages about self-determination and self-esteem. Its February 1989 issue, devoted to "How to Attract a Man Like Crazy," offers the following tips: "Catch a man's eye and then very deliberately look down at his crotch" or "Spill a glass of wine (water, whatever) down the front of your dress while talking to him. Ask for his handkerchief to mop it up."

Coverage of controversial issues is also generally lax. *Sassy* editor Pratt points out that issues aren't addressed until they are guaranteed "safe." She observed that most magazines didn't discuss the environment until after it was embraced by the general population. The coverage of feminism depends on its popular acceptance. While feminism could be popular one season, it may disappear from the pages with the sway of public opinion.

Other magazines get around taking a stand on controversial issues by laying them out in reader polls, as Gloria Steinem points out in her landmark exposé, "Sex, Lies and Advertising" in the August 1990 *Ms.*

But in making these observations, it's hard for me to blame the magazines for not being more political or critical. After all, they aren't political magazines, and feminism is, in various forms, one of their beats. Criticizing them for not being feminist-based is like criticizing *Sports Illustrated* for not mainly covering tennis. Offering some good entertainment and information, they have a role in young women's lives; I myself would rather take a copy of *Vogue* than *The Nation* to the beach any day.

Women's magazines also have a constant effect on raising awareness of readers on women's issues. Stephanie Boatley said that her knowledge of women's rights comes from several glossies. "I heard a lot of it from different little places. I have subscriptions to *Vogue, Elle, Ebony, Essence*, all those magazines. Since those are, all but *Ebony*, basically women's magazines, they push a lot of the issues. They have a lot of articles with questions and answers that shed a lot of light on the subject for me."

Also, women's magazines in general encounter powerful forces preventing them from going over the boundaries: advertisers. According to Steinem's exposé and to others in publishing I have talked with, advertisers typically demand that women's magazines devote a certain percentage of content to beauty and matters related to their products. Many ads also come with the stipulation that they not appear near articles that are controversial or not upbeat in tone.

Pratt knows this risk well, having experienced firsthand the havoc controversy can wreak on a magazine's stability. In 1988, during the first year of publication for *Sassy*, her magazine lost five of its biggest advertisers in six months after being targeted by a right-wing fundamentalist group.

"The Moral Majority didn't like us a whole lot, and we had a boycott of our magazine because of it, and it was amazing to see what kind of power these groups have. Still, when we do something, when we take a stance on an issue, we get a little bit of backlash, not what we experienced before, but if you're going to take stances, that's what's going to happen. At the same time, that's also what makes us stand apart and it's also what makes the reader who likes the magazine, love the magazine. That was really a hellish experience there. It was pretty bad."

She mentioned that one of the offending articles was providing information on birth control, in which the author didn't tell readers to save sex until after marriage. *Sassy* also made waves that year with candid stories headlined "The Truth About Boys' Bodies" and "How to Kiss."

"But really the horrible thing was that when they were sending these letters to advertisers complaining about the magazine, they were talking mainly about stories that had never run. What happens is they have a newsletter, 'Focus on the Family,' and in the newsletter they said we had done a bunch of articles we had never done."

While the uproar eventually led to the magazine being sold to another company (the same one that owns *Ms.*), *Sassy* recovered strongly and its circulation in three years has grown to 650,000. But Elizabeth Larsen, who formerly worked at the magazine and is now assistant editor at *Utne Reader,* reports in *Extra!* that *Sassy* has not been able to continue its frank pieces about sexuality that are not available elsewhere to this age group.

## No Intake Mechanism of One's Own

The list of issues is growing rapidly, and yet no magazine with the goal of serving as a feminist voice for young women has emerged. Young women don't have their own version of *Ms.* as a consistent forum, mode of expression and intake mechanism into feminism during their opinion-forming years. Jane Pratt agrees that she notices a present gap in magazines for twentysomethings. "They say eighteen to twenty-four is the market everyone wants to hit. And for eighteen- to twenty-four-year-old women, there are probably a dozen magazines aimed at that market, and yet there really isn't a feminist magazine aimed at that."

The result is that women in their twenties with an interest in feminism feel like people who have just graduated from college and have lost their campus communities.

"I wonder because we've had, I have some readers telling me that they keep reading *Sassy* even into their early twenties because there isn't really anything for them to go on to. I have gotten plenty of letters saying that. That kind of concerns them. We make them feel aware and where do they go?" Pratt said.

But *Sassy* has only been around since 1988, and has not been an influence on the twentysomething generation. It also does not consciously identify itself as a feminist publication or discuss "the movement."

The only adult magazine taking an obviously feminist stand, *Ms.*, an institution of the women's movement since 1972, does cover an amazing diversity of issues. While presently targeted to all groups, it has in the past been an older women's institution while the twentysomethings have been growing up. During the Eighties, it matured with the Sixties generation that constituted its readership.

Those few people I interviewed who had read *Ms.* during that time said it went over their heads or seemed too old for them. I also remember reading it in college and definitely not feeling a part of its target audience. I felt I had stumbled upon a diary of older women with numerous references to the Sixties.

Even though the perspective of *Ms.* has become more diverse, young women still see it as a publication whose audience is growing older with it. It also is not uniquely tailored to a young audience as a forum for their experiences, as it was for the older generation.

"Not that it's not interesting to people in their early twenties, but [*Ms.* has] a real natural audience in older people who have been feminists for a while," Pratt said. "And I think it definitely has to work to pull in younger women [as well as] younger women who are feminist in their views but would not call themselves feminist. I think *Ms.* probably has to struggle with that."

In a cover story about the struggles of *Ms.* in the November 1990 *Mother Jones*, writer (and former *Ms.* intern) Peggy Orenstein criticized *Ms.* for not fulfilling its original mission as an intake mechanism.

While many feminists say women's studies is performing the job, Orenstein acknowledges that a mass, glossy magazine is more accessible and has a more widespread potential.

Orenstein pointed out the drift of *Ms.* from its central focus as an intake mechanism for casual feminists to being focused more on preaching to the converted and going over the heads of many younger women. She noted that the authors in the first revamped issue in August of 1990 were longtime feminists, such as Adrienne Rich, Andrea Dworkin, Marilyn French and Bella Abzug, with only one main "nod to the uninitiated," a feature about ordinary people made activist by extraordinary situations.

When she persisted in questioning editor Robin Morgan about the inclusion of young women, Morgan replied that the movement originals need their space: "Reaching you women of whatever age is one function," she said. "But another and, quite frankly, more basic one is to speak to our own constituency, which has been ignored by everybody. Some of the feminist media, in trying to do outreach, has ignored the long-distance runners. We deserve some sustenance too."

But, in my interview with her, Morgan stressed that the magazine has received a dramatic response from younger readers, that their issues are being addressed (such as coverage of acquaintance rape and a young feminist dialogue) and that two-thirds of the staff is under thirty. She also said that an intake mechanism is part of her goals.

"It's one of the things I very much want *Ms.* to do. It's not precluding anything else. It embraces women of all ages, as well as races and sexual preferences and classes and nationalities."

## No Room at the Top

Like *Ms.,* the established, visible national mainstream feminist institutions have also matured with their memberships. The result is that certain young women entering them are finding a new conflict.

In the Sixties, the founders used them to develop their personal potential as leaders and carry out their visions. In the Nineties, some young women are limited to another role: that of the office gofer.

Although young women have joined the major organizations, such as the largest and most powerful, the National Organization for Women, at local, state and national levels, the visible spokespeople at the very top are older.

The benefit of such groups is that women have a concerted, united, legitimate voice. They are powerful forces to deal with, establishments, just like the organs of government and private businesses they monitor. But young women wanting to share national leadership can see them as steep structures to scale. Those who founded the organizations twenty-five years ago often are still running things, and there isn't much room at the top. They may even confront a stumbling block given a name by the feminist movement to describe limits in corporations for women: a glass ceiling.

This was pointed out by Mara Verheyden-Hillard, twenty-seven, the organizer of a large event in 1989 billed as the first national young feminist conference. She is also a former director and originator of the Feminist Futures program, a young women's networking arm of the Center for Women Policy Studies in Washington, D.C.

"I see a lot of women who come to Washington and they really want to get involved in the women's movement. They really want to get their foot in the door of the women's movement, and it's very hard. Most end up being support staff, which is okay. That is an entry-level position," she said in a speech at an October 1988 conference.

She and others working in organizations explained that turnover at the top is low, with limited options for the directors in the private sector. They stressed that at the entry level, young women are frustrated at not being able to make a substantial change.

"There are very few places where young women can go where they can say what they think, where their opinions are important and they can have the sort of discussions that lead to developing their ideas, from plan to implementation. They never get to that stage. They are always implementing someone else's plans. They are always assisting people," said Nadia Moritz, twenty-six, director of the Young Women's Project, sponsored by the Institute for Women's Policy Research in Washington, D.C., which has organized a recent conference for East Coast activists at which Verheyden-Hillard spoke.

Of course, for most women interested in activism, the glass ceiling doesn't mean much. Most do not want to be national leaders and naturally expect to pay their dues and learn from those with valuable experience.

But this lack of visible (young) leadership at the top has had an effect on the masses. Young women are missing a recognizable spokesperson personally in touch with their special needs to convey their voices and unite them. With the same older women's voices out there, young women associate feminism with their mothers, not their own generation.

Others around the country said they sensed a lack of concern about cultivating new leaders in the late Eighties in organized women's groups. Talitha Curtis, twenty-six, a third-year law student at Queens College of the City University of New York, said she was interested in attending the meeting of a prominent political group for reproductive rights in New York City. She was interning with a judge, who had been a member since the early Seventies, who she said resisted taking her to meetings.

"I think they failed to build leadership," Curtis said, "to bring people in and build leadership—and let go. That's one of the things I have learned in organizing at CUNY. The first year you join whatever group, and you support them and second year, you lead and bring in new people, and third year, people sort of watch. It isn't always natural. It has to be deliberate."

I asked her if it is still too early to worry about passing the torch.

"It's too late for them," she said. "These are women who were organizing in the Seventies. They're not even together anymore, and they never passed the reins. They know each other, but they don't organize like they used to. There's a lot of women out there in New York City in their forties and when they want something, they call each other. They aren't working together like they did in the Seventies."

Karen Brown, twenty-two, a researcher at the Families and Work Institute in New York and a 1990 graduate of Brown University in Providence, said she also felt this frustration. In extensively searching and interviewing for jobs in nonprofit community work in New York City, she said older women didn't express as a priority nurturing and recruiting new blood—even from someone willing to work at a low salary.

"The older people from the Sixties who have been involved in organizing and community development since the Sixties are burning out, and there is no one to replace them," Brown said. "I have talked about it with other people, and there is a real need for new people to come in. They are very territorial. . . ."

"I wasn't looking to be executive director of the group, but I wanted to learn. There wasn't a sense that we need to really get people in here and nurture them."

Young women also aren't necessarily visible at their own events. At NOW's First Young Feminist Conference in the spring of 1991 in Akron, the diverse and visionary young women who planned it weren't present at the press conference. The event attracted more than 700 people and was the largest known national gathering of feminists of this generation.

Instead, leading the press conference were national NOW president Molly Yard, NOW's vice president and a local NOW official, who mainly rehashed NOW's stances on women in the military.

As a result of this invisibility, others are interpreting what young women's needs are in national women's organizing. "I don't know if the leaders of the women's movement are particularly interested in hearing what young women want to have," Spencer Robinson said. "I think we need to speak for ourselves about what matters to us, and it has to be heard. It's like going through a filter. . . . Women don't want to be spoken for by men, so why should young women be spoken for by older women?"

Some young women have recognized some limitations in older women's organizations and formed caucuses within them or separate networks. Christine Ogu, twenty-two, a staff member of the Feminist Futures program, which at this writing has no budget, was one of several feminists pointing out the importance of initiative.

"You don't really have experience they think is needed to have a voice. That's not true all the time. The question is can you expect to be a leader in an organization which is dominated by more experienced women who have been in the field a long time? I have no idea. But I think that some role needs to be taken, and if it means young women creating their own networks, that might be easier," Ogu said.

Elise Mann, twenty-five, executive director of Women United for a Better Chicago, a grass-roots community group, recognized other limitations. She said the older feminists don't have a model for training leaders. "There aren't training manuals that people can pull off the shelf. They can't say, 'I'm going to do this the feminist way.' A lot of this is undocumented."

## Membership Gaps of the Eighties

Like the leadership, the general membership of mainstream organizations during the Eighties and later has largely been older. This has given the appearance to outsiders of a graying movement and has not been as appealing to new members. While the demographics have recently changed with *Webster v. Reproductive Health Services,* the threat to abortion rights, this gap was most notably felt in the Eighties.

One young woman high in NOW's ranks, Janelle Rodriguez, nineteen, a sophomore at University of California-Berkeley, said she notices this age gap as a state board member. She explains it mostly by the twentysomething generation's more apolitical social climate and the perceived lack of threats to rights in the mainstream—prior to *Webster.* But she also points out a lack of recruitment. Many women's groups seem to have lost the generation that reached their early twenties in the 1980s.

"I think there's a big generation gap," said Rodriguez. "Part of that, I think, number one, there was a lag of organizing after the initial hit of the second wave of feminism and the *Webster* decision. Things died down. I didn't see active recruitment and consciousness-raising being kept up on the same level as they were and at the same intensity as in the early Seventies, late Seventies.

"Now they're starting to take advantage of it again, but we have to start over and so it's like I'm on the state board, I'm the youngest person there."

Many young women interested in joining these groups report a gap in consciousness. As with the older women's magazines, many women new to feminism are starting at a different level.

"What I hear older women saying is 'Where are the younger women?' There is no outreach," Julie Spencer Robinson said. "That's no surprise because there is no outreach to women of color either. There is this group. It's like 'we have to do some things for ourselves, for me, you know.' To me, that's what the women's movement is, in the most part, it's for ourselves, for those women who were real active in the Sixties and Seventies. And they're telling us to go to women's-studies classes—and that's real limited."

In this discussion about women's organizations, I am focusing on NOW as an example of women's organizing conflicts for a reason. It is the most visible voice and is directed to mainstream America.

NOW, with a membership of more than 250,000 and 700 local chapters is also the McDonald's of the women's movement: recognizable and accessible to millions. Many people I interviewed who were not immersed in activist communities said they would first look into joining NOW if they were interested in becoming politically active. Some women involved with NOW, including Kristin Thomson, an organizer from Colorado in the national office, and Janelle Rodriguez, said they turned to it first as a way to get active for women's rights.

For many the impetus was the threat from the 1989 Supreme Court *Webster* decision that gave the states more power to limit abortion rights. Wanting to join in the fight, Ann Bittinger called the local NOW chapter when she arrived freshman year at American University in Washington, D.C. The older women there helped her form a chapter on her campus, which was more accessible to students.

Like more than a half dozen others I know of who started campus NOW chapters after *Webster,* Bittinger said she was attracted by the resources of the group and its reputation.

"NOW has the name too," Bittinger said. "Everyone knows the National Organization for Women."

I talked to older activists, including those at NOW's national headquarters, to give them a chance to explain the apparent lack of recruiting of younger people. At a young-feminist education day sponsored by the American University and D.C. NOW chapters, I caught the attention of Molly Yard. I asked her if this was an example of a continuing national NOW effort to reach out to young women.

"It would be nice to say that, but it wouldn't be the truth," she said. "In organizing the big marches, that's exactly what we were doing. But actually any president of NOW has gone for years to college campuses [to speak] because when we get invited to them we get paid a very decent fee, and it's a way to make money for NOW.

"Ellie [Smeal, the past president] did a lot of it. I do a lot of it. You go wherever you get invited if you can work it into your schedule because I get $3,000 to $4,000 a speech. If I do ten of these a year, it all goes to the National Organization for Women. And they pay all your expenses, so the only thing it costs you is time. But it's also a wonderful contact with women on campus. Any time we have organized a major march, we have done campus organizing. And you know what campus organizing is like. You have to keep doing it all the time. The cast of characters changes."

I nodded sympathetically but still wondered: Money? They want us for our pocketbooks? Or for votes? I felt so used.

She also only mentioned campuses. What about younger women in high school, or those who don't attend college?

But I thought she still needed time to explain herself, say what she really meant, something more noble.

"You talk about major marches," I said. "What about recruiting between that?

"We don't."

"Why not?"

"Because it costs money to organize. The resources are limited, and there's just so much you can do."

She explained that resources were tied up from the late Seventies to the early Eighties rallying to pass the Equal Rights Amendment, which failed to pass in 1982, and in later years, trying to preserve abortion rights.

"We have always known we wanted to have a presence on the campuses, but there just didn't seem to be any vehicle. Remember, that up to 1982, almost 3/5 of our energy was in the ERA. We had hundreds of people working in every state where we were trying to ratify. We literally emptied the national office. We left two officers, and everyone else took off. There was a skeleton force left in the national office. It was a tiring, all-consuming battle to get ratification."

Paula McKenzie, the president of D.C. NOW, also explained that there didn't seem to be as much interest on campuses in the Eighties as presently. She said her chapter tried to organize an educational event at American University in 1986, but received a lukewarm response. In 1990, after *Webster,* Bittinger came to them for help, and they helped her start a chapter. That was received enthusiastically on campus, with 175 people signing up for membership at the beginning of the semester.

Since the 1989 *Webster* decision and an upsurge in student activism on a wide spectrum of issues, NOW and other groups seem to be more conscious of the necessity of including young women and have made a greater commitment to them. At the 1990 summer national NOW conference, the local chapters named as a central priority the recruitment of young women and their development as leaders, according to Rosemary Dempsey, national vice president for action, who explained that the national policy follows the charge of the local chapters.

"Most states have done some leadership training in a variety of ways for a number of years. But what we're trying to do is put that training in coordination so that it's really a factor and on the national level do our best to make those techniques more sophisticated, more available," she said.

NOW's First Young Feminist Conference in February 1991 was an overwhelming success in establishing common ground and attracting interest. Through those in attendance, NOW transcended its stodgy image, represented by a diversity of young women who were leaders of campus chapters and members and officers of other community groups.

Still, barely any young, widely recognizable national leaders have emerged from the tutelage of the older women's organizations. (While I did come across some very impressive, articulate young women leaders, they have had scarce national media exposure.) The degree to which the feminist establishment is willing to share power with these young women will determine their success in providing a voice for the next generation.

## Chapter Three

# The Radical Resistance

## A KINDER, GENTLER ACTIVISM

In the Sixties, people wanting to change the world were inflamed with the rhetoric of revolution.

Today the general vision is more modest and tame: that of a "kinder, gentler nation."

Sarah Turoff observed that this shift in attitudes applies to activists and nonactivists alike. For middle class women in particular, many of the more visible roadblocks have been overcome—such as access to schools and jobs. Women's rights is no longer a central struggle in their lives.

While the goals of activists may be radical, they seem more cautious than those before us, with an awareness that Utopia won't come overnight. They build more slowly on past progress and avoid grand ideologies that could render them inflexible and blind to obstacles.

Turoff, who participated in a few protests of violence against women at the University of Michigan-Ann Arbor as an undergraduate, said older and younger women seem to be engaged in almost two separate movements for women's rights.

She said she sees herself as being as much of a feminist as she is a humanist or environmentalist or antiracist. It is all a part of the same package.

"The older people see it as an issue," she said. " 'We have to fight to get this issue resolved and that issue resolved.' And people of our generation see it as a way of life, an all-encompassing ball of wax, a fair society. Just in the way that we think there shouldn't be racism and save the world and recycling and all that stuff. It's the whole ball of wax, let's just think about making people happy, let's just think of making the world work right."

In not considering themselves radicals, those feminists interviewed also generally feel more comfortable with more mainstream approaches. Many professionally oriented young women have less anger because they have gained access to the system. Also, in working through the system, they have to assume its appearance and character.

"I don't think it's really a smart thing to go out and protest," said Michelle Traupmann. "It's not my way of being. I'm not a person who gets things done through anger. I get it done through being outspoken. I'm going to be better than you and work harder or I'll do it in a smarter way, such that all of a sudden you'll realize, 'Oh my God, this person has some way or another outsmarted me.' I find it more interesting and challenging to do it that way than to just voice my opinion and butt heads with somebody."

While a generation gap is not always present, younger people have a unique approach to feminism. They come from a different place and a different time. Like every new set of young adults, their approaches, issues, identities, social attitudes, pressures and politics are distinct. Even the old issues don't look the same with a set of new challenges.

These forces—along with a particularly cautious and individualistic philosophy—have great influence in explaining the twentysomethings' distinct connections to feminism and activism of any kind.

## Feminist Role Models

The preference for a less "radical" outlook was suggested by the people interviewed in their naming of feminist role models. While the overwhelming majority of people could not come up with any, those mentioned fit a more "mainstream" image.

All those mentioned were praised for their more soft-spoken, businesslike and effective approaches. About five women pointed out Faye Wattleton, forty-six, president of the Planned Parenthood Federation of America, and two cited Kate Michelman, forty-eight, president of the National Abortion Rights Action League, both of whom are seen as mainstream, articulate, inoffensive and focused on a central area of popular concern: abortion rights.

"Faye Wattleton, I think she's excellent. She is everything that I would ever want to be. She's smart, so articulate, calm, even when she's being harassed by pro-life people and she's so level-headed. She has an important job and takes it very seriously. If anybody is a role model, she's definitely the one," said Simone Cooper.

Wattleton has proved herself both in the activist and business worlds. In a March 1990 issue, *Business Week* magazine called her the "nonprofit equivalent of Lee Iacocca," due to her deft management of Planned Parenthood based in New York City, with a budget of $303 million and 178 affiliate chapters. A look through the magazine guide in the library reveals recent profiles in such mainstream magazines as *Glamour*, the *New York Times Magazine* and *Esquire*.

On the more activist side, named by one person was Rep. Patricia Schroeder (Democrat, Colorado), who has provided a strong voice for women in Congress for eight terms. In 1990, she introduced the Women's Health Equity Act, a bill designed to guarantee women greater equity in medical research and the delivery of health services.

A few more conservative political figures were cited, including Republican Elizabeth Dole, head of the Red Cross and former secretary of transportation, and First Lady Barbara Bush.

"I think [Barbara Bush] is awesome," said Paula Barksdale. "I mean, feminism means letting a woman do whatever she wants, and people have to respect her choice and ability to make that decision. Barbara Bush chose to be a wife—a great wife—and chose to be a great mother, and I think *that's* great."

In the popular culture arena, people most frequently cited were Madonna, Cher, several female rap stars and others perceived as having taken control of their lives. In naming its ten women of the year, the December 1990 *Glamour* came up with Schroeder; another health-care advocate, Sen. Barbara Mikulski, a Democrat from Baltimore; Madonna, "for personifying women's power of self-determination"; broadcaster Jane Pauley, "for extraordinary grace under pressure"; Chai Ling, a leader of China's democracy movement; pediatric AIDS-funding activist Elizabeth Glaser; child-care advocate Marian Wright

Edelman, founder and president of the Children's Defense Fund; tennis star and superathlete Chris Evert; and Wendy Kopp, a recent Princeton graduate who set up a Peace Corps equivalent for teachers.

Perhaps one of the more interesting, and problematic, contemporary feminist role models is Madonna. While some interviewed criticized Madonna for the promiscuous image she portrays, a few admired her for her aura of self-control.

"She's a new kind of icon for the Nineties: a smart blonde, not the dumb one. The kind of woman who likes men, but doesn't need them. The kind of woman who likes herself even more," writes syndicated features columnist Jamie Stiehm, a twentysomething herself from San Jose, California, in a September 22, 1990, *Chicago Tribune* article. "I hope Madonna keeps going until she gets her fill. I like a woman who dares to be so brazen. In fact, I think there's a lot to learn from her style: as a strong-minded woman who goes after—and gets—exactly what she wants."

Like Wattleton, Madonna also inspires awe with her business savvy. In an article titled "A Brain for Sin and a Bod for Business," the October 1, 1990, *Forbes* traced her meteoric rise from an almost penniless arrival in New York City in 1978 to her monumental status as the top-earning female entertainer for 1990. That year she brought in $39 million, and since 1986, she has earned at least $125 million.

This group of perceived feminists reflects a feminist movement that is more mainstream and has infiltrated—if not become—the establishment. Some public figures named, such as Faye Wattleton and Patricia Schroeder, work through the political system to elicit change. A great number of the others with political affiliations, such as Elizabeth Dole and Barbara Bush, are conservative and inherently supportive of the status quo. Different pop icons, such as Madonna, are more cultural than political feminists also not striving for radical change. Instead of looking outward at society, they are looking inward for exploration.

## Yes, it *Is* Radical

As a generation more resistant to things that are radical, the twentysomethings naturally avoid feminism.

No one is denying it. Feminism is inherently radical.

Feminist philosophies are based in challenging things at the root, which is what radical means.

The concept of equality for women, which seems basic, is a radical concept. It dares to transform and challenge every institution and tradition of society: politics, religion, the family, the workplace, the law. While it doesn't necessarily mean abolishing all existing orders and traditions, feminism does imply questioning them and considering alternatives.

Personal attitudes are also examined. A woman having determination over her own life and the freedom to form her own identity and being as smart as a man is a radical concept.

Going against the status quo is difficult because it is often a path of much resistance. Feminist scrutiny casts aside the dependable life script that people in the past could turn to in times of turmoil. In planning a life, it is scary to make a choice and not know where it will lead you, or what new conflicts you will confront. Things seem easier when the role of wife and mother is as neatly circumscribed as a job description in the newspaper want ads.

## NEW CHALLENGES ON OLD ISSUES: RADICAL BATTLES

Some of the battles that remain in the women's movement are more radical in nature. Many of the feminist battles have been won with legislation. But other problems that rage on can't be solved as easily.

*New York Times* columnist Anna Quindlen explained that the feminists from twenty-five years ago presented two agendas, a liberal goal of gaining access to opportunities and a more radical goal of changing attitudes.

''The first part of that has come true, and the second part of that I think sometimes never will. I think the way men and women continue to see each other contributes to 90 percent of the problems that we have in terms of some kind of feminist agenda.''

Because much of sexism is expressed subtly, it is more slippery to pin down and difficult to correct. Younger people can't see sex discrimination as easily because other factors may be involved: their skills, their race, their education level, their personality, competitors.

Mary Servatius, thirty, who works for a women's foundation in Chicago, said many of the biases are present in institutions and aren't as obvious. She gave the contrasting example of gaining women's entrance into a men's social club.

"Just about everybody could get enraged about that. But how do you deal with the Chicago Police Department, where there seems to be a pattern in how they treat different types of rape victims, where poor women and minority women are treated worse than white women? So trying to change that seems completely different."

Some barriers also seem too subtle to overcome because they are faced later in life.

"At eighteen, I hit a wall that said can't, can't, can't, can't. I think young women [today] don't hit that wall until they're in their early thirties," Quindlen said. "They can go to Princeton, they can go to Harvard Law School, one of the big Wall Street firms. And, it's not until they're in their early thirties, and they're working like a slave alongside a guy who is working like a slave, and yet somehow has a wife and two children because someone is taking care of the infrastructure in his life.

"And she hits a wall that says can't. In some ways, it's a much more daunting wall. Because 'can't be an op-ed columnist for the *New York Times*' is something you can work against, but 'can't have the time to have a husband without giving up your job' is something much more amorphous and harder.

"The manifestation of sexism that goes on day to day—in noninclusive language, jokes, etc.—is difficult to confront because its individual consequences appear minimal. To address something that small is risking the appearance of being pathological and hypersensitive. What does it matter if it is put 'chairperson' over 'chairman' or spelled 'women' or 'womyn'?"

This is very easy target to ridicule, as evidenced in a May 25, 1990, *USA Today* column by the paper's founder, Al Neuharth: "At Mills College, women students were anything but wimpy. They boycotted (excuse me, girlcotted) classes. . . ."

Another persistent challenge stands in fighting the two most volatile feminist issues at the forefront at college campuses: abortion rights and acquaintance rape. Unlike the struggle for pay equity or child care, these are fraught with more personal complications and stigmas.

Both have to do with sex, a personal topic that hasn't been public for very long. If you fight for abortion rights, you may look promiscuous. If you fight against violence against women, you may look like a prude.

These are also consuming, controversial topics that don't necessarily make one attractive in discussion. A pro-choice stand may alienate one from his or her family, for religious or other reasons. A woman taking an anti-abortion position may find herself shunned by the feminist community.

While those I interviewed were overwhelmingly pro-choice, one stigma attached to the pro-choice side is irresponsibility. Although one strong argument is economics, abortion can be used for back-up birth control for any situation.

Also, many pro-choice activists in public do not reflect their own or the mixed feelings Americans share about abortion. In their battles to preserve abortion rights, they naturally focus on one side of the debate, the woman, and appear not to be concerned about any moral implications concerning the fetus or the woman taking responsibility for her actions.

In *The Second Stage,* Betty Friedan writes about the effects of a militant pro-choice overtone from the past that many perceive today:

> "Still, there was something that went wrong in the terms we used to discuss abortion. Such slogans as 'free abortion on demand' had connotations of sexual licentiousness, not only affronting the moral values of conseratives but implying a certain lack of reverence for life and the mysteries of conception and birth which have been women's agony and ecstasy and defining value through the ages.
>
> "There is a mystique of motherhood; but the conception and bearing of children—the ongoing generation of human life—is surrounded, in all religions, by an awe and mystery that is more than a mystique. Being 'for abortion' is like being 'for mastectomy.' It completely overlooks the life-enhancing value for women and families of the choice to have children."

One difficulty in speaking up on any side of the abortion issue is fear of getting shot down because of compelling views on both sides, stressed Kerry Hughes, twenty-one, a store manager from Hickory

Hills, Illinois. However, she said she would speak out for the pro-choice side.

"It's really hard for anyone right now to take a stand on abortion, because if you say pro-choice and you think it's going to be every woman's choice, there will be people out there who will say you're a baby-killer. But then if you say no, it's pro-life, then there will be those babies on the street that women don't want. Either stand [you] take, [you'll] get backlash from it, so why bother?"

Pro-choice also has the connotation for many people of actually advocating abortion or being pro-abortion. Two male pro-choice activists at the State University of New York in Albany said this is the central argument they face in dealing with other men. "A lot of men don't realize that you don't have to be pro-abortion to be pro-choice," said Charles Monroe, Jr., twenty, of Queens, New York.

Another central issue for college women, aquaintance rape, also poses a substantial challenge. Unlike counseling against rape by a stranger (don't walk alone at night, use your keys as a weapon, etc.), people giving workshops to students about acquaintance rape seem to be interfering in participants' private lives; they are actually setting up new standards for right and wrong for men and women in sexual relationships. They may also put men on the defensive by naming them as the enemy, instead of the distant and unknown psycho stranger who attacks from the bushes.

## True Confessions

In general, sex, which may be difficult to discuss in public, is a big part of "women's issues."

Historically, women's sexuality has been kept mysterious and suppressed. Part of feminists' work has been to give explanations for problems previously considered too private, everything from breast cancer to premenstrual syndrome. It seems that only now, in a much more open society, can many of these private issues finally be properly addressed.

Feminists are known to celebrate a personal discussion of women's sexuality in defiance of past shames and secrets. I remember seeing two male students in a constant state of shock in my senior year "Contemporary Women Poets" class. Instead of reading more erudite poems about nature's bounty or protracted epic battles from the Middle Ages, we read about women's most private and previously unspoken thoughts. For at least two poets, both the uterus and insanity were staple themes. Many people in the class—and even the teacher—shared stories about past lovers that had been evoked by the poetry. At times, I felt as if I had hooked into a late-night 900-number "True Confessions" party line.

## The New Feminist Establishment

While these candid discussions have been going on for a while in the women's movement, the second generation has another challenge in feminist discussion: transforming established institutions into meaningful vehicles for today's feminism.

"The women's movement doesn't have the power of self-discovery the way it had then. The people who go into consciousness-raising now have the burden of history, so it feels like a well-established institution, and the idea of a women's group doesn't carry the same excitement," said Vivian Gornick, who wrote about radical feminists for the *Village Voice* in the early Seventies.

"By now it seems natural for women to say to other women, 'Why don't we form a group and meet once a month and discuss our lives as women, or working problems, etc.' That was unheard of before twenty years ago."

True, women have lost some of the sense of discovery shared by feminist pioneers. However, when young women interviewed have discovered feminism, it has had a radical impact. While consciousness-raising is an established practice, it is naturally new to those who have never done it before.

It is not feminism, but the institutions that may have a more intimidating effect on young people. These are tangible things that belong to the older generation, although they are officially open to all. For example, women's-studies classes, the most powerful forum for young feminists, are run by older people. This academic establishment gives the feeling that to understand feminism, you must be able to have an academic mastery. Even if one studies feminism for a few years, she or he still may not feel it's been possible to scratch the surface in uncovering its layers. While this common perspective from the older generation is not a major obstacle for young women, the subtle message in its pervasiveness could be that this feminism stuff is an older woman's thing.

Some interviewed experienced a difference in consciousness level within the older, established organizations. University of Maryland freshman Heather Macdonald, eighteen, said she felt confused at meetings of a Boston chapter. "I joined because my mother belonged," she said. "It was a little old for me. I was out of touch. A lot of what they were saying went over my head."

Janelle Rodriguez pointed out the additional attention needed for those new to organizing.

"If you go to the local NOW chapter meetings, they say we need to do this and we need to do this and we need to do this," she said. "That's fine for them, but it's not reaching the [new] people. There's no one saying, 'Why are we doing this?' There's no theory behind it. There is theory in the minds of people already doing it. For the people who don't understand it, there's not real outreach to that, speaking of that. I can't say all NOW chapters are like that, that's mostly my experiences. It's not just NOW—a lot of groups are like that."

As a way to provide this consciousness-raising, Rodriguez plans to set up a chapter at her campus. She said even at Berkeley, a reputed hotbed of activism, a multi-issue mainstream feminist group is missing.

## Radicalizing with Age

Some older feminists have said that the desire not to offend men is part of many influences keeping women conservative when they are young. While "social consciousness" is stereotypically associated with the young and idealistic, older women may often find it easier to take a stand.

Gloria Steinem has stressed that young women have not yet had their most radicalizing experiences. In her book *Outrageous Acts and*

*Everyday Rebellions* she lists "entering the paid labor force and discovering how women are treated there; marrying and finding out that it is not yet an equal partnership; having children and discovering who is responsible for them and who is not; and aging, still a greater penalty for women than for men." She and others stressed that while young women can anticipate inequities, they don't really hit them until personally confronted.

Because of the ways in which women are viewed in society, a young woman may also feel more powerful and in control at a young age, Steinem reiterated in an interview published in a 1990 book *After All These Years: Sixties Ideals in a Different World.*

"A woman of eighteen has more power in society, as a sex object and worker and so on, than she will when she's fifty. So it's always been true, in the last wave of feminism, this wave, always, that women get more activist with age, whereas men tend to get more conservative," she said, adding that the idea of college as the time to "sow wild oats" and experiment is a historically male concept.

Anna Quindlen agreed that when women age, they feel more comfortable making connections with older women. "When you're younger, you want to be unique. When you get older, you value the sense of commonality. It's very soothing to know that all the bad things that have happened to you have happened to other people."

## Another View: A Reason for Encouragement

These points make sense in explaining many of the dynamics of forming a social consciousness. It is true that young women haven't experienced much of what radicalizes people yet. But the danger of mainly concentrating on this explanation is overlooking the real potential for awareness and action early in life.

Often a time for thought and fewer responsibilities, college years are a fertile period for new ideas and critical thinking. On campuses, students are exposed to a greater diversity of people with new ideas and criticisms to share. Once they graduate, there is a retreat back to homogenous communities where little is challenged.

Furthermore, many people have had plenty of radicalizing experiences by adulthood. Most people have had jobs before the age of eighteen, usually in places where they have little control or power to fight sexism. Someone working as an office temp or fast-food clerk isn't treated with the same respect as an executive.

Many radicalizing experiences have nothing to do with the workplace, as older feminists keep stressing. As will be discussed more fully later, a surprising number of young women interviewed have been sexually abused or assaulted or had other experiences that alert them to the different challenges of being born a woman. Even people from affluent areas or those studying at Ivy League schools are not as sheltered as one might think.

College is a safe haven to develop ideals. Cloistered environments are always conducive to building awareness, whether it be in a church, synagogue, commune, Catholic high school or historically black or women's college. Those privileged enough to be at a college campus have a separate space and time in which they can build a base and fortify what they believe in. This makes them more resistant to the time after they graduate when their ideals are suddenly assaulted upon entrance into the work force and "the real world."

## A HANGOVER FROM THE EIGHTIES: SEDATED SOCIAL CONSCIOUSNESS

Social consciousness is the base for any political statement: feminist, environmental, antiwar or against racism. But for this generation in particular, this social consciousness has been put under heavy sedation by many distinct and mighty forces—social, political and economic.

The only time this generation ever widely heard the message "We're all connected" said in earnest, it was in an ad for AT&T.

As a result, during the Eighties, the idea of a social consciousness was not in popular fashion. Instead of being celebrated, social consciousness was considered an indication of naïveté or stupidity.

While this is being taken more seriously in the early Nineties—such as with some renewed student organizing—the concept of social consciousness was a dark secret during most of the formative years of the twentysomethings. People did not commonly encounter public or popular dialogue about its existence, implications, development or place in their lives.

Philanthropy and volunteer work were advocated by the Reagan and Bush administrations, but they do not involve a commitment to making fundamental social change. Some renewed discussion about the environment has taken into account a feeling of being socially conscious, but it often stops with making personal changes, such as recycling, instead of reevaluating major policies.

The missing strain is incorporating social consciousness into decision-making and daily life. Instead, with their own particular brand of individualism, the twentysomething generation generally has adopted the philosophy that a connection to others is unnecessary, and perhaps even a sign of weakness or failure. In many ways, this attitude is derived from American culture's historic reverence for self-reliance, as well as a real belief in the opportunities open for many in this unique society. But somehow, during the Reagan era, this individualistic ideology evolved into extremist proportions, blinding people to others' needs—and at times, even their own.

YOUNG people's exposure to social issues has often been limited to whatever happens to fall in their paths at school, or what appears in Thursday's episode of "L.A. Law." This includes issues relating to women or people of other backgrounds and cultures.

"It's as easy as reading a few books and having an open mind, but our generation has not been encouraged to read books in the first place and is not encouraged to have open minds," said Brad Sigal, twenty-one, an activist at George Washington University in Washington, D.C. "We're encouraged to believe that if it isn't in the papers or network news, it isn't happening. Because if people were being killed in El Salvador unfairly, it would be on TV. 'What do you mean? If one in three women were raped, it would be on the front page of the paper, so it's obviously not true.' "

Like Sigal, the most biting social critics of this generation tend to be those actively working for change. I observed a similar discussion of how social consciousness has been devalued in an interview with three women who are members and founders of the Students for Choice group at the State University of New York at Albany. They started out saying they felt like oddballs for wanting to pursue careers in politics and education, but felt they really had some power to improve these systems.

"Our educational system has gone so far down the drain and [has been] so directed toward the sciences for so long, at least in our generation, that we don't value people who can provide us a mirror for this society," said Gina Knarich, twenty, a junior from Nyack, New York. "We are repressing them right now. We don't value the teachers or the people who are allowing us to be reactive and think and expand our boundaries beyond America and think about global issues to be humanitarian. We don't have that these days.

"We don't have enough people to think for themselves. They are like these little robots who go to school, do their homework, go out and get drunk. Their little part of rebellion is getting drunk and sleeping around—and not getting involved in social issues, and they're never taught to think."

She and Laura Tarantini, twenty, a junior from Queens, agreed that there needs to be a mix of Sixties idealism with some realism. "We need people in the middle, thinkers who have a social awareness and a social responsibility," Tarantini said.

But Ilyssa Wesche, twenty-one, a junior from Syracuse, said apathy is the main culprit getting in the way of change.

"I think that a lot of people have ideals and know what they believe in, but I think a vast majority of people won't take the time to act on them," she said. "In fact, all my friends are pro-choice. But God forbid I ask them to come to a meeting. They always have something better to do. They are very individually oriented. They are going to a bar or party or have a biology quiz tomorrow."

"I also see people having ideals, but not feeling like they're useful, not feeling there is a place for them," Tarantini replied. "I don't think we have an educational system or even a social system that supports people for having their own views and going after what they want instead of the expediency of going into professions to get you the money so maybe you'll have the time to think about what you want. But by then, your ideas might be dead, or your heart could be dead."

Knarich and the others gave another reason for more students not getting more involved.

"I think that the scary thing is we're considered radical," Knarich said. "I consider myself very mainstream, just very tolerant. And people consider me a radical, and they're afraid to be labeled radical. They're afraid to go to a Feminist Alliance meeting because goodness knows all feminists are lesbians, or are afraid of joining the radical groups here because we're all neo-hippie, dope-smoking Bob Dylan deadheads. They're afraid of being labeled as radical."

## Backlash

Outside of campuses, and often inside them, the climate has been hostile to activists fighting sexism, racism or homophobia. Insecurities about women and minorities have crept to the surface—with shocking candor and acceptance. Across the country, the number of reported incidents of "ethnoviolence" has been rising since 1986, according to monitoring groups.

The most blatant example of this trend is the rise of former Ku Klux Klan grand wizard, David Duke, who finished a strong second in the 1990 race for Louisiana U.S. senator. Buoyed by the support of college students across the state, he won 57 percent of the white vote. A 1990 poll conducted by the Louisiana Coalition Against Nazism and Racism reports that 52 percent of white Louisianians aged eighteen to thirty-four surveyed said they are in political agreement with Duke.

In popular culture, hateful music once consigned to the fringe has entered the mainstream. Instead of condemning the message, even the "progressives" have rushed to their defense crying "censorship." Performers with bad taste have become national champions of First Amendment expression. In rap, the group 2 Live Crew registered more than two million in sales with their single, "As Nasty as They Want to Be," banned for its violent sexual imagery and profanity.

*Chicago Tribune* music critic Greg Kot points out in a November 18, 1990, analysis of this trend that the music of the Houston group Geto Boys makes that song sound tame. Their "Mind of a Lunatic" describes a violent and gruesome rape. This group sold more than 500,000 records and made the Billboard Top 30 early in 1990 with its album, "Grip It! On that Other Level."

"An album by the California rapper Ice Cube has topped one million in sales with a series of raps that refer to women as either 'hoes' or 'bitches.' In one of its most notorious songs, 'You Can't Fade Me,' Ice Cube plots various ways to commit an abortion on a prostitute who has informed him she's carrying his baby," Kot writes.

Rock music has been less overtly obscene, but it still contributes to a tradition of woman-hating. Kot points out that while many main-stream groups have historically had sexist lyrics, such as the Rolling Stones with "Under My Thumb" and "Stupid Girl," groups today differ in making sexism a cornerstone of their act. He says that today sexism is "not an issue—but the issue."

To avoid being banned like their rap counterparts, Kot says rock bands use "transparent code words" to describe their one-sided lust. He lists Mötley Crüe, Warrant, Scorpions, Skid Row and Aerosmith as culprits, citing Mötley Crüe's demand for a "Slice of Your Pie" on their recent number-one album "Dr. Feelgood."

Comedians such as Andrew Dice Clay and Sam Kinison have also taken this approach, producing variations on the same joke with lita-nies against women. Kot quotes *Village Voice* pop critic Robert Christ-gau as saying these comedians represent a "backlash against the women's movement in which the oppressors are scared and fighting back in sick, ugly ways."

Vivian Gornick agrees that the current backlash against recent gains of women and minorities is rooted in fear, explaining, "It's frightening to give up on the old ways. It's frightening to give up the idea that men are strong and women are weak, that man is naturally smart and woman is naturally less smart, and he will do and she will be protected, and he will be strong and she will be protected. It's hard to give that up. It makes us feel better deep inside in certain ways."

## "Radical" Resistance

While the backlash is recent, twentysomethings are not unresponsive to it, having come of age during a period of rigid conservatism.

This brand of conservatism inherently means resistance to anything sounding "radical" or challenging the status quo. While the mood on university campuses seems to be swinging back slowly from the right, the formative years of the twentysomethings were spent under reassurances from President Reagan that everything was great. Even thigh-deep in scandal, Reagan presented world and domestic affairs under the same soft white G.E. light bulb that permeated the landscapes and faces of children portrayed in his television campaign commercials.

During that time, young people saw the Supreme Court tilt to the right, while fringe, far-right fundamentalists set national moral agendas and the environment crumbled under deregulation and neglect. Politicians preached subsidy of defense contractors, but not child care. Instead of expanding women's choices with health or other resources, the government gave poor women one cure-all word of advice—give up your child to someone who can afford it or "Adoption over Abortion."

While student activism was still strong in the Eighties, a conservative presence was gaining visibility. Steve Klein said that when he was an undergraduate at Berkeley, Students for Reagan was one of the largest campus groups.

Conservatism is also naturally attractive to this generation that grew up with the world in a state of disarray, with failing marriages, drugs and sex that can kill you. Writer Wanda Urbanska points out in her 1986 book *The Singular Generation* that while the Sixties middle-class youth rebelled against conformity, today's young people are rebelling against chaos and seeking more safe and orderly spaces.

Vivian Gornick told me that the mood of the times in the Sixties swept up many people who were not naturally inclined to politics. "In a political time, more people become political although they don't have a real, a natural taste for it. They're infected by the times, the atmosphere. That's what happened twenty years ago. It's not happening now. Most people today shrink from an 'ist' of any kind. For most people, the idea of an articulated political life is frightening."

## A Luxury in Troubled Times

While young people generally lack motivation to redefine others' grand visions, we also don't have the time or luxury to fashion our own.

Under a worsening economy, people are too busy simply struggling to get by. Other responsibilities and priorities that affect one more immediately naturally take precedence. Even students on college campuses, which previously were wellsprings of activism, don't have the same leisure to tinker with grandiose schemes. Instead of taking a liberal arts class in literature, the practical move is a course in welding, data processing or electrical engineering.

"I think students feel uncertain about their economic future," said Marybeth Maxwell, twenty-five, of the U.S. Student Association. "When people talk about apathy on campus, they need to take into account that young people are often working two jobs while they're in school. That's a change since the Fifties, and even since the Eighties—that people have real lives."

She pointed out that the median age of students has climbed to twenty-four, with 43 percent over twenty-five and women students facing additional responsibilities of children and jobs.

"There has been such an increase in nontraditional students, especially in community colleges. Students are not just eighteen- to twenty-two-year-olds anymore. They need child care."

While in college, students have to be cautious for the future. In the Eighties, about a quarter of all college students had student loans, which build up at about $2,500 annually, according to the Department of Education.

Even with a college degree, competition for jobs is fierce. A record 59 percent of 1988 high school graduates enrolled in college, compared to 49 percent in the previous decade. In a 1990 *Time* poll of 602 eighteen- to twenty-nine-year-old Americans, 80 percent agreed that one has little chance of success without a college education.

However, even a professional job does not guarantee security. Nearly four out of ten spring college 1990 graduates—about 400,000 people —were estimated to be taking first jobs that didn't require a college degree, according to the U.S. Bureau of Labor Statistics. In a survey of 1986 college graduates taken a year later, the National Center for Education Statistics found that 36 percent found jobs not requiring a college degree. Among liberal arts graduates, the rate was nearly 50 percent.

Even those graduating from top schools with the most stable majors are jittery about the future. At IBM, 23,000 workers were retired early through incentive programs between 1987 and 1990, according to a July 16, 1990, *Time* magazine article.

"My brother is ten years older [than I], and he had a house and kids at my age," said Chris Jackiw, who has been living with his mother for a year to save money for a down payment on a house. "People had kids at twenty-three, and now they're waiting until they're thirty-three."

During the twentysomething years, people are especially strapped for resources in building their lives from the ground up. Activism—in school or out—for an issue not directly affecting one's present or future is a luxury. When a boat is sinking under economic or other strains, weighty ideals are the first things to be tossed out to lighten the burden.

## Chapter Four

# Generation Gaps: Learning From the Past

CURRENT SOCIAL CONDITIONS and the world view of the next generation can only explain in part why twentysomethings seem to generally recoil in horror at the feminist label.

Young people are missing a critical dialogue about another major source of the generation gap: where older feminists have gone wrong. A serious probe of the past women's movement is vital to successfully forge a future feminist agenda and understand younger women's criticisms of the movement. In her important history of radical feminism, *Daring to Be Bad,* Alice Echols explains: "Fundamental to feminism's decline in the political arena has been its failure to attract large numbers of young women. As in the Twenties—a decade to which the Eighties bears some resemblance—feminists have discovered that many younger women are indifferent if not hostile to the women's movement."

While Echols also outlines many social influences, she points out faults in strategy and substance in the radical and liberal women's movements that left young women more indifferent than inspired. From their special perspective on the margins and as more staunch individualists, the younger women interviewed have stated two major criticisms. They do not see older feminists as having conveyed tolerance for other women's choices and feel that the past women's movement universalized the experiences of the white middle class.

121

## Family Choices

Twenty-five years ago and earlier, a major goal of feminism was to provide women with choices. But in widening the options, feminists were perceived as narrowing them. They fought against confining female roles and seemed to supplant them with confining male roles. The rigid definition of a housewife, which Betty Friedan termed "the feminine mystique," has been swapped for the rigid definition of the antifamily career woman, "the femin*ist* mystique."

"I don't think that we've been clear enough on the question of choice," Anna Quindlen told me. "I don't think women have been clear that the whole point about this was for individual women to step out of lockstep and say this works for me now, this is what might work for me ten years from now, this is what might work for me twenty years from now. We got into a situation where we traded one lockstep, 'The Donna Reed Show,' for another lockstep, the Organizational Woman.

"The potential right now is for us to be able to pick three from column A and three from column B and three from column C. And I hope that we can keep this in our sights so that we don't shortchange our own lives, and so that we don't trash each other for the choices that we make."

Recently, some debate over women's lives has shifted to accepting women's choices. The spring 1990 Wellesley commencement-speaker story caused such a stir, making headlines across the country for weeks, because it touched on that basic, strong nerve. As portrayed in the media, Barbara Bush represented the values of motherhood and tradition, and the enemies of those values were represented as young women with career ambitions, studying at a prestigious school.

Also that spring, tolerance of women's choices was a topic of debate in literary and intellectual circles with the 1990 release of the biography of Simone de Beauvoir, the French author of *The Second Sex*, a landmark feminist work released in 1952. The biography, written by Deidre Bair, revealed that de Beauvoir—who epitomized women's freedom and self-determination and who has been required reading for women's-studies classes of the past twenty years—was a doormat for her longtime companion Jean-Paul Sartre. She tolerated his constant infidelities and elevated his career and writing above her own.

What this controversy most revealed is that no one can live a completely "politically correct" lifestyle, and that even the most senseless of traditions are difficult to shrug away.

In the past, feminist career fixation was rooted in many different factors. First, twenty-five years ago when consciousness was first being stirred, mainly white middle-class women had an extreme reaction against the family, questioning how it controlled their lives. They traced the ways in which they had been socialized to be economically dependent on men and how they were helpless outside this structure. A career was a remedy to gain self-control and power to determine one's destiny, without the official sanctioning of a husband.

Because the role of wife and mother was forced and flawed in many ways, it was indeed oppressive. Women reacted against it like teenagers rebelling against strict parents to seek an identity and gain freedom.

"Of course, our actions were wild and uncontrolled and narrow and impassioned and full of revolutionary rhetoric," feminist writer Vivian Gornick said. "We burned bras and we said, 'Love is an institution of oppression and marriage is rape and women are Amazons.' We said a lot of narrow and bold and extreme and heedless and reckless things, which if you look at them in one minute, you see were said in the passionate heat of sudden, angry discovery."

Examples of the extremist rhetoric can be found in some early writings about the family and motherhood. While the images explored today are more complex and realistic, some earlier analyses of motherhood were simplistic, portraying it as either all-powerful or powerless. One early, strident feminist, Shulamith Firestone, who wrote an influential early feminist book, *Dialectic of Sex,* explained motherhood as the source of all oppression, advocating technology that would eliminate biological reproduction.

Activists also appeared antifamily in the specific issues emphasized to give women control of their lives, such as birth control and abortion rights. Furthermore, women wanting child care seemed to be neglecting their children in favor of "fulfillment."

\*   \*   \*

SOME criticize the women's movement as not being generally responsive or concerned with family needs. Two major feminist books from the past decade, Friedan's *The Second Stage,* and Sylvia Ann Hewlett's *A Lesser Life: The Myth of Women's Liberation in America,* are critiques of second-wave feminism's failure to politically focus on mothers' needs.

NOW and radical feminists have always included in their platforms demands for day care and maternity leave. However, the women's movement has neglected to make the connections to these issues as feminist concerns. These are "bread and butter" feminist issues that have been the underpinning of movements in other industrialized countries. The reality has been ignored that most women work, that from 1989 through the year 2000, two out of three new entrants to the labor force will be women.

"We should have clearly reached out to the working class, the poor, minority groups and we should have more clearly talked about day care and parental leave and health care and adequate housing and jobs for everybody," said sociologist Ruth Sidel. "That placed us on the fringe."

Taking this view, some blame an emphasis on cultural feminism over political feminism. Instead of focusing on child care or parental leave or the material needs of masses of women, the feminism of the past focused instead on personal liberation and behavior.

"What is more supportive of women's equality than affordable and accessible child care? What could be more liberating for a woman than a life-sustaining wage?" writes feminist Felicia Kornbluh, a research scholar at the Institute for Policy Studies. "And conversely, what good is consciousness-raising—indeed, how possible is it—if you can't get a sitter on Tuesday night? Someday we will deal with the challenges posed by more ambitious theoretical and ideological critiques of patriarchy and its cultural consequences. Today we have no choice but to join with Rep. Patricia Schroeder and Marian Wright Edelman, the respective chief sponsors of the Family and Medical Leave Act and the Act for Better Child Care."

Waiting in the wings to assume the role as guardian of traditional family values were the right-wing fundamentalists. "And by ceding the territory of the family to the Right," Kornbluh argues, "we not only missed an opportunity to expand, but allowed feminism itself to take much of the heat for the family's supposed 'breakdown.'"

Still, many activists younger and older cannot deny the real study and attention feminists have given the family. Barbara Ehrenreich said she was first drawn into the movement because of health and family issues directly relating to her children. She saw problems in prenatal care at New York Hospital and faced challenges getting child care. Her contribution was teaching women about their health and helping to organize a child-care collective.

"I don't think feminism has been antifamily. I think that was the first image that males could point to," maintained Ehrenreich. " 'Look, you're walking away from the family. You want your own life. How terrible.' "

She also points out that in general, criticism of the women's movement fails to take into account the enormity of the challenge.

"It's true we haven't achieved our goals in terms of childcare. But, you can't blame a movement for what it hasn't succeeded in yet."

## The Tyranny of the "Politically Correct"

While they were fitting for their times, radical feminists from the Sixties and Seventies seem too militant in their rhetoric to young observers today. With their focus on personal lifestyles and extreme reactions against traditional ones, the radical groups seemed to disdain any behavior that wasn't revolutionary. They dictated a militant view of what was acceptable in terms of jobs to take, clothes to wear, issues to promote—and even sexual partners.

One central issue was lesbianism—presented by some as the only alternative to total dependence and oppressive relations with men. As radical feminists struggled for common ground, they suffered many political divisions over issues of sexual politics. "There were times where there were schisms and splits and splits within splits, the gay/straight split, the child-bearing or child-free splits, the old/young splits, the racial and ethnic splits. You name it, it was there," Robin Morgan recalled.

In the early part of the movement, much of the rhetoric of the fringe groups was also revolutionary and against capitalism—described as an instrument of the patriarchy to keep women down. Groups issued manifestos and preached subversion of the system. Certain activists stormed and disrupted American institutions across the country, from the Wall Street trading floor to bridal fairs.

Much of the more militant rhetoric included separatism and male-bashing, an approach that offends most people's current sensibilities. Although it was meant as tongue-in-cheek, an excerpt from the SCUM (Society for Cutting up Men) Manifesto printed in 1970 left an enduring mark on perceptions:

"Life in this society being, at best, an utter bore and no aspect of society being at all relevant to women, there remains to civic-minded, irresponsible, thrill-seeking females only to overthrow the government, eliminate the money system, institute complete automation and destroy the male sex."

Morgan explained that some of the "politically correct" and extremist approach occurred because the more radical women had their activist origins in the antiwar movement. "We had suffered a kind of brain damage from our years in the male left. There was a sort of jockeying for who is more radical than thou," she says, adding that the feminist dialogue has matured with time.

Still today, many are also turned off to feminists because of their militant "enforcing" of what is "politically correct" (or what follows often euphemistic, strict, official doctrines). Some claims are valid. Like in every political group, extremist and intolerant factions exist. But often, this label of "PC" is a guise to discredit any suggestions or criticism that challenge the status quo or make society more inclusive. Both sides—the feminists and those they address—stop serious dialogue when they automatically label and denounce others as "sexist" or "PC," without serious consideration of their points of view.

## Single-Issue Politics: Pornography

Through the formative years of the twentysomethings, the late Seventies and Eighties, the central issues of the women's movement did not reflect the priorities of the masses of young women. The movement seemed to focus on single issues appealing to limited sectors of the population and neglecting the spectrum of concerns in between. For example, the existence of pornography became a preoccupation of intellectuals who were actually divided over its significance. The debate, in an oversimplified and diluted nutshell, was about whether pornography of different extremes reflects women's sexuality or oppresses it. While they were meant to address universal issues crossing lines of sex, race and class, the actions against pornography served to alienate most women from feminism and even attach a stigma to the movement. Those feminists opposed to pornography and seeking bans on it— through both legal means and public pressure—put themselves on the same side of the fence as right-wing fundamentalist groups, stereotyped as narrow minded, insulting and oppressive. A fixation on pornography as the root of evil also made feminists look paranoid and simplistic in reasoning.

While some people I interviewed mentioned exploitive media images as a priority issue, no one uttered the word "pornography." This is not to dismiss the work of antipornography activists, who provide an analysis that is useful in determining the effects of pornography on gender perceptions, in addition to monitoring sexual exploitation.

Like most of the younger women I interviewed, Ruth Sidel was sympathetic to the issue, but saw other concerns as worthy of more attention. "If I were to choose the key issue of the twentieth century, [pornography] wouldn't be mine. I would say, 'Are we going to spend X number of hours on pornography or X numbers of hours on day care?' "

## ERA MAYBE

While I was researching this book, I spoke with an older NOW official, who drove up to meet me for an interview. But before the tape recorder even went on, she'd given a hint of a generation gap I would later find talking to younger women with the message on her license plate: "ERA YES."

A young woman's version would be "ERA MAYBE."

This is the issue some older liberal feminists still seem fixated on, even after a consuming decade-long battle that ended in defeat. But only a handful of young people interviewed—both apolitical and activist—mentioned it. And, when questioned, they described the Equal

Rights Amendment as representing their main conflicts in priorities and strategy with older feminists.

Still, those young women who brought it up generally supported it and expressed outrage that something so basic has not yet been adopted into the Constitution. The ERA means that "the sex of a person could no longer be a factor in determining that person's legal rights," according to *Rights and Wrongs: Women's Struggle for Legal Equality.*

An Equal Rights Amendment was first introduced to Congress in 1923, but support for it then was lacking. In 1972, Congress finally passed it. But fitting the requirement of any new amendment, thirty-eight states, or three-fourths of the state legislatures, had to pass it by June 30, 1982. It just missed passing by three states.

Advancing ERA has been the priority of liberal feminists, those who believe in making do with our present system by reforming it, such as the National Organization for Women. The only younger person mentioning ERA as a top priority was a student leader of a NOW chapter.

Most young people interviewed were unfamiliar with ERA's purpose or its potential power. Before writing this book, my only memory of it was some hazy pictures from television of a group of women chaining themselves to the capitol building in Springfield, Illinois. When I was in high school, I had a chance to go downstate and march for it with my best friend and her feminist mother, but my parents nixed the plan as too radical. I didn't protest, though; I didn't even know what ERA was.

And even today, ERA remains a mystery for this generation. "I really don't know about the ERA," said Sarah Edmunds. "I don't want to clog up the courts. Why do we need that? I don't see what it will do. It does seem to be an obsession, that all is lost unless we get this amendment. I don't need the ERA."

One fear created by conservative opponents that remains about the ERA—and feminism itself—is that it would mandate women be drafted into the military and fight on the front lines with the outbreak of war. But ERA advocates point out that Congress already has the freedom to draft women, and even considered it during World War II, but didn't reach a verdict before the end of the war. And if women were drafted, ERA would only prohibit discrimination based on gender, not on a person's abilities. Also, the military has special discretion to assign its own rules because of the "war powers" clauses of the constitution.

To young activists interviewed, the argument went further. ERA is a sore spot representative of the generation gap with older feminists. It seemed to be a prime example of the dangerous, single-issue focus of the women's movement that has sapped its energy and blinded feminists to more immediate and vital battles.

Elise Mann echoed this view and also questioned ERA's power. Mann says her generation sees ERA as more of a symbolic gesture than a cure-all. In her view, the younger generation has learned to be skeptical about laws designed to create sweeping change. "We know that the civil rights acts didn't eradicate racism, and it's safe to say that the ERA is not going to eradicate sexism," she said, adding that during the long battle, ERA supporters neglected the needs of low-income women and women of color, who were falling further behind other women due to the increasing feminization of poverty.

This gap in perceiving ERA as vital is present in the office of NOW, which led the drive for ratification. At NOW's First Young Feminist Conference in 1991, national president Molly Yard focused on plans to reintroduce ERA and voiced confidence that it would pass after the year 2000, when enough female politicians are in place. But that weekend, during hours of floor debate about important issues, no one else uttered those three letters.

Kristin Thomson, twenty-three, an organizer in the national NOW office, said young women are looking more toward individual solutions.

"I think of ERA as a dated term," Thomson said. "When they failed to pass it in the mid-Seventies, it was a disaster. And it was also something that made me feel women have succeeded through sheer tenacity and in court cases and exposing discrimination. We may not have a constitutional guarantee, but women are overcoming this discrimination in individual ways."

Jane Mansbridge, who wrote *Why We Lost the ERA*, argues that ERA is more symbolic. She explains that an exaggeration of its power was what led to its defeat; as some feminists boosted it as a cure-all, traditional women reasoned it must be mighty enough to create a uni-sex society and threaten their ways of life. However, Mansbridge does grant that ERA would have provided a boost for women and legislators to address issues of equal pay for equal or comparable work.

The younger generation may also be resisting issues of pornography and ERA as mainly ideological or philosophical. Unlike past feminists, young people today seem to be shunning ideology—except that of individualism. They have learned it can provide answers that are too simplistic to explain this complex world and blind people to the real, shifting issues at hand.

But the real tragedy with the fight for ERA is that it wasted tremendous resources. Along with other social issues, the recruitment of younger women was put on the back burner and left there until recent years when the fight for abortion rights rekindled youth participation in the women's movement.

## Abortion Rights

Many younger activists also criticize the past women's movement for its narrow outlook on abortion rights, another example of single-issue politics. As older activists are now also stating, abortion is but one, although vital, component for expanding choice for women.

"Looking at the way reproductive rights have been treated showed me the shortcomings of feminism," said law student Talitha Curtis. "For a long time, it was just the abortion issue, and it was a white middle-class woman's issue, and that's what feminism for a long time has been—a white middle-class woman's approach to life."

She said the fight ignored a wide variety of other issues critical to women who want the choice to have a child. "What's scary about focusing on the abortion issue is that you lose sight of other issues equally as important to women. The right to abortion doesn't mean everyone out there can get an abortion; you can go out and get one if you have the money."

Felicia Kornbluh also argues that abortion rights have to be connected to other issues that give more choices to women, and, in the meantime, have to be supported as an economic necessity for women.

"Seventy-five percent of minimum-wage workers are women," she argues. "In 1987, the median salary for a woman employed full-time was $16,909—little better than the poverty line for a small family. 'Choice' is no answer to these problems; class-sensitive politics that include the abortion option come a lot closer."

## The Gender Gap

One fundamental way in which the generations are dissimilar is their emphasis and openness to the question of difference. Before, the women's movement's focus was on how the sexes were the same. When women wanted to enter the job world and seek opportunity, they had to prove that they had the same capabilities as a man. This often translated into mimicking men to get a crack at their institutions.

Over the past ten years, the major developments in feminist scholarship and literature have explored the ways in which men and women differ. Harvard education professor Carol Gilligan studied a possible gender-based difference in moral decision-making and made waves with her 1982 book *In a Different Voice: Psychological Theory and Women's Development.*

However, some caution that a celebration of difference can lead to overconfidence in women. Some health-clinic defenders from Detroit who attended the NOW First Young Feminist Conference in 1991 blamed NOW's leaders for believing that "women think from their uteruses." The health-clinic defenders felt that relying on women's differences is too simplistic a view.

## Race and Class—and Sexism

The young activists I interviewed passionately stressed the importance of looking at the links between sexism, racism, classism and other prejudices. This would make the dialogue within the women's movement more inclusive and address issues with greater depth and relevance.

Julie Spencer Robinson, who is white, stressed that a multicultural focus and class sensitivity is a matter of survival for feminism. "As far as I'm concerned, multiculturalism is it," she said. "I see our country getting more diverse. If we want more women to identify with the women's movement, then we have to recognize diversity, and that means a diversity of values and opinions."

In her book *Sister Outsider,* Audre Lorde explains the inherent relation between the 'isms': "Racism, the belief in the inherent superiority of one race over all others and thereby the right to dominance. Sexism, the belief in the inherent superiority of one sex over the other and thereby the right to dominance. Ageism. Heterosexism. Elitism. Classism."

Both white activists and those of color I interviewed voiced a sensitivity to these connections. The single most common book that young activists recommended I read was *This Bridge Called My Back: Writings by Radical Women of Color,* a classic anthology. At the three young feminist conferences I attended, issues of diversity and race were generally brought to the forefront by those in attendance.

"I think the reason black women have a hard time identifying with feminism is that a lot of white women who claim to be feminists tend to be racist," said Jamika Ajalon, twenty-three, a black writer and artist from St. Louis living in Chicago. "Or when those issues are brought up, they get really defensive or don't look at themselves to see how some of these issues are true, or how black women have a different issue to deal with when it comes to feminism."

But Ajalon, who works at a feminist bookstore in Chicago, and other women of color I interviewed said they personally notice younger white women acting less defensive about issues of race. Ajalon sees more and more people of all ages buying books that address other women's experiences.

After heated dialogue at a young feminist conference in 1989 about race, Leslie Wolfe, director of the Center for Women Policy Studies in Washington, D.C., was encouraged. "Thanks to all the anguish that we've gone through, young women are more willing to confront this issue," she said, adding that feminists twenty years ago were more defensive.

This apparent enhanced dialogue, while still not substantial enough to heal past divisions has many explanations. Perhaps our society has become more focused on issues of multiculturalism as the population continues to grow more diverse. Young white middle-class women may not be as preoccupied with sexism, feeling less affected by it than their mothers. Also, during their intellectual development, today's young people were greatly influenced by an explosion of accessible and relevant feminist scholarship by women of color. These writers retain the revolutionary and dynamic spirit that has been lost in some of the more obtuse academic works. They also provide strong critiques of the mainstream women's movement that alert readers to pay attention to issues of racism both in issues addressed and in the ways women relate to each other.

It is difficult to explain why this visible organization and expression of women of color has happened at this point. Ajalon saw it as an effect of consciousness building that has been happening in all parts of the black community. She said the separate organizing also reflects the movement of white feminist activists in the Sixties, who saw their issues weren't being addressed by male "progressives."

"Black women were tired of beating their heads against the wall having to defend their own issues. Instead of defending their own issues, [the alternative was] coming together to talk about them, being validated in them in order to reach a higher potential and continue to grow and help other people too," explains Ajalon.

The greater visibility of works of highly respected black writers such as Alice Walker, author of *The Color Purple,* may have also helped validate and inspire the voices of people who have been most silent. While their writing has always been influential and ample, women of color intellectuals seem to be performing the same function now that white intellectuals did twenty-five years ago. They are articulating the concerns of their sisters and creating a movement.

Much recent scholarship documents how racism has been at work historically in the women's movement, alienating women of color. Some is being exposed from specific battles, such as the fight for abortion rights. One anthology about making an inclusive reproductive rights movement, *From Abortion to Reproductive Freedom: Transforming a Movement,* edited by Marilyn Gerber Freid, includes an essay by black feminist Angela Davis. She documents past conflicts that make women of color resistant to joining present activism. Described is an article published by feminist pioneer Margaret Sanger, founder of Planned Parenthood, in the American Birth Control League's journal, who defines as the "chief issue" of birth control "more children from the fit and less from the unfit." Davis writes that in the same journal, white supremacists pushed the development of birth control to limit the reproduction of the black race.

But most criticize the mainstream women's movement for more subtle forms of racism.

"Black women have been standing on the sidelines to begin with. When the suffrage movement began, they were there, but were not welcomed and had to start a whole series of black women's clubs and did the same types of activities these suffragettes were doing," said University of Illinois student Tiffany Ferguson. "Black women have been there struggling the whole time and have never been invited into the fold, and when there has been a supposed invitation, their issues have never been addressed."

Many women of color criticize early theorists for speaking for all women based on the experiences of one sector: the white middle class. Especially influential and groundbreaking has been black feminist theorist Bell Hooks, thirty-seven, who is a frequent lecturer at college campuses nationwide. On the first page of her book, *Feminist Theory From Margin to Center,* Hooks describes how the landmark feminist work of the Sixties movement, *The Feminine Mystique* by Betty Friedan, did not address the specific conditions of women of color, who have had the least voice in trying to fight daily struggles.

"Betty Friedan's *The Feminine Mystique* is still heralded as having paved the way for the contemporary feminist movement—it was written as if these women did not exist. Friedan's famous phrase, 'the problem that has no name,' often quoted to describe the condition of women in this society, actually referred to the plight of a select group of college-educated, middle- and upper-class married white women—housewives bored with leisure, with the home, with children, with buying products, who wanted more out of life. Friedan concludes her first chapter by stating: 'We can no longer ignore that voice within women that says: I want something more than my husband and my children and my house.'

"She did not discuss who would be called in to take care of the children and maintain the home if more women like herself were freed from their house labor and given equal access with white men to the professions. She did not speak of the needs of women without men, without children, without homes. She ignored the existence of all nonwhite women and poor white women. She did not tell readers whether it was more fulfilling to be a maid, a babysitter, a factory worker, a clerk or a prostitute, than to be a leisure-class housewife."

Hooks concedes that some radical feminists originally had a vision of solidarity between all women. Robin Morgan, who is white and the editor of *Sisterhood Is Powerful*, one of the works Hooks cites for its broad vision of women's solidarity, argues that diversity has always been stressed by the women's movement. "Consistently throughout there has always been a very strong African American presence, Asian American, Latina, lesbian, old women, young women, it has been an extremely diverse movement in this country and obviously internationally."

Morgan further said that within the radical women's movement, for many, who, like her, came up through the struggle for civil rights, there has been a constant awareness of racism. "More than any other movement I have ever been involved with, in a life of political activism, at least women tried to deal with [racism] in a variety of ways and creativities."

But Hooks and others write that within the organized radical feminist movement, after the early Seventies, the commitment to "sisterhood" was generally forgotten as political views turned more personal. Women of color didn't find this change attractive because their issues weren't being addressed.

"These sentiments, shared by many feminists early in the movement, were not sustained," Hooks writes. "As more and more women acquired prestige, fame or money from feminist writings or from gains from the feminist movement for equality in the office, individual opportunism undermined appeals for collective struggle. . . . Privileged women wanted social equality with men of their class; some women wanted equal pay for equal work; others wanted an alternative lifestyle."

Other women of color writers have documented their personal experiences of not being taken seriously by white feminists. In the introduction to *This Bridge Called My Back*, co-editor Cherrie Moraga, then twenty-seven, writes: "What drew me to politics was my love of women, the agony I felt in observing the straitjackets of poverty and repression I saw people in my own family in. But the deepest political tragedy I have experienced is how with such grace, such blind faith, this commitment to women in the feminist movement grew to be exclusive and reactionary. *I call my white sisters on this.*"

In the Eighties and Nineties especially, women of color have given new breadth and depth to all aspects of feminist analysis. Race and class questions run deep into questions of economics, attitudes and values. Considering race and class, all the issues look different. Hooks explains why the early feminist reaction against the family was especially threatening to nonwhite women:

"While there are white women activists who may experience family primarily as an oppressive institution (it may be the social structure wherein they have experienced grave abuse and exploitation), many black women find the family the least oppressive institution. Despite sexism in the context of family, we may experience dignity, self-worth and a humanization that is not experienced in the outside world wherein we confront all forms of oppression."

## Not Separatist

Under these analyses, radical feminists' traditional advocacy of gender separatism becomes more impractical and threatening. It is simply not possible for those who depend on men, emotionally and financially. Many perceive separatism as a simplistic solution, blaming men for all the problems, when women experience other conflicts among each other that are rooted in society.

This awareness also affects how white women organize. A small group of white pro-choice activists at the State University of New York-Albany brought up these points on their own and explained why diversity and building a broad base of support is key.

"We're not separatists. We don't believe that at all," said Gina Knarich. "Because we're not the only ones with the problems. It's not men oppressing us. It's the fact that men have been socialized to oppress us and therefore they need healing just as much as we do, and we need to help each other."

Laura Tarantini added: "We're not saying women should not have their own place. But it's taking that understanding and taking it to the groups involved. It's understanding what your own problem is, but that's not the need in itself. The end is communicating it."

However, Hooks and others continue to see the value of separate space as a way to raise consciousness and explore identities. It performs the same function as, for example, a Catholic school or a black youth group. The difference in their vision is that separatism isn't an end unto itself, but a means to achieving unity.

With this diversity, young feminists are resisting defining one issue as most important, or one approach as best for all women. They recognize that people have a variety of perspectives, tastes and personalities, and that the best route is the one each individual feels comfortable taking.

In other movements too, young people are expanding the definitions of their issues. At the national student environmentalist Catalyst conference in October of 1990, a major issue addressed was racism. A male Tufts University student explained the connection:

"The environment is more than grass and trees and air and water," he said. "For people of color, it includes communities infested by drugs, a lack of affordable housing, a lack of medical care, a lack of social services and an absence of meaningful work. . . . It is imperative to realize the same options open to white [people] are not the same ones open to the poor and people of color. People of color will die of ecological devastation even if we buy environmentally safe diapers."

While there are still tensions, young activists are more willing to acknowledge the tremendous challenges to be faced in achieving a new solidarity and building awareness to confront prejudice. But outside these circles, in the mainstream, the task is more monumental. While activists have moved on to discuss the effects of oppression, there are others who have yet to recognize its existence.


## The Generation Gaps

Activists and non-activists also experience different types of generation gaps with older feminists. Those looking to the surface of the women's movement may be turned off perceiving past and present "extremist" rhetoric as representative of all older feminists today. Younger activists also may confront an actual difference in their approach to, or understanding of, feminism.

But, because older and younger people are learning about organizing together, generation gaps, for some, are becoming more like a sliver. Closer ties have been visible in demonstrations over the past few years. The 1989 march on Washington for abortion rights drew a crowd of about 600,000 people (according to NOW estimates), at least half of whom were women under twenty-five.

At the Catalyst conference, student organizers depended on the wisdom of their elders, including former Vietnam War protesters and decades-long leaders of the environmental movement.

"We're more accepting of older people because our parents were activists," said Beth McKay, twenty, who drove fifteen hours to the Midwest conference with friends from the University of South Carolina in Columbia. "There are women sixty-five years old heading environmental groups, and we see that. We realize they have the knowledge to bring to us, and we don't have all the answers.

"But we can look to the past to what our parents did, and we're building on that. We're not an exclusive movement."

♀ PART THREE

# FEMINISM IN "REAL LIFE"

## Chapter Five

# A Feminist Report Card

## GENERAL PROGRESS

To really learn about what the women's movement means to young people, I didn't ask professors and I didn't go to a university.

Instead, for a report card, I visited the real world, the Southwest Side of Chicago neighborhood of Mount Greenwood, where the word "feminist" isn't commonly used. Living there is the family of my friend Jean Lachat. To me, they reflect some of the most fundamental changes made by the women's movement in the past twenty-five years.

Yet, from a visitor's perspective, things at Mount Greenwood don't seem to have changed. Many families like Jean's have lived in the same area for generations and still strongly identify with the heritage and traditions of the scarcely remembered relative from a European Catholic country who settled near there long ago. ("South Side Polish, yes!" says Jean.) You can see it in the corner tavern with the Fighting Irish Notre Dame flag on the wall, or at the rectory down the street. On the December day I interviewed the Lachat family, the small brick houses looked pretty much the same, with their concrete driveways—only wide enough to accommodate a compact car—strings of Christmas lights and well-groomed streets dotted by police cars or the utility trucks some parents take to work.

Like other girls in the neighborhood, Jean and her four sisters, aged fifteen to twenty-seven, attended Mother MacCauley High School and went to mixers on weekends with guys from nearby Marist or Brother

Rice, the all-male schools in the area. But unlike their parents and those before them, the three oldest sisters have gone to college, the fourth attends a university out of state, and the youngest, Nicole, already has her sights set on a New York college.

"Education is probably the biggest change," said Jean's mother, Felicia, fifty-two. "Probably parents realizing that these kids can do more than the norm. Pushing them, never saying no, that they can't do this."

Now her daughters, one of whom is married and another engaged, are working in or planning to enter careers or companies that in the past have been dominated by men. Felicia Lachat, who is a nurse, doesn't look down on traditional female careers, but appreciates that her daughters are able to pursue and develop their own individual interests.

"The first female came in ten years ago maybe," said Jean, twenty-three, a photojournalist who is describing the South Side daily newspaper where she works. "Still I'm always with guys. I was thinking about that at the Hawks game last Thursday night, I was eating dinner in the media room and I was the only girl with about thirty-five guys. I looked around and said 'Holy cow.' I'm the only woman photographer shooting the Bulls and Blackhawks. It doesn't bother me. It just makes me work harder to prove that I can do just as well as they can."

Chrissy, twenty-one, is studying in Colorado to become an athletic trainer and enter a largely male field. "Most of what we do is exercise and rehabilitation. After they get hurt, we tape them up. All through high school, I was in sports and went to a camp in Colorado where I got interested in it. I've always been athletic. I love sports."

The oldest sisters, Michelle, twenty-seven, and Susie, twenty-six, interjected that athletic prowess does not run in the family. Both work as sales representatives and hope to climb the corporate ladder in their male-dominated departments.

"The whole thing is that when I graduated from high school, it was limited," said Felicia. "You either went into education or into nursing or you were a secretary or social worker or whatever—back in the Fifties. Now when these kids graduate from wherever they graduate from, the parents have more of an outlook on them. I don't think the girls, women, themselves are put in a little category where they can only be a nurse, a teacher, a social worker, a secretary; the world is open to them. They can do almost whatever they want to do—as long as they're good at it.

"My kid can shoot hockey games. Susie has cracked into a man's world in sales. Michelle has also cracked into a man's world working for Amoco Oil. And they're doing quite well."

But working outside the home is not new to this family. As with a great number of American families, including a larger proportion of immigrants and minorities, working hasn't simply been a matter of glamour. Like most women, they work because they have to. Jean's grandmother, Esther Pietrowicz, seventy-six, started work when she was a child at her parents' corner grocery store on the South Side. During her teen years, she worked "from six in the morning to seven at night, six days a week and half a day on Sunday," Felicia said.

"One time Grandma killed a mouse by stepping on it," Jean said.

"We bought the store and we didn't know if it had little mice in the floor, but one day I saw one and stomped on it, like that," Esther explained.

Felicia started filling in there when she was thirteen and worked part-time while attending nursing school in 1958. She worked as a nurse between having children and a year ago returned full-time.

During that time, she was affected by the struggles for women's rights although she didn't feel part of any women's movement. She was already working, and saw it mainly as a struggle for those wanting to have flexibility with the traditional roles of staying at home.

"I had a bunch of munchkins when that whole system was going. The only thing that it did was raise my consciousness that my kids could do what they want to do because these women now are fighting for them."

The Lachats also felt that they were ahead of their time with their father, William, fifty-two, looking after the family several days a week when Felicia worked. Mr. Lachat had a job as a foreman with an electric company that required twenty-four-hour shifts followed by two days of breaks.

"We would come home for lunch and Dad would be home making fried baloney sandwiches for us, because I think that's the only thing he knew how to make," remembered Michelle.

And still, as in the rest of the country, change for this family is slow and incomplete. While appreciating some changes in opportunities, Jean's grandmother prefers to hold on to her traditions.

To illustrate this point, Jean asked, "Grandma, what do you think of Geraldine Ferraro?"

"Oh, I hate that. I hate to see a woman in politics. They have a home to take care of and should stay home. Politics. That's a man's job, not a woman's job!

"There was a lady alderman in our neighborhood, and then there was another fellow, Fitzpatrick. I signed his petition immediately and said, 'I want that man in there!' "

Like the Lachats, both women and men, with traditional and unconventional views, voiced appreciation for gains made in career opportunities for women over the past twenty-five years. Whether or not they have been on the front lines of the struggle or just sympathetic to the tactics used is really irrelevant. Almost all those I interviewed agreed that feminism has been injected into the mainstream of America and given it a transfusion of values, expectations and ambitions.

"Militancy has its own rewards," said Resa Hare, a Los Angeles teacher. "If you strive for 150 percent, and you end up with 50, you've gotten somewhere. You probably wouldn't have gotten that 50 percent faster if you hadn't been so militant.

"It's probably made men aware that women have brains and women can succeed. It took away a lot of your typical woman-as-barefoot-and-pregnant-is-the-best-place, etc. attitudes."

The positive responses to the women's movement I found reflected the results of a December 1989 *Time* magazine survey. Of the 1,000 adult women polled, 94 percent agreed that the women's movement has helped women become more independent, 86 percent agreed that it has given women more control over their lives, and 82 percent believed that it is still improving the lives of women.

## Opportunities in the Work Force

Older women interviewed recognized something that younger women have mainly taken for granted: a sense of entitlement to opportunity.

"They've got more coming to them than we did. We didn't think we had anything coming to us. And that's what a lot of our consciousness-raising was all about—hey, I deserve this," said *San Francisco Examiner* columnist Stephanie Salter.

Younger women can get right down to the business of making decisions.

"In fact, many, many, many people, young women, whether they recognize it or not, they're living different, different lives," said Vivian Gornick who teaches college across the country. "They are leading lives where they think about taking themselves seriously in a way that they never would have twenty-five years ago. I love the idea of women talking about—as seriously as young women do when they do—how they'll deal with the career. They struggle because feminism put that desire into them. They think more about—whether they know it or not, consciously or unconsciously—what is it going to be like when the children grow up. They think about the life ahead of them."

When asked specifically about what gains the women's movement has made, interviewees put education and careers at the top of the list. While almost all pointed out the main reason for working is survival, not fulfillment, they said women have wider options and more legal protections. Over half of all bachelor's and master's degrees are now earned by women; for doctorates, the percentage is now 40 percent. Among blacks, more than 60 percent of master's degrees go to women, according to the Institute for Women's Policy Research.

The entry of young women into the professional fields has skyrocketed. In a fall 1990 special edition of *Time* magazine on the status of women, Barbara Ehrenreich first comments on women making their mark in high positions, although in limited numbers, and not enough to transform the workplace. She recognizes that women's participation in medicine, management and law has increased by 300 to 400 percent since the Seventies.

"Women lawyers have spearheaded reforms in the treatment of female victims of rape and of battering," she writes. "Women executives have created supportive networks to help other women up the ladder and are striving to sensitize corporations to the need for flexible hours, child care and parental leave. Women journalists have fought to get women's concerns out of the style section and onto the front page."

Several people I interviewed noticed that women are indeed increasingly calling the shots from high places. "I think we've definitely come a long way because we've got a female governor now, female senators, a judge on the Supreme Court and that's great, instead of seeing all those male faces running everything. I think it's just like a household; in order to make a household run, you need two heads and for running this country, I think everybody has to be involved," said Stephanie Boatley, twenty-one, who hopes to someday own a business.

But women are still far from running the show. As Ehrenreich concludes, women in elite, fast-track positions are still scarce. A July 1990 *Fortune* magazine article from July 1990 that revealed that the highest echelons of corporate management are less than one-half of 1 percent female. After the November 1990 elections, the progress of women in government office proved slow; still only two senators, three governors and twenty-eight House members—down from twenty-nine.

Also, despite dramatic career gains for some, ironically, a large group that seems to have gone relatively unadvanced is young women. Most continue to work in relatively low-paying female-dominated jobs—as secretaries, nursing assistants, data-entry keyers and so on.

## A Question of Necessity

The main difference between women's status today and that of women two decades ago is increased participation in the labor force. In 1989, 72 percent of white women and 74 percent of black women aged twenty-five to thirty-four were in the work force, up from 44 percent and 58 percent respectively in 1970, reports the Institute for Women's Policy Research. Today, roughly 58 percent of women are in the work force.

Of those I interviewed, nearly everyone who was not already working was preparing herself for a future job.

"I've decided self-fulfillment doesn't matter; it all boils down to the bottom line," said Bonnie Bieze-Adrian, twenty-five, an insurance representative in the Chicago suburb of Downer's Grove. Her new husband works two full-time jobs, as a waiter and construction worker.

"We have three incomes coming in between the two of us, and we have a mobile home. We don't have a new car. He drives my 1988 Omni I got for a college graduation present. I drive my company car. I don't have incredibly gorgeous clothes. I have the furniture my parents gave me from their old house."

Career plans were described as necessary even for those who would prefer to stay at home. According to the Virginia Slims/Roper Organization poll published in a 1990 issue of *American Demographics* magazine, most women and men surveyed said ideally they would stay at home until their children were ready for school, but that as a practical reality, few believed they would be able to do this.

ONE reason women's need to work has increased has to do with changes in earnings. Over the past twenty years, those under thirty have been the big losers. The median income of families headed by people in that age bracket plunged 30 percent from 1973 to 1987, according to the Children's Defense Fund, a non-profit advocacy group based in Washington, D.C.

Particularly hard hit are blue-collar males who have suffered with the drying up of industrial jobs. Author Sylvia Ann Hewlett sums it up as follows: "One well-paid smokestack job with health insurance has been replaced by two service jobs without benefits. Burger King doesn't provide as well as Bethlehem Steel." In the fall 1990 *Time* special women's issue, Hewlett cites dramatic statistics charting this phenomenon. Between 1955 and 1973, the median wage of men leaped from $15,056 to $24,621. Then, quite suddenly, it started to drop. By 1987, the male wage, adjusted for inflation, was back down to $19,859, a 19 percent decline. She notes that wives pouring into the market had no major effect. Although twice as many wives were at work in 1988, the average family income was only 6 percent higher than in 1973.

THOSE interviewed also recognized that higher costs of living are driving women to go to work outside the home. In a July 1990 *Time* poll, 65 percent of those surveyed between the ages of eighteen and twenty-five agreed that "given the way things are, it will be much harder for people in my generation to live as comfortably as previous generations."

Two-income households are now a virtual necessity to buy a home, as concluded in a 1990 survey by Chicago Title and Trust. Among all home-buyers nationwide, 79.3 percent came from two-income households, and among first-time buyers, more than 88 percent were two-income.

Auditor Chris Jackiw sees the need to plan ahead. He is already concerned about his pension, predicting that Social Security will be but a fond memory by the time he reaches his golden years.

Although her husband makes a solid income with his own business, Karen Berling, thirty, a middle manager at a Cincinnati company, explained that she could not quit her job because of future expenses, such as her son's college. Her son Brian is one and a half years old.

"They say by the time he grows up, it will cost $100,000 to send your kids to college. We know people won't be able to live like that. Something has got to change. If you have two middle-class people with two incomes, you still won't be able to send two or three kids to college for $100,000 each," she said.

"You have to start saving for it. You can't wait until they're in high school."

With this long-term view in mind, women today are more resistant to leaving the work force. Even if a woman can afford to quit temporarily to look after a child, she takes a risk in terms of lost work experience or not being able to find another job.

In some cases, leaving a job can render someone less marketable than when she or he left college. Jodie Jones, a Cincinnati systems analyst, said that a five-year leave in her computer field would be devastating, since the technology changes so rapidly.

## The Feminist Establishment

Perhaps the most unrecognized but most pervasive evidence of the women's movement's mainstream presence is an abundance of feminist institutions. These organizations are such a common part of the twentysomethings' landscape that they often overlook how revolutionary they were just twenty-five years ago. They don't realize that the women's movement is responsible for that class with a women's perspective they have the option to take, or the health information they have at their disposal, the women's shelter they can turn to, or the crisis line that's available for support.

In *The American Woman 1990–91*, a yearly progress report of the women's movement, Sarah Harder lists the contrasts:

—In 1970, no one even knew what a "battered women's shelter" was. Now there are at least 1,200 such centers or shelters.

—In 1970, no one had ever heard of a "women's center" (campus- or community-based social service center for women). A recent compilation by the National Association of Women's Centers has discovered that there are at least 4,000 women's centers.

—In 1970, the idea of a rape crisis center was in germination in perhaps three minds in the United States. There are now 600 rape crisis centers.

—Displaced homemakers (women left without means for support) were first recognized in the early 1970s. Now there are over 1,000 displaced-homemaker groups, programs or services in the United States.

Women's-studies courses are now offered at over two-thirds of all universities, nearly half of all four-year colleges and about one-fourth of two-year institutions, according to 1984 statistics from the American Council on Education.

"The world of feminist scholarship includes over fifty centers or institutes for research on women, numerous professional journals for the bulk of the new knowledge and more than a hundred feminist bookstores across the country," writes Mariam Chamberlain, president of the National Council for Research on Women in New York in *The American Woman 1990–91*.

While women of color have always organized together to support each other, they are also becoming more visible with their own institutions, many at the same stage of mushrooming growth that the National Organization for Women achieved in the early 1970s.

Among the most famous and revolutionary is the National Black Women's Health Project, based in Atlanta, which has expanded from a local shoestring operation into a respected national organization. It has formed a model for health-education programs and self-help groups "where women stand up and talk out loud about what's happening to them," says Byllye Avery, fifty-one, the charismatic founder of the organization and a longtime women's health activist.

The self-help groups that have spread across the United States and beyond during the Eighties provide the unique function of relieving isolation of poor women and empowering them with information about their mental and physical health. The National Black Women's Health Project has ninety-six self-help groups in twenty-two states, six groups in Kenya, and groups in Barbados and Belize.

"I think the greatest news of the past fifteen years has been the development of feminist organizations made up of women of color, like the Mexican American Women's National Association, and Asian Women United, and the National Political Congress of Black Women. This has been an exciting development that has gone almost unreported," said Leslie Wolfe, the director of the Center for Women Policy Studies.

This profusion of groups was quickly evident to me as I perused the regional *Directory of Milwaukee Area Women's Organizations,* Eighth Edition, published by the Center for Women's Studies of the University of Wisconsin-Milwaukee. It lists more than 200 support organizations for health care, counseling and family services, professional networking, political action, women of color, domestic and sexual abuse advocacy, and cultural contacts for art, literature and music.

## Women and Men: A New Respect?

Most people I interviewed pointed to changes in attitudes as the major influence of the women's movement on young people. Notable were two common new ethnics cited by both men and women: sharing housework and enhancing the fatherhood role.

Because of the enormity of the task of working and keeping house, young women interviewed were overwhelmingly adamant about their future husbands' equal sharing of the load at home.

Lisa Seidlitz, twenty-one, a junior at the University of Illinois in Champaign, is not married yet. But, like others, she knows what she will expect. "If he won't share it, he's not my husband," she said.

I asked her if she thinks this will be possible to achieve.

"I kind of hope that it is. If it's not, then I don't think I'll die not having a husband. I hope I won't need a husband to exist. I'm not afraid of living alone or with female friends."

The good news is that young men overwhelmingly know this will be expected of them. Their consciousnesses do not need to be raised about what is fair in the household if the woman works.

Many men had mothers who set standards for parity with their husbands or had their children equally divide chores. Arthur McAdams, a Birmingham lab technician, was one of four men interviewed who said he was trained well by a single mother.

"All of us had to do work. When I was small, I had to clean up my room. We were raised to pick up after ourselves and do work. I know about domestic things."

Either way, men said they expected to feel pressure from their wives or from themselves to share the burdens.

"My dad cooks and cleans," said Columbia University student David Tepper. "I will probably end up being my father whether I want to or not."

"[I don't] naturally go up and do the dishes," said his friend Justin Lundgren. "I have to will myself to do it, that's all. I come from a family where I have never had to do chores."

I asked him if it would be hard to share the load.

"Yeah, sure. You have to marry a woman who won't let you get away with shit."

Thomas Nishioka, twenty-one, another Columbia student, replied that sharing is a matter of ethics. "I think I'd like to be that way, and I'll try to marry a woman who won't let me get away with anything, or I'll feel guilty."

"It's a feminist superego we have," Lundgren added.

It must be noted, however, that this question of equal housework is a question of privilege. Four million single women aged twenty to thirty-four, nearly one-third the total, have children. For the three single mothers I interviewed, who were by far among the poorest of the sample, the question of getting any help from someone else was a fantasy.

But for those who were married, equally sharing the work in the home was a definite ethic (even if not consistently practiced). Seven out of nine members of working couples surveyed said the work around the house was divided equally. Rick and Debbie Jaskolski, a Kenosha,

Wisconsin couple who lived together before marriage, said that they had an easy transition keeping up the roommate habit of splitting chores. Rick has the benefit of working a twenty-four-hour shift as a fire fighter, after which he gets two days off and looks after the children.

They both said they enjoy taking care of their infant twins, but are relieved to hand them over to the other parent when the shift ends.

## Fatherhood Focus

Others interviewed have noticed some fathers taking more responsibility and making fathering a priority in their lives.

"My husband is very, very involved," Karen Berling said. "I traveled a few times when my son was young. I can leave, but I don't have to leave a list for my husband telling him what he eats, what he wears, what time he goes to bed, what time he gets up. I don't have to leave any instructions about his daily care and I think that's wonderful. You can't say that about a lot of husbands—twenty years ago or now."

Even the two men interviewed whose wives don't work outside the home admitted the importance of more equitable child-rearing. Renee Boots said she appreciates the commitment of her husband Todd, a carpenter, who helps take care of the baby when he comes home, although he is exhausted from eight hours of physical labor.

"After four o'clock, [the baby] pretty much shifts hands every couple hours," Renee said.

"It's important, so that she knows who is who, who the parents are," said Todd.

"It's important for me that he does things with her."

"I don't want to turn out like Renee's dad did."

"That's what I'm scared of, because my dad was no father at all. I can count on two fingers how many times I heard him say 'I love you.' And it's a terrible thing. It's terrible. And I don't want to have her miss out."

The four male Columbia students interviewed all said they were taking that into account. Thomas Nishioka said he changed his major from biological research to banking. "I really got into biological research, and I've been working in a lab with a couple of Ph.D.s and scientists. I looked at their lives and they work too much. They don't have enough time. Despite the fact that I think it's really noble, and I enjoy it, I just don't want to do it because I don't want to be so manically engaged by my work that I don't have time to raise kids and have a family."

## Friendships

Many also indicated that according to their experiences, marriages and relationships between men and women have improved. Women working in a variety of places—whether in the military or in the corporate world—say that men of their generation are more comfortable with them as peers.

The young men working in traditionally male fields noticed the most dramatic difference among generations. While recognizing conditions could be different at other sites, Todd Boots said that men on his carpentry crew only judge women according to how they do the work, and that he has never seen harassment.

"I just got through with my apprentice training, and probably 20 percent of [the apprentices] were women. You go through an apprenticeship with women, and you get out on the job, and it's no big deal. I see the guys in their sixties, they're still like 'she'll never make it.' They see it the old way."

Outside of work, young men and women seem to enjoy more genuine friendships, which were reported by at least half of the nonactivists interviewed. These were real trusting relationships, not just the old routine of two people breaking up, saying 'let's be friends' and never laying eyes on each other again.

While the attitudes are still light years away from being transformed, the reason for a seemingly more common mutual respect is that much of the mystique of who men and women are has diminished. Those interviewed explained that their parents stressed that sisters and brothers share kitchen tasks equally, that they had been told they were equal in school, that they had attended college as peers, and had often lived in coed floors in residence halls.

While also recognizing that complications or misunderstandings can develop, a great number of people doubted the validity of the 1988 movie *When Harry Met Sally,* based on the premise that men and women can't be friends. They didn't understand the big deal about the long-running sitcom of their youth, "Three's Company," which revolved around men and women trying to live together platonically.

Typical was a group of five women acquaintances who work in different departments of a large company in Cincinnati. All said that they have male friends whom they see regularly, much to their parents' confusion.

"If I even mention I did something with a guy, my parents are like, 'Oh, what is he like? Is he nice?' " said Rachel Kirk, twenty-four.

Another, Cheryl, who preferred not to have her last name used, agreed. "My parents used to do that but not anymore. I yelled at them too many times about it. I warned them."

"There are also the rumors that fly at work, people are like 'Are you going out or what?' I say no, we're just friends. Can't I have a friend?" said Suzanne Hiernaux. "Everyone wants to believe something."

This newfound notion of friendship seemed to extend to the marriages of those interviewed. Todd and Renee Boots said they both expect to communicate and respect each other more than their parents did. "Sometimes I thought in my family there was a general lack of respect for one another," said Renee. "I see it between my mom and dad. My dad is the boss and does whatever he wants, and my mom is supposed to accept whatever his answer is."

## Confusion: Sit, Stand, Kneel?

While some relations between the sexes have reached détente, other tensions have emerged as roles are expanded and challenged.

"I think it's given women more choices, probably, to improve [their lives] in the end. That's the one thing that the women's movement has done. When I was growing up, I was told you can do anything you want. If I wanted to be president, I could do it. If I wanted to have kids and be a mommy, I could do it. If I wanted to be a policewoman, I could do it," said business student Amy Strassler.

"I think that's really great, but it also makes things more confusing. Because you have to say I do want to have a career, but I still want to have a family, but how do I combine it. A man doesn't worry about how he's going to make the combination. It's kind of taken for granted that if he wants to emphasize the career a little more than the family, there will be someone there to balance the family part."

Making a difference for women in terms of stress was one additional and uncompromising pressure: a biological time clock. This is most felt by women planning to enter traditionally male professions, whose demands are set up for people with wives at home.

Graduate student Rachel Spector discussed the stress of trying to fulfill their ambitions without being blinded by them.

"You're supposed to stay home, raise your kids, do nothing else but raise your kids," Spector said. "Suddenly you're supposed to have a career and put it off until you're thirty-nine and have to go to these fertility clinics. Suddenly the question is 'How am I going to balance as a woman my desire to have a family and my desire to have a career and not be stuck at age fifty never having done anything in my life, or not be forty and say I have never had children.' It's also how to involve the man. Where does his responsibility lie, or is it all up to me?"

Like many others, a theme of the conversation was the difficult challenge of having children while younger to avoid fertility problems —whether for medical reasons or because no man was yet in sight to help get the process moving. All the painful images of older couples on television paying thousands of dollars to specialists have had a major impact on younger people's psyches.

Men notice this turmoil. One young lawyer said that he was sad to see his unmarried female co-worker in her thirties considering having "a baster baby," one conceived by an anonymous donor with artificial insemination.

Some women wanting careers find themselves in the self-defeating mode of constantly comparing themselves to others to make sure they are on track. They worry when a friend moves, gets promoted, gets engaged, has a child.

"At twenty-four, no matter how sure of yourself you are, life sometimes seems like the final race of the Kentucky Derby—everything is at stake and it might be over in a flash," writes Jill Neimark in a December 1990 *Mademoiselle* article about young women's ambitions. "I couldn't help but compare myself to others my own age, not so much because I wanted to beat them at anything, but because I wanted to be reassured that I wasn't falling behind in my own life plan."

For those who are married, confusion about expectations is also common. While in Cincinnati, I asked Rick Jones, twenty-four, an accountant, and Jodie Jones what advantages she has over her mother.

"She's more fulfilled," Rick volunteered.

"I am?" said Jodie. "In my career? I hate my job."

"At least you plan on being more fulfilled. Our mothers didn't necessarily expect that. You have these expectations that aren't being met so it's creating tension in your life."

"Thanks, doctor."

"Mom and Dad never had to deal with that," Rick said. "Before, just dads worried. Now moms *and* dads worry."

Changing expectations for roles have also caused confusion for men. However, one man interviewed explained that he prefers women to define their own identities for themselves—whatever they end up being.

"What hurts and really makes things difficult is that there is such a wide variety. If you meet someone who has traditional, old-fashioned-type values, you kind of have to get in the traditional, old-fashioned mode." said Mike Brooks.

"If you run into someone who's a feminist, you have to treat them as a feminist, as someone who will insist on being treated as an individual, and you have to accept that that person believes in the principle that they don't need you."

I later asked him which he would prefer.

"Oh God . . . I think everyone would prefer having their goals and their wishes predefined. The problem is it's not possible anymore. In a situation where roles are so uncertain, I guess I prefer someone who has a mind of their own and can think for themselves."

Others were not only confused, but angry about the organized women's movement. Renee and Todd Boots agreed with a minority of others interviewed that it only made matters worse.

"I think it's all ridiculous, to be honest with you," said Renee. "I think women got themselves in trouble with all the women's lib stuff. It all comes down to respect. Here I am with groceries in my hands and a baby stroller trying to get through the door, and I don't care if it's a man, woman, boy, a girl, old person there to open it for me. It's nice to have the door opened for you. But I don't expect it. If you want to do it for me, fine. If not, I'll do it myself.

"There are some men who think women have bad attitudes. I think maybe we've lost our positioning. If we hadn't fought so hard for it, I think maybe it would have come eventually anyway."

Her husband turned and asked me, "Did you ever see that show 'Love Connection' on TV? They don't know if he should open the door or not open the door."

"The men are confused," said Renee. "I really think they're confused. They don't know how to act."

"It's like during the church service," said Todd. "Sit, stand, kneel. Sit, stand, kneel. No one knows what in the hell is going on."

The largest "negative" effect discussed by both females and males was affirmative action, or special consideration for hiring women, designed as a balancing agent to make up for past lack of opportunity and any discrimination within institutions.

Resa Hare echoed the sentiments of both white men and women who said that affirmative action is too much of a "sledgehammer approach." While voicing strong opposition to any discrimination, they said that gender, along with race, should not be a factor when it comes to hiring. Many also expressed confidence in the laws for protection.

"It stigmatizes women," Hare said. "It will do the same thing to us that it has done to our minority populations, saying that you didn't get the job because you're a bright, intelligent, educated human being. You got the job due to the extra ten points you were given because you were born female."

Still, most women who mentioned affirmative action spoke of it positively and appreciated the break. "If you can get your foot in the door just because you're female, more power to you," said Jean Lachat. "But they're not going to keep you there if you're not going to do the job."

The group with the most resentment for affirmative action was white males. But both white and black males spoke strongly about feeling reverse discrimination directed toward them.

One engineer, who came from a working-class background, said that friends at his state university often discussed how women and minorities received preferential treatment at hiring time.

"People talk about it a lot," he said. "In college, what do you think a bunch of white guys do? We griped about it and it was a fairly legitimate gripe. It was just so bad, it was so blatant, you just laughed at it. It's just disheartening. It's like, it would be nice that someone gave me a scholarship because I'm a white male. But I don't see any white male scholarships. 'You're a white Protestant male, we want white Protestant males, we'll give you $5,000 more than anyone else.' That would be sweet. I'd take it, no problem."

Others say women's needs will be met by a force more mighty and just than affirmative action or organizing: the free market economy.

"It doesn't seem like there is a real need for feminism because economics is going to change everything. It really is. You don't need the real outspoken women," said Rick Jaskolski.

But his wife Debbie, twenty-seven, a city clerk, was more hesitant in her reply.

"I don't know," she said, trying to settle her crying infant twins at her feet. "I think our relationship is really healthy. But I think there are lots of cases out there where both husband and wife have to work and the woman is still expected to do everything else. Rick and I are in a minority."

## Proceed with Caution

While notions of career and family are changing, so are views on marriage.

The National Center for Health Statistics reports that men and women are marrying, on the average, three years later than they were in 1970. In 1987, the average age for marriage was twenty-five for men and twenty-three for women. Studying the twenty- to twenty-four age group in 1988, the U.S. Census Bureau found that 77 percent of men and 61 percent of women had never married, up sharply from 55 percent and 36 percent, respectively, in 1970. For those aged fifteen to twenty-nine, the unmarrieds included 43 percent of men and 29 percent of women in 1988, vs. 19 percent and 10 percent in 1970, according to the July 16, 1990, issue of *Time.*

Young people are understandably wary. Over the past fifteen years, half of all marriages ended in divorce. As a result of their general skepticism about commitment and its loss of meaning, many women are facing more responsibilities than ever before without the stability and security that ideally comes with a relationship.

After my interviews, I realized that a substantial number of those who were involved in a serious romantic relationship were living with their boyfriends or girlfriends (nine); sixteen were married. The cohabitation arrangement seems to be the only rational alternative for those who have enough confidence in marriage to consider it. While this pre-marriage screen test isn't a guarantee that a marriage will work out, it can give a definite red light warning if it is destined to flop.

Michelle Traupmann, a teacher who lives with her boyfriend in San Diego, said that she has learned to be realistic about what to expect from marriage. Her parents divorced early, and she was left struggling with her mother.

"She worked her tail off," Traupmann said. "She worked a lot. She got her Ph.D. when I was in third grade. We went through a lot of hard times. We were on food stamps for a while."

Traupmann said that her views are representative of our generation, even those without divorced parents have learned from others' warnings.

"I think if you interviewed these same people five or ten years ago, they probably wouldn't have said that they would be living with their boyfriends in their twenties," Traupmann said. "Yet, as they grew older, they went to college and they went to college in the Eighties, a time when living together became more and more and more acceptable. In fact, more and more people said, 'Boy you should do this instead of getting married or before you get married because how can you possibly make a decision about getting married to somebody if you don't know what it's like to live with them day to day?'

"I have always felt this because I came from a situation where my parents didn't know what it was like to live with each other day to day. And look what happened: They got divorced right away. I thought: 'How silly, why didn't you just live together?' But obviously at that point, it wasn't the thing to do."

## DECLARATIONS OF INDEPENDENCE

Many interviewed noticed another sweeping change in attitudes. Twenty-five years after the outbreak of the civil war for women's rights in this country, a great declaration of independence is being drafted.

Women of the next generation from all walks of life are individually and uniformly determined to realize some of the movement's most fundamental goals: self-sufficiency, self-definition and self-determination. More than any other word or philosophy, independence describes the next generation of women, their goals and their ideals.

For those prepared to achieve it, this state of independence can be an exhilarating and endless source of confidence. Cheryl, a Cincinnati business writer, explained that this makes her a feminist. "That has been a point of pride. I can do it myself. I can do it myself," she said. "That's why I feel really strong about independence, and I think women should be independent at least once during their lives."

Nodding in agreement were her four acquaintances, all young female professionals, who were sitting around the table in the old apartment in the urban Hyde Park district.

"I have seen so many women who have always been taken care of by someone else, and they are afraid to do things on their own," said Cheryl, who grew up in Dayton. "That makes me kind of sad to think that perpetuates a lot of attitudes. I have a younger sister who is like that. She has always been protected. She's the baby."

I asked her if that independence was too much of a demand to put on herself.

"I don't think so, really," she said. "I think men should be able to take care of themselves too. They seem to still need a wife to help them cook and clean and are pretty much clueless about taking care of themselves."

But more than being valued as a personal statement, independence is prized as an economic necessity.

Both traditional and nontraditional women young and old have come to recognize that the old female standard of dependence just doesn't work anymore. Instead of being considered a privilege of womanhood, dependence is now more often feared as a trap. They've seen the examples of women before them who have been left helpless— in losing their identities in relationships, being abused within them, or struggling, once left, to face life on their own.

Confirming these findings is a 1990 study on the status of the thirty-five million young women between the ages of eighteen and thirty-four in this country. "The most prominent development over the past two decades has been the increased independence of young women and the assumption of responsibility for their own support," concludes the study issued by the Institute for Women's Policy Research.

The report documents how women are working more, marrying later and less, assuming more family economic responsibility and more frequently raising children without partners. This is the only known comprehensive current research about that status of young women.

"Women have come to realize that whether because of divorce (which leaves some on the average 73 percent poorer, and men on the average 42 percent richer), childbearing outside of marriage, the inability of many men to earn an adequate 'family wage' or their remaining single—either through design or circumstance—they must be prepared to support themselves and anyone else for whom they feel responsible," writes Ruth Sidel in *On Her Own.*

The potential for independence is naturally valued no matter what one's present situation, whether rich or poor, committed or uncommitted in a relationship. For those relying on others—whether a family, a boyfriend, a husband—knowledge of one's ability to be independent is a premium insurance policy to withstand future turmoil. Young women interviewed expressed that in this uncertain and changing world, the one thing they can always depend on is themselves.

Almost all have been taught this lesson by their parents, even those in more traditional homes. Stephanie Boatley said that her mother, who has been with her father for twenty-one years, drilled this concept into her.

"If my mother had to do it by herself," said Boatley, "she would lose her mind."

In the process of seeking independence, young women are facing a variety of new challenges and responsibilities—some faced by men in the past and others unique to this generation.

## The Struggle for Personal Autonomy

For many like Cheryl, living on one's own provides the space and time to define oneself. The twenties are often a time of constant struggle against inner and outer demons to achieve personal independence. In those years identity becomes filled in and reinforced so that it will be strong enough to endure any future compromise or pummeling from others.

A challenge is taking charge of making your own mold and ensuring that it is not disturbed while the shape sets. The ongoing battle is to strike a balance between the natural human need to connect with others and the necessity of not losing oneself and one's needs in the process.

The rest of the Cincinnati women I interviewed said the ideal of personal and emotional independence makes them resist options that may jeopardize this opportunity, such as living at home with their families or depending too much on a boyfriend.

"Sometimes it bothers me," said Suzanne Hiernaux, a systems analyst, who said she moved home after college to be with her close-knit family. " 'Where are you going? When will you be back?' You walk in at 4:30 in the morning and they say, "Do you know how late that is? I woke up at three and couldn't go back to sleep. I almost called the hospital to see if you were there.'

"It's to the point where it's too much. I need to get out and do exactly what Cheryl said everyone should do—find out what I can and cannot do. Can I push my limitations? Can I just be by myself and enjoy it? It's comfortable, safe and secure. And I need to get uncomfortable and unsafe and unsecure.

"You can be a slave to the fear of being alone," she added. "Then you will do whatever you can to always have a boyfriend. That really limits you."

Other women and men interviewed stressed the importance of living on one's own to establish an identity. Chris Jackiw said he can finally afford to move out of his mother's home, where he lived for a year after graduating from Northern Illinois University in DeKalb.

"You lose who you are," he said. "You've been on your own for four to five years and developed this personality, and no matter how much you were what you were when you lived at home, your room is not the same. You have no belongings. It's not your house.

"Even if your parents say, 'You can stay out as long as you want, we don't care'—they really care. You always feel that burden. You almost feel like they are conforming you back to the way you were—and you're not that person anymore."

Facing strong economic constraints, Jackiw is part of a large group of men and women of his generation living with parents in adulthood. During the 1980s, householders under the age of twenty-five were the only group to suffer a drop in income—a decline of 10 percent.

As an apparent result, over the past twenty years, the rate of females and males eighteen to twenty-four living at home has been rising, according to U.S. Census data. In 1980, 42.7 percent of females in that age group were classified as "child of the householder," compared to 48.4 percent in 1988. The number of men in 1980 was 54.3 percent and in 1988, 60.7 percent.

## Isolation

When a young person moves out to be on his or her own and seek independence, this self-sufficiency can often mean isolation. In entering the work force after college or high school, he or she may suddenly be without the support networks of others of the same age.

In seeking their career fortunes, young women, as men have in the past, often find themselves settling alone in new cities or towns because of school or careers. Instead of patterning their lives after their husbands' ambitions, they are more often following their own and facing a new set of complications in leaving a potential partner or parents behind.

In finding the best livelihood, four out of five of the young women from Cincinnati are starting lives on their own. One in the group, Rachel Kirk, twenty-four, a systems analyst from the small town of Bradford, Pennsylvania, said she was following her older brothers' pattern of mobility in her career choice. One moved to Dallas and another to Phoenix.

"It's pretty far. It was kind of hard because I didn't know anybody here. But my family has always been really spread out. There weren't any jobs in my hometown, so I couldn't stay. I probably could have looked somewhere closer, but I was interviewed, and this is where I ended up," Kirk said.

Sarah Turoff, who works at a Chicago bank, said she sees the isolation even for those who don't move far from home. A general loss of community in American life means the loss of a support system, source of tradition and even a predetermined route to a mate. "I think there's isolation because you no longer grow up in the same community, marry from the community and die in the same community," she said.

## A Pioneering Task

Women also have some additional pressures that working men have not faced. One major change from twenty-five years ago is that women expect to be able to accomplish what they want with little or no help from others. For many women, such as those in the Cincinnati group —with solid training, access to opportunity, no major life disasters and avoidance of early pregnancy—this challenge of self-sufficiency is possible.

But, for many, many women, this firm expectation of independence is often a tremendous struggle, considering the pioneering quality of the task.

Generally individualists, they expect to achieve it all on their own. To some, it means that they must be able to face unforeseen circumstances by themselves and be in charge of all facets of their life, including job, home and family. No one since the beginning of time in any civilization I know of has been able to live with these expectations.

"Men usually did not 'make it alone,' " Ruth Sidel writes in *On Her Own*. "They did not, as the image goes, tame the West, develop industrial America, and climb the economic ladder alone—and they certainly did not do it while being the primary care-giver for a couple of preschoolers. Most of those men who 'made it' in America, whom we think of when we reaffirm our belief in the American Dream, had women beside them every step of the way—women to iron their shirts, press their pants, mend their socks, cook their meals, bring up their children and soothe them at the end of the hard day. They did not do it alone. They still don't do it alone."

With this exalted idea of independence, women are facing an awesome challenge. They are striving to fulfill new ambitions and make it in a world that has changed little to accommodate them.

## Independent with Children

For women with all degrees of responsibilities, one major difference in expectation from twenty-five years ago is that women today are generally less confident that men will support them. As a result, by circumstance and choice of being on their own, more are facing the world without partners.

Some cautiousness is derived from their personal experiences of men not taking commitments seriously. Those who were not prepared for independence said they learned from harsh struggles that they must take charge and maintain control of their lives from now on.

Diana, twenty-three, who is white, works at a credit union in Wisconsin and did not want her last name used, said that she is wary of ever getting married or depending on anyone again. After becoming pregnant her senior year of high school in North Carolina, she married right after graduation and never acquired the skills necessary to be self-sufficient. Two years ago, her husband walked out on her and her daughter; he is now in prison where he can't pay support.

"It's scary, very scary financially doing it on your own, emotionally too," said Diana. "Especially when you've gone straight from living with parents to living with someone else as a wife. I think that you have to experience things on your own before you can decide to jump into something like that. It needs to be for all the right reasons too."

Kim, also twenty-three (and does not want her real name used), of Dallas, stressed that women can't depend solely on men for financial support. She was recently forced to move with her son back home with her mother, who lives in a public housing development in a dangerous neighborhood on the West Side. Like Diana, she said she will avoid marriage in the future.

"After I had the baby for about six months, [my husband] just told me he wanted his freedom. I didn't know how to take it. I didn't know how to deal with it, so I have been through some counseling, whatever you want to call it, I was there. Everything is getting back on track, thank God for that," said Knox, a day-care worker who is attending a local college to get a teaching degree.

"I don't think I ever want to get married again. I know that's being negative, but I feel like what happened might happen again. Or a second marriage might work out, who knows? But I feel I would rather do bad on my own than do it with a man," she reflected. "Hmm. Hmm."

Kim and Diana are representative of an enormous demographic group of their generation. While the proportion of women in this age bracket with children is falling, the proportion with children outside marriage is rising. Four million women between the ages of twenty and thirty-four, nearly one-third of the total of single, divorced and widowed women, have children.

Between 1960 and the early Eighties, the divorce rate rose steeply, and since then it has remained relatively stable. While younger people may tend to consider divorce as something their parents do, a lot of women who get divorced are under thirty, as evidenced by National Center for Health Statistics figures. For women, 16.3 percent of divorces in 1986 were in the twenty- to twenty-four-year-old age group; 22.8 percent fell into the category of women twenty-five to twenty-nine. Over the past fifteen years, half of all marriages ended in divorce.

Women are also having more children outside of marriage. The Institute for Women's Policy Research reports that in 1986, 23 percent of births were to unmarried mothers, compared to 11 percent in 1970. Black women in this category had a higher rate, with 61 percent of births to unmarried mothers in 1986, compared to 38 percent in 1970. For teenage mothers in 1986, 61 percent of births were to unmarried women compared to 30 percent in 1970.

Making it alone under these conditions is a struggle. Families with a female householder are three times as likely to be poverty-stricken. For families with a young woman householder, the proportion in poverty is over 50 percent. And for families with a female householder who is both young and a woman of color, the poverty rate is over 60 percent, according to the institute.

The stress can be overwhelming. "I get depressed a lot," said Diana. "I've been in a rut a while now. The bills really get to me, not being able to do for [my daughter] what I really want to do. She wants a lot of love, and that I can give her. But I know she wants to do things. She wants to go here, go there, and we can't always do that. I mean the job, the home life, having to worry about her father."

## A Personal Story

Many young women feel isolated by both an absolute, theoretical belief in self-reliance and a real necessity for it. In many cases, they justifiably see the state of being alone as the only sure thing in their lives, and don't hope for or expect anything more. Many, especially women in low-income situations, have lost faith in other sources of support, including a partner, family or the system.

Mary, twenty-three, a single mother from Brooklyn, who did not want her real name used, personified this Nineties ethic of complete independence. Her confidence only in herself and insistence on being alone has been reinforced by some long and painful trials in her life.

Like others interviewed, her troubles were hidden below the surface. I met her through a professor I interviewed who offered to recruit subjects from her sociology class at one of the campuses of the City University of New York. I went to her office and found one volunteer, Mary, who told me she believed women should help each other. She was a black woman who spoke slowly with a Caribbean lilt to her voice. Her hair was pulled back and she was dressed in a bright pink sweater and jeans.

We went down to the cafeteria, talked about her class and teacher, got some food, and came back to the office. I took out the standard questions about feminism, but first asked her the vital statistics— name, age, date of birth. She told me she had a three-year-old daughter and lived with her boyfriend in Brooklyn.

I remarked on how difficult that must be, and she agreed. For about a half-hour, I forgot about my original set of questions and listened to her react to that one statement.

I slowly learned about the disappointments that explained her strong convictions about why she must make it alone. Like others I talked with, she had been living in silence and was eager to finally share her experiences.

"People ask me how I do it," she said. "I say I have my ups and downs—I have a lot of ups and downs.

"People say, 'Aren't you married yet?' I say I want to wait until I finish school and get a job. Because right now a job is more important to me. I don't want to go to [my boyfriend] and ask him for money, to give me things. I want to be independent. I always think of being independent, doing things myself."

"But can't you have a job and be married?" I asked.

"I want to do that. But if I'm not married and just work, there will be no pressure on him. I don't want to depend on anybody. I want to depend on myself."

"What about still trying to find a job? What does it matter?" I persisted.

"I want to do that, get a job and carry out my goals. But getting married right now . . . I don't have a job. I don't think that's good."

"What about him helping you?"

"Him helping me? I don't know about that. Especially with him. He has other problems. He has his car, his insurance to pay. He always has some excuse why he can't help me."

She explained how she came to her present situation. "My parents are very old-fashioned. They come from Trinidad. I come from a very old-fashioned family. My father was very strict. He was constantly beating me. He was very abusive, my mother also. There were times when I wanted to commit suicide. There were times when I just couldn't take it anymore."

When she finally attempted to get outside assistance, it took three calls to the police before they arrived and she watched her mother tell them nothing was wrong.

Soon after, she ran away and was placed in a group home on Staten Island. But then the court assigned her back with her parents, where she was abused for another year. Finally she was placed in a foster home, which proved to be less than a comforting environment. At that time, she met her boyfriend, who introduced her to his family.

"I told them about my problems, my difficulties. And his mother, who I'm very indebted to, she helped me a lot. She fought for me to stay in her home."

She has been living with her boyfriend's family since she was eighteen. Now she helps him pay rent and child care with her income from public aid, $209 every two weeks.

I asked Mary about her goals now, and she explained that she didn't want to be dependent on her boyfriend, as her mother had been on her father.

"My mother was scared to leave my father because he brought her to this country. He suffered to bring her to this country and she's indebted to him. I didn't want to go through the same thing. I did not want to be indebted to my boyfriend. I wanted to do it by myself. I want to do it because I have a child. I want to be secure if he leaves me tomorrow, I want to say I can stand up on my feet and support myself and support my child. I don't want it to come, but it's a matter of getting yourself ready. In this society, to me, you can't depend on anybody. You can't."

"Even your boyfriend?" I asked.

"I think he cares about me [but] I still feel insecure. I still feel— another thing. Some things he does I don't agree to. He hits me."

"He hits you?"

"If I say, 'I don't agree with that,' my point of view is not honored. His point of view is more honored than anything else. I start getting angry and cursing at him. He starts getting mad, and the first thing he does is hit me. He knocks me."

But, meanwhile, until she can become independent, she will have to put up with this treatment.

"I was talking to my friend, she said she would not take that. She said she would not let a man hit her. I said I was with it for a lifetime with my parents. I saw the problem with my mother, and my mother never raised a hand. I feel like I'm going through the same cycle. And she said, 'Why don't you leave him?'

"I said to her: 'Leave and go where?'

"I don't have anybody to go to. And I have a child now. Then someone will take my child. I don't want to leave my child with him.

I'm not going to do that. I've gotten in the situation and I'm going to school. I'm now dependent on him, on his family. I'm locked in. If I do one thing, everything else falls apart. I can't finish my school. I can't get a job. Why can't I do that? Why can't I put up with it a little bit longer? You know what I mean?

"Then she said to me: 'But do you love him?' "

"I said, 'Yes, I love him. I really love him. Yes, I do.' "

"Then she said, 'If he knocks you once, he's going to knock you again.' But if I find a job, I will have more of a choice than I have now. Now I have no choice."

Mary told me that people can't accurately judge her on her life by first appearance.

"People can tell you all these things—don't do this, don't do that. But you have to put yourself in the situation. I'm in the situation I'm in, and people don't know the whole story. You have to know the whole story in order to judge me. You know what I'm saying?"


WHILE Mary has been through an unusual set of trials, she is most representative of the ethic held by everyone else interviewed. The women's movement's principles of self-sufficiency are not an experiment or a phase; they are being applied for survival and are evolving with present social conditions.

♀ PART FOUR

# TODAY'S ISSUES

*Chapter Six*

# Work and Family

IN COMING TOGETHER to discuss their lives through the years, women have generated significant power in voicing what has gone unspoken. Some of the greatest achievements of the women's movement of the early 1970s were merely to name issues: pay equity, maternity leave, sexual harassment, wife-battering.

With these namings, they were also making political statements about women's rights to take control of their destinies and identities, to go beyond the status of "the second sex." Even the title "Ms.," regularly used today in even the most straitlaced of Fortune 500 and Business Week 1,000 companies, was a radical call for women to be recognized in their own right, not in their relationship to men.

Those interviewed stressed the importance of discussing new issues and angles, along with some of the same concerns women have been working on for centuries.

As with feminists before, bringing the private to the surface for exploration is a priority. Young Americans have constantly witnessed attitudes changing about the legitimacy and importance of women's concerns. This is reflected in the media. Recently, even breast cancer, previously taboo in a public forum, has received wider news coverage, including a January 1991 *Time* magazine cover story. Also that year, the former television series "Thirtysomething" delved into the hidden subject of ovarian cancer by chronicling the story of a character who had become a victim.

With some of these private issues, the next generation is working to transcend old myths. On college campuses, more students are realizing the realities of acquaintance rape, going beyond the stereotype of the mysterious stranger on the prowl. To promote change, discussions are focusing inward to explore social attitudes about aggression and domination.

Some people stressed that the feminist agenda needs to address greater issues of social justice that are disproportionately hitting women, such as poverty. This involves a web of interconnected concerns, including housing, employment, reproductive rights, drugs and racism, among others.

With a great number of concerns, women of color are also often hardest hit. The most dismal statistics about prenatal care, sterilization abuse, discrimination, poverty and AIDS get even more dismal where women of color are concerned. In these areas, coverage has not yet adequately broken the surface of the mainstream press.

The twentysomethings I interviewed also constantly emphasized men's roles in addressing feminist concerns. Many are recognizing that "women's issues" are really "people's issues" that happened to more directly affect women in the past.

Touching both men and women are the most common issues discussed: work and family. Those interviewed generally recognized that struggles to achieve equality in these realms are far from over. With the traditional, primary care-giver now in the work force, new questions remain about gaining acceptance, equal compensation and flexibility from both private and public institutions.

## PERSONAL ATTITUDES

### Making Choices

To make life easier in home and work realms, many stressed a fundamental change that involves no legislation, agency monitoring, special task forces or appropriations of tax dollars. Part of the overhaul needs to come from changes in attitude. While progress has been made over the past twenty-five years, old prejudices against women and their roles remain, as mainly stressed by those entering or working in professional careers.

In pushing for equity in the workplace, feminists have been trying to expand women's choices. A related issue for those interviewed was valuing those choices that women decide to make.

Speaking in a hushed voice from inside her office cubicle, Amy McPherson, twenty-nine, a program administrator at a Chicago company, said she is personally struggling in making choices for the future.

"Traditional women and men are changing," she said. "For almost anyone to survive today, you both have to work. But those who choose to only have one working are suffering because society looks down on those people. If you choose not to work, you're looked down upon. And if you choose to work, you're looked down upon."

Women who have made these choices about how to raise their families report feeling some negative judgment from others. Renee Boots decided to quit her job as an insurance sales representative to stay home with her daughter. She said it was worth the financial sacrifice of staying in their small suburban Chicago apartment and putting off buying a house.

"I feel a lot of women look at you like you're wasting your time. I can't think of anything I would rather do [than] "waste" my time on my baby. They need so much attention, and I couldn't stand it if the first time she sat up someone else told me about it."

Specifically, many people commented on the need for motherhood and what has been viewed as traditionally female to be more valued in society. One woman stressed the seriousness of the role by calling her mother "a houseworker" instead of a "housewife." Men brought up this issue in equal numbers.

Even people who have already invested thousands of dollars and years of vigorous study to enter the most high-powered professions stressed the value of a traditional role. At the University of Chicago Pritzker School of Medicine, about half the twelve medical students interviewed separately or in pairs raised this point as one of the most important women's issues of the Nineties. They expressed the idea that traditionally male-dominated professions should not set the standard for what merits respect.

"A lot of people, even when I talk to them today, especially women, say, 'My mom was just a housewife,' and they put a 'just' in there. My mom was a housewife. She was a very good mother. She took pride in it. She worked until she got pregnant and then was always busy at home," said Mike Pyevich, twenty-three. "A woman doesn't have to be a nuclear physicist just for the advancement of women's lib."

Two students with strong ties to other cultures said in separate conversations that they have noticed this devaluation in American society.

Magda Kryzstolik, twenty-four, of Szczecin, Poland, said she greatly appreciates being in the United States where women have more freedom in defining their roles, but she is still critical of some attitudes she has noticed.

"In Poland, in some ways women are more liberated. Women are more proud of being a woman and being a mother than they are in the United States. Here, being a housewife isn't such a good thing to be. People say: 'I am only a housewife. I am only a mother.' And that's belittling yourself."

Asra Khan, twenty-three, whose parents are from India, said that women shouldn't have to explain themselves in choosing full-time motherhood. "If you decide to be a homemaker and stay home with your kids, it's like, 'Oh, you don't have a job.' In India, it is considered a job. It's very highly regarded. You are taught to respect your parents and older people."

One common plea for tolerance was that every woman is different. While some would much prefer to stay home full-time to raise children if affordable, for others such an arrangement could seem like a sentence.

While Sarah Edmunds, twenty-eight, said she would prefer to stay home with her children, she understands how that choice depends on each parent.

"A girlfriend of mine who works here just had a baby three weeks ago and plans to come back after two months," said Edmunds, who works at a New York advertising agency. "She's going crazy. She can't stand being home. She just had this baby and can't hold a conversation with an adult. She's alone a lot of the time."

But many added that attitudes valuing motherhood have to change more at the workplace. Amy McPherson said that even though her firm offered more flexible benefits for mothers, employees would likely be looked down upon for taking them.

"I think I would still have in the back of my mind: 'Would this hurt my career?' " she said.

One Chicago medical student, Nancy Marks, twenty-four, said that she has seen medicine become more tolerant of mothers, but it still has an unprofessional stigma. "There is still something to be said about going to a residency interview pregnant. Will it look bad?"

Debora Kaylor, twenty-four, who worked at a major corporation before leaving to take care of her baby, said she regularly sensed this macho ethic "through grapevine talk."

"Men are still the big directors. The VPs are mostly men. Every time a woman goes on leave, it's like: 'Oh God, here we go.' I've heard it before, and it's ridiculous," said Kaylor. "But I understand that it leaves the company in a bind; you can't hire anyone else and everyone has to do double time."

Kaylor came from a male-dominated department in which she was the first ever to raise the concept of maternity leave. She said much of the pressure actually came from herself, in feeling she was letting down her boss when she told him about her baby.

Men confront even more of a stigma in leaving a job to care for children. While a great number interviewed expressed willingness to take time off, most men already working in professions said they would limit it to a few days or weeks partly because of bad feelings they would generate for not "taking [their] job seriously." Only the great minority of those interviewed had careers flexible enough to permit even thinking about this option.

## Anti-Role Models

But with this dominant call for tolerance, many recognized a backlash against the choices of older women (and men). Many of those interviewed in the professional world were especially critical of women pioneers a generation ahead, who happened to have paved the way for them, for having little family life.

While not all women want families, this has often been a necessary sacrifice for many of those who have made it to high positions. They are competing with married men who are free to work marathon work weeks with someone else tending the personal side of their life.

Anna Minkov, twenty-three, a systems analyst in Cincinnati, said she bristled while reading an article about women on the top rungs of the career ladder in a July 30, 1990, issue of *Fortune*. She referred to the following quotes that conveyed the costs of success, which she said she never wants to pay:

> "I don't take care of the house. I don't cook. I don't do laundry. I don't market. I don't take my children to malls and museums. And I don't have any close friends," said Phyllis Swersky, the executive vice president of AICorp.

> Claudia Goldin, the first tenured woman professor at Harvard University, was one of many who had to sacrifice family altogether. "I am at the top of my profession," she said. "I don't know if I could have made it if I were married and had kids."

In discussion, many people brought up as a negative role model the example of an older woman they knew from the office.

"There are many women in this field in their late thirties who don't have a family and their entire social life revolves around the job and people [on the job]. I think that's horrible. It's kind of fake. It's a fake life. If you change your job, you've got no life. You've got no permanence," said Sarah Edmunds.

Rick Jones described the attitudes of people of his generation in viewing their office elders. "The girls look at the women and call them 'career bitches,' and most of the young women there are different than they were ten years ago. They are more normal, regular."

Jones said that younger men in his office feel the same way toward their older male counterparts, and many plan to quit after a period of paying dues for a more balanced job.

"We sit around and talk about how screwed up all the partners' kids are," said Jones, who still says he has ambitious career aspirations. "One partner comes in and treats us like we're his sons, and I asked one of the managers one time why he did that, and he said: 'Well, because his kids are so screwed up because he was never there.' We're his fulfillment!"

But the harshest words and most definite intolerance was leveled at women with more of a career focus—even those near the age bracket of those interviewed. Sarah Turoff noted that at her last bank job in

Chicago, people in the office regarded one unmarried woman with suspicion.

"They'll say things about the fact that she's still single, which still shocks me. Like 'she's one of those.' It's hard to put your finger on it, but it's like there's just something wrong with her. 'What's behind it? Why isn't she married?' "

## Challenge of Balance

Since career and family are in the future schemes of those interviewed, the greatest challenge is how to balance these responsibilities with the least possible guilt, stress, fatigue and financial duress. Any detectable change from the past—at least for those who can afford it—seemed to be shifting some of this attention away from work to home.

Of those surveyed in a fall 1990 *Time* magazine poll of adults eighteen to twenty-four, 51 percent put having a long and happy marriage and raising well-adjusted children ahead of career success (29 percent). A large number of men and women said if they had the opportunity, they would be interested in staying home and raising children; this included 66 percent of the females and 48 percent of the males.

Along with a shift toward the family is a loss of career machismo for women and men. The significance of this attitude to employers is to better accommodate working mothers to keep them satisfied on the job. Especially in the corporate world, people seem to be putting more limits on work in order to be with family—and feeling comfortable with that decision.

Karen Berling said she puts less pressure on herself, knowing she can't be a superwoman—achieving maximum success in her job and also having a family.

"I know I've done a good job during the day. Sure, I know I could do a hell of a lot more if I stayed four more hours every day. But I also know I want to go home and take care of my family. I want to spend time with my son. I want to get supper ready and do puzzles with him and read him books. It's not hard for me to leave at five o'clock. It's not hard for me to say I'm not going to be the vice president of this company, because I want to be something else."

Making decisions to be with family is easier with less of a prevailing workaholic ethic from peers, said Nancy Hybert, twenty-nine, a corporate research analyst in Chicago.

"All of the pressure is coming off women to shoot for the absolutely highest level. A friend and I coined a phrase, 'power skirt.' You don't have to be this incredibly independent, 'Wow-I'm-shooting-for-the-top' woman of the Nineties type. You are allowed to have balance. Look at Connie Chung dropping off to have kids. What is she, forty-four?"

This younger generation seems especially cautious in marrying themselves to their jobs. Like Hybert, many interviewed were not shy about their opinions. Visiting major corporations, I was constantly surprised at how outspoken they were in criticizing their companies—even at work and out in the open when a supervisor might easily be strolling by. I was worried that some of the offices were bugged and I would leave a trail of broken careers behind me.

But many didn't seem to worry about conveying their skepticism. In her office on the thirty-seventh floor of a soaring white marble building, Hybert has hung a sign in her cubicle: PROUDLY SERVING MY CORPORATE MASTERS.

So far, in her short career, she has changed jobs five times when not satisfied—and has profitted with a 33-percent pay increase for each move. "At a certain point, you don't want your resumé to look like a bouncing ball, but I have yet to have that be a problem," she said.

Hybert has made these career moves against the advice of older people, who she said seriously warned her she might be giving the appearance of not being loyal to a company. She explained the realization young people are making.

"I think there's an attitude that was definitely not prevalent in our parents' generation," Hybert said. "I think people are a little bit wiser early on, maybe because they grow up quicker. But I was taught very, very early on that corporate loyalty is always, always, always one-sided.

"And if you remember that, you can be loyal to them, but [know that] basically there are not too many people in the structure who are not replaceable. A corporation will not love you, no matter how much you give it."

Others of this generation seem to display the same attitude when polled. In the *Time* magazine survey published in July of 1990, 58 percent of the 602 people polled between eighteen and twenty-nine agreed with the statement "There is no point staying in a job unless perfectly satisfied."

## Women Compromise

When the question of career compromise was raised, it was most often the woman who assumed flexibility. Men were much more reluctant to actually take time off work, if affordable, to take care of children. Men and women agreed that careers are more socialized as an element of the male ego, a basic part of how he defines himself.

Amy McPherson said she is learning this lesson in discussing family plans with her new husband. She started at her company at the age of eighteen as a secretary and has worked her way up to administrative status. But she says if she has children, she would be the one to take off and threaten her career.

"Hypothetically, I asked him if he'd be able to take off a few years if my career was growing," she laughs slightly, "and if I quit work to have a family it would hurt my career. He had a very difficult time with that, and I'd say he's very liberal in his views.

"It's so instilled in men. They almost think that if they lose their job, they lose their manhood."

A few other men told me that their jobs are too basic to their identities to ever quit. "I would get out of the marriage before that would happen," said Seth Michael, twenty-eight, an engineer in suburban Chicago, who said he would still share duties with his wife while working. "For me, to be fulfilled, I would not give it up. I wouldn't ask my wife to do it either. You have to be fulfilled in what you're doing."

Several young professional men said their work was too much a part of their identity to ever leave. Realizing this, they are looking for more traditional wives who would prefer to stay home with children, if this was affordable.

But this preference was not perceived as a problem for many women interviewed, who overwhelmingly preferred to be the one doing the compromising. Each expressed the belief that in her case, she would be better at taking care of the kids—whether because of natural ability or conditioning.

"The sexes are instinctually prone to certain things," said Greg Beaubien, twenty-seven, a public-relations writer in Chicago. "When I was a kid and I was sick, my mom knew how to take care of me. She knew how to assuage me when I had a fever and my dad was clumsy with that. From my narrow point of observation, she was instinctively better. Just like female animals are in the wild; they take care of the babies. I don't think there is anything sexist in that."

Most people, though, pointed out that social conditioning was a factor in explaining why the woman was best at taking charge of mothering when given a choice between parents.

"As little kids, girls are crowding around the babies and newborns and playing with Barbies, and all the guys are playing with GI Joes," said Mike Kaylor, twenty-four, whose wife recently quit her job to stay home with their infant. "I was walking around the mall yesterday carrying the baby, and everyone was just looking at me, and I don't think everyone would stare if Deb was carrying the baby."

## At Home: Sharing Work

One key to balance is sharing work with a partner at home. But achieving equality can still be a battle for those not brought up with that standard.

"When you get married, you become the mom again," said Bonne Bieze-Adrian, a twenty-five-year-old woman from suburban Chicago. She said her husband did more when they were living together, and then changed his ways after the wedding. "I'm now a mom to a thirty-two-year-old man! That's how I feel sometimes. They say they're Nineties-type people, but deep down they want that Fifties lifestyle—to have their wives work and still be Mrs. Cleaver."

Old habits do die hard for men, and women are angry. In a 1990 Virginia Slims/Roper Organization poll, next to money, "how much my mate helps around the house" was the single biggest cause of resentment among women who are married or living as if married, with 52 percent citing this as a problem.

Considering their extra housework load, Berkeley sociologist Arlie Hochschild, author of *The Second Shift*, tabulated from major studies

that American women in the Sixties and Seventies ]
roughly fifteen hours longer each week than men. In her ov..
one hundred two-income families in the Bay Area, published in 19&>,
she described a "second shift" of housework for the female. By closely
observing them day to day, she found that only 20 percent of the
husbands were sharing work equally.

Others recognized the mighty force of socialization keeping them in
the kitchen. Karen Berling, who works the same hours in the corporate
world as her husband of the same age, says she understands how socialization has affected their sharing of housework. She observed that even
when men help, it's usually the women assigning what has to be done;
with children, the father is often more of a playmate than a primary
care-giver.

"I'm manager of our social life," said Berling, "and I take care of the
house. I keep thinking if I wasn't around, and my son kept growing, I
guess one day Steve would go out and buy him clothes."

## Attitudes on the Job

Once on the job, many women find a need for co-workers to change
their attitudes about taking women seriously. In trying to process the
interview data collected, classifying the types of sexism people described was like mastering a form of advanced botany. It all came in
different strains that took a meticulous eye to label: Was it harassment,
discrimination, just joking, the person's imagination? Whatever it was,
it had the same effect of causing stress.

The most common form of sexism experienced was harassment on
the job. (The other most typical forms were found in sports and academic pursuits.) Women described harassment in a variety of forms
from the most subtle such as being called "honey" or "sweetie," or
seeing pin-up posters on the wall, to the more blatant, including constant emotional or physical gender-motivated attacks. All were difficult
to fight or protest.

All types of sexism and harassment described did not differ in intensity according to class or economic background. While the old stereotype is of harassment at blue-collar jobs, such as construction workers

leering from atop steel beams, women from all walks of life described almost the same incidents.

One of the most blatant and distressing cases was described as having occurred at a prestigious private Eastern university, the kind that costs $20,000 a year to attend. Susan, a twenty-five-year-old graduate student interviewed in her New York apartment, said she was constantly harassed as the only female in a science department. Like two other women in traditionally male fields, she was a novelty in the lab. As a result, her work suffered, and with every routine situation, she had to think ahead in terms of prevention.

"I would be sitting at a desk, and someone would say '[Susan], you look so tense, let me.' And I would say, 'No, I don't want a back rub. I don't want a back rub!' Then they would put their hands here," she said, pointing to the two sides of her chest under her arms. "That's not the same as like this." She moved her hands behind her to touch her back.

She often also felt helpless in stopping it herself, and then in not getting a response from her boss: "I did go to my boss one day because I was very upset over something he said in a meeting. He made a very sexual joke, and my reaction was to blush like crazy. I said, 'This is hell working on this project. It's like working with a bunch of three-year-olds. I can't handle it.' "

Then, like others who describe harassment, she wondered if she should blame herself. "He said, 'Boys will be boys, and you have to understand the way you look. Look at the way you are.' "

She went to her room and showed me a picture of herself from two years ago: thin, blond and exuberant all-American good looks, the type of face you might have seen on the cover of last month's *Seventeen*. She said she felt like she might have been leading them on with her attractive appearance. If she was being treated badly for being a female, she would make herself look less like one.

"I don't know if it was something I consciously decided, but one day I didn't wear makeup, and I was treated a little bit different," she said. "And the next day, I didn't put on makeup and wore baggy clothes. Life was made easier."

But finally, after cutting her hair and even gaining fifteen pounds, she realized that the harassment wasn't her responsibility. One day, she was driven over the edge by the constant whistling of one co-worker and threatened to file a lawsuit.

"And it stopped. Not only that, but everything stopped. Things I didn't even complain about stopped."

But soon she found out that this wasn't an end to her problems. She learned the price of making waves, which so many people I interviewed described as a central worry in speaking up on feminist issues.

"My job was made completely unbearable. I was ridiculed. I was embarrassed. So I left."

In recent years, victims of harassment haven't been as alone in calling attention to the problem. More companies are taking notice as it becomes a pervasive and costly problem for American business. Women have been emboldened by laws to report it. Since 1980, when the Equal Employment Opportunity Commission published historic guidelines on sexual harassment, 38,500 cases have been filed with the federal government. In 1986, the U.S. Supreme Court unanimously upheld the guidelines in the landmark case *Meritor Savings Bank v. Vinson,* which found that sexual harassment is a severe enough problem to create a hostile or abusive work environment that violates the law.

The December 1988 issue of *Working Woman* magazine documented the seriousness of the problem with a comprehensive survey given to human resources officers who represented 3.3 million employees at 160 giant corporations. One of the conclusions was that companies were being held more accountable. Some 90 percent of Fortune 500 companies had received complaints and more than a third already had been hit with lawsuits. Nearly a quarter had been sued repeatedly. Sixty-four percent of human resource executives interviewed said that most complaints of sexual harassment were valid.

Companies with the lowest percentage of women workers registered the highest complaint rates, reported the article. This is one constant factor described by women's employment advocates as keeping them from the higher-paying nontraditional jobs. Women especially in the nonprofessional male fields seem to be in the same position of breaking barriers and establishing credibility as those in the professions twenty years ago.

An interesting variable in all types and rungs of occupations was the age of the harasser. Women and men said they noticed it as more of a problem with members of older generations who were not as accustomed to or accepting of female interlopers in the workplace. Only a small minority of those women who had experienced sexism on the job said they ever had problems with men their own age.

"It's frustrating," said Nancy Hybert. "I can remember walking into a meeting and sitting down at the table with a bunch of men, and at one point, one of them looked over at me and said: 'Can I help you?'

"I said, 'I don't know. What are you offering? No, I don't smoke cigars. . . .' "

Stephanie Boatley, who recently completed her service in the Navy, described a similar phenomenon in the characteristic perceptions of a retiring officer who envisioned a "man's Navy."

"He's been there for thirty-five years; he's seen the navy come from having no women, except coremen, working with the doctors and stuff. That was the only thing then, and they had them in the offices for administrative work because the men couldn't type.

"As things started changing, they started letting [women] go into the fields for working on the airplanes, and they started letting them on the ships, and that really drove [the men] crazy. So they have seen it come a long way, and now they're probably thinking it shouldn't be like this."

She said she didn't generally feel the same resentment from men her age. "Even though they tried to hit on me and that kind of stuff, I never felt anything discriminatory from them. I don't know if it was the age thing or what, or if it had anything to do with them thinking: 'Okay, we're the same because we're the same age. Why should I treat her any differently?' That could have been part of what was going through their minds."

Most of the sexism Boatley and others observed from the older men was not as blatant as Susan's harassment. Many women said they were surprised at how commonly older men made sexist jokes that degraded them.

But the older generation of men wasn't the only startling source of insensitivity. One ironic observation by two medical students was their discovery of discrimination from older women. Kathryn McLeese, twenty-eight, said she noticed older women physicians as being extremely unsupportive of a female colleague who had a family—to the point where she was driven away.

"They looked at her and thought: 'Why can't she hold her life together?' Sometimes you do get the most resistance from [women] who want to show people they can be as good as any man. They don't want a woman who wants to have a family and work only sixty hours a week to reduce their image in other people's eyes. I think that is a very significant problem."

## The "Glass Ceiling"

The two oldest women I interviewed, who seemed the most savvy about corporations, said that disparaging attitudes toward working mothers create a "glass ceiling," at middle-management levels, not only in the upper echelons of CEOs and vice presidents, as commonly described in the media. A July 1990 *Fortune* article also documents such discrimination and sexism. Nearly 80 percent of 241 respondents to a survey conducted by Catalyst, a group that does research on women in the workplace, said there are identifiable barriers, such as stereotypes, that keep women from reaching the top.

But few of the people I interviewed, who are still at lower levels in companies or don't have stellar ambitions, mentioned the glass ceiling at the top as a serious concern in their lives. In a 1989 *New York Times* poll, young women were much more optimistic about who has power in this country. Only half agreed that "men still run almost everything and usually don't include women when important decisions are made," a view held by substantial majorities of older women.

Some explained that they thought the glass ceiling was so high that by the time they reached those points, the older men dominating them would have retired, and women who have only recently entered the job market would have had enough time to infiltrate their ranks.

But Nancy Hybert and Karen Berling said their lower-level "glass ceiling" is serious in affecting a much greater number of women in the present who don't have aspirations to be Citizen Kane or Gordon Gekko and run the company from the executive suite.

For young women of childbearing age—not even those who have

children—sexist attitudes can create barriers. The mere possession of operable ovaries often marks a woman as potentially unreliable, not to be counted on in the future.

This may also stop some employers from hiring women. But as far as researchers have been able to tell, managerial women aren't more costly to employ than men. "As far as we can determine—with the help of the Business and Professional Women's Foundation and Women's Equity Action League—there is no published data on this point," write Barbara Ehrenreich and Deirdre English in the July/August 1989 issue of *Ms.*

Hybert said she was appalled to feel this underlying suspicion when she became engaged. But she said she will be the main wage earner for her family; her fiancé is a graduate student and is looking into academia.

"When a man gets engaged, it's like: 'Oh great. Now he's got that final missing piece that's going to make him balanced.' When a woman gets engaged, she kind of sees this glass ceiling closing over her head very quickly—'Oh, well, she's going to be home and making babies soon.' You definitely get that feeling. What, should I not wear the ring around the office and keep it a secret?"

This attitude seems to be a shadow trailing young women in business. Another woman in her late twenties working at a Fortune 500 company in Chicago, who did not want her name used, said she was shocked when her boss gave her a warning about what she has to do to succeed. "I was told I would go very far if I didn't have ten kids. I'll never forget it. I heard it as plain as day."

The definition of sexism that I've come to after having conducted my interviews is "not taking women seriously." This describes both the subtle and blatant treatment many women in the work force have described at all levels. For most women, sexism at work was the first jolt in their lives about how serious the problem is.

The massive 1990 Virginia Slims/Roper poll (with an older sample of women from both generations in the work force) found that more women today than in 1970 believe sex discrimination is holding them back in the workplace and are encountering more obstacles than expected.

Men, especially those past college age or in the work force, answered just as strongly as women that they noticed discrimination. One gave a textbook example of sexism at the hiring level, but didn't call it that. He explained that his small engineering firm in the Chicago area would never hire a woman because of its all-male atmosphere. Apparently, it is often true in male-dominant fields that the "old boy network" can include the new boys as well.

"Considering what goes on in this office, with guy talk or whatever, I'd imagine they would feel pretty uncomfortable," he said. "It would cramp our style, change our environment somewhat with a woman in here."

"What do you talk about?"

"Oh, what do girls talk about when they get together? Guys talk about girls." He pointed out the window to the parking lot three floors below. "For example, if we see a good-looking girl get out of a car, everyone has got to see her."

I nodded and thought that the federal Equal Employment Opportunity Commission would find the hiring attitudes rather interesting as well.

This example illustrated how invisible discrimination often is. While a woman submitting an application at this company might suspect she was being turned away because of her gender, she would be called paranoid to mention it because of a lack of concrete evidence. These are questions women often ask themselves but then shrug off.

With the recent Persian Gulf War, discrimination against women in the military has been central in discussion of sexism on the job. Many have reported that they feel like second-class citizens with a combat-exclusion policy that limits women's advancement to senior ranks. The U.S. military began recruiting women in large numbers when it abolished the draft in 1973. Since then, the percentage has grown steadily —particularly in medical engineering, key support and other intelligence specialties.

Some women named another mighty and established institution that has failed to be an equal opportunity employer.

"I used to want to be a priest," said Clare Sullivan, twenty-three, who described her childhood ambition to me during a summer hiatus from Peace Corps duty in the Dominican Republic.

This shocked me because Sullivan had been one of my four housemates during the final two years of college, and I never heard a word about this. I asked her if she was joking.

"I really did, and then I realized that if I'm Catholic, I can't be. I considered going to another church for that reason, but I don't know. I found other ways I can do what I want to do, not just with the church. I got involved in other social justice things."

Like Sullivan, several Catholic women mentioning this issue voiced no hope of women gaining entry to the priesthood. Even the federal authorities don't have enough clout to lobby the Pope. While the heads of the Catholic Church are scrambling for recruits and closing down seminaries across the country, they are losing sight of valuable human resources.

In most cases, though, discrimination is less obvious. For one particular group, women of color, this is especially true.

Even the *Wall Street Journal,* a major daily capitalist tool, recognizes this barrier. "While white women complain about the glass ceiling that keeps them from the very top ranks, women of color are hardly present in the management pipeline. Faced with both racism and sexism, they're still struggling to land middle-management jobs," said a July 25, 1990, article.

While black women made up 10 percent of the work force in 1988, that year they made up just 2 percent of managers in companies with 100 or more employees, compared with black men, who accounted for 3 percent of this group and white women, who totaled 23 percent, according to data reported by the Equal Employment Opportunity Commission.

Women of color are often bypassed for promotion and relegated to staff positions that aren't on the fast track. They suffer from isolation, lack of mentors and being stereotyped as "twofers," or fulfilling two affirmative action obligations, which undercuts their credibility and respect for them. While being a "twofer" could help get a foot in the door, as with white women, it doesn't guarantee that they will be taken seriously or have any voice or power.

## THE SYSTEM

In discussing the balance of career and family, many said change starts with personal attitudes.

But that could take some time. Until the epoch of individual enlightenment and/or the feminist messiah arrives, many children and women are having to tolerate present inequities. For heads of households, reform is especially urgent.

In general, the shift of women into the work force has been dramatic, but the move to accommodate them has not. Work institutions are still largely set up as though every family had its own selfless Barbara Bush at home taking care of the family. As people interviewed at all levels of work pointed out, women are still seen as a minority group that has to conform to past male standards to be accepted.

While 12 percent of mothers with children under age six worked in 1950, 56 percent did in 1990. Projections are that by 1995, two-thirds of mothers with preschoolers—and three-fourths of mothers with school-age children—will be working, as reported in *Working Mother* magazine in October 1990.

By the year 2000, white males born in the United States will be a small minority of those entering the work force. Of the total new labor force entrants in 2000, 52 percent will be women. Fifty-seven percent of those who will leave the labor force will be men—only 43 percent will be women. Women of childbearing age will account for 41 percent of the growth in the female labor force according to statistics from the U.S. Department of Labor.

## Equal Pay

A persistent problem cited by those I interviewed went right to the meat and potatoes: equal pay for equal work.

The fact that women earn on the average 68.4 cents to the male dollar (according to 1990 U.S. Census Bureau Statistics) seems inconceivably unjust for this generation taught from birth that via the American Dream, you can get ahead if you work hard enough.

This was pointed out by people from all walks of life with all ambitions. Diana, a single mother who works at a credit union in Wisconsin, said she is struggling to keep off welfare, although she recently got a promotion as a department supervisor. She became close friends with a male manager at her level, and was enraged when he told her how much he was making. She has since found out about others.

"There are men in that establishment who have been there for a shorter time than I have," said Diana. "They don't have any degrees; they have the same education as I do. And they are paid a great deal more. I'm not sure, but I think I'm the lowest-paid supervisor. No one ever talks about pay in front of me because they know how mad it makes me."

Diana was talking about a difference of three dollars an hour—she makes seven dollars an hour, the male manager makes ten dollars—that she feels deeply. After paying for loans accrued during her marriage, car installments and lawyer's fees for her divorce, she only clears $230 to $250 every two weeks. She is now $700 behind in child-care payments.

But she said protest of the unfair pay would be too risky. "If I fought it, I think that I would be fired, or I would be reprimanded because the pay in our institution is hush-hush. No one is supposed to know what everyone else is making. But I do know."

Women at the highest income levels of those interviewed also pointed out discrepancies.

Nancy Hybert said she and a friend confronted their boss when a man with similar qualifications who had a family was hired and given a higher salary and a separate office.

"[The boss] was going on and on, and I said, 'He has two things I don't have: a male reproductive organ and a family.' I have the type of boss [to whom] you can say things like that."

Rick and Jodie Jones gave me an article from the October 29, 1990, *Business Week* about business-school graduates' salaries. In sorting through responses from 3,664 business-school graduates, the magazine found a general 12 percent gap in male and female first-year earnings. In information systems, there was a 29.5 percent difference, and in management, 13.6 percent.

Men, even those skeptical of feminism, were generally sure that this discrepancy was real. Steve Abernathy, twenty-four, an engineer in Cincinnati, said he saw his mother's work devalued while working as a bookkeeper in an office.

In total, young women workers earn 60 to 75 percent of the salaries of young men aged eighteen to thirty-four, according to U.S. Census bureau data. The median annual earnings for year-round, full-time workers in 1988 were: $27,228 for white men, $20,371 for black men, $17,819 for white women and $16,538 for black women, according to a 1990 study by the Institute for Women's Policy Research. It concluded that women do not reap the advantages of work experience to the same degree as men, pointing out a decline in women's earnings relative to men's as they age. While the figure is seventy-six cents to the dollar in the twenty-five to twenty-nine age bracket, the figure drops to sixty-four cents to the dollar from age thirty-five to thirty-nine to a low of fifty-four cents to the dollar from age fifty to fifty-four.

This difference can be explained by many factors, such as blatant sexism and more subtleties in the system, including which jobs women are socialized to enter. Most women work in female-dominated occupations, with women of color further concentrated in the lowest-paying positions. For example, in 1989, a secretary was paid on the average $327 a week (99 percent are female and 12 percent are black and Latinas); nurse's aides earned $239 a week (90 percent female and 33 percent black women); and child-care workers received $179 a week (97 percent female and 19 percent black and Latinas). In 1989, black women constituted 5.5 percent of the civilian labor force and Latina women 3 percent of the total, according to statistics from the National Committee on Pay Equity in Washington, D.C.

More "men's" careers have the benefit of unions that boost salaries of low-income employees—whether city employees, truck drivers or reporters. Thirteen percent of all female workers compared to 22 percent of men are in unions. The male high school dropout earns on the average $26,045 yearly, which is $1,000 more than the average college-educated woman, according to 1988 statistics from the U.S. Department of Labor.

To balance their family responsibilities, women more commonly seek part-time or temporary work, which is relatively low paying and offers little chance for advancement. More than 25 percent of women workers work part-time and 62 percent of temporary workers are women. These workers make only 59 percent of the earnings of full-time employees, according to statistics from the National Commission on Working Women.

Some movements are trying to address systemic discrimination. Many feminist advocates encourage women to go into nontraditional fields, in which women earn 20 to 30 percent more than women in traditionally female occupations. While more women have entered nontraditional professional fields, progress has been slow in the traditional occupations in which 74 percent of working women are employed. Between 1983 and 1988, the number of women in nontraditional jobs remained relatively unchanged at only 4 percent of the total work force.

But the barriers to entering nontraditional and nonprofessional fields, such as construction, are often overwhelming. Women are socialized to traditional female jobs, often lack information about how to get education and training, and commonly feel isolated or are harassed on work sites.

One remedy to make pay for women fairer is "comparable worth." Advocates state that even if women achieved equal pay for equal work in the same jobs, they would still on the average be making significantly less than men.

This practice is accomplished through collective bargaining with a union, individual litigation or legislation. Measures are instituted to try to ensure that people are paid according to their skills, efforts and responsibilities and the working conditions required by the jobs they perform—and not according to their race or sex. This means that a union for all workers at a university might raise the salary of a secretary to that of a grounds keeper, a traditional male position at that institution, if it was determined that they were of comparable worth.

But while it has proven successful in many cases where implemented, comparable worth is a complicated and controversial approach. The primary objections to comparable worth are cost and difficulty in measuring how much each job deserves.

Another legal response to inequities in male and female fields is affirmative action, which got mixed reviews from those I interviewed. Men especially seemed to be suspicious of it as an unfair hiring process.

Affirmative action comes in a variety of forms, ranging from special recruitment and training procedures to preferential treatment for individuals who are basically qualified for particular positions and are members of underrepresented groups. The strongest requirements have typically grown out of court orders or litigation settlements; weaker forms have resulted from voluntary employer action and federal executive orders. They are commonly directed at government contractors and grantees to establish goals and timetables for hiring.

## Child Care

Many people interviewed brought up the need for more family-friendly policies from the government and private industry.

As mentioned, one of the biggest restrictions women have on their earnings is their lack of flexibility in caring for children while working. With more and better child care, women, who are more than ever heads of households, would be able to increase their earnings potential. It would be easier for them to train for better jobs and not lose experience gained in present positions by having to quit to care for their offspring. Children of the working poor would also generally benefit with higher-quality child care.

One woman interviewed, Kim, reveals the desperate need for improved child care with the irony of her present dilemma. She works two jobs as a child-care worker, yet she can't afford quality child care for her own infant son.

At her first position, at a Dallas health club, she is paid $5.25 an hour for forty hours of work, which is considered a part-time job and does not include benefits. Her second, a temporary job at a youth agency, pays a dollar less an hour.

Since she was on public aid when she had her son, right after her husband walked out, she is eligible for government-financed day care. But, still on a waiting list, she doesn't expect to get it for another six months to a year. Meanwhile, her younger sister, who works as a prostitute, is in charge of taking care of him in their home in a West Dallas public housing development.

But if she wants a chance for a better future, Kim said she can't afford to stay home and care for him. She also attends a local community college, where she is working on her teaching degree, which would lead to a higher-paying job in two years.

"I filed for child support six months ago, and haven't heard anything," Kim said. "That's why I have to take two jobs and take two incomes—to provide a better environment for my child to live in.

Where we're at now, it's bad. It's drugs, prostitutes or whatever you name, it's there."

Her ex-husband, who works as the manager of a pizza restaurant, refuses to pay support.

Diana also said she went to the social services offices to find out about getting day care for her daughter, but she was told she could only get it if she went on public aid. Since the money would be the same in the end, Diana would rather work. She is preparing to go back to school for an accounting degree to get a better job. She recently dropped out because of stress from her marriage and other personal pressures.

Many women emphasized the need for government to pick up more of the cost for child care for low-income parents or single mothers. Some national polls reflect this consensus. In a *Washington Post* ABC News Poll in August 1989, 61 percent of those surveyed said the federal government should increase spending on programs to take care of the children of working parents who cannot afford it. In a Yankelovich Clancy Shulman poll for *Time* and CNN, an overwhelming 90 percent of women polled at the end of 1989 said day care was a very important issue for women today; day care ranked second behind equal pay for equal work as the most important issue.

Some of the objections raised to government day care were cost and fear of bureaucracy management. Ruth Sidel estimates that per-child quality care ranges from $3,500 a year for preschool care to $6,500 for toddlers, and for those younger, $7,800.

One woman interviewed suggested that immediate family take care of children. Currently, 37 percent of children are taken care of privately by relatives, and 6 percent by nonrelatives in the home. Forty-nine percent are in day-care centers or licensed facilities, according to the Child Care Action Campaign.

But some others gave the other view that if people really care about valuing motherhood, they will put their money on the line for it and make it a national priority.

"I have a girlfriend who is married—she has to work too because her husband can't meet the bills. Things are too expensive and people have to work. There has to be child care set up, within limits, for everybody. It's usually too expensive, or you can't trust the people, or it isn't obtainable. Everything, I think, should be based on the family. I'm a very family-oriented person," said Renee Boots.

Boots perceived child care as pro-family, instead of a means of breaking it up, as is the stereotype. As long as mothers are in poverty, so are the children, she recognized. Currently, in female-headed families, one in two children is classified as poor. This compares to the general 1990 figures of one in seven if white, four in nine if black, or three in eight if Hispanic, according to the Children's Defense Fund.

This organization also reports that the trend applies to children of two low-income working parents. According to 1990 figures, wives contribute an average of about 30 percent of their families' total income, but wives of husbands who earn between $10,000 and $15,000 a year contribute over 40 percent.

When people think about child care, another fear is that it will encourage women to work, and that the child is better off with the mother at home. But the reality is that with one-half of single mothers in poverty, they have no hope of improving their situations if they stay home and collect welfare. Child care is a basic support system to allow them to climb out of the depths of poverty. A mother can't stay home and take tender loving care of her children if she can't afford to pay the electric bill and her roof is caving in. Another absolute is that people should be self-sufficient. But with the demands put on a single parent, considering a failing economy and other social ills beyond one's control, this is a fantasy for anyone to achieve.

Given that working is a common necessity, a mother has to leave her children with whatever care is available. Investigations by the Children's Defense Fund reveal that much of the care being given to children of the poor is inadequate, and that state regulations and standards are generally poor. Although parents place quality at the top of their child-care concerns, only twenty-nine states in 1990 maintained staffing requirements for the care of infants in child-care centers that meet the professionally accepted minimum-safety standards.

In other industrialized countries, day care is superior and often contains an early education component, which families value as important to their children's development and socialization. The American preschool program counterpart for low-income families, Head Start, has proven successful, but in 1990 is only available to fewer than one of six eligible participants.

The child-care costs are overwhelming for single parents and low-income households. Proportions of salary spent on child care vary widely according to income. Families with incomes under $15,000 spend 20 percent of their incomes on child care; those earning $15,000 to $29,000 spend 9.2 percent, and families with incomes of over $50,000 typically spend less than 5 percent, according to 1990 figures from the Child Care Action Campaign. Of course, with more children, the bills get higher. One study found that a single parent earning 100 percent of the median income for a single parent and requiring full-time care for a preschooler and a toddler could pay as much as 36 percent of gross income on care.[1]

While day care is a huge investment, child-care advocates argue that it is financially beneficial to the country. With it, women are working, training for better-paying jobs, getting off welfare and contributing tax dollars to the system. The Children's Defense Fund estimates that every public dollar invested in quality child care for a low-income child saves more than three dollars during that child's lifetime.

America is a wealthy nation. Like every other citizen need, providing child care is partly a matter of making priorities and reallocating funds. Just like gun owners, automobile companies, foreign oil barons and the military, families are a formidable constituency.

"If bankers can get $164 billion to bail out deregulated, imprudent savings and loan institutions, and if we can afford the $5 billion in tax breaks for inherited capital gains for the wealthy, then this nation can afford to lift its twelve million poor children out of poverty," concludes the Children's Defense Fund's 1990 report.

## Child Care for the Middle Class

While the need is most urgent for women in poverty, good and accessible child care improves the quality of life for others as well.

Nancy Hybert mentioned the importance of child care at private sector companies. Working for a Republican U.S. representative as a researcher, she saw enhanced long-term productivity with child care in hospitals. In 1990, while only 220 corporations nationwide provided on-site or near-site child-care centers, 800 hospitals and 200 federal and state agencies provided the service.[2]

Workplace studies have shown that problems with child care reduce productivity, increase absenteeism and contribute to low morale and rising levels of stress among workers. While the average American worker is estimated to typically miss seven to nine days a year, mothers with child-care arrangements miss about thirteen days a year.[3]

Still, while companies are making more efforts to provide or supplement the service, day care in the private sector is still sparse. An annual survey of the best companies for working mothers by *Working Mother* magazine reported in October 1990 that only 5,400 of the six million U.S. employers offer some kind of child-care assistance, up from 110 in 1978.

However, it also reports that more companies than ever are recognizing that family needs aren't the sole responsibility of working parents. In 1990, it expanded its annual list of the best companies for women from thirty to seventy-five to accommodate these improvements. One company in the vanguard was IBM, which has committed itself to spending $22 million over the next five years on child care and another $3 million on elderly-care programs; one project involves training the elderly to work in child-care centers.

The article also noted that some companies were reporting a payoff for their efforts. An example is SAS Institute, which currently runs two 100 percent–subsidized child-care centers and has an employee turnover rate of 7 percent—less than one-third the 24 percent average in the software industry.

"The real danger is that we want the private sector to become more involved, but we can't let the government off the hook," Fern Marx said in a *Chicago Tribune* report.

The federal and state governments, especially in the past decade, have a dismal record in making commitments to child care. During the 1980s, as women's participation in the labor force swelled, the government actually cut child-care support, which had a profound effect on the supply of child care for low-income families in many states.[4]

Family-rights advocates have had to lobby vigorously and constantly over the past decade for any response from the federal government. But finally, in October of 1990, Congress passed the first comprehensive child-care legislation since World War II, a $22 billion child-care package of tax credits and grants. As far as child-care advocates are concerned, the heart of the legislation is a three-year, $2.5-billion block grant program for states to distribute to parents and day-care providers. Sen. Christopher Dodd, a Democrat from Connecticut and one of the principle architects of the legislation, acknowledged it as the base of the nation's first child-care policy.

While grateful for this measure, some experts were previously calling for no less than $10 billion to make a substantial difference. Still, they had beat a strong resistance.

"Both the Bush and Reagan administrations attacked the block grant approach as a throwback to the Great Society Programs of the 1960s with federal standards and large new bureaucracies. The Bush administration wanted little more than tax credits for the working poor," reported the *Washington Post* in an October 28, 1990, article.

Politicians need to be held accountable for their promises to the family. In their rhetoric, they put the family on a pedestal, but in their actions, place it on the back burner.

## Other Family Benefits

Quality child care is one component of a policy needed to help accommodate the changing needs of the family. Considering the rest of the package, including family leave, the United States is behind almost every other industrialized country—and some Third World countries.

"The principal difference between the American working mother and her counterpart in the rest of the industrialized world is that the American woman gets virtually no help. She's on her own," write Vivian Cadden and Sheila Kamerman in a September 1990 *Working Mother* report about benefits abroad.

In total, sixty-three nations worldwide provide family allowances to workers and children, and seventeen industrialized nations have paid maternity/parenting leave programs. Seventy nations worldwide provide medical care and financial assistance to all pregnant women. While the United States does indeed boast the number-one army, it finishes almost last among its industrialized peers when it comes to family care.

Ruth Sidel stresses that in other countries, family packages are at the forefront of politics, not considered to be on the fringe as in this country. "Virtually every other industrialized society has a family policy," she said. "Every country like us, France, England, Germany, Canada—Canada is much like America, right?—has much more in the way of human services for families than we do. Canada has children's allowances for every family. Human services are not considered far-out in much of the industrialized world."

Throughout Europe, working mothers are guaranteed paid leaves to stay home with their infants, and are then helped to return to work with a variety of government-sponsored fully or partially funded childcare arrangements.

The United States has no basic national policy that guarantees parental leave. In May of 1990, Bush, "the family president," vetoed the landmark Family and Medical Leave Act. The act, covering 5.9 percent of American businesses that employ 61.8 percent of the nation's employees, would have allowed workers in businesses with fifty or more employees to take unpaid leave to deal with family emergencies, personal illness or the birth of a child. Workers would have been guaranteed up to twelve weeks.

The United States and South Africa are the only industrialized nations without such a family-leave policy.

The 1990 veto was obviously a concession to Big Business, which voiced hostility to the plan. A Bush spokesman explained before the veto that the president opposed it because of his belief that such issues should be decided by employers and their workers, rather than by the federal government. Business groups that opposed the measure, including the U.S. Chamber of Commerce, asserted that the bills were too costly and would give employers too little flexibility.

But also speaking in business terms, Republican Marge Roukema of New Jersey, member of the House labor-management subcommittee, voiced her wonder at how President Bush could object to it.

"In a day and age where most families need two paychecks to get by, it is inconceivable that we do not have a minimum guarantee of job security when a medical emergency strikes," she wrote in a June 20, 1990, *New York Times* op-ed. "The debate over the Family and Medical Leave Act is not about federal mandates or benefit packages. It is about values and a standard of decency, and protecting the jobs of workers who are trying to hold onto the American dream."

Roukema added that as a person with a solid record of support "for and from the business community," she did not foresee the policy threatening industry; not one state or business that has adopted similar or even more far-reaching leave policies has reported to Congress disruptions or declines in productivity, she said.

Instead of American business, it is American women—the workers who keep these companies going—and their children who are suffering financially. The Institute for Women's Policy Research has estimated that the incomes of working women and their families lose $31 billion annually in lost or reduced wages because of a lack of parental-leave protection.

After Bush's 1990 veto, the *St. Petersburg Times* excoriated the president for his hypocrisy and lack of commitment to the family.

"President Bush, while seeking votes during his campaign, said he favored family leave," stated the August 2, 1990, editorial. "But in his veto message, he made it clear he favors it only in the abstract. He opposes any law that would require it, which is the only way most workers ever would get it."

## Maternity Leave Rations

With a lack of provisions for leaves, taking off time for care for a family member or newborn is a stressful and haphazard process.

"She negotiates a maternity leave with her boss and patches it together with vacation days and sick time," report Vivian Cadden and Sheila Kamerman. "Then, with little or no guidance, let alone financial help, she orchestrates an infant-care arrangement. The government shows little interest in her family unless it is on the verge of financial disaster. The prevailing attitude in this country seems to be 'Okay, lady. You want to have children? You want to work? That's fine. But your children are your problem. Work it out the best you can.'"

This is not *Socialist Review* or a fringe feminist publication I'm quoting. This is mainstream *Working Mother,* which I picked up at the library in Kenosha, Wisconsin.

The magazine also reports that only 40 percent of employers even have maternity-leave policies, and those that exist are often insufficient. The days for leave are rationed meagerly like cigarettes in a World War II prisoner-of-war camp. The great number of mothers begging for the scraps, living from paycheck to paycheck, are unable to protest.

The prevailing miserly policies also affect "professional" women. Sarah Turoff, twenty-three, who was making a solid wage at a major household-name national bank, described her company's maternity-leave policy, which is the average: six weeks off with sick days tacked on. As a result, women across this country are afraid to take off when they are sick.

"A lot of women probably didn't take a lot of sick days, whereas a man wouldn't think about it, because what else would he be saving it for? When I was at that job, I literally thought that I should not just take random sick days because I wanted to save them up. That was my first year there, twenty-two years old, and I was thinking about saving for maternity leave," said Turoff, who is unmarried and not planning for childbearing in the near future.

One medical student, Kathryn McLeese, said she saw this phenomenon at a prominent hospital in Chicago. "I have a friend who is a resident. She had ten days after the birth of her baby. Ten days, and she was back at work. This was her vacation time. She happened to schedule it so that it was convenient for her first baby. That was outrageous. They didn't have any policies."

The lack of national policy affecting private employers has a great effect on motherhood in this country. It forces women to make a choice between their job and their family—there is no room for compromise.


## Paternity Leave?

If mothers are agonizing over decisions about caring for their children, fathers, for the most part, don't have the chance to consider them. While gaining in acceptance and allowance, paternity leave is a rare opportunity. Like other family benefits, it is strictly limited to the most prestigious and flexible professional careers. For example, three out of four men from Columbia University interviewed, who are all from affluent backgrounds, will probably have this freedom in their planned careers as professors, which will allow them, to a certain extent, to make their own hours and spend more time at home.

The handful of foreign governments offering this option include those of Finland, Sweden and Italy. Paternity leave is even a relatively new concept in the vanguard European countries.

To illustrate how privileged this concept of paternity leave is, I asked the four men working in blue-collar jobs about their opportunities to take off time from work to care for children.

Tim Evans, twenty-seven, a construction worker from Vallejo, California, laughed. "They give you maybe $100 at Christmastime," he said, summing up his family benefit package.

"They don't even give you paid holidays in the union," said Todd Boots, twenty-four, a carpenter from Chicago Ridge, Illinois. "If you don't work, you don't get paid at all."

"If your wife happens to deliver on a day when you work," said Rick Jaskolski, twenty-eight, a Wisconsin fire fighter, "they let you have the day off."

"Paternity leave?" asked Frank Capasso, twenty-three, a mechanic from McHenry, Illinois. "I was lucky when my grandfather died to get those two days off."

Even when provisions are made for men, they are often condemned for not being serious about their jobs. Even in Sweden, which has offered paid paternity leave since 1974, tradition endures, with only one-fourth of men taking advantage of it.[5]

But most men don't even have the luxury of turning down provisions for parental leave. *Working Mother* reports that only three companies in America provide paid paternity leave for new fathers: Lost Arrow (eight weeks), NCNB (six weeks) and HBO (one week).

One critic, James A. Levine, the director of the Fatherhood Project at the Families and Work Institute in New York, points to the utter slowness of corporations to recognize the "working father." Their policies do not reflect the "redefinition of fatherhood going on in virtually every arena of American life for more than a decade," he writes in the March 1986 issue of *Across the Board*. "While more and more companies use the term 'working mother' to describe a growing segment of their benefits packages, almost none use the term 'working father.' 'Working mother' immediately signals conflict, stress, potential losses in productivity—an identifiable problem to be addressed by human resources. But 'working father' is taken as a redundancy."

Much of the myth that men have a choice is perpetuated by the media, which mainly concentrates on the upper middle class, who have much more flexibility. In its fall 1990 report on women, *Time* is bubbly with optimism about the next generation taking command: "The next generation of parents may be less likely to argue over who has to leave work early to pick up the kids and more likely to clash over who gets to take parental leave."

For women, the lack of men considering leave as a possibility reinforces the norm that when family time comes, the burden of career compromise rests on the mother.

## Flexibility

Many interviewed stressed that flexibility for both parents is needed beyond the first several weeks after pregnancy. Karen Berling, who was most passionate about this point, already works for a corporation that ranks in the top twenty for providing family benefits. Its policy, which has been lauded by *Fortune, Working Mother, Family Circle* and *Cosmopolitan,* allows a generous year of unpaid maternity leave. But Berling points out that it does not take into consideration care after that time off.

"It's wonderful that you have the ability to take off a year and still have your job. But it sure would be nice if you did have some compensation or if you could work some type of reduced schedule until the child is six years old, instead of just one.

"Who says that when they turn one, they still don't need someone there? What's to say that you still can't be a productive employee as well as a good mother? Until industry recognizes that, they're not going to be giving women the support they need."

She said she would expect to make sacrifices for a more flexible schedule, including proportionate pay and risking losing promotion.

"I'm not looking to be vice president. I still think that I'm a good deal for them here. I think I do a good job. All the women around here do a good job. We are valuable people for this company who I believe they don't want to lose. I can also be valuable if they give me flexible time to work with my family."

People in other traditionally male professions said that they would be willing to make the trade-off between absolute career success and a more humane schedule to be with their family. University of Chicago medical students said that those going into medicine should expect to work long hours, but that some basic flexibility is still needed.

"I think the main thing is if you're willing to work like a single man with no other responsibilities, you're entitled," said Kathryn McLeese, who discussed the period before someone has enough experience to open their own practice. "The problem is there isn't much leeway for people who want to approach it in different ways."

Out of the twenty-five corporate women interviewed, Paula Barksdale, twenty-five, who works in marketing at a St. Louis company, had that option available. She said she plans to take advantage of her company's plan, which allows a woman to work three days out of five for three-fifths the pay.

"Personally speaking, that kind of thing is very appealing to me. I can see myself attaining a certain level in my career and consciously making a plateau."

But like everyone else, she explicitly cautions about "the mommy track," or special work arrangements for mothers: It has to be something the woman elects for herself. Feminist analysts are cautious and skeptical about "the mommy track" with the fear of women being branded with a capital "B" for breeder. This would give employers an excuse to pay women less and not promote them. They also say this option should be more like a "parent track," open to men and women.

"It has to be my decision," Barksdale stresses. "That's something I never want forced upon me or expected of me."

## Sequencing

Without flexibility in their schedules, most women are faced with the possibility of sequencing, the most common strategy voiced by college students planning careers. This means working until pregnancy, quitting and then coming back when the child enters school.

But this plan has drawbacks. For women with careers in mind, it may mean falling back dramatically behind competitors and losing earning power. Karen Berling said it also makes life unbalanced for the mother.

"If you have a family, you can contribute to your workplace also. They don't understand that. You might be able to do a better job at both if you have both. You look at the moms at home and some of them are going nuts. I love my child to death, but sometimes when you're with them twenty-four hours a day, these kids can drive you crazy. Sometimes work is like that too. You can only get so much into it."

But career ambitions aside, sequencing for most people, including the great number of single mothers in poverty, is not possible financially.

"What we must develop are options for the millions of women who must work and the millions of women who want to work," states Ruth Sidel in *On Her Own*. "Not the illusion of options applicable only to that minority of women who are part of affluent two-parent families and are willing to sacrifice their careers, their earning power and often the real pleasure they obtain from work because the larger society is unwilling to meet women and families even halfway."

## Optimism for the Future?

Many I interviewed were optimistic about changes being made over time in the workplace and in terms of attitudes. They generally noticed more of a friendship between younger men and women that could help disrupt old-boy networks or suspicion of women that have kept them outsiders.

Another tidal force—economics—might help change attitudes of employers seeking quality workers. The twentysomething generation has demographics on its side. In coming years, it will be more of a seller's market for labor, and women, men and families will be in a position to make more demands for sensitivity and accommodation.

During the seventies, the work force grew by three million workers a year, but will increase by only 1.6 million new workers a year in the coming decade, according to the U.S. Department of Labor. By the year 2000, there will be 8.2 million fewer Americans in the young adult age group (eighteen to twenty-four) entering the work force than there were in the mid-1980s, a decline of 14 percent.

Women in particular will be in a better position with employers, since over the next several years they will constitute a majority of new skilled and educated workers.

Many men and women interviewed in the corporate world made this prophecy. Nancy Hybert, who describes herself as a Republican, stressed that this is becoming less a matter of benevolence and more of common sense. In dealing with younger people who have learned not to be blindly loyal to companies, making provisions is a long-term investment.

"I'm not saying they should be jumping out of their way to see where I want to be in life," says Hybert, "but if you want to keep people, you have got to keep them happy in a career path and cultivate them and at least be aware of their needs, or you're going to spend a lot of money in training."

Many younger people interviewed, who described balance as a priority, considered family benefits to be important. They also attached less of a stigma to taking advantage of family benefits than their older counterparts. Typically individualists, they also seemed to care much less about how others judged them.

Perhaps the greatest hope for women and families is that young men also seem to believe in compromise and family attention, an attitude that wasn't as pervasive with the previous generation.

I asked UCLA law student Robert Renner, twenty-four, what he would look at in finding a job as a lawyer.

"I'd say in ranking it would probably be: the area of practice, the people and then definitely the salary and benefits. Let's be honest. I'm not doing this for pure enjoyment."

I asked what specific family benefits are important.

"A kind of novel concept, out here at least, is paternity leave. I would look at that. It sounds strange as I'm talking, but I don't think the woman should be the one automatically to stay home. It should be the couple saying: 'How are we going to deal with the kid?' "

While he stressed that he would rather not take time off, he would definitely consider it if his wife "were adamantly devoted to her career."

But what if it would jeopardize his career, as it has done with his sister, another lawyer, I asked.

"That would be something that we would talk about. I'm not going to close that door."

But would he lose his identity not working?

"I think that if I chose to marry, that is what I would most define myself by. Jobs would be second."

As with all the issues discussed around the workplace, the most active change may be needed for low-income women. Their employers usually have less incentive to be flexible or start task forces or caucuses to rid the place of a social evil, such as harassment or lack of diversity.

Also, more provisions need to be made for the tremendous setbacks in support systems for those in poverty, whose recipients are mostly women. The only real social policy of the Reagan/Bush administrations has been deregulation or dismantling of existing programs. Between 1979 and 1988, the proportion of American children living in poverty grew by 23 percent, with one in five now in that bracket. The reality is that people are falling through the cracks, which have more recently become craters.

Speaking in strict capitalist terms of expediency and international market competition, the United States will need to invest in every individual who has been neglected and marginalized in the past. Now family-friendly policies for parents—especially concerning child care, family leave and health care—are sorely needed to nurture a throwaway generation of children. Investing in the family should be considered a part of the country's real strategic defense initiative.

To make changes on a large scale, people, on a personal level, need to value women as workers. Then they have to extend that attitude to political action. Those I interviewed wanted more of a valuing of motherhood and children, but is this limited to their own personal motherhood and children? If Americans want to make these things a priority as a society, they have to make a commitment and pressure policymakers.

Among the most important attitudes to be examined are Americans' conflicting feelings behind family leave and child care. These demands, like many feminist concerns, seem radical in going against the tradition of women staying at home.

But other provisions for families that were feared in the past to be antifamily have now come into acceptance. Unlike twenty-five years ago, shelters for battered women present in almost every city in America are not questioned. Society has recognized the social ills behind them—violence in the home—and looked to collective supports to actually help preserve the family. Common-sense feminist drives have helped to break stereotypes in the past. It is to be hoped that in the near future we will also be able to look back at more persistent national myths with the same irony.

## Notes

[1] Citing 1984 estimates by the City of Madison, Wisconsin, Day Care Unit (Marx, 1985); Fern Marx and Michelle Seligson, "Child Care in the United States," *The American Woman: 1990–91* (New York: W. W. Norton & Company, 1990), p. 148.

[2] Milton Moskowitz and Carol Townsend. "The 75 Best Companies For Working Mothers." *Working Mother.* October 1990: p. 31.

[3] Cited by Child Care Action Campaign, New York; Ellen Galinsky, "Child Care and Productivity," New York, 1990.

[4] Marx and Seligson. "Child Care in the United States," p. 135.

[5] Cited by Ruth Sidel, *On Her Own,* p. 201; Jan Trost, "Parental Benefits: A Study of Men's Behavior and Views." Current Sweden (Stockholm: Swedish Institute). June 1983: pp. 1–7.

*Chapter Seven*

# Reproductive Rights, Sexual Violence and Other Battles for Control

WHEN DISCUSSING ISSUES of work and family, the older twentysomethings answered with the most urgency. More of them were experiencing the baby bottles and the carpools and the food stamps, and had a greater awareness of these challenges.

But for people of all ages within the sample, the issues more frequently mentioned involved women's self-determination and control over their bodies. Among these, no concern touched a nerve as strongly and widely as abortion rights.

In recent years, the legal assaults waged against women's reproductive rights have hit this generation as unexpectedly and fiercely as a lightning bolt on a sunny day. The past decade's unofficial anthem, "Don't Worry, Be Happy," had drowned out much of the apparent urgency for many to address women's issues.

In 1989, the Supreme Court's *Webster* decision upheld various provisions of a Missouri anti-abortion law and invited states to impose new restrictions on access to abortions. One was the limit of abortions at publicly funded hospitals, which disproportionately hits poor women and women of color. This helped illustrate to the mainstream how seriously access constraints affect women's choices, even if abortion is not completely outlawed.

Adding to the urgency was the indication by several justices of a willingness to reconsider—and for some to overturn—the 1973 *Roe v.*

*Wade* decision, which invalidated nearly all the existing laws restricting abortion and ruled unconstitutional any restriction on abortion during the first trimester of pregnancy.

Many of those women I interviewed said after *Webster,* they suddenly realized how tenuous their rights were and how seriously they must fight for them. As a topic of discussion, for many, abortion became more than just a removed, academic subject of debate to be studied in the same unit as the death penalty and euthanasia.

Another startling blow to follow was the May 1991 Supreme Court decision that flirted with First Amendment protections of speech. The ruling was that federally funded family planning clinics could no longer discuss abortion—even if the life of the mother was in danger! This also would deny information to young or poor women who didn't have access to factual and dependable counseling services. Unwilling to comply with this demand, clinics across the country, including the massive Planned Parenthood, pledged to give up this important resource.

Those who spoke with the most anger and fervor about such rulings were women. Personally, they felt threatened with a challenge to the control they exercise over their lives. Depending on their age and income, decisions were no longer theirs to make or, in the near future, would quite possibly be made for them by a distant tribunal of faceless and overwhelmingly male judges. Some also realized that abortion rights marked only one part of the fight for women to be able to have true choices in life. With this debate came more discussion of the other restrictions women face in having children, such as with access to birth-control, availability of affordable child care and lack of adequate health care.

Any restrictions on abortion rights affect large numbers of women. Each year, almost three out of every hundred women aged fifteen to forty-four has an abortion. In 1988, there were 1.6 million abortions in the United States. Women under thirty, especially those eighteen to nineteen have the most abortions. Abortions are also more common for unmarried women, who are four to five times more likely to have abortions than married women, and the poor, who are three times more likely.

But, no one interviewed—and I mean no one—spoke more passionately about abortion rights than one young man, Bill Bell, Jr.

At first glance, Bell, twenty-one, does not appear to fit the fringe stereotype of a political activist and critic. A commuter student at Indiana University/Purdue University in Indianapolis, the city where he was raised, he mixes in naturally with others at his school. He is tall, sandy-haired, wears a brown leather jacket and speaks with a slight southern Indiana twang. Two role models in his life, his parents, were homecoming king and queen when they were in high school together in Indianapolis.

When asked about his activist leanings, he also assured me he wasn't a radical. "I'm as normal as you're going to get. I hunt, fish, play basketball. I work out. I play Nintendo quite a bit. You know?"

But his easygoing nature fades away when he starts talking about his younger sister, Becky.

On the last day he saw his seventeen-year-old sister in 1988, she had been sick for a week. His family assumed she had the flu, which his father had suffered from the week before.

"As she got sicker and sicker, she got to the point where it was very hard for her to get up and move things. The last thing I remember saying to her, the last time I saw my sister alive, was Friday, September 16.

"And I was getting up like I did every day to go to work, and my sister was lying on the couch. 'Billy,' she said, 'get me a pillow and put it underneath my back.' And I got it and said, 'I love you, Beck, and I'll see you tonight.'

"I never saw her again until the funeral."

The day after, the coroner called Bill's parents and told them Becky had been killed by a massive deadly infection—the result of a back-alley abortion.

In shock, her parents traced Becky's steps during the last weeks of her life. They found that when Becky learned she was pregnant, she went to a clinic. She was told about Indiana's parental-consent law for teenagers that requires one parent's written permission for an abortion. Her friends warned her that her alternative of seeking permission in court from a judge would probably be a wasted effort; in Indiana, only a dozen waivers had been granted each year since the law was enforced in 1985.[1]

Becky told a friend she couldn't bear to tell her parents and disappoint them, and instead resorted to an illegal abortion.

The Bells also learned that Becky had told a friend she thought she didn't need protection because the young man she had dated told her that he was sterile. Her friend confided that when Becky told him she was pregnant, he turned his back.

Bill Bell, Jr. said his sadness about his sister's death turned to rage when he learned the cause: a law he and his family never knew existed. "I would never wish that pain on anyone," he said. The devastation that these laws create in the family is incomprehensible.

"And not only do I have to accept the fact that my sister has passed away and I will never see her again, I accept that the law was the culprit in forcing her into a back alley to acquire an abortion, which could have been done in a clean and sterile environment," said Bell.

In 1991, Bell joined his parents' two-year national campaign against parental-consent and notification laws, which have become a growing concern in the ongoing abortion-rights battle. In 1990, the Bells appeared in *Rolling Stone, Time, Newsweek, People* and a flurry of other publications.

He is aware of the challenges. While the numbers fluctuate as the fights continue state by state, as of June 1991, parental consent laws were enforced in sixteen states; also at that time, they were on the books of twenty others, but then blocked by executive decision or court order or not enforced.

In the summer of 1990, the Supreme Court invited these and other states to follow suit in limiting minors' access by upholding the constitutionality of restrictive parental-consent laws in Ohio and Minnesota. Specifically, the court's decision upheld not only mere notice for permission, but requirements that impose a forty-eight-hour waiting period and stipulation that both parents be notified as long as there is a legal system in place for judicial bypass.

The Becky Bell case has alerted many nationwide that back-alley abortions are not a relic of the past, limited to horror stories of older people. In the nineties, young women under eighteen are also dying.

Since these younger women are often the most voiceless and secretive about abortion, many do not realize the extent of the threat of parental consent, which was exclusively mentioned by the activists I interviewed.

"There are people who fall through the cracks that you hear about, but what about all the people you don't hear about?" said Nina

Chamyan, twenty-three, an organizer of Students Organizing Students, a national reproductive-rights network, which was formed days after the *Webster* decision.

Bill Bell, Jr. joined the national student council of SOS right before I met him at NOW's First Young Feminist Conference in Akron in 1991, at which his appearance was a highlight. There he made a bold step and admitted in public that he had "come out as a feminist."

The limiting of teenagers' access to abortion is a commonly recognized strategy to divide the pro-choice consensus in this country and chip away at abortion rights. Teenagers, who are those with the least resources to take care of a child, are a target for their high rates of abortions. Each year nearly a million teenage girls get pregnant, and 42 percent elect to have abortions.

It is true that at first glance these laws seem as if they would help teens and parents. Reflecting the results of other surveys, a *Newsweek* poll published in July 1989 showed that 75 percent of the respondents believed that teenagers should have parental consent for an abortion. Supporters reason that abortion can be a traumatic operation for the teen to endure alone and without support. Parents also may feel as if they have a right to know; a common argument is that if a teen needs a parent's consent to get her ears pierced, why not for an abortion?

But the data and all major medical organizations have concluded that such restrictions actually do more harm than good. The health and safety consequences have led associations such as the American College of Obstetricians and Gynecologists, the American Academy of Pediatrics and the American Psychological Association to oppose these laws.

While the advocates of parental-consent and notification laws argue that they help foster family communication, the result is that they have little effect. Fifty-five percent of teenagers under age eighteen who obtain an abortion do so with their parents' knowledge—the younger the teenager, the more likely the parents are to know, according to the Alan Guttmacher Institute, a nonprofit research organization in New York City. Those who don't tell their parents often have compelling reasons: fear of abuse, physical violence, being thrown out of the house or even disappointing their parents.

The alternative is often a lone journey to another state, a petition for a court bypass or an illegal abortion.

"These laws look good on paper," said Bell, "but in reality, they are nothing more than a death warrant."

Or it could mean a dangerous delay in the abortion while waiting for a judge's decree. After a Minnesota law was enacted in 1981, there was a 26.5 percent increase in later, more costly, higher-risk second-semester abortions.[2] Also, because some minors travel out of state to get abortions in order to circumvent their own states' laws, the chances of receiving adequate follow-up care are reduced.

The insistence on one or two parents' notification or consent is also a denial of reality. Not everyone comes from a functional family, or even has contact with the one or two parents required for notification. In Minnesota, though both biological parents are required for consent, only 50 percent of minors live with both parents.[3] This state is one of four with laws requiring the notification or consent of two parents, and has the most punitive law with the demand for biological parents.

The alternative, judicial bypass, is also discriminatory. It frequently does not work, and those who most often attempt it are white, middle class, college-bound and self-confident. The requirement of two parents also discriminates against certain groups. Only four out of every ten black children, compared to eight of every ten white children, live in two-parent families, according to the Children's Defense Fund.

Parental notification or consent also doesn't necessarily take into account the most horrifying of circumstances, as one sixteen-year-old interviewed commented.

"I think that if a young woman is raped or molested, and it's by a parent, by her father, I think it's ridiculous, because it will only cause more violence," said Sarabeth Eason of Toledo, Ohio, who was on the planning committee for the NOW conference.

Even in the most functional and healthy of families, the teenager may resort to desperate measures to avoid notifying parents, as in the case of the Bells. Bill Bell, Jr. and his parents stress that they had an unusually close family.

"Let me put it this way," said Bell. "My sister and I were best friends. We were also worst enemies, just because we were brother and sister. 'Hey, you get on that side of the sofa!' Or 'Don't cross this line!' The whole bit.

"It was a typical brother and sister relationship. We could talk to each other when we had problems. 'Oh, Mom, she's being uncool today, she won't let me do this.' Or 'I got into trouble.' It was the usual thing like that."

He said he understood why his sister didn't tell him, assuming she feared that he would go to their parents.

With other health-threatening and controversial issues, states have recognized how consent laws prevent minors from receiving health treatment. States have recognized minors' rights to seek certain services on their own that would be discouraged with parental consent. In almost every state, for example, minors can seek treatment alone for drug abuse, alcoholism, sexually transmitted diseases and prenatal care.

Gaining access to and navigating the judicial system alone can be overwhelming for a teenager. The analysis of court bypass also shows that it varies wildly according to state and the specific judge on the bench. While the grantings of permission in Indiana have been sparse, in comparison, Massachusetts courts have denied only thirteen of the 8,000 petitions filed in the nine years after the parent-notification law went into effect in 1981.[4]

The teenager's basic right to privacy is also violated as she is forced to go through the criminal procedure of judicial bypass. In a small town, she may not trust the clerk in charge of forms. While going through the process, she may go through a maze confronting dozens of people. A few of those interviewed also voiced objection to the bypass because of how it further isolates and traumatizes the teenager during a time of crisis.

The restrictions also have a social cost to teenagers. One in four teenage mothers drops out of high school, and only one in fifty finishes college. Children of teens are twice as likely to die in infancy as those born to women in their twenties or forties. The total cost to American taxpayers for families started by teenage women is $20 billion annually in public aid, including food stamps and Medicaid benefits, according to statistics compiled by the Fund for the Feminist Majority in Washington, D.C.

But while activists are addressing the loss of rights for the young, many are also recognizing that poor women have not had this option for years. The first severe restriction on the poor was the Hyde Amendment, first passed in 1976, which prohibits federal Medicaid funding for abortions except in cases involving rape, severe illness or situations in which the life of the pregnant woman is at risk. It was followed by campaigns in many states to prohibit state funding, and in 1990, only thirteen states continued to fund abortions. The 1989 *Webster* decision also had the dramatic effect of permitting drastic restriction of abortions at publicly funded hospitals, a base of support for the poor.

As Becky Bell has come to symbolize the threat to middle-class America of teenage access limits, Rosie Jimenez is a figure representing the poor and women of color. In 1977, Jimenez, twenty-seven, was the first woman to die as a direct result of the cutoff of Medicaid funds provided by the Hyde Amendment. She was a young Mexican-American mother in McAllen, Texas, who found herself pregnant and confronting a difficult choice.

A semester away from graduating with her college degree in education, and pregnant, she could use her $700 scholarship check for a legal abortion, or to finish her degree and get out of poverty with a better job. She chanced it on a back-alley abortion and was reported to have died with the money in her purse.

But when discussing their pro-choice views, many talked in terms of principles, not in terms of the threat to their own lives. The overwhelming majority of women and men who were pro-choice voiced two reasons for their stance: the issue of privacy and a confidence in the woman to make the right decision for herself. Many women considered the restrictions a personal affront to their intelligence and judgment capabilities.

Sarabeth Eason, sixteen, made a stand at the age of eleven when interviewed about parental-consent laws for two seconds on the local news. She then refused to take back her statements and was kicked out of her Catholic school.

"It is insulting because I feel that I am able to decide for myself what is going to happen in my future. I decided to go against the church when I was eleven years old, and that was a very good decision, my right as an American citizen," said Eason.

"And that's just one example, that we as women are being shot down and treated as second-class citizens. And just because we are young, that's where the ageist factor comes in. We are treated as though we were brainless!"

A large number of those interviewed from all walks of life, who have been less publicly vocal, expressed similar indignance.

"It's scary to think that these sixty-year-old white upper-class males can decide for me," said student Lisa Seidlitz. "That itself is pretty alarming."

"I would do almost anything for pro-choice," said Paula Barksdale, a St. Louis manager. "To me, everything is important. Child care is important. So many things are very, very important. But it's the one that scares me the most, the idea of not having freedom of choice. It frightens me to the core. It just feels so Orwellian. It's such a fundamental right. To think of it being taken away, it absolutely terrifies me."

Of course, a great number stressed that they were not "pro-abortion" in being "pro-choice." While many said they could never go through with the procedure, they pointed out that they could not practically impose that judgment on others and were aware of the realities of the back-alley abortion.

"I wouldn't because I couldn't live with myself," said Bridget Johnson, 20, a University of Illinois-Champaign student, who described herself as "a practicing Catholic." "But I don't think a judge on the Supreme Court has a right to tell me. I think the law is totally unrealistic."

University of Chicago medical student Asra Khan took a typically cautious view, saying that resources are better utilized treating the causes of abortion instead of fighting laws. "I'm against abortion, but I wouldn't want to totally illegalize it. I don't think it's a question of pro-choice, pro-life or whatever. I think we have to ask why do we have all these unwanted pregnancies? It's ridiculous to illegalize because you're still going to have all these problems. People are going to get abortions anyway."

Like others, she recognized that criminalization would also be useless to stop wealthy women—who can more easily travel out of state—and it would be the poor who would most suffer.

She mentioned the need for discussion of other factors leading to abortions she said aren't often addressed. "In this society, people do not take enough responsibility for their actions. That should come first, the morality part of it and then the responsibility part of it."

When I asked those who did not name abortion rights as a priority, about one-third of the sample, about their views on the issue, they gave mixed responses. Like Khan, a large number from this group was indeed pro-choice, but didn't recognize themselves as having that stance.

A minority of the women said that they didn't consider abortion primarily a woman's issue or as one of privacy. "I don't think about it as [a matter of] women's rights as [much as] I do in terms of murder or not," said Beth Berkowitz, twenty, a Columbia University student. "The complication for me doesn't lie in the women's rights. It's peripheral."

Her friend Rachel Stoll, twenty, agreed. "People who are radical feminists or anyone who is pro-choice and says things like: 'It's white men telling us what to do with our bodies,' I think it's so wrong. Because look at the women who are also telling us that."

But they also recognized the realities of what happens when abortion is not accessible. "My dad is a doctor," said Berkowitz, "and tends to take a conservative stance on issues. When he was on call in the emergency room, they would get case after case of incomplete abortions of women who tried to perform abortions and got infected and were in bad shape. That's what decided it for him, that you need access to it."

There is a small faction of the anti-abortion movement that calls itself feminist. A central belief is that abortion is direct violence against women and children, whom feminists are supposed to be protecting.

## Reproductive Freedom

While recognizing the particular urgency today of the abortion fight, the pro-choice people interviewed strongly emphasized that merely keeping abortion legal, or even ideally accessible to all, would not cure any social problems. Abortion, a last resort, is a symptom of many other ills.

In recent years, those at the vanguard of the pro-choice movement have tried to broaden the spectrum of issues addressed. The goal is a transformation from "abortion rights" to "reproductive rights."

"Reproductive rights is a [relatively] new political term," said Andrea Rose Askowitz, twenty-two, a pro-choice organizer. "It is not just the right to have an abortion, but all the rights that come along with having a child—if that's the choice."

Activists also stress that focusing on other issues can provide a larger base of support for the pro-choice movement. Those on both sides of the volatile abortion debate more naturally agree on the necessity of reducing the demand for them. Younger women are also suspicious of a single-issue battle, which often means excluding anyone not white and middle class.

## Prenatal and Postnatal Care

Askowitz, like others, mentioned demanding better prenatal and postnatal care.

As with other family issues, the record of the United States in caring for its children's health is abysmal. In 1988, it ranked nineteenth in infant mortality rates, with one in ten babies dying for every 1,000 live births. In mortality rates for children younger than five, it was twenty-second. For low-birthweight births, it was twenty-ninth.

The rates are worse for people of color. Overall, in 1987, 79 percent of white mothers and 61 percent of black mothers received early care. Five percent of white women and 11 percent of black women received none, according to the Children's Defense Fund.

A commitment on a national level is missing to help alleviate the problem. In 1989, a White House Task Force on Infant Mortality report, leaked to the *New York Times,* recommended eighteen specific steps, with a total price tag of about $480 million a year, or roughly one-tenth of 1 percent of the total spent annually on personal health care in the United States. By applying known procedures and modestly expanding related health-care programs, the committee estimated that the nation could reduce infant deaths by 25 percent and cut the number of disabled infants by 100,000 annually.

In early 1991, President Bush made one front-page proposal to devote a total of $58 million to combat infant mortality in ten cities. The bad news was that it would be taken from other, strapped programs that serve pregnant women, poor children and the homeless. (Congress later rejected that proposal and instead appropriated $25 million from undesignated sources.)

## Birth Control:
## Development, Access, Education

To prevent abortions, a common need pointed out was the development of better contraception and easier access to it. Forty-three percent of women having abortions become pregnant even though they are using some form of contraception, either because of inconsistent or incorrect use or because of a method failure. For teenagers, more prevention is especially essential. The United States has one of the highest rates of teen pregnancy in the industrialized world, twice as high as that of other industrialized countries, according to the Children's Defense Fund.

More research for methods to suit the wide variety of women's and men's needs is also needed. American University student Lisa Scheeler, eighteen, said her mother was one of the unknown numbers of women who was damaged by the Dalcon Shield IUD, marketed from 1971 to 1974, and then could not have any more children. In early 1991, 85,000 of the total 195,000 Dalcon Shield claims were still pending.

Those interviewed discussed birth control with a remarkable openness (even though it does still seem to carry something of a personal stigma for singles indicating a "loose woman"). While riding on a bus on the campus of the University of California, Santa Cruz, two classmates behind me were talking in intellectual terms at the tops of their voices about men's preferences of condomwear.

Many speaking out are critical of alternatives available. In the fall of 1991, both *Mademoiselle* and *Glamour,* two major mainstream young women's magazines, featured extensive coverage of the lag in new methods introduced.

Writing in the October 1990 issue of *Glamour,* Peggy Orenstein discusses the limitations.

"American women have fewer contraceptive options—and pay more for them—than women in any other industrialized nation. During the three decades since the Pill and IUD were introduced, European women have been offered a variety of barrier methods and injectable and implantable contraceptives, while our major new options have been the sponge and cervical cap. So sorry is the state of contraceptive 'choice' in this country that our most popular form of birth control is sterilization."

Strangely, while there is a massive consumer need, this is one area the free market has failed to accommodate. "Why, in this age of miracle medicine, don't we have a contraceptive for every woman's—and man's—needs, for not only the 'average' consumer but the woman with the special health concern, the breast-feeding woman, the woman over thirty-five who smokes?" Orenstein writes.

Her explanation: "Politics, money and fear."

Some of the resistance is from the government. Taking inflation into account, she writes that the Bush and Reagan administrations have reduced funds for Title X, the nation's family-planning program, by 40 percent since 1980.

The Reagan and Bush administrations, both avowedly "pro-life," also demonstrated their indifference to developing contraception with a lack of research funding. The annual average for contraceptive development from 1980 to 1989 was $16.6 million, and all other research in that area $20.3 million. (The annual average of economic and military aid to El Salvador in that period was $364.1 million. In 1990, it cost $486 million for one Stealth B-2 bomber.)

The administration's stance was also evident through appointments of anti-abortion advocates to high positions in family planning. For example, in 1989, a former official for the National Right to Life Committee was appointed assistant secretary for public affairs for the Department of Health and Human Services. Her job is to approve all public literature and statements distributed to the public through Title X, Orenstein reports.

Also, the private sector is intimidated by the prospects of lawsuits and an extensive research and development period. To follow government regulation standards, the process to develop a new contraceptive takes at least eight years.

Both private and public researchers have been suppressed in their efforts by a strong and organized anti-abortion lobby. They advocate a form of contraception that requires no research funds, "natural family planning," a method that scores low on statistical charts for effectiveness.

Since then, early in 1991, the Federal Drug Administration took a major step in approving the first new type of contraception in thirty years, Norplant. Hailed as 99 percent effective by family planners, it comes in the form of six silicone capsules inserted into the upper arm that secrete the hormone progestin. This blocks ovulation and can work against unwanted pregnancies for five years.

Still, besides some standard side effects, another drawback is that it may not be necessarily practical for the poor, teens or women in their twenties, who have the highest rates of unwanted pregnancies. The implantation requires forethought and access to a doctor for removal. At an estimated cost of $500, it will only be feasible for many if offered at reduced cost through public clinics.

Some also fear its abuse. In a Dec. 12, 1990, editorial, the *Philadelphia Inquirer* recommended that welfare mothers be given incentive to use it with the suggestion that it could help solve the problem of poverty among blacks. "That suggestion treads dangerously close to state-sponsored genocide," criticized Vanessa Williams, an *Inquirer* reporter and president of the Philadelphia Association of Black Journalists.[5]

## Sterilization Abuse

One of the reasons Norplant was welcomed, though, was that it is a reversible form of sterilization. A great fear, especially in communities of women of color, is of abuse of this procedure.

Often sterilization is the most economical method for impoverished women who cannot afford abortions. Unlike abortions, it irrevocably destroys a woman's ability to have children.

When the federal government stopped reimbursing states for Medicaid abortions in 1977, it continued to pay for sterilizations, free and on demand. When examined closely, the relationship between abortion and sterilization is clear. When the Illinois government cut funding for Medicaid abortions in 1980, the number of government sterilizations doubled in the state, as reported in *The New Our Bodies, Ourselves*. With the *Webster* decision in 1989, which further curtailed poor women's access to abortion, this fear of sterilization abuse has been amplified.

The abuse of sterilization is also a concern when it is involuntary or women aren't informed of the consequences. In the 1970s, lawsuits exposed a broad pattern of sterilization without consent of poor women by government-funded clinics and private doctors. One notorious case in 1973 involved the involuntary sterilization with federal funds of twelve- and fourteen-year-old black sisters in Alabama without their parents' knowledge or consent.

The fear of sterilization abuse is strongest in communities of color, which have been disproportionately hit. Since 1974, studies by individuals and the government have documented a pattern in women of childbearing age, fifteen to forty-four, from different groups: About 24 percent of Native American women were reported sterilized in 1976, according to testimony from Dr. Connie Uri in a Senate committee hearing; statistics from the Department of Health and Human Services show that in 1988, 21.6 percent of black women and 16.1 percent of white women had been sterilized for contraceptive reasons. In 1972 alone, the federal government performed nearly 200,000 sterilizations on women.[6]

Only since 1978 has the government required a series of precautionary steps for federally funded sterilizations, including the furnishing of an interpreter for women who speak a different language than the physician, information about the procedure's permanence and the alternatives, the provision of a thirty-day waiting period and a witness present.

## Teen Pregnancy

In controlling reproduction, young women are especially vulnerable without education.

"Why don't we have sex education in the schools? Why aren't we fighting for this tooth and nail?" asked Janelle Rodriguez, nineteen, a Berkeley sophomore. "If boys and girls who become men and women have no idea who [they are], then we're perpetuating teen pregnancy."

A 1985 Lou Harris poll commissioned by the Planned Parenthood Federation showed that 67 percent of the parents polled had never discussed birth control with their children, and a follow-up survey the next year showed that 31 percent of sixteen- and seventeen-year-olds surveyed had never talked to their parents about sex.

Writing in *The Nation,* Planned Parenthood president Faye Wattleton warned that teenagers must get straight information about birth control, even when abstinence is the best choice. While the abstinence method is indeed unsurpassed in effectiveness and economy, as major national studies have proven, this cannot be the only component of education for teenagers. Wattleton stresses that people who oppose educating teens about birth control are taking too simplistic a view: "Their one and only solution to the problem of teenage pregnancy is, 'Just say no!' But just saying no prevents teenage pregnancy the way 'Have a nice day' cures chronic depression."

Another expert on teen pregnancy, Ruth Thomas, thirty-seven, who has been a counselor to girls at an inner-city youth club in Dallas, also emphasizes the need for communication between parents and children. At Girls Incorporated, a central component to the program is a parent/ daughter workshop meant to deliver the facts about sexuality. Thomas said this is an alternative to a common source of information: friends from the streets, who are often the girls' boyfriends.

"One of the really popular myths is that if a guy gets a hard-on and doesn't ejaculate inside a girl, then he'll die," she said.

"Kids believe that, especially if a girl is being fed all these wild myths by her boyfriend—somebody she's in love with—if she hasn't gotten factual information or doesn't have that mom somewhere she can go to and test this question out."

But Thomas stresses that just objective facts aren't enough. She says at a young age, girls must be taught the consequences of their actions or a view of "the big picture."

While many conservative critics have pinned the blame for out-of-wedlock births on the "breakup of the black family," deeper economic factors must be taken into account. Faye Wattleton says that teen pregnancy is more directly proportionate to class than to race: "The majority of poor people in this country are white, and so are the majority of pregnant teenagers."

She reports that even when the rates for teen pregnancy are calculated for whites only in the United States, they far exceed those of other countries, such as England and Wales, America's close competitors.

Another influence is unemployment, which makes a father a liability to a family, rather than a pillar of support. In the 1990s, when skilled labor has been increasingly needed, one of the best solutions for single mothers is training and education for both sexes. Writing in *The American Woman 1990–91*, Harriet Pipes McAdoo, a Howard University professor in the department of social work, documents studies that have shown that adolescent black men tend to marry the mothers of their children when they are financially able to provide for them.

Also, often facing a lack of opportunities elsewhere, many young people who are in the depths of poverty plan pregnancies. During our interview, Tina, twenty, who lives in a public-housing development in Dallas, mentioned that all her friends have children, and I asked her what could be the cause.

"For a lot of us, when you have a child, it's good in a way, because you feel the only thing you have to love is that child," said Tina, who didn't want her real name used. "That child is going to keep you going, keep you on your P's and Q's. Because there's a whole bunch of us that feel we are not loved, we are not worth being loved, and having a baby, for many of us, that's the answer."

Underlying the problem of unwanted pregnancies is Americans' "fundamental discomfort" with sexuality, which confuses teenagers, Wattleton says. While they are as sexually active as teens in other countries, American teenagers get more mixed messages. As society suppresses messages about sex, the media exploits it. And the message is often one of lack of restraint and precaution, as actors are swept away with romance.

In watching more than my share of television and movies over the past twenty-three years, I have rarely seen anyone mention contraception. So in real life, for many people, this seems like an unrelated concept.

The lack of precautions on television and in movies continues as sex gets more common and explicit. Even Batman did it with Kim Basinger's character on the first date! And I don't remember seeing any Bat-Trojan in his utility belt.

## Women's Health

Many health concerns dealing with pregnancy are encompassed by the women's health movement. More than ever, people are realizing that women's health is a political issue.

"The main event in my life that really made me feel like women got the short end of the deal was my mother [dying] of ovarian cancer four years ago," said Sarah Pressman, twenty-nine, a student at Rush Medical College in Chicago, who said she has also become more sensitive to disparities since studying medicine.

"My mom was very sick. She was a very healthy person. And for some unknown reason, she got ovarian cancer, which is a very deadly form of cancer. Because the ovaries are so internal, it's hard to diagnose until it's very late. And a year and a half after she was diagnosed, she died. I felt that she died because there wasn't enough research into the treatment and prevention of ovarian cancer, and I felt it was true because it was a women's disease, and there wasn't as much interest."

Activists are pushing for more research money for breast and ovarian cancer, contraception, osteoporosis and AIDS; more health and social services for pregnant teens; and Medicaid coverage for mammography and Pap-smear screening.

Some progress has been made since a 1990 study revealed that the National Institutes of Health, the nation's principal source of money for biomedical research, was largely not including women in its studies.

That year, the same group that proposed the inquiry, the congressional Caucus for Women's Issues, introduced more than a dozen bills on health issues. As a result, in 1990, the National Institutes of Health established an Office of Women's Health Research and developed a policy requiring the inclusion of women in government-sponsored studies unless there were specific reasons for the exclusion.

Still, in medical research in general, women are considered a special-interest group. The male is the norm subject and defines the symptoms and treatment of the illness.

A central issue is breast cancer, which kills almost a third of its victims and is increasing. The American Cancer Society estimates that one of every nine women runs the risk of developing it, compared to one of every ten projected in 1987. The incidence of cancer in blacks has risen 34 percent over the past twenty-five years, as compared to 9 percent for whites.[7]

Cancer-prevention activists have taken note of the influence of ACT-UP, the AIDS Coalition to Unleash Power, a direct-action AIDS funding activist group, which during the 1980s demonstrated the power of organizing. A disparity in funding has become noticeable: $1.1 billion in federally financed AIDS research in the 1990 fiscal year, for a disease that killed more than 23,000 in 1989, versus $77 million for breast cancer, which killed more than 43,000 Americans that same year.

"That's not to say that we should take money away from AIDS research, because it's obviously an incredibly critical health issue, but one of the reasons AIDS is so well funded [in comparison] is because of ACT-UP, and we have to do the same thing," Sarah Pressman said. (In a January 6, 1991, *New York Times* article, federal officials noted that AIDS is a contagious disease, and the death toll is likely to surpass that of breast cancer in the future. They also said that breast cancer receives more government money than any other cancer including lung cancer, which claims 142,000 lives each year.)

Women's health advocates are also demanding that research adjust to including women as subjects, or to specifically addressing special conditions or complications of their illnesses.

With breast cancer, this has been a constant battle. "There's no research on the normal breast," said Dr. Susan Love, an author and professor of surgery at Harvard, at a 1990 national symposium. "Therefore, we don't have a clue when carcinogens are acting."[8]

Criticism has also been leveled at a lack of research about how AIDS affects women and how diagnoses are not adjusted according to the symptoms women experience. Once diagnosed, women have shorter life spans: White men live twenty-four to thirty-six months on average after diagnosis; for women, it's fifteen weeks to six months.[9] With AIDS, women of color have been particularly hard hit. Fifty-two percent of all women with AIDS are black; 75 percent are women of color.[10]

Janice Pemberton, twenty-three, a counselor at a Los Angeles AIDS clinic, said women also have to fight stigmas to talk about the disease.

"Cancer is okay to have. You can go out and tell people you have cancer and everyone feels sorry for you. You tell someone you have AIDS and they say: 'What did you do?'

"I talk to people in the cancer community, and there was a time when cancer was the same way: 'What did you do? I never knew anyone with cancer before.' But it doesn't seem to be getting any better for people with AIDS who are HIV positive."

## Eating Disorders

One medical epidemic hitting a disproportionate number of young women and young people is eating disorders. The two most prevalent eating disorders, anorexia nervosa and bulimia, occur most in women (90 to 95 percent of cases). They are frequently associated with teenagers and adults preoccupied with weight.

Anorexia is characterized by extreme and compulsive behavior toward food and losing body weight. In this case, self-consciousness can lead to suicide; it is one of the few psychiatric disorders that can start an irrevocable course toward death.

A high proportion of these patients (30 to 50 percent) has bulimia, binging followed by vomiting. The effects of this purging are often sores in the mouth, rotten teeth, swollen gums and enlargement of the salivary glands near the lower jaw, giving a chipmunklike appearance.

The most comprehensive recent studies indicate that 3 to 5 percent of women between puberty and the age of thirty are seriously afflicted with bulimia and that 1 percent suffer from anorexia nervosa.

While eating disorders hit people of all sexes, races and incomes, the majority of victims are white teenage girls from privileged families. Especially at high risk are people whose careers require a certain weight, such as dancers or models, as well as college women and older women with high-power jobs and socially demanding lives.

A University of California-Santa Cruz student made an apt comparison to describe the pervasiveness and hidden qualities of eating disorders. She said that finding out about people's eating disorders is similar to the way in which you slowly discover a string of people being sexually assaulted or abused or who have had alcoholic parents. You find out about one, and then another, and then another, until the pattern seems like it won't stop. She also noted that her sister's sorority house at a large university in Oregon had to have its pipes replaced because of so many people vomiting regularly after eating in order to lose weight.

Often eating disorders are manifestations of feelings of perfectionism or insecurity already present in the victim. But the overwhelming dominance in women should provide a clue about some of the special pressures they face in society and how important appearance is in determining a woman's worth.

Vomiting to lose weight is an extremist, desperate, health-threatening, lonely, horrible act. For many women, weight takes on monumental importance, with appearance seeming to more directly define one's actual self-image and self-esteem. In their eyes, controlling their weight is equated with being able to control their lives.

From every direction, women are bombarded with messages that looks are everything. The definitions of beauty are generally strict and rigid, making the thin, tall, white blonde the standard. Everything else is a deviation from the "norm."

A few people noticed that overemphasis on women's looks is one societal attitude the women's movement has yet to put a dent in.


## Sexual Violence

Next to abortion rights, the topic that came closest to generating the most anger and electricity was sexual violence.

Many people said they knew someone who had been assaulted, abused or attacked. Even those who had not been victims spoke with fervor, living in constant fear keeping them prisoner.

Heidi Friedman, twenty-two, a student at Hunter College in New York City, described why rape is such a serious violation. "Property is really irrelevant. The bottom line is what you have is you. If you can't have you, I think you can't have anything. You are being stripped of your rights to be human."

While this issue was mainly mentioned by women, one man said this constant fear is how he most detects the presence of sexism in society. "My [female] friends can't go outside alone after nine P.M., and I can."

It's indicative of the whole situation," said Justin Lundgren, twenty-one, a student at Columbia University.

The most ironic description of the fear came from medical student Asra Khan. We were reflecting on the Persian Gulf War going on at that time, and talking about the restrictions put on women in Saudi Arabia, under its particular interpretation of the Koran.

But Khan, a Muslim, said Americans should also reserve some pity for women in the United States.

"Here, you can say: 'The woman has freedom.' But what does she really have the freedom to do? I mean, I'm terrified to be by myself in almost any area of campus at night," said Khan, who attends the University of Chicago in a heavily patrolled South Side neighborhood.

"What kind of freedom is that? I'm glad that I'm living here; I would never want to live there, but you have to realize there are things wrong with this society too."

She is not alone in this constant feeling of being powerless. In a stirring 1989 book, *The Female Fear,* authors Margaret Gordon and Stephanie Riger study this phenomenon:

"The only crime that women fear more than rape is murder. And while rape is not often uppermost in the minds of women, it is ever present. Most women experience fear of rape as a nagging, knawing sense that something awful could happen, an angst that keeps them from doing things they want or need to do, or from doing them at the time or in the way they might otherwise do."

They documented the extent of the fear interviewing 299 women, finding that it was a day-to-day concern of about a third of the women, a sporadic concern for a third, and of little concern to another third, who still took precautions to prevent it.

The fear of rape is especially strong because of two fundamental differences between rape and other crimes: It involves sex, a taboo subject, and guilt. Unlike when a woman gets mugged and her rage is directed at the mugger, with rape, the anger is also directed toward herself: What could she have done to prevent it? How differently could she have acted?

Many interviewed also freely quoted the staggering statistics about the epidemic nature of sexual violence. When people pronounce that all women's problems have been solved, and that the women's movement is now obsolete, they must never have heard of sexual assault. It is the single most convincing proof that women are still oppressed.

Violence against women hits people of every class, age, race and physical description, in every part of this country, rural or urban. In 1990, a record number of rapes were reported, totalling 100,433 across the country, according to a study by the Senate Judiciary Committee. Statistics from every state showed that rape increased four times faster than the country's overall crime rate over the last decade, indicating that twelve rapes occurred every hour that year.[11]

Those interviewed also seemed to fear a more common kind of rape often overlooked in discussion: acquaintance rape, or rape by someone the victim knows. While the popular term is "date rape," activists prefer acquaintance rape, which more accurately includes the wide spectrum of assailants: boyfriends, co-workers and family members, in addition to dates.

The reality of acquaintance rape has been established most notably for this generation in a groundbreaking study released in 1988, which was sponsored by the *Ms.* Foundation and the National Institute for Mental Health and published in *I Never Called It Rape,* by Robin Warshaw. Researcher Mary Koss headed the work of surveying 6,100 undergraduate women and men at thirty-two college campuses.

The most astonishing statistics reported were that one in four female respondents had an experience that met the legal definition of rape or attempted rape—and 84 percent knew their attackers. Fifty-seven percent of those rapes happened on dates.

But all rape researchers caution about the difficulty in gathering statistics. Rape, especially by an acquaintance, is one of the most underreported crimes. Also, those raped by someone they know are not as likely to classify the experience as rape. Only 27 percent of the women whose sexual assaults met the legal definition of rape thought of themselves as rape victims in the *Ms.* Foundation survey.

For men, there also seems to be a lack of awareness in distinguishing forced sex from rape, and in recognizing the seriousness of this act. In 1986, UCLA researcher Neil Malamuth reported that 30 percent of the men he questioned said they would commit rape if they knew there was no chance of getting caught. When the word "rape" was changed on the survey to the phrase "force a woman into having sex," more than 50 percent gave that answer.

But much of the work done in the media in the past ten years about acquaintance rape has just established it as a reality, rather than fought for its prevention. Many attribute initial press recognition of acquaintance rape to the book, *Against Our Will* by Susan Brownmiller. In 1982, *Ms.* magazine broke ground with an article about "date rape." But the mainstream press has only very slowly caught on with coverage, which has mainly been accounts by anonymous victims, to establish the seriousness of the problem. The social factors leading to acquaintance rape and men's responsibilities in prevention of it still have been barely explored.

Even academics did not address rape, a "women's issue," with research until recently. It has only become a legitimate scholarly topic since the mid-1970s, when the National Institute for Mental Health established the National Center for the Prevention and Control of Rape and began funding research.

Like abortion, this is a most private issue that has been brought to the forefront of public debate. People now have a name to describe this experience, and women's boldness in discussion has increased with the growing women's movement and openness in society.

"I have a friend who was raped, and she got pregnant, then had an abortion, and no one ever knew," said Heidi Friedman. "The guy is here on campus. This kind of thing happens all the time. The fact that this can happen makes me angry."

"So many women I know have been raped, and how many other women this has happened to, I don't know," said Santa Cruz student Robyn Chapel, twenty-two.

The interviews that conveyed to me the extent to which awareness had grown were at my former school, the University of Illinois-Champaign. In 1988, I was considered radical for writing about the subject in the college paper. But now this is common knowledge, and even those I would consider mainstream are mobilized for prevention.

At the Phi Mu house, Bridget Johnson explained to me why she has taken a lead in providing education on the subject to her sorority. "That is one thing I feel very strongly about. There is no way I will ever let anyone take advantage of me. In that way, I guess I am very much of an activist. Some people call it prudish, but I think it's more like having control. It's a self-esteem thing."

"I know someone it happened to," said Suzanne Mayer, twenty, a junior at the University of Illinois-Champaign. "She passed out, and when she woke up, she was like: 'Oh no.' I think that if we weren't educated about it, then people would think it was her fault—'she shouldn't have gotten that drunk.' "

But this movement against acquaintance rape is indeed radical in its mission to shatter a universe of myths about sexual assault. First, activists go beyond the stranger to look at other men as potential assailants.

The movement is radical in calling for a new sexual revolution. While the old one of the sixties seemed to exalt the right to have sex, this one is a demand for quality. It sets new standards of what is acceptable, with the discussion of articulated consent, communication, respect and sensitivity to the other person's privacy, as well as a new honesty.

The movement is radical in terms of shifting the blame. Instead of guilt being placed on the woman, it goes to the man. "Bad judgment is not a rapeable offense," as Robin Warshaw stresses. It doesn't matter how she's dressed, how much she drank, how far she had gone with him in the past or even if she had birth control in her purse and was planning to have sex that night.

The movement is also radical in defining what is unacceptable sexual behavior in women's terms. The classic definition is forced sexual intercourse. But women experience violation with a wide spectrum of unwanted attacks—and want to be taken seriously for these protests.

Others also say any attempt at attack demands outrage. Marita Vasquez, twenty-six, a Chicago bartender, told me how violated she felt by sexual abuse that took place while she was driving south on the expressway from work. Her case illustrates that acquaintance rape is not mainly a campus problem, as it is almost always portrayed in the press.

"One day this guy was really, really drunk, and I felt obligated to give him a ride home, and he kept harassing me all the way home, like touching me and stuff. And I said, 'Cut it out. I'll leave you here on the Dan Ryan [expressway].' "

When she got to work the next day, she told others about it, but was kidded by co-workers about the way the man had "scored." Often people involved with any kind of sexual abuse or assault find it hard to be taken seriously and have the repeated humiliation of having to face their attackers in everyday life. "I was the bartender, and no one goes out with me, only if we're friends," Vasquez said. "He actually got to touch me and stuff."

Like others, she wondered if she was overreacting. "This could have been a date rape kind of thing, but it was only date molestation." She thought, " 'I don't care. It doesn't have to be rape for me to talk about it.' But I ended up being the butt of jokes for a couple of weeks because I opened my mouth and said this is what he did to me."

In the end, she saw this as a political experience, showing how women are socialized to tolerate this behavior and be passive. "This guy, he took advantage of my sweetness. I could have been a bitch and said, 'Get off on Eighty-seventh and the Dan Ryan.' No, I was nice. You're supposed to be good. You aren't supposed to argue about that."

One form of acquaintance rape mentioned was incest. As one activist told me, "incest" is a common euphemism for rape. Researcher Diana Russell cited a study done by a research company in the Bay Area that documented that 38 percent of women had been subjected to unwanted sexual contact before the age of eighteen, with 16 percent of it from a family member.[12] Like other rape survivors, people who have suffered this type of abuse often internalize the blame and feel especially helpless. This happens in households of all classes and races.

## Domestic Violence

While women are less likely than men to be victims of violent crime in general, they are far more likely to be attacked by someone with whom they are intimate, according to a study released in 1991 by the Justice Department's Bureau of Justice Statistics. The report said 25 percent of the violent crime against women is committed by family members or people they have dated while the figures for men are only 4 percent.

Domestic violence is so widespread that a report in the *Journal of the American Medical Association* in 1990 called it the most common cause of injury to women. It reported that 22 to 35 percent of women who visit emergency wards have abuse-related symptoms, either physical or stress-related.

FBI crime statistics from 1987 showed that 26 percent of married couples surveyed reported violence in their homes in the past year.

Sixty percent reported violence at some time. Another finding was that 34 percent of all female homicide victims older than fifteen years old are killed by their husbands or intimate partners.[13]

Like rape, domestic violence is a hidden crime surrounded by many myths. So I was startled to hear descriptions of battering by a woman my own age, twenty-three.

While she never called herself a victim of domestic violence, it was clear when she was telling me the story of how she got to be a single mother. Her experiences illustrated that domestic violence, like rape, comes in a variety of forms and extremes.

Diana, who did not want her last name used, and her husband came to Wisconsin with their newborn child right after high school in North Carolina. They were seeking better job opportunities in his carpenter trade.

But isolated from family and in a new town, she soon felt him take control of her life. He limited her contact with others, not letting her get a job. "With the house, he felt it was a woman's job. That's what I should be doing. Having kids, not having a job." She said she had worked before that, since the age of sixteen, and was used to having her own money. Instead, her husband gave her an allowance of ten to twenty dollars a week.

When she went out with friends, she faced the consequences. "He didn't want me to go out with my girlfriends and do this and that. I went out with my girlfriends once, and he didn't talk to me for a couple of days after that. I didn't go out. I didn't want to do things because I didn't want to be punished. Do you know what I mean? Not talked to or grouched at all the time."

As time went on tension mounted as he started drinking more. "When he went out to drink, and he came home when the bar closed, you are darn right that I would be sitting on the couch waiting for him. I would say, 'You've been out since after you got off work.' He never even used to come home to change. He would blow a lot of money."

Then the violence started. "He'd throw things. We went through a lot of glasses. We went through about three phones. He ripped them out of the wall.

"At one point, he got right in my face. That used to make me really nervous because he was a fairly big man. He got right in my face and started yelling at me. I don't know if it was a reflex, [but] I pushed him away, and he just grabbed me and went *whooosh* right across the wall, and I fell on [my child's] rocker and broke it, like into four pieces. I crawled into the bed after that. I couldn't even get up. I was in too much pain.

She said that the next day was a turning point in ending their relationship. "That night, I looked at him and said: 'You asshole.' And he just looked at me and said: 'You deserved it.' He tried to help me up, and I said 'Don't even touch me.' I walked into the bedroom.

"For the longest time, I bet close to a year, we didn't even sleep in the same room. I slept in the bedroom. He slept on the couch."

She said the alcohol compounded every problem, and made every normal situation into a trauma. "It was just that when he was drunk, he was really depressed and would start crying. Then he'd get angry and get mad and start throwing things. At one time, when we first moved up here, he was out at a Christmas party. He never even told me that there was this Christmas party he was having. He went right after work. I made dinner and everything.

"We were living with his parents at the time, and he said I told him that I could just kill him. I don't remember saying that. He ran into his dad's bedroom and got his dad's gun. At that point, I lost it. I had never—this may sound incredibly naive—but I had never seen a gun. And for him to take it out. I tried to lock myself in the bathroom. And he got in.

"I was sitting on the floor and I said, 'Get away from me!' And he said, 'No. You're going to sit here and watch me blow my head off.'

"I can't tell you what it was like. It was awful. It was really bad. I thought, 'Oh, you weirdo! You psycho!'

"After that, I was ready to leave him and just not come back. Take [my child] and go. She didn't need that. I didn't need that."

I asked where her husband is now.

"He's in prison."

At that moment, I looked out the window of her ground-level apartment and saw a large man approaching. "That isn't him, is it?" I asked, getting ready to flush my tape recorder down the toilet.

"No, he won't be out for a couple of years," she said.

Her husband had recently been arrested after unsuccessfully trying to kill himself on the expressway. He had gotten drunk, laid down in the front seat of the car, and gone head-on into two other vehicles.

Miraculously, only one of the other drivers was injured. Diana's husband ended up with a crippled leg.

This case illustrates how invisible domestic abuse and violence is; Diana said she never felt it was serious enough to go to the emergency room or a domestic-violence shelter. I had met her through a counselor at a local technical college. Diana had been taking classes there until she dropped out because it was too much to handle.

While this case sounds serious to me, she never got help. Part of the resistance to seek help through her years of abuse was due to her incredible isolation.

"I didn't know what marriage was like, and I wasn't sure if that's how it was supposed to be. I never experienced anything. I went straight from high school to being a mother and a wife, and I never got to do anything on my own. In high school, all I did was work and go to school, and never really went out and did anything."

In conversation, three men mentioned knowing about domestic violence as third-party witnesses. Rick Jaskolski, a fire fighter, said these cases were routine calls. One California, construction worker, said his co-workers often brag after work in a bar about hitting their wives.

Like women, men also expressed helplessness in fighting domestic violence. "I've lived in some pretty seedy places, and also some okay places. And never—I've had seven or eight apartments, including some in which I've lived with my girlfriend—was there not someone in earshot getting the crap beat out of them," said Ken Kurson, twenty-three, a Chicago musician.

"I called the police once and this woman swore nothing was happening. I met the police at the car another time and said: 'She will say nothing is happening. What am I supposed to do?'

"What is anyone supposed to do? Beat the guy up? She barely speaks English. She has all these kids. She's doomed. She's had it."

## Sexual Schizophrenia

As myths about violence abound, so do myths about women's sexuality in general. It is still something widely suspected, feared and misunderstood, as many interviewed have commented.

One persisting obstacle is the old double standard. Marita Vasquez observed that women who are single and have sex are still judged differently than men.

"Either they're complete sluts or whores. Why can't you be a normal person and have sex and feel okay about it, and not feel scummy or that something was taken away from you, like you were raped or something, even if you did consent to it?

"I think guys deal with it a lot easier," she added. "Sex is not a big deal for them. It's like a conquest for them.

"For a woman, it feels like you're having something taken away. I don't know. I feel like they're taking a little bit of your soul, really."

Mixed messages about sex tell women to do it, but since it is wrong, they shouldn't plan for it or do it consciously.

"That message is so strong that millions of women will go through an abortion they do not want or a pregnancy they do not want—that can be very painful in many ways—rather than get the pill," said Nina Chamyan of Students Organizing Students.

"That's the message. A lot of women, why don't they use birth control? Because they feel like sluts if they use birth control. That means that you want to have sex."

Chamyan said this is a particular dynamic in the New Jersey neighborhood in which she grew up.

"A lot of women I know feel like this. If a guy knows that she is on the pill, then that means that she is predisposed to having sex. In a lot of communities, in the Latino community, the fact that a woman is not a virgin is the biggest deal in the world. It might even make it difficult for her to get married. Yet like so many, women have sex in this community. But they all have it with their boyfriends, which they think is okay because their boyfriends tell them they love them. Okay, fine. All right. But they won't get birth control, because if they get birth control, that tells the guy that he's not the first one. And that's like the biggest thing in the world.

"So therefore, all these young women get pregnant. All these young women have to look for abortion facilities. And they aren't made available because it's a hush-hush thing in that community. You can take that example, that microcosm, and use it in every kind of scenario in the United States and the rest of the world."

## Gender: The Other Half

Another continuing personal battle for women is to feel comfortable with themselves.

During adolescence, something happens to drain their self-esteem. While women generally enter adolescence confident and assertive, they often leave with a poor self-image and a deflated belief in themselves. These are the results of a major 1991 survey of 3,000 children commissioned by the American Association of University Women. When elementary school girls were asked how often they "feel happy the way I am," 60 percent answered always. But by high school, it dropped to 29 percent. For boys, the figures changed less drastically, from 67 to 46 percent.

In just glancing at what girls are exposed to during that time period, some influences become clear. One obvious factor seems to be the especially tremendous pressure for girls to concentrate on their appearance and be part of a couple. The role models who teenagers constantly see profiled in their magazines, in fashion spreads and special contests, are models, not people who do things with their minds.

For women, this pressure is so great that they often feel as if they have to deny parts of their personalities or subvert their intelligence. In preparing to write this book, I talked to my feminist role model, Kristen, twenty-three, one of the most assertive and individualistic people I know, a graduate student at a Southern university.

Even she put on an act in high school as a "dumb blonde" for popularity's sake.

"My parents raised two sisters to believe boys are not better than girls. They were always encouraging us to do whatever we wanted to do," she said.

"Meanwhile, I was really affected by social aspects of school. I didn't feel accepted. I felt out of it. I wanted to have a boyfriend. I know I really changed a lot in order to be attractive to date guys, things like acting less intelligent than I was. I was blonder then, so I had long, blond hair and people would view me as a dumb blonde, and I would play the role."

Her appearance then was markedly different. In high school pictures, she resembles the classic prom queen, which is not a bad thing to be, but is a direct contrast to her present, more "hippie" self. I laughed because I couldn't imagine her looking any other way.

While growing up, the benefits of this "dumb blonde" behavior is constantly reinforced for all women. Acting intellectual gets you an electric jolt. Just think which has more prestige in most high schools: winning a state speech tournament or being a cheerleader. Think of who the "socialites" or popular people were at your school. On what standards was this based?

While Kristen became true to her identity, many women get so consumed in their men-pleasing roles that they neglect to please themselves. "One of the issues that I find is women become audiences for men in relationships," said Heidi Friedman. "Their words revolve directly around the men's choices and decisions. In terms of what goes on, you have women who say I want a career, not a man. But the desperation to find one is still here. I know many girls who went to college to find a husband."

"What's wrong with getting married?" I asked.

"There's nothing wrong with it, but if it controls you, it becomes the essence of what you're about, you're literally living with someone else's goals in mind. That's absolutely preposterous, and I would never settle for that."

The pressure may even intensify later in life in the "real world." One Cincinnati woman said tension from her family has continued since college at holiday time, with her other siblings paired off or married. "They say things about it, and you know everyone is thinking about it and you feel self-conscious. I thought, maybe I should just invent a boyfriend. I stopped going home for a long time because of it. I just couldn't deal with it."

Another pressure young women find hard to resist while growing up is the need to demonstrate certain socialized feminine traits, which may belie their own confidence and assertiveness. From all directions, girls are bombarded with subtle images portraying the traditionally feminine ideal of being passive. Sarah Edmunds, a television-commercial producer, pointed out how even the products her ads sell may have influence.

During our interview in her high-rise Manhattan office, she pointed to her shelves, which were stacked with videotapes and sugar cereals and snack foods.

"Right here, we have two products," she said, pointing first to one of two identically shaped boxes standing on the shelf before me. It was dark-colored with sharks as illustrations. "We have Shark Bites, which is a fruit snack aimed at boys, and it's kind of violent and it's aggressive."

Edmunds pointed to the other box, which was pastel. "And then we've got Berry Bears, which is aimed at girls. It's cuddly, a little family of bears, as opposed to the great white shark."

She pulled out a little plastic family of bears from the second box that were offered as prizes.

"It's the same exact thing. It's just different shapes. It is just marketed differently [with the thought] that little boys are going to prefer this, and little girls are going to prefer this. And little boys won't eat this because it's for girls."

She added that assumptions about what boys and girls like may also reinforce the stereotypes. "How can a four-year-old have an attitude about much? Or a six-year old? Why would they have an attitude, except for watching their parents."

Of course, snack foods aren't the only products instilling social norms. "You look at GI Joe and you look at a Barbie doll," Edmunds said. "You dress them up and play with them, but they do very different things. Barbie dates. GI Joe doesn't date; he fights battles."

## Language

While it is the area that most often makes feminists look trivial, language is an important and rich focus of feminist study. On a basic level, it can convey how deep-rooted sexism is as reflected in our culture's attitudes and values.

Just the common use of the male as the standard in forms of speech such as "*man*kind," "he" as a general pronoun or "chair*man*" illustrates society's perception of woman as "the other."

As with other women's issues, language reform has been an ongoing battle. Here is a convincing argument presented against the term "co-ed" by a University of Chicago student:

"There is a custom prevalent in western colleges where co-education exists of calling the young ladies attending such institutions 'co-eds.' Aside from the barbarity of this expression, it is discourteous and vulgar. As a joke, it is even too cheap for the average college wit. It is consoling to think that 'co-ed' has not yet received a place at the university. . . . The whole weight of the best public opinion at the university should be unfalteringly arrayed against any attempt at introducing this relic of the medieval way of looking at the position of women into the conversation and writings of the students."[14]

Although this appeared one hundred years ago in the *University News,* Nov. 1, 1892, it is still relevant today.

But this term is even more "medieval" now in referring to women, as they make up a majority of all undergraduate students, 54.8 percent, and 53 percent of all graduate students in this country, according to the 1991 Digest of Education Statistics.

In using inclusive language, people are making statements about women's identities. This feeling of not wanting to be "the other" is one reason some women keep their own names when they get married. Historically, society has defined a woman according to her relationship with a man.

Different ethnic and racial groups that have been seen as "others" are also defining themselves on their own terms, not on those of the dominant white culture. One movement is to substitute "women of color" for "nonwhite" or "minority." Using "nonwhite" is like using "non-Christian" to define a Jew or Muslim. It ignores a unique history, tradition and identity.

While "people of color" deliberately invokes the historically derogatory term "colored" people, advocates note its uniting power.

"We are women from all kinds of childhood streets: the farms of Puerto Rico, the downtown streets of Chinatown, the barrio, city Bronx streets, quiet suburban sidewalks, the plains and the reservation," write Cherrie Moraga and Gloria Anzaldua in *This Bridge Called My Back.*

This movement also follows a growing emphasis in feminism on recognizing differences in people. In the larger popular culture, the term "African American" to replace "black" is also more connotative of a unique shared culture and history.

But using nonsexist language isn't just a matter of principle. Insensitive terminology can show a real lack of respect for someone. On a deeper level, it can give women a subtle and continuous message that they indeed are the "other." This is one of a multitude of subtle effects forming women's identities.

But those interviewed, most nonfeminists and feminists alike, conveyed a sharp awareness of language and its effects. Those who were aware of the dynamics discussed feeling resentment when it showed lack of respect and exclusion.

Stephanie Boatley described why the use of "girls" felt condescending when she heard it used by Navy officials.

"I had to remind my commanding officer one day. He had addressed us as 'girls.' The first thing I think about when they call us girls is that you have to be eighteen before you can even join. If you're seventeen years old, they want your parents to sign. They want *women*."

Two women I interviewed at Columbia University told me they feel so strongly about uses of language in religion that it affects their choice of synagogue membership.

Theodora Langbaum said she was distracted when she came home during her school break to a synagogue without a gender-sensitive text. "I can't believe what I'm reading. 'He,' 'God,' all the kings. I don't say it out loud. I split it up. I say: 'My father, our Queen.'

"I found a synagogue twenty blocks down with gender-neutral language," said Beth Berkowitz. They say: 'Abraham, Isaac and Jacob, Sarah, Rachel and Leah.' I feel comfortable, but if I have to hear a traditional congregation, it pisses me off a lot."

## Poverty

With these feminist issues discussed, their connection to women's lives seems clear-cut. A definite factor of sexism is involved. But one of the most urgent and increasingly recognized feminist concerns is the feminization of poverty.

Some say this is the most widespread and continuous form of violence against women. The statistics of the especially high numbers of women hit by poverty give all the explanation needed. While the women's issues previously discussed affect everyone, women in poverty often face special complications, feeling more isolated and consumed in daily struggles.

With all women in poverty, no matter what the occupation or circumstance, the myths abound. Growing up in the Reagan era, many of my generation are apt to judge all poor people the same way, according to two-second, nightly news glimpses of inner-city life. The stereotype says that they are all black, have child after child to get welfare, and while away their days before the television set. The inclination is to blame the poor person for moral or mental deficiencies, instead of taking a hard look at education, employment and other societal factors.

Some of the stereotypes of poverty are rooted in stereotypes of race. Interviews with more than 200 white, black and Hispanic middle-income Chicago area residents in 1990 found widespread beliefs that race and poverty were linked, an assumption that makes it more difficult to create concern among white people for dealing with poverty issues. In a study commissioned by the Chicago Council on Urban Affairs, blacks were more likely to make distinctions between types of poverty and not lump everyone together in one hopeless group. They distinguished between temporary poverty, generational poverty, the working poor and the dependent poor. Blacks were also more likely to point out that the poor could be of any color and view the country's economic system as being unjust.[15]

The word "underclass" helps promote the stereotype that people in poverty are helpless, with their problems too complex and deep-rooted to ever be solved. But as reported in a three-part front-page series in the *New York Times* in early 1991, the late 1980s have produced "a wealth of research" and many new proposals for helping the poor.

While no one has any simple answers, what is most critically missing is a will to help, which includes: "a passionate leader to articulate it, taxpayers willing to pay for it, special interests that sacrifice for it, skilled administrators to apply it," writes the *Times* series author, Jason DeParle.

"It's a lie that nothing works," said Marian Wright Edelman, director of the Children's Defense Fund. "I think more and more people are realizing that. The fact is that we made dramatic progress in the sixties in eradicating hunger and improving the health status of children, and then we just stopped trying."

None of the prominent government and academic experts from all political realms quoted in the article advocated that funding would solve everything or turn our country into a socialist or communist state. But there was general agreement that our country needs some investment if we are to relieve poverty. People have turned their backs on the inner cities and moved to the outskirts, where they think they are not affected by the problems of others. With the gulf between rich and poor expanding during the Eighties, our country has been transformed from the United States of America to the United Suburbs of America.

No one will deny that there is a significant number of people shamelessly exploiting the public-aid system. But as with every system, there will always be exploiters. The newspapers regularly feature the conviction of the week of America's most esteemed financial wizards and pillars of the community for insider trading and embezzlement. This corruption and depravity would seem to indict the financial system. But, unlike with the public-aid system, no one from the mainstream press talks about dismantling the stock market or the savings and loan industry.

Some factors of poverty are traditionally women's problems such as those experienced by Diana (who was quoted in the section on sexual violence)—teen pregnancy, discrimination in pay and single motherhood. Like other single mothers, she has the additional burden of a lack of child support.

"He said he would rather rot in jail than give me money," Diana said.

For women in poverty, violence takes on a new dimension. While many from all backgrounds discussed the fear of violence as a constant stress, it is far worse for others. One Dallas single mother, Kim, conveyed the danger of her neighborhood in describing it as "just like New York." Like others interviewed, she is afraid to go out at night alone. But she is also afraid to go out during the day, even if someone is with her.

"You can be walking and minding your own business and shooting can break out," said Kim, who added that she has been in the line of fire several times.

Like the two other public-housing residents interviewed, she said she was at least grateful for what she has. The growing rate of homelessness, more and more affecting women, is also a "women's issue." While families in the United States typically own homes, three-quarters of those headed by women under forty-five are renters. They are also more likely to be discriminated against as renters with children and spend more of a proportion of their salaries on housing, according to *The American Woman: 1990–91* status report.

Kim's sister Tina told me that she once defended herself from a robbery with a knife. "There's a whole bunch of people who carry knives. But, see now, they don't carry knives no more. They carry guns. Because if you stab someone and you don't kill them, they'll get you whenever they get well."

For Kim, drugs are a women's issue. She explained how they affect her life as a single mother trying to raise her son, as well as others'.

"That's what our environment is full of today, and drugs is the most important issue. Just for example, if you have a single parent or a married woman who is involved with drugs, that is what's messing up the baby's life as well as her own life. That is why I would say drugs."

Kim had acknowledged that she was lucky in personally avoiding many traps of poverty. She has managed to enroll in a community college to get a teaching degree and is confident about being able to pull herself up.

But her sister Tina may not be as fortunate. Tina dropped out of school at the age of twelve to answer the siren call of the streets.

"I think that school is good for everybody," Tina said. "But then again, everybody ain't good for school."

For young women in high crime areas, the pressures to stay down are strong, and are getting stronger, observed Ruth Thomas, an administrator at Girls Incorporated, who knows both the sisters.

"It's hard for me to say this without a heavy heart, but [Tina] is pretty much typical of what is happening, with the drugs and prostitution. That is really happening to more girls now. Some of the girls who might have just been borderline, they still have a possibility of making it out, escaping some of those traps," said Thomas.

"But the traps are bigger now, in that particular area of town. It used to be just fourteen, fifteen, sixteen. And now it's eleven, twelve, thirteen. They're getting caught in these traps by thirteen."

Prostitution is an invisible but massive women's field, which has been both a last resort and chosen vocation. One section in *The New Our Bodies, Ourselves* quotes estimates that 1.3 million women in this country earn part or all of their living as prostitutes. This includes housewives and secretaries trying to make ends meet.

In the inner cities and other poverty-stricken areas, many forces are at work that set the stage for prostitution and drugs, which are often linked. Thomas described how the pressures worked differently to affect the two sisters. She said both started off with the same vulnerabilities in being in an unsupervised home; their father and mother, a housekeeper at a hotel, was usually away.

"[Kim], early in her life, she discovered God. She was a goody two shoes. Sweet Polly Purebread. [Kim] was not real, real, real smart in school, but she pushed herself. She tried real hard."

But she said Tina, "who is academically smarter than [Kim]," needed more attention.

"Tina took advantage of her freedom, whereas [Kim] would spend time at Girls Incorporated. [Tina] would just happen by. She was the kind of kid who was harder to get in and keep because of the pleasure she was having on the streets with men. She started dabbling with alcohol first, and then drugs. She discovered herself, discovered her body. She wore real heavy makeup, very heavy, as long as I've known her, tight, tight, tight clothes."

Tina explained that the streets are the best place for her. Although she said she has been raped, put in jail and almost stabbed, she said a life of prostitution offers her fulfillment she didn't get in school. She also denies that she has ever taken drugs.

"I may not be here tomorrow, I may not get everything done I want today, but most of it, yeah. When you're out there, you learn a lot."

Tina said her experience makes her a stronger person. With this job, she is guaranteed a roof over her head and dependence on no one. "I always made sure I had enough money to get me some decent clothes and underclothes and all that good stuff. I have always [taken] care of myself, and nobody can do it as good as me. Because I do it well."

She gave an example of how she protects herself.

"The best thing to do not to get diseases is to not have sex. But I do the next best thing: I have a suitcase full of condoms. Every time I go to the clinic, I get about forty-five of them. They give me about forty-five of them."

I asked how she decided to take up prostitution, and her answer was more bitter. "When you're out on the street, and you don't got no money or home to go to, it just pop right in your mind. That probably be the one part I hate about living my life, but then again, if I don't . . . ," she said, stopping for a second.

"I was looking at it then, and I still look at it now: ain't nothing comes for free. Everything has a price tag. And that's how I'll always look at life. You get some and give some."

Thomas was regretful about Tina and many others she has seen living in danger and wasting their great potential.

"But I have seen a real soft side of [Tina], where she cried and really opened up and really wanted something different," Thomas said. "I remember, it's been some time ago—she must have been fourteen at the time, before she became a real hard-core hooker and drug user—when she really wanted to do something different. She tried to get into alternative school–type programs and stuff like that. She was really needing a mentor, someone who could just take her over, who would just mother her.

"But the children, younger people, their needs outgrow what you're actually able to give them in reality. Their problems get bigger.

"[Tina] has always been emotionally weak, where she needed that extra arm around her. She didn't get it. She is looking for it right now. She really is. She's still a young lady. She's still very young."


## Racism

As with poverty and housing and health care, racism as a feminist concern may not be obvious at first to middle-class white women and men.

Barbara Smith, a distinguished feminist writer and editor, helped elucidate this at a speech in 1980:

"The reason racism is a feminist issue is easily explained by the inherent definition of feminism. Feminism is the political theory and practice to free all women: women of color, working-class women, poor women, physically challenged women, lesbians, old women, as well as white economically privileged heterosexual women. Anything less than this is not feminism, but merely female self-aggrandizement."[16]

MANY younger activists of all races, including about half the twenty-five women of color I interviewed mentioned racism as a problem feminists need to address. They generally agreed that it was more of a serious and ever-present problem in their lives than sexism.

As a white person in this society, I know well that white people are widely skeptical that racism is a serious problem. Many I talked with who brought up affirmative action in their discussion of the women's movement generally had this opinion: The civil rights laws are in place, the structure is there, and what is needed is to stop complaining and get to work.

This is a similar argument used to dismiss the importance of being vigilant against sexism. Laws don't change attitudes, and the efforts against racism go beyond issues of hiring practices. And to hurt someone, racism doesn't have to be expressed in a violent or blatant form, such as a full-scale burning of the cross on the front lawn.

As with men looking at sexism, whites also recognize the existence of racism. But they take it less seriously, are less apt to have examined and questioned their own attitudes and are much less troubled by it.

The very first step in confronting racism is recognizing it as a serious problem. As with sexism, many who are not the targets of racism do not realize what a constant and gnawing presence it is in others' lives. White middle-class people are not generally accustomed to putting themselves in the shoes of those looking on from the margins.

One person in particular conveyed this consciousness gap to me most strongly, like no other. She wasn't among those interviewed in the inner cities struggling to emerge from poverty. She wasn't from the South and directly confronting the Ku Klux Klan, like three black women I met at a conference who headed an antiracism group in North Carolina.

The person who taught me the most about the pervasiveness of racism, Nancy Harris, came from the same predominantly white, upper-middle-class suburb where I grew up.

We both attended and were competitive in the same grade school, high school, university and graduated with degrees having to do with communications.

But her experience with the same people and the same institutions —work and school—was different. Racism was a major variable. She expressed nothing life threatening, but enough to add another emphasis to daily life.

Like most other women of color interviewed, she indicated that racism was more of a problem than sexism. She seemed to waver and gave an answer representative of many people interviewed when I asked if she had been affected by sexism.

"I can't think of a specific instance, but I'm sure I probably have been since I have just gone from school straight into the working world, and where I'm working, it is all women—except for the people at the very, very top, who are all men, and I find that very interesting."

"What about racism?"

"That, most definitely. If I [thought] of anything, I would automatically think of racism. Oh yeah. Yeah. Most definitely."

I asked how, and she gave examples from her past four years working at a chain of women's clothing stores, one of the most popular of its type in the United States. She started out in sales during high school then worked there during college breaks. After graduation, while pondering the rest of her life, she was presently working as an assistant manager at various store locations.

During that time, Harris said she faced trouble with customers and bosses when she was stationed at two malls in white middle-class suburbs. But she said she still had problems at her current job in a more racially diverse shopping center.

At first she mentioned the most routine examples. "You don't get the respect. Everyone thinks that you're the salesperson. 'You're the manager? You've got to be kidding.' People really don't believe that. Or a lot of times I help people, and [then] they blatantly said that nobody was helping them, and that kind of stuff. I notice that. Why do you say no one is helping you, and I have been helping you for the past fifteen minutes? Even though we don't work on commission, it's probably the principle of it. I worked to try to help you, and then you say no one is helping you.

"And then I've heard of racist comments made by other managers. People have told me when they didn't know I was black on the phone, and they have said things about blacks and Hispanics shopping at their mall—how they only like the sale merchandise, etc., etc. I've heard a lot. I've heard an earful."

I asked her to elaborate.

"There was just one instance where another manager was talking on the phone, and she talked about how she hated her mall, and went on to explain why she hated her mall. I said, 'Oh that's very interesting.' She said people there were cheap and all they wanted to buy was Spandex, and she had all the blacks and Hispanics shopping at her mall, and all they bought were the tight, sleazy outfits and all the Mexicans were fat, and they would say: 'Oh, does this look good on me?' And it looked awful. She went on and on. I said, 'I have heard enough, thank you.' All this happened with her not knowing if I was Hispanic, black, anything."

I asked her if she confronted the same attitudes at all four stores at which she had been stationed. She said much depends on the person she happens to wind up with as her boss.

"Still we have one district manager that's over us, and she's in charge of your hiring and your promotion, and if she's prejudiced, you're not going to move as you possibly could."

Like those discussing sexism, she also cautioned that she doesn't blame racism for every setback in life.

"The thing with me, you don't know if it's because you're a woman or because you're black, or because you're both. You can't say. I hate when people jump and say everything and everybody is racist. You can't say that. You can't put the blame on anybody.

"But you must admit, there are a lot of things that happen and you have to ask why they happen."

She talked about the manager in one exclusively white middle-class area where she worked. Like others, Harris said she is able to sense when someone is especially racist.

"She was prejudiced. She treated me great, but I knew she was prejudiced."

"How did you know?"

"She made a comment to another girl working with me. And it's funny because you never know who you're talking to. She just made a comment about going to Bennigan's, and that she didn't want to take her friends there because it got a little bit dark at night. Her friend said, 'What do you mean?' She said: 'There are a lot of black people there at night.' "

But the complaint was not about hurt feelings. Harris said while the hiring of managers came from higher on the corporate ladder, those on other levels could be affected by the manager's prejudice.

"If she has that kind of attitude, what is going to make her hire black people to work there? Nothing. Why would she? You don't have to. If you can have a whole staff with no black people, you will. She didn't have a black person there until I was there."

I thought how when I worked different jobs, I never had to worry beforehand if the atmosphere would be hostile to white people. And I had sympathy, knowing the suburbs in which Nancy Harris had worked. She was not paranoid. As in the city of Chicago, many are segregated according to race, and a constant, often unspoken current of fear toward outsiders keeps them that way.

I asked her if she first strongly experienced racism in the work world. I thought about how our high school had no major publicized incidents of racism and how I never really noticed it there. I don't even remember ever seriously discussing the topic with anyone from there until after college graduation.

"I think I faced some in college too. I think I faced it in high school too, most definitely."

I asked her how.

"Even in just trying out for things, you notice that, it seems that they only want one black girl or one black guy and that's about it."

"What kinds of things, plays?"

"With plays, my God, unless you want to be the maid or something. With cheerleading, any kind of dance thing. It's amazing, in retrospect what you see. A lot of times, especially in the situation of this type, you think, 'Oh if I didn't make it, I wasn't good enough.' Then it brings down your self-esteem. Maybe I wasn't good enough. Maybe I am very bad. Maybe I can't sing. Maybe I can't dance. Maybe I can't act either. Maybe I can't do anything. That kind of stuff can really bring a person down."

I asked why she never discussed this back then among our scattered group of friends.

"Back then, I didn't talk about it, but I did notice things. In retrospect, you notice even more. In what you think, in what you think maybe you didn't think. Oh well, maybe it wasn't racism, or then you think I don't know what else it could have been, when you look back on it.

"As people grow and they mature, you can talk to them more about it. And if I can't talk to my friends about it, then they aren't my friends. If they don't feel comfortable talking about certain issues, then they can't possibly be a true friend."

## Lesbian and Gay Rights

Another "ism" that the activists mainly emphasized, but others did not, was "heterosexism" or "homophobia." Confronting this powerful force requires the same recognition and commitment as battling the other "isms."

Many explain that this is a women's issue because oppression of lesbians is based on the most extreme sexism imaginable. A lesbian is defying the most sacred traditional female role of male partner, and she pays for it.

These voices also have been invisible and isolated. When "in the closet," a woman may feel as if she is leading a fake life, and when out, the ostracism is strong. Family, friends, any past order can be shaken.

But conditions have changed dramatically in terms of visibility in the past twenty years. One remarkable example took place at the University of Minnesota-Twin Cities, the largest university in the country. In 1990, Susan Denevan, twenty-three, an "out lesbian," won the election as student-body president. A charismatic and dynamic speaker, she gained the endorsement of the Greek system and won the office by more than double the votes that any candidate had received in the past four years. Her campaign inspired students with a platform of co-leadership, activism and self-determination.

Such visibility is having an effect on the next generation. Lisa, a law student in California who didn't want her last name used because she fears later consequences to her career, said that more lesbians are feeling comfortable about living their lives honestly and openly.

"My clear view is that women have always—this number of women have always been dissatisfied with heterosexual relationships," said

Lisa. "The thing is that now it is a more visible issue—homosexuality —and they realize they don't have to be in heterosexual relationships."

She added that other social and economic changes made for women in the past twenty-five years have made this possible. "And now women aren't completely dependent on men to survive in this world. You don't have to get married anymore. So women who you are seeing as lesbians, seventy-five years ago they wouldn't have been."

As a result, she observed that unlike older lesbians, who were mostly married at one time to men, the younger women have more of an alternative path before them and don't go through that denial stage.

But she cautioned that the backlash is still strong and ever present, even living in a large city on the West Coast. "I have felt a lot of it. I have felt very isolated and alienated at school, to the extreme. I have felt ostracized and basically shunned by the general, more popular heterosexual students in law school."

The three women interviewed for this section said that they had also suffered strained ties with their families. "I'm lucky that they didn't disown me or something like that," said Jamika Ajalon, twenty-three, a Chicago artist. "Still, the initial response was that it's a white man's disease type of thing. It's abnormal. That's a part of me that they still struggle to accept."

The pressure to stay straight is so strong that coming out may require years of struggle.

"I didn't come out until I was twenty," said Lucy Baruch, thirty, a Rutgers University staff member. "Before that, I was very much trying to be 'straight and strong.' I already figured out that being a feminist meant that you'd take extra blows."

Coming out can be more of a challenge for women of color, said Ajalon. She said a great fear is the loss of support within their communities. "As a black woman, you know the whole thing: First of all, you're a woman, so you're discriminated against because of your sex, and you're black so you're discriminated against because of your race.

"At least in the black community, you can get support along the race issues and get fulfillment within that community. But because homophobia does exist to an extreme extent in the black community, even in the liberal organizations, it's hard to come out, because once you do, you're very ostracized."

She added that it is also more difficult in the Midwest and smaller towns and cities where a lesbian presence isn't as visible.

But all three voiced relief in finally making their decision to come out. "I mean, who wants to be a part of an oppressed group if you don't have to be?" said Baruch, who is also the organizer of a lesbian social and education group. "On the other hand, now that I'm a lesbian and comfortable with being a lesbian, I'm living an incredibly rich life. I have lots of friends I feel great about and work in an environment where I can be out."

Ajalon also said that she made the right choice in coming out, for herself and others who feel isolated. She gained strength through some women of color lesbian writers, and wants to provide the same hope. "That's one of the reasons why I think it's important for black lesbians to come out, because if there are more of us to say, 'We're very much a part of the community, and we're doing this and we're doing that, and we're strong and we're able,' more will come out. Pretty soon it will be like the Queer Nation," she said, describing a militant gay and lesbian activist group.

"Their slogan goes: 'We're here, we're queer, get used to it.' Soon people *will* get used to it."

## A Final Word

In naming "priority" feminist issues, the challenge was in narrowing down the list. I realize that everyone's most important issues are different, and a multitude were not discussed.

## Notes

[1] According to a 1990 study commissioned by the Fund for the Feminist Majority in Washington, D.C., done by an attorney, a former Indiana commissioner of Health and Human Services and a women's-rights activist.

[2] Fund for the Feminist Majority statistic. Measuring a year's time, taken from the footnotes of a legal brief, from American Civil Liberties Union, lead litigants.

[3] Ibid.

4 "Teenagers and Abortion," *Newsweek*, January 8, 1990, p. 34.

5 "Newspaper Apologizes for Editorial," *Chicago Tribune*, December 22, 1990, section 1, page 6.

6 Angela Davis, "Racism, Birth Control and Reproductive Freedom," from *From Abortion to Reproductive Health*, edited by Marilyn Gerber Fried, Boston: South End Press, 1990, p. 23.

7 *From Abortion to Reproductive Freedom*, from figures compiled by Dazon Dixon, Loretta Ross, Byllye Avery, Sabrae Jenkins, p. 157.

8 "Panel Decries Lack of Knowledge on Female Biology," *Chicago Tribune*, December 9, 1990, section 1, page 20.

9 Dave Gilden, "Different Stories: Women with AIDS." *San Francisco Bay Guardian*, November 19, 1990, p. 17.

10 *From Abortion to Reproductive Freedom*, from figures compiled by Dazon Dixon, Loretta Ross, Byllye Avery, Sabrae Jenkins, p. 159.

11 Linda Campbell, "Senate Study: Rape an 'Epidemic,' " *Chicago Tribune*, March 22, 1991, section 1, p. 11.

12 *The Secret Trauma: Incest in the Lives of Girls and Women*, Basic Books, New York 1986, p. 72.

13 "Domestic Abuse Leading Cause of Female Injuries," *Chicago Tribune*, August 22, 1990, section 1, pp. 1, 2.

14 Lynn Gordon. *Gender and Higher Education in the Progressive Era*, New Haven, Connecticut: Yale University Press, 1990, p. 396.

15 Sharman Stein, "Study Targets Stereotypes of Poverty," Chicago Tribune, January 30, 1991, section 1, pp. 1, 11.

16 *This Bridge Called My Back*, edited by Gloria Anzaluda and Cherrie Moraga, New York: Kitchen Table: Women of Color Press, 1981, p. 61.

# INFLUENCES AND ACTIVISM

*Chapter Eight*

# The Feminist Influences

IN CALIFORNIA, THEY know how to put on a real production. Even this concrete lecture hall, perched on a hilltop on the oceanside campus of the University of California-Santa Cruz, has the bustle of opening night in Hollywood.

As 2:00 P.M. approaches, a few teaching assistants race across the floor in front of the room as if they are trying to change sets between scenes in the theater. Behind them, operated by remote control, six enormous white slates used as blackboards, aligned three on the right and three on the left, shift places up and down over one another. The appointed students quickly rub off the lessons from the class before that were written in marker and list announcements: a book sale outside, a debate about the impending war in the Persian Gulf, a new discussion-group meeting. From the production booth in back, technicians are checking the microphones, video and sound.

A steady stream of women and men students flows through the side doors and takes up every seat. This is the type of capacity crowd that many college students have only seen form on the last day of class, when the semester review for the final takes place, and fresh, guilty faces fill every previously vacant row.

But the motivation here is not grades, and no one is taking attendance. This is the final day of the term in Bettina Aptheker's introduction to feminism class, which has become a cult course at the school. On the first day of the term, 850 students showed up, but only 500 were able to register. And this particular day is the most awaited session of the year, when volunteers give presentations to share what they have learned in the class, about women, society and themselves.

Aptheker, a writer and activist, walks to the stage with the same instantly hushing effect on the crowd as house lights dimming. Already, from past interviews in different feminist communities in the state, I have heard some refer to her as "the goddess" for her power to inspire and incite learning among the masses. She is a dramatic presence with a long yellow scarf, deep and commanding voice and large gold earrings.

But I will have to take the word of her students as to her teaching skills; immediately she hands over the mike to the first presenter and retires to the sidelines. By this time, sitting remains room only in the side aisles. This means that dozens of people are squatters like me, not enrolled in the class.

A young woman, Tara Somerville, quickly takes her place behind the podium and says that she is going to tell a story about her mother and her art. She explains why she never before gave her mother's passion the appreciation it deserved.

"At home, we never really talked about her art that much—except with maybe my dad grumbling about the price of another canvas or whatever. Not that he was a bad person or anything, but I think that we didn't respect her art as a career because she never made any money, really.

"After taking this class and doing research on women and art and discrimination, I realize how sad it was that we denied her support."

Somerville says she had dismissed the art, judging it by the established standard that something has to be commercially successful to be good. But then she discovered that throughout history, and still today, very little of women's art has ever been recognized. Although 40 to 50 percent of professional artists are women, the number invited to exhibit their work rarely exceeds 15 percent, according to a 1990 report by Eleanor Dickinson, national vice president of the Artists' Equity Association.

"I know that it is difficult for any artist to achieve a reputation, male or female. But I realized how important it is to celebrate women artists because they don't have a fair chance."

Then she announces "the long overdue celebration" of her mother's work.

The lights go off and a slide of the face of an old woman painted in watercolors appears. The crowd oohes and aahes as if they are seeing an unexpected fireworks show. While the skin on the portrait is pale and every wrinkle highlighted vividly, a witty and dignified personality emerges. In this close-up, a universe of experience can be traced in every line.

She announces the title: "Sometimes Broadway, Sometimes Catskills," and then others with elderly people in New York scenes: "Cold Afternoon in Central Park," "The Old Woman and the Toad." Some get laughs, such as "Do the Right Thing," of a stern old woman before a porno shop in Times Square.

Then the mood shifts from humorous to fanciful, with the muted colors turning bright, some paintings with abstract shapes and others with surreal scenes of people dancing around broccoli stalks.

Suddenly the gaping, huge lecture hall has been transformed into an intimate gathering. I have seen that through the semester, people have learned to trust each other, now feeling free to tell about personal experiences without hesitation or fear of betrayal.

After months of journeying, I had found women's-studies' Shangri-la.

But the dynamics of this class are not unique. As in other women's-studies classes, which have been multiplying across the country over the past twenty years, the old academic boundaries are being crossed.

Women's studies has mushroomed so dramatically that some call the discipline the reproductive organ of the women's movement. Since the first program started at San Diego State University in 1970, programs have grown to the count of 621 in 1990. From 1988 to 1990, there was a 20 percent increase alone, according to figures from the National Women's Studies Association. This number does not include the multitudes of other institutions that offer women's-studies classes without full-fledged programs.

With the added effect of the mutual growth of women's social-service centers and women's research centers, feminism has become an academic institution. At universities, it is becoming both a part of the system and a catalyst to change it.

Here and elsewhere, a tide of new forces that build on past organizing are combining to change the face of feminism for young women. Consciousness-raising in the Nineties looks different from what older people remember from the Sixties. But the inner workings of the process are the same. The new feminist influences still provide a safe space for exploration. Here, young women are teaching each other the meaning of the feminist phrase "The personal is political" by making connections between themselves and society.

And throughout, young feminists are also still generating the same controversy, fury and skepticism from outside critics.

As the class in Santa Cruz goes on, more presenters share their experiences and questions they have asked while learning about feminism through the semester. Like a few other students, Lee Rosenberg, one of the men, who make up about 10 percent of the class, discusses art's meaning to women in society. He contends that women are commonly portrayed as passive and victimized objects in popular culture, and begins by paraphrasing radical feminist and antipornography crusader Andrea Dworkin:

"A woman asks, 'Why doesn't woman create great art?' The traditional male replies, 'Because they are great art.' "

Rosenberg first explains that although he is presenting rap music lyrics, sexism is not unique to this medium, and it comes in the same proportions with heavy metal or punk rock. While he says he does not advocate censorship, he does stress taking a stand and being vigilant against woman-hating music.

"As you will hear," he says, "explicit lyrics essentially objectify women, glorify rape, condone and normalize violence that renders women inferior and nonhuman, and makes frequent and unconditional use of women's bodies.

"Finally, this basically reduces making love to two barnyard animals in heat."

The music follows, replete with every nonclinical word ever invented to refer to parts of female anatomy. Afterward, some women tell Aptheker that they were deeply offended to be subjected to this litany. But at the end of the class, while recognizing these objections, Aptheker also stresses the importance of education and exposure to form a feminist critique.

Another woman, Angela Hancock, appears on stage to give voice to other invisible women: "Hi, I'm Angela, and I'm going to do a slide show on lesbian imagery."

I look around, expecting to see people gasp and flinch but everyone here is completely attentive. She explains that both heterosexual women and lesbians from the class helped dramatize the scenes of people in regular everyday situations.

Before beginning, she quotes poet Audre Lorde: "Visibility which makes us most vulnerable is that which also is the source of our greatest strength."

The scenes begin with different humorous panels: "Aren't Lesbo Queers Cute?"; "Lesbians and their Cats, Of Course"; "Memory of Today's Love," with a sole older woman at a cello; "The Classic Park Bench Scene" of two women meeting.

The next speaker, Ayisha Knight, also dramatically breaks barriers in communication. She starts to motion with her hands to an interpeter sitting at a table before her.

"This class has been a real learning experience for me," says the interpreter, "in that it has taught me how to see myself as a woman. In terms of history, it has taught me that in order to move into the future, we must first learn about our past and how it relates to our present and future.

"It has raised the question: 'Who am I?' And is it okay to be who I am? I am a woman! But am I wrong? I am a strong woman! But am I wrong? I am a strong, black, deaf, beautiful woman."

She introduces one of the poems that she has written. "I think this class teaches us that in order to live and grow, this is a safe place for people, a safe place to trust one another. If I can't trust you, who can I trust?

"The invisible bond that links us together/ The key in our lives that unlocks the secrets in our lives/ But promises that open doors will never be exposed/ The relationship between you and me is very strong/ Because of the many invisible opened doors that you and I share . . ."

"My next poem is a tribute to interpreters, all interpreters. I'm sure that all of you have noticed that I'm not standing up here speaking."

The class laughs.

"I'm signing, and this is my own language. It's separate from the spoken language. The hearing and deaf world are basically separate worlds. But they come together through an interpreter."

She reads "The Magic Hands Speak," and the class responds by raising their arms and waving their hands. The motion sweeps over the seats. This is sign language for clapping.

"All right, you all know what to do!" she signals.

Some people share even more personal thoughts. One woman reads a poem about when she was raped. "Not all of life is pleasant," she says, in introducing her work, "as most of the lectures in this class were pleasant and easy to listen to.

"But, as my mother once said, 'Pain is what makes the soul grow. You need a little heat and a lot of tears just as the flower needs a little sun and a lot of water.' So, in order to grow, I wrote a poem about the rape."

Others also show the importance for feminists to look outward, as well as inward. The last speaker, Mary Whitney, brings home a political message.

"Children are the single largest group in the American society—and they have the fewest rights and quietest voices. We talk about children being our future and our promise. Political races are run and won over the issues of children and family, yet children are the most downtrodden of any group."

She lists statistics on infant mortality, budget cuts, and state laws about abuse.

With these issues, Whitney's stress is the importance of going from the passive to the active. "The treatment of children is a distinct issue because it is personally relevant to every single human being here. You either will have a child, have a child, were a child or live in a world that is going to be run by the children of today. The issues of child abuse, neglect and oppression will decide the consistency of the next generation, to make a decision that will govern our future. This is everyone's issue."

She becomes more passionate over the importance of social consciousness and seeing past one's own life. "To secure these rights, we must begin to see ourselves as child advocates, friends of children who speak out. It's not enough for any one of us just to do a good job with our own children or the children we know. We must have allegiance to children, all children. There is a pressing need for everyone to present children's needs to friends, relatives, labor, business, government— state and local and national—and to the press, radio and TV, to all of our citizens who ultimately decide how we spend our money. We must help children now."

She also provides some concrete tools for help: some contact numbers for children's agencies that had been written on one of the slates in front.

Afterward, Ayisha Knight, twenty, the author of the trust poem, sums up why women's studies can be so effective. The word "empowerment," which may already seem trite for its common use, is the key.

"I really love this class because it shows you how you can love yourself and respect yourself and be proud of yourself as a woman and not be afraid to be a woman.

"Oftentimes I take other classes and I walk around outside, it's a night class, and I'm alone. I've had various experiences where people have tried to knife me and different types of things, so I tend to be nervous. With this class, I just feel more confident to handle things better. It has improved my life in general."

For Knight and others, this class was emotional because of the detailing of many people's experiences. She suggests that I should take it to really understand the class's enthusiasm. "You're just going to cry a lot. Trust me. A lot of people after class, you see them crying, with tears in their eyes, walking home. I live on the other side of campus, and will be crying as I walk all the way.

"It felt good. It felt good to get things out. Many of the issues that were brought up in class made me feel uncomfortable. I wanted to leave. But I just had to sit there and get through it. Bettina gives you the feeling that life is hard, but you can get through it."

She says the class goes with her personality as a radical thinker. "I am the only deaf woman in the university. Last year I was the only deaf person here period. But I tend to think of myself as a trendsetter. I have to go out and break every rule. It's my responsibility."

Later, I visited another Santa Cruz women's-studies professor, Marge Frantz, sixty-eight, who explained why this class has such a powerful effect on so many young women. We spoke at her office, another reflective atmosphere. It was filled with an overflowing wall of books and had a spectacular view of the mountains. Santa Cruz is set up in the form of residential colleges, which each have the nature of a Thoreau-like retreat, set off in clusters from each other in the woods.

While Frantz attributed part of the enthusiasm for the class to

Aptheker's rhetorical skills, she stressed that the popularity of other women's-studies courses on the campus, at local community colleges and across the country attests to the appeal of the material studied.

"What's significant is she is offering people something for which there is a real hunger, which is enormously resonant in their lives," Frantz said.

"I don't think the answers are out there in the world just waiting to be plucked off a tree. I think you have to struggle for them. And I think that the success of women's-studies classes across the country is just phenomenal."

She stresses that what has been missing for young women is a chance to see what feminism is genuinely about. "What I really think about the subject of young women and feminism is that if they're exposed to it, they'll embrace it."

## Satisfying a Hunger: No More Junk Food

Other observers have noticed the phenomenon that happens when young women are exposed to feminism's fundmentals, without the distortions. Robin Morgan, the editor of *Ms.* magazine, said that she has received passionate responses from younger readers, who she said are starved for quality feminist information without artificial fillers.

"I think that what has been shown in the response to the new *Ms.* is that there is a real hunger for real food, no more junk food. Letter after letter says: 'I have been nurtured by this. I finish reading and I feel satisfied. I feel filled.' "

As in women's studies, empowerment is the motivating ingredient. She paraphrased young readers' letters: " 'It gives me stuff to argue with. It gives me statistics I can take out into the world and argue with others. It gives me that sense of ammunition.' And that's precisely what it ought to be doing."

This response challenges critics' underestimations of younger women, Morgan said. Instead of being self-centered, they have been interested in the wide social focus of the new *Ms.*—international women and diversity.

"I was told that young women wouldn't be interested in this because of course, they're all yuppies," Morgan said. "These are the media myths that are continually propagating 'postfeminism' and 'They won't care.'

"I have to tell you the response has been staggeringly wonderful," she said, giving a report in early 1991. "The subscriptions continue to pour in at the rate of about one thousand a week, newsstand sales are up when no one thought it could sell at all—without movie-star covers."

Morgan said the hunger is strong for a sense of social connection, even for those who don't necessarily feel great personal oppression.

"A lot of the mail is from women who are under twenty-five who say: 'Oh, well, so this is what feminism is about. I wasn't interested in feminism if all it meant was getting paid more, and that's important, but I have parity in my job.

"But if this is what it's all about! If all issues are women's issues, if I can in the process read about and learn about my sisters in countries I have never heard of. This is a real form of educating my life, and also the spirituality aspect of it, the fiction, the poetry, the theoretical analysis."

This hunger for feminism that has been observed can partly be explained by its self-affirming analysis for women. When women are put at the forefront of discussion, they feel new insight and inclusion.

As with analysis of race and class, a feminist analysis into identity can be an especially heady experience for young adults who are trying to figure out who they are.

"It was interesting to me because feminism addresses those kinds of issues of identity and values," said Debra Schultz, twenty-nine, assistant director of the National Council for Research on Women in New York. "That was my main preoccupation during those years."

One longtime activist, Susan McCarn, twenty-nine, a graduate student at the University of Maryland-College Park, explained how feminist analysis relieves isolation. She said it can expose personal attitudes and social forces influencing women's lives.

"We aren't being overtly blocked from opportunities, but our internal lack of belief in ourselves is still sustained by the culture. We're still presented as sex objects," said McCarn. "Even with professional positions, we're still presented as incompetent or unintelligent [even though] society pretends to change."

McCarn stressed how self-defeating self-blame is for women. "We go into that old place inside of ourselves as women to say it's our fault if we're not succeeding. It's still a sex-role issue, but it's not as evident anymore. So it becomes a therapeutic issue for young women, ready to come to this issue of self-discovery and self-growth, to recognize that our rights are still impinged upon."

McCarn added that feminist analysis could even expose self-blame in the most routine situations. "When men fail at something, they say it was chance or they asked the wrong question or it's an unfair task. When they succeed, they say, 'I did a good job.' When women fail, they say, 'I'm not good enough. I wasn't prepared.' When they succeed, they say, 'I was just lucky.' "

After hearing feminist theory, many are politicized or more politicized by issues in their lives; those most often mentioned were violence against women, abortion rights and being raised by a single mother.

Writing in a 1990 student anthology, *Now Hear This,* a Santa Cruz student from San Diego describes how analysis from feminist classes shed light on her family. After her parents' divorce, her mother, who had always been financially dependent, struggled to support the family while her father, a professional, shirked his responsibilities.

She writes that she learned to see her mother's helplessness in terms of how women have been socialized. "I do not claim to have all the pieces of the big picture, but I certainly have more now than I did when I left San Diego. Placing your family under the microscope of your political thinking does a lot to alter the way you see them. I know now that the change in each of my parents' economic condition after their divorce reflects a statistic in the United States that the man's income shoots up while the woman's takes a plunge."

But making the connections involves more than being aware of a single issue or problem. It takes making political connections, putting things in an overall perspective. For example, a fraternity sponsoring a workshop on acquaintance-rape prevention may not be feminist if not making connections to sexism and how it is a socialized attitude. It may be misleading to interpret the overwhelming pro-choice response of those interviewed as an indication that they are overwhelmingly feminist. While they could be feminist, they often don't see the issues in a feminist way, such as with women's rights being involved.

"There are a lot of people who are really aware of women's issues, or race, or talking about things like abortion, but they haven't put it into a bigger context," observed Tobi Walker, twenty-three, a graduate student at Rutgers University.

But many are making the connections between feminist issues and others. In becoming aware of and recognizing the dynamics of the united triumvirate of sexism, classism and racism, the world may never be the same. Young feminists interviewed say that it has a great effect on their lives in constantly transforming perceptions.

"All of sudden, things you never thought about before make sense. It just clicks, and you can never think the same way again. You look at things from a political viewpoint," said Walker.

She gave an example of how she makes feminist observations in everyday life. "You go to a film, and you think how this film deals with women. I went and saw *Pretty Woman,* and I really enjoyed it. I got out of the film, and I thought: 'What are you doing? What are you thinking? Why can't I go out and earn the money to take myself through Beverly Hills?'

"I get in this debate all the time with people I am involved with. They say, 'How could you always talk about this?' Like, it is just a part of my consciousness that I can never stop thinking about. Sometimes —I hate to say this—I wish I could stop thinking about it because it's so exhausting, so overwhelming. There are so many problems. It's depressing. You can think about rape, battered women, how women are being treated in the university. . . ."

This feminist consciousness can complicate life. Feminists are constantly trying to maintain integrity about their political beliefs with their most regular routines. Often the hardest and most vexing sexism to fight is one's own.

"That's the hardest thing, to live with feminism personally, structure my life so that I value other women, that I value other women's contributions," Walker said. "The hardest thing is when you see another woman walking down the street, and your first instinct is to say: 'What a bad outfit.' It's things like that I grew up with in high school where women were bitchy to each other. And it is the personal things like that I have to deal with on a day-to-day basis."

For feminists, trying to tolerate others' sexism is also a constant challenge. Anger appears in the most inconvenient of places. Different feminists have mentioned to me a "consciousness gap" between them and romantic interests. On a simple, harmless date, one can get suddenly annoyed with attitudes that were earlier tolerable. The challenge is separating oneself from fundamental feminist thoughts in trying to relate to people who have never thought about sexism. A comparison would be a black person trying to form an intimate and trusting relationship with a white person who hasn't thought about racism.

"I think what it does is it limits the kind of men I go out with because I expect them to be cognizant of the issues," Walker said. "And if they're not, they had better get cognizant."

Many feminists have come to the same conclusion in dealing with this new awareness. Walker said that she has found her own niche where she can personally make the most progress.

"You can start out really angry at the world, really angry at everything, but then you slowly have to sort of channel it together. You see the compromises and you see the realities of the situation, and you say, 'I can't change the world as much as I would like to. I can't rework it completely, but this is what I can do.' "

And she recognizes that every part of one's life can't be "politically correct." "I have a good friend, and we had a discussion a long time ago [about the fact] that there are so many things that you can boycott, and if you did, you would cease eating!

"What I have to do is pick the battles I want to fight. A couple of things to me that are very personally important: women's issues and within that, women in politics, women in leadership. And I work really hard at those," said Walker, who coordinates a leadership program for undergraduate women at Douglass College.

Many other feminists interviewed expressed confidence in a similar approach: cautious idealism. Like Walker, they stressed that a feminist view is so fundamental to them that it will last a lifetime. I asked Anne McMillan, nineteen, a student and feminist at American University, if she has any fears that her idealism is a phase she is going through.

"No, I don't think so, just because if I were to say: 'I will only eat brown rice to save the planet,' that might be a phase. But this is basic stuff about equality and tolerance for people's beliefs. It's relatively solid.

"I would be surprised if I woke up one morning and decided that I didn't want to be a feminist."

## Men as Feminists

I also found about twenty men, mainly in activist communities or who had attended "progressive" colleges, who stood firmly by their feminist beliefs. As with many women, instead of looking at feminism as their core philosophy, men tended to look at it within the realm of civil-rights issues.

"To me, it's the struggle for equality," said Tad Stephenson, twenty-seven, a graduate student working on his doctorate in political science at American University. "The women's movement in America stretches to the furthest reaches of the struggle for human rights."

Like many women feminists, he had a politicizing experience that has made him particularly intolerant of discrimination and aware of life on the margins. He is white and grew up in a predominantly black school district in North Carolina, where he felt constant tensions of racism.

"Coming from a closed society like I did, you either got along or tried to avoid black people as much as possible, and I learned to get along and appreciate the differences," Stephenson said.

Another motivation expressed by many feminist men is to improve the lives of men, who have also been harmed by unhealthy sexist attitudes. "I think men suffer because we have these stupid ideas of what it means to be a man," said Stephenson. "Each guy thinks he has to be a football star, excel in athletics, whatever, go out with an incredible number of women, be sexually proficient with everyone. It's just ridiculous. Men are so consumed with being macho that they can't even sustain a meaningful relationship."

A minority had experiences that made them empathize with women. An example was a friend who had been raped or had an abortion. Mark Halperin, twenty-five, a reporter in Washington, D.C., said he became a feminist while coping with a body image problem in college. Like women, he said, he illogically based his self-esteem on how much he controlled his eating and his appearance. Six women's-studies classes he took in college provided the base for his current intellectual framework.

For men, being feminist has different complications than for women. One leading feminist male writer, John Stoltenberg, has written about the special isolation these men feel. Their masculinity is often questioned, and other men are suspicious of their motivations.

I asked Stephenson if he gets trouble from other men about his feminist stance. "Yeah, I do. I get a lot of razzing. They say I'm an opportunist, that I just want to hang out with a lot of women."

But in some progressive communities, such as Santa Cruz or Amherst, Massachusetts, more men actually find it a popular stance. This makes some women wary of their motives.

"Before I got to school, I heard people warn to watch out for feminist men. 'They're just trying to get you into bed,' " said a student at Hampshire College in Amherst, which is also known as "the Happy Valley" in the western part of the state for its abundance of liberal thinkers.

Halperin explained that the biggest challenge for men comes from inside. While intellectually he is a feminist, he is constantly embroiled in a mission to seek and destroy his natural sexist attitudes. He said an early example of inner confict came from some experiences in the laundry room at college. While he was critical of other men letting physically attractive women jump the line for dryers, he found himself giving them the same privileges. Even today, overcoming his gut-level thoughts is a struggle.

"On one level, I feel distinct from most men, that intellectually, I know these things," Halperin said. "But I don't mean for a second to pretend that I haven't been coded. And I react to social situations, visual images of attractive women, taking orders from a woman in the workplace, in ways that are not dissimilar from men who I consider to have Neanderthal attitudes. While I don't behave the same way they would, I do have initial visceral and psychological reactions that don't differ in a lot of instances."

He added that feminism doesn't offer him the same personal understanding as it does for his female friends. "They are going toward a temple built for them, intellectually, emotionally and psychologically," Halperin said. "I can intellectually get there, but emotionally and psychologically, it just doesn't speak as directly to my concerns."

A few men also said that they feel pretentious calling themselves feminists and speaking for women, and prefer the term pro-feminist.

But the women were more definite in their reactions to the question of men being feminists. They overwhelmingly said they don't care what men call themselves, but they need their commitment to fighting sexism. An analogy is leaving only black people to fight racism, while the white people feel too "unqualified" to address it. But they also stressed that men should be careful not to monopolize debate or organizing because a vital concept of feminism is women taking control of their lives.

Women activists also gave uniform responses in pointing out the special personal challenges for male feminists. They emphasized that awareness or mastery of female rhetoric isn't enough, and that real feminist men have to constantly take on Mark Halperin's battle of confronting their own sexist attitudes. Men who are too confident about having overcome them may not understand the extent of the problem or may be complacent.

Farnaz Fatemi and Robyn Chapel, students at the University of California-Santa Cruz, said their greatest criticism is when male feminists lack commitment or integrity to their professed beliefs.

"Men will criticize women's images in the media and say, 'Oh yeah look at that.' And I'll say, 'Oh, good they're noticing,' and then you just wonder. Sometimes you know it's crap," said Fatemi.

"Sometimes you wonder if they go back with the other men and if they will stop a rape joke if it happens. If they don't stop a rape joke, all that criticism means nothing because they are letting it go on in their completely personal lives."

"Don't make me believe there's 'another man for feminism,' and then turn around and not be because it takes a lot."

Robyn Chapel said men face the same challenge as others in fighting for the rights of other groups. "If you're a man, you can walk away from feminism. And if you're white you can walk away from racism."

In discussion of feminist men, feminist women also made a strong comment according to what they didn't say. No one voiced a desire for men to become the rampant popular stereotype of a feminist man, a type I've seen comedians describe as "the Alan Alda sensitive man of the Seventies." The call was for a questioning of attitudes, not a change of personhood. No one wants men to change their personalities to become effeminate, pliable, castrated, squeamish and hypersensitive. A comparison again is that black people expecting white people to examine attitudes about race don't expect them to try to become black or abandon their own culture. The "sensitive man of the Seventies" is a media stereotype that is perhaps more inflexible and misleading than the one of female feminists.

## Women's Studies: On the Edge of Mainstream

For men and women, the most common form of consciousness-raising described was women's studies. These classes uniquely embody the same dynamics of consciousness-raising sessions of the Sixties, and are adjusted to people on the entry level in the Nineties. Starting at a common general stage of awareness, young people in the class have the opportunity to develop ideas together. Of critical importance is that they are seeing more than the stereotypes, which have often been their only frame of reference about feminism. For what is often the first time, they are meeting real feminists in person, who are suddenly demystified and humanized.

While women's studies performs this radical function and exists as the result of an experiment from the women's movement, it is losing its "fringe" stigma. Besides strict studies of feminist theory, women's-studies classes are usually cross-listed in other areas. People interviewed mentioned being influenced by law, history, anthropology, English, sociology, psychology or ethnic-studies classes that made links to women's issues or perspectives.

The classes are also growing in scope in terms of access. While the stereotype is of women's studies being established only in the refined cultural cradles of the Northeast, they are spread throughout the country. The largest region of the National Women's Studies Association is the Great Lakes (Illinois, Minnesota, Michigan and Wisconsin) with eighty-nine programs. Next are the mid-Atlantic states (Delaware, Maryland, New Jersey, Pennsylvania and Washington, D.C.). The New England, New York and Southeast regions follow closely, with the other regions having between twenty-two and fifty-five programs. The state of New York has the most, with sixty-nine programs of its own.

Students also are showing that they take women's studies seriously with majors or minors in women's studies. The most popular type of concentration is a minor, with 425 of the 621 programs offering either a minor certificate or area of concentration. One hundred eighty-seven of the programs offer majors.

One of the areas of most dramatic recent growth is graduate emphasis, which is most often done with a minor. In 1986, only twenty-three institutions indicated to the National Women's Studies Association that they offered graduate-level work in women's studies, but the number grew to 102 in 1990. Six institutions offer master's degrees in women's studies, with two being added in the last six months of 1990.

While the classes are still a luxury for most, in recent years they have gained a new accessibility to people of more diverse backgrounds and interests. This was conveyed to me in January of 1991, on the first day of an introductory class at Northeastern Illinois University, a state commuter school located on the North Side of Chicago. The course was being held at an accessible time—the evening, at an accessible location—El Centro, an extension in the Latino community, and in an accessible language—Spanish. Irene Campos Carr, the women's-studies program director who grew up in Nicaragua, was teaching, in English and Spanish, this first women's-studies class to be held there.

Compared to the Santa Cruz class setting of tropical splendor, this room on the second floor of El Centro is a different world. While the doors in the California hall could have been left open, the weather outside here is about ten degrees. Any presence of green life has turned brown for the winter. Two blocks to the east is the busy Edens Expressway, with traffic also heavy outside on Fullerton Avenue. During the lesson, every few minutes, the building shakes with a passing truck and, from time to time, a siren.

Outside, El Centro is inconspicuous, part of other storefronts on the block. Across the street is a gas station and to one side, a corner diner. I have to circle the block three times in my car with trucks tailing me and honking at me to speed up before I locate the door.

But inside, it is warm. The students, who appear to range in age from early twenties to midthirties, have their winter coats spread out on the backs of their chairs, which have been arranged informally in a circle. Like other women's-studies classes, the first day begins with defining the most basic concepts. In Spanish, Campos Carr asks: "What is women's studies?" She turns to the fifteen students looking at her with some doubt.

One woman answers in Spanish: "The way a woman develops and grows."

Campos Carr looks at one of the two men. *"¿Y tu Cesar?"*

He doesn't answer.

She persists. *"¿Que quiere decir? ¿Porque estudiar la mujer?*

*"No se,"* he answers.

One woman helps. Also in Spanish, she says, "Before, the men told her what to do. But, as the years have gone on, it doesn't have to be like that."

The next person speaks in English:

"It reminds me of the slogan, 'You've come a long way, baby.' That's what women's studies is all about. Our role is not only the wife and mother. Now it's that plus being where a man is. The focus is where we should be going with that."

Campos Carr nods and explains in Spanish some of the background. She says women's studies grew out of a focus of the women's movement of the 1960s and 1970s that put value on women's point of view, and also traces its large growth through the past twenty years. At Northeastern alone, there are sixty classes offered by many departments. One professor from the Criminal Justice Department conducts a women's-studies class that includes field-trips to women's prisons.

The women's-studies classes are often distinctive because they are not only about women who were famous, but about women's experiences in everyday life. "You all may only now know about Sor Juana de La Cruz, Queen Isabela of Spain, and maybe a few others," Campos Carr points out.

The methods are also important, she says. Women's-studies historians have gone through whatever they can find to reconstruct their realities, including personal artifacts, such as diaries and letters. Her recent work is about Mexican women working in factories in the Midwest.

One important principle is to be proud of being a woman, *elser mujer.* Campos Carr says that defying the stereotypes, feminists like her would not prefer to be men.

She goes through some basic definitions: gender roles, what society has defined as male and female; what a feminist is; what the stereotypes are of feminists.

"My favorite definition of a feminist, of feminism, is that it is a philosophy of working to change human relations between men and women, women and women, men and men, so that our relations will be more egalitarian, on the same level," says Campos Carr.

But she says she has had the tendency to avoid the label. "Here in the United States, we label everything. You're white, you're black, you're Asian, you're Puerto Rican. You have to have a label for everything. More than in any other country, we have categories. We need categories—'Who are you? How do you define yourself?' I don't like that.

"But it occurred to me, if I did not define myself as a feminist, it would be cowardly, like running away."

To illustrate the concepts she has defined, she points out some common experiences that show differences in the way men and women are socialized, such as aggression being looked at as a positive trait in males but as a negative one in females, and men acting confident and women apologizing when they speak.

The class offers other traditional characteristics of being female: gullible, shy, passive.

One student points out that what is described as manipulative is just a desire for equality. She says that her brother accuses her of being calculating with her boyfriend in wanting to have the same say in where they go together.

But another woman expresses some doubt about getting too involved with feminism. Tradition is too important. In her marriage, she prefers her husband to have the final say and earn more of the money; that's how she has been raised.

As with the other points, this raises a flurry of questions.

For many women's-studies students, part of the power of the class, as with the issues discussed by Campos Carr, comes from analyzing the current issues in their lives. But, as she mentioned, some of the attraction is filling in the gaps of lost, neglected and forgotten history.

Tobi Walker said that her identification as a feminist began after a class at Northern Arizona University in Flagstaff.

"I didn't become cognizant of being a feminist until I took my first women's-studies class, until I took 'Women in Western History.' I loved history when I was in high school, and when I got into the class, [the teacher] just ran off a list of women from Western history. I didn't know one, maybe Pocahontas or Sacagawea. It was like someone had broken this big intellectual bubble I had about what a history machine I was, and said: 'You didn't know anything. You haven't had an education.' "

Marge Frantz said she noticed that most students have a large gap in knowing history, especially that of women.

"If you take a class with one hundred students, and ask them who hated high school history, 90 percent will raise their hands. They just hated it. It was a lot of memorizing and rote stuff, and it did not include women—except for Betsy Ross. Give me a break."

But a sense of women's history can give women a new feeling for the discipline. Schultz said that it inspired her to become a historian.

"You read this stuff and you see how it relates to you, to women and your family, to friends. For me, being a historian, to think that we're having experiences today women 2,000 years ago were feeling and experiencing. . . . Also, a lot of it is different. What is it about women's experiences we can know and share and understand?"

Women's studies is also a unique medium for passing the torch, with the sharing of experiences between older and younger women. When asked to name a feminist role model, the most common people mentioned by those identifying themselves as feminist were their women's-studies professors.

Carla Pommert-Cherry, twenty-eight, a graduate student at Texas Christian University, said that she is still inspired by her feminist teachers at the University of Virginia in Charlottesville whom she knew more than six years ago. Now she is considering becoming a professor to provide a similar strong role model for young women.

Pommert-Cherry especially remembers one unconventional women's-studies professor who brought her baby to class, and put it under the care of a student who would go outside at the threat of disturbance. What she admired was the professor's approach to uniquely and defiantly combining her family and work life.

"I just thought that she must have a lot of confidence in herself and didn't care what other people thought," said Pommert-Cherry. "Because it was her baby and her classroom and her life and she wanted to combine those things. She wanted her child to be exposed. She wanted to be around her child as much as she could, and as long as her child wasn't distracting other people, she wanted to make that happen. I thought it was a brave thing to do."

The several women's-studies professors interviewed said they find meaning in serving as role models and also passing the torch to the next generation of feminists. Marge Frantz, a longtime labor organizer, said that now many women who were activists twenty years ago have finally been in academia long enough to get tenure and feel bolder in their teaching.

"I try to make room in my class for all kinds of opinions, but nonetheless I make it clear to people that I have point of view and I express it," Frantz said, "and it's very strong and I get people excited about radical political movements and activism, and it's just incredible to me. I just feel wonderful about it. Because you can't help but care about passing the torch if you are a political activist. If you have led a worthwhile life, you care about passing the torch."

Pommert-Cherry stressed another common lesson of women's-studies that is especially jolting for the white middle class. For the first time, many are being exposed to and studying the experiences of women with different backgrounds or pressures.

In one class at the University of Virginia, "The Psychology of Oppression," she especially remembered shattering stereotypes. One of the requirements was to work with women in a domestic-violence shelter in Charlottesville. The students' duties were general coverage of the shelter, answering phones, babysitting and helping the women become independent. Pommert-Cherry said this last part helped her to better understand the behavior of battered women and the importance of empowering them. As in other women's-studies classes, the boundaries between college and the "real world" were often crossed.

"There is always that question why a woman would tolerate such abuse, especially if her children are being abused as well. I think, after talking to those women, you could see the kind of trap that they would fall into.

"You could read about that in a book, but if you could see firsthand a person who doesn't even know, who hasn't the vaguest notion of how to find a place to live . . . If they don't get some help and they don't have somebody to take their hand and help them through the process, they are never going to get out of that abusive sitation. If you don't have a checking account or a job, how are you going to get out of an abusive sitation?"

In the classroom, along with those at the vanguard of feminist theory, women's studies generally seems to be encompassing a broader and more inclusive analysis. Women's studies is slowly changing with feminism to have more of an emphasis on diversity.

Back at the University of Illinois in Champaign, I talked with Carol Neely, who has taught an introductory class for three years. When she started, women of color writers and lesbian writers were grouped in a separate unit of study. Now they make up the mainstream of people studied throughout, with half the writers studied being women of color and 15 percent lesbians. I know personally that this is a dramatic change. Three years ago, when I took two women's-studies literature classes there, almost all the authors were white and the other forms of oppression or diversity were hardly an issue.

With this generally increased emphasis on inclusion, women's studies is taking on even more power. Women of different backgrounds and experiences are finding it a safe place to explore all facets of their identities.

"I think it's important that people be validated. As a lesbian, it's important that my life be validated. To a black woman, it's the same thing. Our life experiences as women are very different," said one former Rutgers student.

But across the country, women, especially women of color, are indicating that the change has been too slow. Candy Wilmot, twenty-five, a student at Brooklyn College, who is in a minority there, being black, said she was frustrated in a series of women's-studies classes at different city universities that only featured one woman of color writer.

"All the women writers they throw out to me are white women," said Wilmot. "Everyone's like, 'Yeah!' but I say, 'I don't understand.'"

Wilmot said many don't realize that her identity is not addressed without this emphasis. "It's like being in a room with sixty-six people and three are people of color and sixty-three are of European descent. And they say, 'Why do you always raise that issue?' I say, 'That is the issue of my life. It is the issue.'"

To compensate, she is making her own minor in African studies, conducting separate research and doing an internship at nearby Medgar Evers College, which is 95 percent black.

But many women of color are no longer sitting back when they feel racism is not brought to the forefront. In women's-studies classes across the country, the atmosphere is growing increasingly volatile. The

1990 National Women's Studies Association national June conference was an indicator. It came to an abrupt halt when a group from the Women of Color Caucus walked out in frustration that their issues and racism within the organization were not being addressed adequately. Since that time, the pages of feminist publications have been filled with open letters from both sides calling for a truce and deeper dialogue.

In Carol Neely's fall 1990 introduction to women's-studies class, the atmosphere has been charged with tension. Neely, who is white and has a classic training in Shakespeare, describes her class three years ago as "placid and polite." But now, with the numbers of men, of activists, of older students and students of color growing, discussion is more heated and confrontational with more challenges to the curriculum. While Neely said much of the effect is positive, with more voices being heard and more meaningful connections being made, it has been a rough battle. Often students express anger openly and Neely has also been a target of criticism.

Attending a November class, I felt the familiar dry radiator heat of the English Building, along with a new tension in the air. The assignment was a group presentation on the representation of women, gender and sexuality in a song by a popular performer as a way for students to analyze gender roles in the culture they live with. One group of several people of color took pains to explain the relationship of racism and sexism as barriers in one blues singer's life. A man who asked a question was blatantly ignored by another male giving the presentation. One white woman appeared almost in tears when she told about the misunderstanding in one singer's life that reflects the misunderstandings in the classroom.

After class, in her office, Neely looked beleaguered. She said she does not know how to make the class more inclusive. New conflicts had also appeared that semester with clashes between groups wanting their issues addressed. She said one group of black students complained that they felt they were taking "Lesbian Studies 111," which caused bitter feelings among the more silent lesbians in the class. Some students said they did not see the connection between homophobia and oppression; a lesbian could choose not to come out while a black person has no choice.

Neely was concerned that the intense arguing over a variety of issues had intimidated some of the freshmen. They had been silent, unable to understand the connections between issues without even a basic understanding of sexism. She quoted one exasperated freshman who finally raised her hand and said: "I'm a freshman, I don't understand any of these issues. What do you want me to say?"

One of the most outspoken people in the class, Susana Vasquez, twenty, explained why she and others are trying to make race a stronger emphasis. While she agreed that the authors in the course were diverse, she said analysis of the white authors had to go deeper, such as in questioning an assumption that was racist or classist.

She agreed with Neely that the tension in the class was also reflecting the overall campus atmosphere, which is growing more tense around racial issues. People of color are becoming more visibly organized and vocal, and white people are feeling more threatened and confused. The women's-studies classes provide a needed forum for them to discuss racism and connections with sexism.

Vasquez explained why the class was more conducive to this discussion. "I think that in women's studies the reason that these issues come to the forefront is one, out of necessity, and two, because it's a comfortable environment. The tables are turned. The class is predominantly women, so you don't feel silenced by men. Also, other classes won't say that they are going to address sexism and racism. Here, it's acknowledged that these issues are fair game, maybe."

She also said that finally the numbers of women of color have made a difference. "And then in our class, I think that women have spoken up because there are seven of us in the core vocal group. It's a magic number. When there are two, you aren't strong enough."

Another challenge for women's studies is the inclusion of men as students. One Mount Holyoke student said that when women are first learning about feminism, they often feel anger, which males could easily interpret as being directed toward them. They also often talk about personal matters and might feel inhibited by the presence of men.

"I don't think it would work with men in the class," said Katherine Woolverton, twenty-seven. "We do so much tearing down of the power structure that men's lives are based on, that they gain their power and identity from, they would just feel attacked all the time."

Of the six males interviewed who have taken women's-studies

classes, about half said they felt tension in their women's-studies classes. Mark Halperin said he didn't let it stop him from making women's studies a minor while he was an undergraduate at Harvard. He mainly had to watch that he didn't talk too often and generate resentment by taking over discussion.

"Some women totally rejected me out of hand, and said I was making a mockery of it and was a voyeur, based on some psychological manifestation," he said.

But he also pointed out that what most mattered was the teacher accepting him, which usually happened once he turned in his written work, which conveyed his interest and dedication.

The most resistance to women's studies seems to come from those who have never taken a class. Only a small minority of the core group of one hundred nonactivists interviewed had taken a women's-studies class. The most common reasons were lack of space in the schedule, lack of interest or a suspicion that it would be biased or "a bitch session" filled with complaints or cries of victimization. Like other feminist concerns, women's studies is often perceived as "preaching to the converted."

"My roommate had a women-in-politics class, and she said it was the most irritating class she ever had," said Suzanne Mayer. "The woman who taught it was a domineering figure. A lot of what was there was interesting, but a lot of it had a lot of hype in it too."

Some who major in women's studies also commonly talk about being accused of their work not being as academically rigorous. "My parents were outraged I was a women's-studies major," said Jennifer Callahan, twenty-six, who teaches English to immigrants in New York City and attended Brown University in Providence, Rhode Island. "They made me have a double major, history or English, or they wouldn't pay for my education. I really lost a lot of respect for them that they would do that."

Women's studies has also been the target of criticism at a larger academic, theoretical level. As a feminist institution, women's studies often defies tradition. Opponents contend that these subjects are a form of political brainwashing and censorship of ideas conspiring to foment anarchy in the curriculum. The main voices of this view have come from columnists from the major newspapers and the newly formed National Association for Scholars. One argument is that they don't mind working toward multiculturalism, but objections arise when other cultures are glorified, or study of them is made compulsory with special classes or supplants the traditional studies.

Writing in the winter 1990 National Women's Studies Association newsletter, editor Debra Humphreys answers in defense:

"Those of us who want to discuss issues of race, gender and class and who dare to suggest that American society is a less than an equitable one are accused of political indoctrination. By contrast, courses taught primarily by white men on history, English and all the traditional disciplines with scarcely a mention of women, people of color or nonwestern cultures are somehow 'objective.' "

Despite the criticism, women's-studies' philosophies are growing to reach other disciplines and create a more inclusive curriculum. In 1990, there were a reported one hundred projects at different universities to restructure their curriculums. Columbia University has restructured its "Contemporary Civilization" curriculum; one student there said she appreciated reading Simone de Beauvoir's *The Second Sex* as an important volume in Western civilization. In 1988, Stanford's required course on Western civilization was renamed "Cultures, Ideas and Values," and was revised to include women and minorities as well as studies of non-Western cultures.

While welcoming this spread of fresh and more inclusive ideas in the classroom, many working within women's studies say that separate women's-studies classes are still important. They help compensate where progressive integrated curricula are not present and also provide a feminist critique lacking in many disciplines. While a work by a woman could be read in an English class, it might not be looked at with a feminist analysis.

Other feminist institutions on campuses—women's research centers and social-service centers—are building bridges between the academic and practical worlds. In 1990, 818 higher-education centers had at least one of the three, which accounts for 25 percent of all the accredited institutions in the United States, according to statistics from the National Women's Studies Association.

The research centers, which number more than seventy, mostly are housed in academic institutions. They often feature forums on women, libraries for scholarship and grants for research. Some of the first were established in 1974 at Stanford and Wellesley, with the National Council for Research on Women forming in 1982.

Schultz described the gap filled by the research centers. "There was no central place collecting and promoting research on women. There was very little research done on women to begin with, but what was done was done by a few isolated individuals who had no sense of other people asking the same types of questions."

Like women's studies, the focus of research is also growing to be more multicultural. In March of 1989, NCROW launched a project to introduce research on women of color into undergraduate curricula at thirteen member centers.

One center that represents the pinnacle and culmination of efforts from women's research is the Center for American Women and Politics at Rutgers University. Founded in 1971, it has been a respected clearinghouse for information about women and politics.

Even the geography and appearance of the center command the respect of an established institution. It is housed inside the Eagleton Institute, a dignified three-story white house at the end of a winding road on the edge of campus. Inside, the flowered red wall and Victorian furnishings have a stately aura.

I climbed three flights to the CAWP office, where I talked to Lucy Baruch, thirty, the information services coordinator, who explained how the center serves as a bridge between academic and political communities. Through its scholarly research, educational and networking programs it helps women of all political bents to get ahead.

Like other research centers, it serves to empower women through knowledge and mutual support. The premise of CAWP and other programs is that more women in leadership will lead to better representation of women and their special concerns.

Director Ruth Mandel is employing the same principles for women to help each other get ahead as men at Harvard and Yale have historically been doing for each other for centuries. The old-boy networks are being emulated with some new-woman schemes.

"There's a very basic underlying view here," Mandel said, "that the only way in which women are going to make any progress in the public sector, or in any other domain, will be through mutual support. Women must support each other, whether through votes, with money, through contacts and access, or information. The more women come together across state, party, age, racial or ethnic and class lines, the more they will help themselves and women everywhere.

One program associated with the center involving young women, the Political Leadership Education Network for women, helps get women started as leaders. Established in 1978 and housed at fourteen women's colleges around the country. It sponsors training and skills workshops, mentoring and internships.

One PLEN participant, Lisa Harris, twenty, a student at Douglass College, an all-women's college within Rutgers, said she noticed a difference with her summer internship through the program. While she doesn't call herself a feminist, she said she appreciates the emphasis on women helping each other. She worked with another black woman, Diane Lynch, the chief of staff of the Department of Health in New Jersey.

Harris compared the experience to a past internship with a man, who didn't take a personal interest in her learning. "She made sure I had everything I needed, that I had all the research, made sure I knew who to get in touch with. Daily she asked: 'Are you okay?' Not because she doubted I was capable or competent, but to assure me that she was there. She was constantly encouraging me."

Like the women's research centers, women's social-service centers are fulfilling old needs in innovative ways. But more than women's-studies classes or research centers, they are based in student communities. The purpose is to provide for the underlying personal needs in women's lives that may affect their academic studies and to provide an established political feminist voice.

Jennifer Callahan said that a primary feminist force in her life was the Women's Center at Brown University in Providence, Rhode Island. "I went to the women's center with a friend. I liked it there. Everyone there I had so much respect for. They were so articulate and interesting and honest, and I wanted to be like them in a way."

One of the primary functions is to provide resources, whether reference books, health information, counseling or rape crisis hotlines. The space at Columbia University resembled a handful of others I had visited throughout the country: a narrow room in a student-activities building, filled with rows of books and made hospitable by posters with images of women and comfortable chairs for lounging.

At Columbia University, some women hanging out after a meeting explained the function of their women's center. "A woman can be a feminist, and she can know other feminists, but it makes a difference having some place or some structure that you know is going to be there, whether a woman's-studies class or support group," said Megan Bartsch, twenty-one.

"It definitely provides a medium for people to talk," said Carolyn Farhie, twenty. "If I say, 'Yo, I'm fucking really mad and want to talk about something,' I could bring it here and maybe they can help me solve it."

This feminist presence is even invading the most traditional of schools. Organizers at Harvard/Radcliffe emphasized the purpose of advocacy for a women's center they were pushing to establish. In June 1990, petitioners made the *New York Times* by gathering more than 1,000 signatures for a center to be built in or near Harvard Yard. Organizers said one goal would be to pressure the administration to increase hiring and granting of tenure to women and minorities.

At Hampshire College, the women's center is serving another political purpose. Staff members said they want it to expand its focus and become a catalyst for thought on other issues of social justice. Like the women's movement, women's centers are taking on broader issues and seeking alliances with other activist groups. The Hampshire center had recently sponsored a panel on racism, classism and homophobia and was beginning to network with others interested in human rights.

"One of the big problems Hampshire has is working on single issues. It's not that people don't see a larger issue, but I definitely believe they can get overwhelmed trying to deal with it all at the same time," said Tracy Turner, twenty, a student who works at the center.

She and a friend showed me other work being done by the women's center, including a literary magazine, *Jane Doe,* and a brimming monthly calendar of programming.

The women's center at Hampshire was the most centralized of any I visited, located on the main level of the airy student-services building, across from the library and food stop. Like the University of California-Santa Cruz, Hampshire College was built as an alternative, experimental college in the early Seventies. It occupies an expansive field, formerly an apple orchard, and has simple, boxlike concrete buildings that defy the traditional qualities at nearby Amherst, Smith and Mount Holyoke colleges.

At Medgar Evers College in Brooklyn, the women's center is also evolving with student needs—but serving a more essential purpose for daily survival. From the outside, the college resembles an oasis. The building is modern and angular, looking as if it belongs on the Upper East Side of Manhattan as an addition to an art museum, but it is surrounded by more downtrodden storefronts in the Crown Heights section. The Center for Women's Development is housed inconspicuously in a narrow hallway of offices within the confines of the counseling center.

Here, academic struggles are usually only the surface problems of students, said Safiya Bandele, director of the Center for Women's Development, who also does work with the National Black Women's Health Project based in Atlanta. Seventy-five percent of the students are women, and a majority of that group are single mothers.

"When we talk to the college administration, [we say the center] represents the difference between staying in college and dropping out of college," Bandele said.

The average student is twenty-eight to thirty-five years old and is adjusting to returning to school. They are often saddled with added responsibilities as the heads of households, live in substandard housing and work in the lowest-paying jobs. Many are also immigrants from the Caribbean with special challenges to gain access to the educational system and become independent.

As with other women's-student programs and centers, establishing this one did not come without a fight. In 1982, demanding child care and a women's center, the students took over the college as a result of "insensitivity on the part of the college administration—insensitivity to the needs of women at the college," Bandele said. For students, the center now provides counseling, advocacy for dealing with government agencies, health information and moral support.

While black women have always organized in their communities, the women's center is a prime example of their more recent visibly organized feminist presence. A thick brochure about the center's programming sums up its philosophy of empowerment, which is based on a women of color counseling model. One quote from Lillie Allen of the National Black Women's Health Project says it all: "For too long now, we've been told to keep our business to ourselves. . . . Well, the business of silence is killing us. We must begin to tell our stories."

In relieving this isolation, Bendele said the center is effective with its holistic approach, in not separating a woman's academic needs from her personal ones. "We look at a woman's life experience when she comes in for help, whatever the obstacle in the way of her empowerment," Bandele said.

Arlene Parker, forty-three, a program associate with the center, said the center hands out doses of self-esteem and self-knowledge for empowerment.

"Our major concerns and the major reasons why the center is here, is that we see women, our sisters, coming in here with very, very low self-esteem and low confidence," said Parker. "And those things are disabling, and the consciousness-raising and the education in a formal and informal setting affords women the power of personal empowerment. That personal empowerment kind of transfers to economic and social empowerment, and those things are important to all people, in particular for women in this society, in this world."

Bandele also emphasized a spiritual approach that is often an essential ingredient in organizing among women of color. During my afternoon there, the sense of sisterhood between women was so strong that it was almost tangible in the air. "We take into consideration the fact that African women, most women, we suppose, but African women we know, are very spiritual," said Bandele. "And in their healing, we must take into consideration their spiritual needs."

The work of the center also extends to the community in advocating for housing, prenatal care and child care. It gains strength networking locally, nationally and internationally with other women of color groups. One new education program extends to men, prisoners in pre-release centers, who are in the transition phase between maximum-security prisons and their old communities. The center educates them and raises their consciousness about rejoining a family with a single mother and the pressures she has faced.

"We fill in a gap. These are men that have been in ten, fifteen, twenty years. They don't know the reality of black family life. So we talk about the issues, particularly women's issues, how women's issues have evolved and women's concerns and how it's something they shouldn't be afraid of or fear."

She said so far the reaction has been positive. "They write us and say so: 'It was an eye-opener.' They didn't know black women were doing these things."

## Women's Colleges

The feminist institutions of women's studies, women's centers and research programs are sometimes seen as a balance to build equity at co-ed schools. But at women's colleges, the entire institution is already inherently feminist.

As with other feminist academic structures, young women are building on the work of their elders. Like historically black colleges, women's colleges were originally founded to provide an education for those shut out of institutions of higher education. As women have increasingly entered the mainstream over the past three decades, the number of women's colleges has fallen from a high of 298 in 1960 to 94 in 1991.

Although other colleges are open to women, the nineteen women I interviewed who attended or who had graduated from women's colleges across the country voiced no regrets. They said they appreciate the power of separate spaces for women to develop their identities and form a consciousness about the world around them.

"I think so many women's colleges have become radical—in fact, it's all about subconscious dynamics—but, in fact, women are put down so much in this society, that when you put a bunch of women together and invite them to take each other's ideas seriously, they can't help but realize they have been oppressed and they begin to challenge the oppression," said Susan McCarn, who spent a year as an undergraduate at Barnard College in New York. "It's endemic to the nature of putting a group of women together."

But I really didn't understand the feminist sense of these schools until I personally visited a women's college. While in Massachusetts in the fall of 1990, I decided to get to the heart of women's colleges by checking out one of the oldest, Mount Holyoke in South Hadley, founded in 1837. With a deeply religious foundation, the school was originally a "seminary" school for women. Its purpose was to train women to earn a respectable living outside the home, mainly as teachers, in the changing industrial economy, and to enhance the public sphere with their "inherently" moral characters.

In my wildest stereotypes, I imagined a feminist commune Utopia atmosphere, each student sitting under a weeping willow, her hair pulled back in a band to resemble Virginia Woolf. They would be reading depressing poetry by Sylvia Plath and Anne Sexton, most likely, and buying things with Susan B. Anthony dollars.

And what about the real issue here: the lack of men? I remembered my friend's co-ed dorm floor at Northern Illinois University that I had termed "the Den of Iniquity." How did these schools attract so many women who were willing to live without guys, especially in these most experimental years of one's life?

But my most serious fear and criticism before visiting was that these women's colleges were isolated and sheltered. I was thinking about this point as I arrived at the Mount Holyoke campus one Tuesday evening in October at dusk. The drive from Amherst in the student shuttle was a thirty-five-minute journey down winding rural roads. We entered the campus, a classic collegiate public-relations-pamphlet paradise of winding hills, streams and falling leaves in rich decorator colors. I walked across the lawn between the seemingly ancient buildings and residence halls, all encrusted with ivy.

I walked up the steps of the residence hall and looked at the pillars and the wide wooden porch. It was so quiet, too quiet. No stereos blasting, no motor scooters knocking me over on bicycle paths. I thought how painfully dull it must be here as a college reporter without fraternity gang rapes, CIA research or NCAA violations to investigate.

Once in the door, I met my contact, Heather O'Connor, seventeen, a sister of a student I had recently interviewed in New York. Although she had little idea who I was, she gave me a warm welcome.

We went to the eating hall, where dinner had just started. We sat around one of the long round tables with O'Connor's friends, and I was startled when a waitress came to take my order. O'Connor said that some were fighting against this service. Another vestigial tradition was the nightly ritual of the residence hall staff putting out milk and cookies. I remembered O'Connor's brother's warning that the campus was an eerie facsimile of the set of "The Facts of Life," a television sitcom.

People at the table were friendly and curious about what I was doing. I asked how they knew about this school. Many had family, aunts and grandparents who had been there before. After dinner, for the first time in a few weeks, directly following my New York trip, I was actually relaxed, with the conversation coming easily. We walked up the stairs, which looked like those inside a house, not an institutional residence hall, and went to the room of O'Connor and her roommate. I talked briefly to their friend Jennifer Rochles, seventeen. Like everyone there I interviewed, she didn't choose the school for its all-women's status. Instead, she liked the less competitive atmosphere.

She explained how people's contributions were valued in the class. "If I'm in a class and if I don't feel like talking that day, they will single me out, and teachers will encourage people who don't talk to speak up. I think that's important to learn when you're in the first year because you feel intimidated by the new environment."

I thought how mature she was to say this. The reason I liked my classes freshman year was that I was usually left alone to contemplate life in peace.

Another woman at a women's college told me later that she couldn't explain why, but it was also easier for her to speak in a group of women. They both said it was easier to take a risk and be wrong and not spend so much time going through the answer in their heads before speaking.

Rochles also added that she was a science major and felt more supported in a setting in which a quarter of the women had the same concentration.

Then I asked her the big question: What about having no men?

"As a matter of fact, I really don't even notice it," she said. "That might seem strange because it's really evident that there aren't any men around. But it isn't like when I see one, I go: 'Gasp! A man! I haven't seen one in so long!' "

She said that she has a boyfriend anyway, and the strong feeling of friendship among the women there was important. "I think my friends in high school were good, but here it's this huge family, and I really love it. Everyone here is so supportive, so interesting."

Next on line was Radhika Ramanan, twenty. She told me she had a women's-studies discussion session, a virtual gold mine of material, and I could sit in and interview people.

We entered another ivy-encrusted building across the campus, and the class trickled in, on time. Ramanan said I wanted to know about women's colleges, and the response was strong.

"I have learned to appreciate it more," said Ramanan. "The first year, college in general is new to everybody, so when I came here, I didn't notice it as a women's college. I liked it, I had a lot of fun, but I would have had fun anywhere.

"I didn't suddenly wake up one morning and realize anything. But during my second year here, only after learning more about myself and society and this school, did I come to appreciate it."

"I really, really ended up loving it here. If I could do it over again, I would," said Diane Greenfield, twenty-one.

But will it be a shock when they enter the real world?

"This is my first year here, but I'm a Francis Perkins Scholar," said Katherine Woolverton, who explained that that meant she was an older student. "I've been out in the real world and this is a wonderful haven. For the first time, I'm reading history and reading about women. I'm taking an anthropology class and reading about women. I have been at community colleges and art schools, and it's the first time the focus has been on women. It strikes me how subtly validating that is to me as a woman, spending all my time studying about women, no matter what the subject of the class is."

Kimberly Cate, twenty-one, said that she feels a similar boost in science classes. "I'm a chemistry major here, and I really notice the difference in science. When a machine breaks down here, it isn't automatically assumed the guy has this mechanical or mathematical mind to fix it. You're expected to try to fix it. You're just treated very differently here."

I said I didn't want to sound corny, but did they have a feeling of "sisterhood" here?

They nodded, but qualified the answer. A few said that it doesn't compare to the exuberant sense among the older alumnae who visit.

"I think part of what we're doing here is we have to be very focused on ourselves so we can't be as embracing as we could be out of school," said Woolverton. "You are alone in the academic goals and avenues you are pursuing, and there is a lot of opportunity to come together— but there is a lot of pressure and a lot of work."

After talking longer, I went back to the residence hall and interviewed two younger people who said much the same, but also had some different angles.

O'Connor agreed that the women's college allows students time to explore their own identities. "I definitely feel I'm forced into a place where I have to develop my own points of view. For instance, I was dating a man for two years, and we broke up two weeks ago, and I realized that over those two years—I was sixteen when I met him—I hadn't developed any true opinions, that we shared all the same opinions. Most of them I developed because he had such a strong argument for them. And I didn't have any strong arguments back. Now I am beginning to realize that."

Two students interviewed at Mills College in Oakland agreed that the women's college experience is unique. They were even willing to help shut down the school the year before when board members threatened to make it co-ed.

"It's hard to put it into words," said Angela Gibney, twenty, "but when you have the opportunity to be in an environment where you are looked at for your mind and you are challenged by other women mentally and academically and you have a lot of role models who are women, it takes away all those extra things: what you are looking like, all the sexual pressures, a lot of the things that women have to deal with first."

At Douglass College, Lisa Harris explained why she doesn't mind being "sheltered" at an all-women's institution. First, she recognized that Douglass has the benefits of being part of Rutgers University, which is co-ed. (She also pointed out two other women's schools, Trinity and Mount Vernon colleges, in Washington, D.C., which are in an urban and more diverse setting.) Contrary to popular belief, Harris feels that her school actually better prepares women for future turmoil by building their confidence and making them more aware of how to face the "isms." Without competition from males, women also get more practical experience in taking leadership roles within the college, such as with student government or school publications. Harris said she hopes this training will help her in her future goals to enter public office.

After these conversations, I understood why many leaders have emerged from women's colleges, such as Geraldine Ferraro, who ran for vice president in 1984, Gloria Steinem and Betty Friedan.

Douglass College dean Mary S. Hartman emphasizes this point in an article in the July 5, 1990, *Chronicle of Higher Education:*

"We have undeniably impressive data on women's colleges. Their graduates are twice as likely as female graduates of coeducational institutions to earn doctoral degrees; their alumnae made up 42 percent of the women members of the last Congress; they graduated fifteen of fifty leading corporate women cited in an article in *Business Week,* even though they accounted for only 5 percent of all college-educated women in the relevant age group."

Other less famous graduates from women's colleges interviewed told how they are still influenced by their education. Besides the help in careers, they mentioned an influence in their identities.

"In retrospect, I feel that it has really shaped me," said a graduate of Barnard, Sarah Pressman, now attending Rush Medical College in Chicago. "This is kind of silly, but I'm going skiing tomorrow, and I want to bring a sweatshirt, and I have both a Rush Medical College and a Barnard College sweatshirt. I decided I would bring the Barnard College sweatshirt, because Rush Medical College is what I am—I'm going to be a doctor—but Barnard is who I am.

"I think it really has influenced me. The whole message was that we could do whatever we wanted to do as women, and that there was support for us."

While Douglass is a public school, at other women' colleges that are predominantly private, the cost is more prohibitive. Many of the colleges mentioned that are private, such as Mount Holyoke and Barnard, cost—with room and board—upward of $20,000 a year. While 55 to 60 percent of students at both institutions are receiving financial aid, the dilemma is the same as with most private schools. Besides the poor, they often exclude middle and even upper-middle-class women who don't qualify for scholarships, yet cannot afford to pay this vast sum.

Like all schools, women's colleges suffer from a declining pool of students of college age. And women's colleges have a special challenge in attracting students while maintaining high standards. Currently, according to statistics widely quoted in 1990, just 3 to 11 percent of high school women say they would consider a women's college. This attitude was partly behind the crisis at Mills College, which almost went co-ed. In 1990 the undergraduate population was 777, more than

200 under the 1,000 total the administration claimed it needed to meet its $23 million operating budget.

The stereotypes of women's colleges also run deep. One nineteen-year-old woman from a Catholic co-ed but formerly all-women's school said she is constantly asked if she wants to be a nun.

Heather O'Connor said when she chose Mount Holyoke, she was the target of jokes at her high school. "Oh, yes, at first it really upset me, and it still does. I get so sick of it. I really shrug it off. This one young jerk that I know, whenever he sees me, he says, 'What are you, a dyke, going to a women's school? You go to a dyke school.' I never really thought it was funny, and when I asked him to stop, the more he did it."

## Take Back the Night

Beyond and on the college campus, older women planted the seeds of feminism around specific issues. Young people are following their lead in organizing and breaking the silence on what was forbidden only a decade ago.

As stated in previous chapters, one of the most politicizing issues has been sexual violence. Farnaz Fatemi and Robyn Chapel, who edited *Now Hear This,* an anthology of feminist essays at the University of California-Santa Cruz, said that violence against women was the most influential factor cited. They were compiling autobiographies of women's-studies students tracing the growth of their political consciousnesses.

Fatemi and Chapel said that the politicizing effect was stronger than the pro-choice issue because liberal feminists often see the latter as an issue of privacy more than women's rights. With violence, women could more easily see a personal threat in the present system.

The impact was universal, whether people had or had not been directly victimized by violence, Chapel said. The contributors often recognized violence as a constant fear that made them feel dependent on men and powerless. Starting from this issue, they made connections to other forms of violence and harmful ways women and men are socialized.

While similar investigations are being made in women's-studies courses, perhaps the major catalyst for feminist analysis of sexual violence occurs at rape crisis centers. Every middle- to large-sized city has one, with others being housed in hospitals or shelters, according to the National Coalition Against Sexual Assault. These institutions embody the most basic of feminist philosophies as visible institutions that relieve the isolation of survivors. They also give legitimacy to a crime that others had suspected and not seen as real.

In uncounted communities and towns, feminists fighting against sexual assault have also taken to the streets with their message. Across the country, annual events largely sponsored by rape crisis and other women's centers—"Take Back the Night" marches—are building solidarity and awareness. They commonly take place as educational rallies and then marches down the most public of streets as a statement of women taking control over their lives.

In a 1990 documentary by a former Santa Cruz student, Jenai Lane, twenty-three-year-old Jamie Lee Evans, who works in Oakland, explained that the message goes beyond warnings to strangers:

"When women are out there marching in Take Back the Night, they are telling not only the man in the bushes, but they're telling their husbands, they're telling their boyfriends, they're telling their brothers, their uncles and their guy friends: Stop doing this. We're not going to take this anymore."

As with other feminist institutions, what was most radical before has now penetrated the mainstream. The first Take Back the Night march was in San Francisco in 1978, undertaken as a stand against pornography and violence against women. More than 5,000 women from thirty states who had met for a national conference entitled "Feminist Perspectives on Pornography" staged a march through the city's pornography district. The march spread the next year to New York City under the auspices of Women Against Pornography. Take Back the Night is one of the most powerful remnants of the now diminished antipornography movement.

The concept for marching against violence has even gained popularity in Waukegan, Illinois, a factory and naval-base town between the Chicago and Wisconsin border, partly surrounded by a string of wealthy suburbs. In the fall of 1990, the Lake Coalition Council Against Sexual Assault (LaCASA) held its second annual Take Back the Night in Waukegan's downtown area on the Lake Michigan shore.

On that clear September evening, while the sun was distant but still shining, the first speakers, young survivors of sexual assault, told their stories. Standing on the rolling green hills and around the white park gazebo, a large crowd of mothers, fathers, high school students, young adults and children stood at attention. On the sidelines, an interpreter for the deaf did sign language and another spoke Spanish.

I saw three teenagers with a long banner reading "Youth for Peace and Justice." A family with a husband, wife, son and dog also joined the crowd with signs. Present were representatives from the Girl Scouts and local churches. About a tenth of the 400 people there, as tallied by LaCASA, were men.

As we marched through town, one counselor boomed through a horn: "No more date rape, no more lies. We will not be victimized!"

A few men in business suits exited a bank with perplexed looks on their faces. The crowd chanted: "Wherever we go, however we dress, no means no, and yes means yes."

Passing the Lake County Police Department they yelled: "Don't blame the victim, change the system!" and stopped to hear speeches by the county sheriff and city police chief about making the process less traumatic for victims.

The next stop was the Lake County Courthouse, where the state's attorney and then a judge spoke about LaCASA's strides in the community in building awareness.

"I want to thank LaCASA for sensitizing me as a judge to meet your needs. Never give up on the children, give them a second chance," said Barbara Gilleran-Johnson, an associate judge assigned to juvenile court.

During the march, children were a common theme. LaCASA has sent volunteers to educate 5,000 students in public schools throughout the county.

Nightfall came minutes later, and against the sounds of a band's drumming in the background, I talked to two young college women. They had come with an independent group from suburban Rosary College, a Catholic school predominantly attended by women that had become co-ed a few years ago.

Like others interviewed, this march was their first, and it assuaged some of their fears about feminism.

"I've never felt this much energy outside of high school pep rally," said Ann O'Hagan, nineteen, who comes from a small Idaho town. "It's great to see adults with a common goal coming together for something other than a football game. I enjoy seeing that a lot."

She was also impressed at the diversity of people at a feminist event. "I enjoy seeing men here. I really didn't expect as many men. I like to see the children, parents bringing their children. I'm really impressed with the energy, the community coming out and cheering it on."

O'Hagan said this is the first time she has felt this sense of the power of people organizing together.

"I'm an education major and want to work with children. I want to know what I can do, and I like the spirit and knowing that other people care about children as much as I do.

"To me, a child is a strange and beautiful gift. I would hate to see anyone hurt or abused in any way, especially sexually. It's such a demeaning act, I don't know, it's an awful crime. So I'd like to know how to prevent it and see others [who] feel the same way I do, from all walks of life. We have got everybody here."

She looked to her best friend, Brigid Maher, nineteen, from another large Catholic family and a small town, this one in central Illinois. Both had dark hair and freckles and were dressed preppy, with penny loafers and cardigan sweaters. O'Hagan held a white carnation.

"With important issues, we stick together," said O'Hagan. "We do these things together, and it's important. It gives you a really good feeling, like you're doing the right thing."

"It feels good," said Maher. During the march, she said she was making a stand about the sexual harassment that all women have experienced.

I ask O'Hagan about the black button on her shoulder, which said "Just what part of no don't you understand?"

"I get real frustrated with people who make me explain myself when it's something you can say yes or no to," she said. "If I tell somebody no, I don't have to explain myself. I say no. That's it.

"This is my favorite button in the whole world."

They had made the trip to Waukegan because of a friend who lived in their dorm who interned at a nearby social-service agency. "We were at a hall meeting, and she told us there was this great march going on against sexual harassment, and you can't tell us there isn't a person here who hasn't been harassed, if not abused, in any way. It's important. We need to make a stand. We have to do something. We have to let people know we aren't going to take it," O'Hagan said.

I asked them if they consider themselves feminists, but they said they still didn't know enough about it. Still, the march was educational.

"One of my educators started bringing it up and said, 'Now people are going to start accusing you of being feminist if you take a stand' and all that. And I never thought I was a feminist. Seriously, I thought feminists were people who never shaved their legs and burned their bras and fought for votes," said O'Hagan.

"I learned they are not an eccentric group. They are a group fighting for the rights of women."

She said that she has recently started to take some flak in her hometown for the new views she developed at school.

"When I went home for the first time, a lot of people accused me of being that. But I don't know if I should say 'accused.' In a way, it's kind of exciting. And I felt yes, I've learned a lot more.

"People have got to learn that feminist is not another 'F' word. It's a movement, and it's a powerful, good movement people have to give credit to instead of being scared and saying, 'Those dykes from hell.' They have to say, 'There are a lot of young women working toward things that our daughters are going to thank us for and appreciate.'

"You can be a small-town girl from Idaho and still be a feminist," she declared.

For others with previous feminist exposure, the Take Back the Night march was also a source of support. I asked another young woman why she was attending.

"I'm here for the spirit of unity and people united," she said. "I'm here because I'm a volunteer and a rape survivor, I find a lot of comfort in women and being with other people who have gone through similar experiences that I have gone through."

Throughout my interviewing, other people recounted similar scenes of antirape marches that galvanized their feminist instincts. Take Back the Night was especially mentioned as a growing phenomenon on college campuses.

Leslie Gates, twenty-two, a researcher for a nonprofit group in New

York City, said she got involved with feminism while helping to organize two Take Back the Night marches at Princeton through the women's center there. In 1989, after members of all-male clubs jeered a small march of 100 people, 1,000 rallied for a second action.

Back at Columbia University, one student said that a Take Back the Night march there helped demystify feminism for him, especially seeing other males rallying in support.

"It helps to break down the image of 'castrating bitches'," he said.

As at some Take Back the Night marches, at Columbia, only women were allowed to march. For educational purposes, men could attend the rally. Gillian Greensite, a rape-prevention educator at University of California-Santa Cruz, explains in Jenai Lane's documentary that this separation is a political statement about women taking control.

"Take Back the Night is an occasion where women can experience safety without it being on the grounds of a man being around, and obviously that can't happen when men take part," says Greensite. "So it's not an antimale statement. It is much more an expression of the one moment in your life of feeling safe without the accompaniment of a man. And that's really eye-opening."

The Columbia student said he didn't mind the separation: "I don't know what it's like on other campuses, but the first time I went, I was really moved by it. It was really powerful.

"There was a woman explaining an incident that happened. She said maybe it was her fault, and everyone said it wasn't her fault. She kind of stopped, and the crowd forced her to say it wasn't her fault. It was the first time she probably said that to herself. It provided an amazing function."

But while Take Back the Night marches have become more acceptable and widespread, they still have not lost their radical edge. One common observation is that these marches seem to threaten and alienate male onlookers. During one I covered at my university, I remember passing through the freshmen co-ed dorms and hearing a litany of obscene shouts and threats from all directions.

Christine Porter, nineteen, a sophomore at the University of Maryland-College Park, described a similar scenario at a recent march of about seventy-five people on her campus. She said outsiders interpreted the event as bashing males, and one participant received a threatening letter afterward that warned she would be raped.

"We were marching past male dorms, and we would yell, 'No means no,' and they would yell back, 'No means yes.' People were really hostile," said Porter. "People were offended."

For participants, no matter what the reaction from onlookers, another jolt can come after the march. The feeling of security is so strong at the event that leaving it can be a letdown.

After the Waukegan march ended, I went to a gathering in the basement of a church, where people were drinking cider and handing out information. In a corner, children were coloring. One girl was drawing a peace sign with the label: "Pease."

On my way out, one of the organizers, Valerie Walker, told me, "Be safe." As soon as I climbed up the stairs to the sidewalk, I realized I wasn't sure how far away I was from my car. But instead of asking for directions, I thought I would find my way by myself. I had parked on a major street and knew it had to be close.

As I walked on, I saw the streets were deserted, with lights on banks and city buildings shut off. I could hardly even see the sidewalk. Soon, while feeling for my keys in my coat pocket, I started moving more briskly and then was almost running. After a few blocks, I found my car, standing alone by a meter on the wide and empty street. I quickly opened the door, did my cursory check for the looney stranger hiding in the backseat, got in and secured the lock.

Immediately after leaving the group, reality had resumed. Now, back to our regularly scheduled programming.

## Pro-Choice

As discussed in previous chapters, a more visible feminist influence of the past decade has been the abortion-rights movement. Through the media, Americans have seen a glimpse of its power in public media-transmitted marches. While all forms of organizing are important, marches, like those against sexual violence, have the unique power to convey the spirit of the masses and educate others to the issues at hand.

A surprisingly high number of the feminists and activists I interviewed recalled a particularly memorable consciousness-raiser, the

April 9, 1989, massive abortion-rights march in Washington, D.C., which was sponsored by the National Organization for Women.

While covering the event as a college reporter, I seemed to be witnessing a clear movement right before my eyes in the tidal wave of people sweeping through the Mall. I had gone from writing about abortion under fire to feeling the overwhelming support and energy of thousands and thousands of others my age.

The makeup of the crowd revealed a particular group that older feminists before had hardly, if ever, publicly recognized: college students. NOW president Molly Yard estimated that between 100,000 and 200,000 students, both male and female, many of whom officially represented their fellow students from more than 500 colleges and universities, took part.

Many schools, especially those on the East Coast, sent relatively large proportions of their students, who arrived in several bus loads. One student told me that Macalester in St. Paul, Minnesota, and Brandeis University in Boston were represented by about 10 percent of their student populations, and about 1,000 students from Harvard/Radcliffe rallied behind their schools' dual banner.

Janelle Rodriguez, nineteen, a sophomore at Berkeley and a member of the state board of California NOW, said this was her first exposure to feminism. On the day of the *Webster* decision, later that summer, she got arrested with twenty-five other people from ACT-UP, the AIDS activist group, at the foot of the Supreme Court stairs.

"Those were probably the two most empowering experiences of my life," she said. "It was like I was taking a stand. I was saying in the only way that it could be said at that time that I knew how, that this was intolerable.

"And I remember when we broke the police lines and got up there, there were hundreds of people there, and everyone started chanting and clapping."

Like others interviewed, Rodriguez said the pro-choice movement was a channel for her to follow her yet unexpressed feminist convictions.

"This was the first way I knew how to get involved. There were no active groups in the area. I had no idea. I always wanted to get involved, but didn't know how to do it, until I heard about the April march, just by chance. So I said this is it, and this is how it starts. That is something I had always wanted to do with my life, be an activist."

Others have been mobilized by local and campus pro-choice organizing. In Albany, at the State University of New York, I interviewed five members of the new Students for Choice group, who told similar stories about the pro-choice movement's influence on their becoming feminists. After the *Webster* decision, as at other campuses, a group had formed that has become a major presence in campus politics.

One member had been influenced by the Washington, D.C., rally and brought the fight back to campus. "It was so wonderful to see all those men supporting women's reproductive rights," said Robert Purvis, Jr., nineteen. "It really makes me crazy that men have the nerve to put laws on women's bodies. It's so sexist."

Purvis, one of two men attending a Students for Choice meeting of about twenty people, said he first became political about the issue in high school when two friends, a man and woman, told him "they were in trouble and needed help." He gave them money, his car and helped them locate a clinic.

"Right after that, I became active in the pro-choice movement to make sure every person has the right to have an abortion because I saw that not having an abortion could have ruined their lives. It was very scary to me."

As it had for Janelle Rodriguez, the movement gave these activists the support of a feminist community. "It introduced me to people who thought the same things I did, and that's empowering," said twenty-year-old Gina Knarich. "It's not [just] a crazy thought of mine."

One student became more aware of the threat to abortion rights and went to a meeting of Students for Choice, which she had heard about from friends. After getting more involved, she took a semester off from school to organize a campus pro-choice newsletter.

"For me, it was very much a politicizing issue. In December of 1988, my mother was raped, and so there were a lot of issues of anger, of why is it that women are taken for granted and are such a usable commodity, that this is encouraged by people's passivity.

"And then I found the pro-choice issue, and it gave me a channel to work for women's rights and to work for my self-respect and the worth of my body to me. There is nothing as politicizing as seeing an entire institution—meaning our government and medical institutions—built on your demise."

Another leader of the group, Ilyssa Wesche, twenty-one, attended a meeting after seeing a flier. She said that before becoming active, she would not have called herself a feminist, thinking that men and women had achieved equality: "This is the only thing that ever politicized me at all."

All agreed that they have learned to see new connections between issues. The group has done educational forums on the spectrum of reproductive-rights issues: sterilization abuse, Medicaid funding, birth-control access. "It has politicized me in that it shows me how encompassing this issue is. It's not just abortion. It has to do with poor women, with so many issues that affect me and this world," Knarich said.

Fellow pro-choice activist Laura Tarantini concurred. "I entered at this almost small point and began to connect other issues and saw it opening up to a global perspective of different people's struggles."

## Youth Groups

Other forms of organizing around the most vital issues for women are not as visible. They aren't expressed with public demonstrations. Those being politicized don't necessarily call themselves feminists.

In the inner city of Dallas, Ruth Thomas is utilizing the most basic feminist principles to fight the most seemingly hopeless social problems for teenage girls. She is an administrator at a chapter of Girls Incorporated, a youth group for girls eight to eighteen years old, in a high-crime part of town that others have abandoned. Thomas said people wouldn't start businesses in the area even if given the buildings for free.

Since the first girls' club affiliated with the group was founded during the industrial revolution in cities for young factory workers, others have been providing the same function of refuge. A national federation of nineteen of these clubs was founded in Massachusetts in 1945 under the name Girls' Clubs of America, which changed its name in 1990 to Girls Incorporated.

Girls Incorporated, with the slogan "Growing Up Is Serious Business," is one of many established, national female-oriented agencies that have evolved to take on an increasingly feminist and advocative focus. Since 1980, with the establishment of its own research agency in Indianapolis, the group has had more of an educational component—with tested programs on substance abuse and teenage pregnancy prevention, math and science education and health care—in addition to its regular recreational and educational activities. While the programs have been geared toward low-income girls, Girls Incorporated serves a wide diversity of ethnic and economic backgrounds, with 125 local affiliates in thirty-three states.

Another well-known institution working for social justice is the Young Women's Christian Association (YWCA), based in New York City, which was founded as a national organization in 1906 and has 400 chapters. Featuring programming for women over twelve, the common purpose of all chapters is empowerment of women and elimination of racism. Girls Incorporated and YWCA are also planning to work together more in the future to devise programs for girls.

After interviewing four young women to whom Ruth Thomas had referred me, I tracked her down at her home by phone to ask about them and Girls Incorporated. When she answered, her voice was weary and cracked. She explained that she was in a recovery period from work. But as we talked about Girls Incorporated, her voice regained its vibrancy.

Thomas stressed that the power of the club comes with the space girls get to form identities. She learned this lesson herself when she started work there fifteen years ago. Like others, she was forced to grow up too fast.

"I thought I'd stop and peek in and pretend I was kid. I was a kid even though I was already married and everything."

She said it filled a void in her life to learn about herself and pay attention to her own needs. This type of understanding is powerful in helping girls define their goals for the future and resist later pressures. With the center's sports activities, they can also have a safe environment to build confidence and take risks where they won't be judged.

"In the world as we know it now, women are going to be having the babies. And women, they need to be equipped as girls. They need to know more about life than physical attraction and living for men.

That's a real strong feminist statement," she said, laughing a bit, because I had told her how strongly feminist her group seemed to me.

"The girls get sidetracked, and start living for other people, and it's
usually boys or men, and they get way off track. That's a skill, if you
can learn how to live for yourself as a woman, and as a young woman,
your chances for making it as an adult are more likely."

The center also fosters the feminist ideal of being able to make
choices. The programs are designed to help build self-esteem and a
feeling of entitlement. "It isn't teaching girls to stomp on boys and
shut them out, but it is teaching them identity and feeling good about
being a woman and contributing to all facets of life, not just mothering
and nurturing, but building and making, inventing, deciding, dictat-
ing, even politicking. It teaches them that life is out there, and it's
filled with choices, and you can choose whichever route you want to
go."

All four young women I interviewed who had gone to the center as
teens had a strong feminist sensibility, although three did not recognize the word "feminist." All had clear ideas of their goals and what
they stood for.

Kim, twenty-three, a single mother quoted earlier who was working
part-time at the center, was training at a community college to get a
teaching degree. In my standard battery of questions, I asked her if
women are better off now than twenty years ago.

"I think it has improved tremendously, because twenty years ago, I
heard most people say that a woman had to stay home and take care of
her child. Now, they have training. Whatever we want to major in, we
can do that. We can take up that trade to better ourselves, to get a
skill. And I feel strongly about that. I always wanted to be a teacher. I
love working with kids. I love working with people period."

While Thomas said all these girls started out with talents, the center
helped them realize it. "I think for Kim, the number-one thing she got
out of Girls Incorporated was the assertiveness, how to stand up for
herself. Now she's going through a divorce. She married after high
school, you know all this kind of thing. She's still in college even now,
speaking up for herself, [but] she was really shy. If she had an idea or
comment, she wouldn't say it. She'll say, 'Girls' Club taught me how to
speak up for myself.' "

Cemetria Hayes, seventeen, who was born to teenage parents and raised by her grandmother, plans to be an architect and attend a major state university. Now she is earning money for college selling some of her paintings. I asked her if she knew any feminists, and she mentioned the people at the girls' club.

"They're more decisive and they know who they are," she said. "They are more energized and less afraid of showing the men how they are."

Thomas also expressed her confidence in Hayes, who had almost no parental involvement growing up. "You should see her drawings. She has the portfolio of someone who lives in Paris or New York. I told her that when she goes to those places, don't forget Girls Incorporated."

Throughout the years, Thomas has seen other examples of girls with no support go on to fulfill their career ambitions. Many in Girls Incorporated go to college, some becoming cheerleaders or campus Homecoming queens.

"This guy who is executive director of another agency called me up, and he was right in the middle of an important meeting, but he wanted to tell me that a young lady had made campus queen," said Thomas. "To his surprise, we already knew. I already knew. I'm usually the first to know when the girls make big accomplishments. They will call you up and say: 'Oh, Ruthie! So and so happened in my life!' "

But Thomas didn't mention another function of the group, which is to provide a strong female role model for young women. Kim said that she appreciated the hours of conversations with Thomas when she was going through bad times. They often talked in the center's van while Thomas drove girls home at night.

"I feel she is a very good role model because she is always there to 'conquer' me and no one else does. 'Conquer' means she's there for me to be encouraged: 'Don't give up, you can do anything, whatever you put your mind to,' " said Kim.

Like all services to low-income people I have reported about, Girls Incorporated in Dallas has funding problems. As in other cities, boys' clubs are more apt to get contributions. Widely published 1988 statistics from the New York-based Woman and Foundations Network reveal that less than 4 percent of philanthropic dollars in the United States and Canada have gone to programs that specifically serve girls and women in the last decade.

## **Oral History**

Often women don't have to go too far to find the most influential feminist role models. Besides professors and friends, for many of the women I interviewed the most common ones named were mothers.

Influential mothers were not always activists, but inspired their off-spring with their strength as single parents. Some women learned to appreciate activist mothers later in life.

Valerie Walker, twenty-five, a rape-crisis counselor at the Lake County Council Against Sexual Assault in Gurnee, Illinois, was raised by her activist, divorced mother on a Native American reservation in Michigan and then went to live with her father in the area of Chicago. She only understood her mother after getting involved in the feminist community at the University of Iowa in Iowa City.

"My mom has been the major influence. I haven't always liked it," she said. "Because when I was in high school, a lot of the things I saw her do were embarrassing to me. I had to explain to my friends why my mom was in jail, things like that. But when I got away to a different environment in college, I learned to appreciate it."

Sometimes this discovery of older people's experiences can happen with a simple conversation. One women's-studies professor, Marge Frantz at Santa Cruz, realizes the power of the older generation's influence, and has made oral histories an assignment in one of her classes. She directs young women to talk to their grandmothers, an often overlooked resource, and learn from their strength.

"A lot of the connections between the generations happen at Thanksgiving, and there is this very superficial conversation, and young people really don't find out what's happening. They really don't know their grandmothers at all," Frantz said.

She said that she recommends the grandmother, because often mothers and daughters have too many other unresolved issues between them clouding a clear dialogue. She said grandmothers give more of a sense of connection to the past to the interviewer, and feel appreciated after they are finally convinced to tell their stories.

"You will say, 'I want to interview you, Grandmother.' And they will say, 'There is nothing special about me. I mean why would you want to interview me?' And that's the immediate response of 95 percent of women. They don't think they're worth interviewing."

Johnnie Griffin, forty-seven, a teacher and grandmother in Washington, D.C., said that young women can also gain strength in their personal lives by making the connection to their grandmothers. They learn that balancing work and family life is not a new concept. She said she learned that her challenges pale in comparison to those experienced by her ninety-three-year-old grandmother.

"Not only did she have to go out and kill the hogs to get the bacon, she had to feed the hogs. Before she could feed the hogs, she had to plant the seed for grain to get the hogs' food."

Frantz emphasized the strength that activists receive from talking to elderly women who have led political lives. Students in her class interviewed older women who were active in labor movements in the Thirties and Forties, but then silenced during the McCarthy years. Robyn Chapel, a student of Frantz's, said that learning the stories of "ordinary" women involved in social movements was inspiring, showing that such idealism is not necessarily a phase of one's life, but can be an enduring commitment.

Chapel added that the assignment taught her that people do have power to change things. Most valuable, she said, was "the idea that they could create a vision of how they wanted to make the world."

## A Chasm

While in Santa Cruz talking to Chapel and Frantz and attending Bettina Aptheker's class, it seemed that all the world was feminist. I also had this sense at conferences for young feminists and in every other "progressive" setting.

But I want to introduce caution in making an assessment of the feminist presence in this country. It is a delusion for activists to universalize the experience of visible feminists and describe them as representing the mainstream. At one conference, people said over and over that the attendance represented young women in general as converted to the feminist way of life. This is like saying all men are plumbers at a national plumbers' convention.

This overly optimistic estimation of feminism and young women risks complacency. While they often support feminist principles, people living in "mainstream" areas or without the support of a feminist community have less of this identification. Older feminists should not forget them because of the continuing need to build a broader base of support and commitment to women's issues, especially in the political realm.

The women I interviewed who most identified themselves as feminists often seemed to be a segregated slice of the population. Some of the gap in consciousness was in age. Generally, those who were twenty-three and older, who more commonly attended school during the height of the Reagan years, did not have access to the feminist networks that sprung up after the *Webster* decision.

Also, some of the most visible feminists are located far from the mainstream at liberal schools, such as Hampshire College or Brown. As in women's-studies classes in general, feminists there often "preach to the converted."

A challenge for feminists is to recognize the chasms in perceptions between activist and mainstream communities in articulating and recognizing feminist convictions. Many who would be open to feminism are lacking the organizing and thinking environments that nourish and define feminist thought. It is also crucial to recognize that the ugly "feminist fatale" image is still alive and powerful, acting to isolate feminists and block personal exploration of feminism for others. The struggles of many of those I interviewed to overcome the pervasive stereotypes and backlash attest to its force.

## Chapter Nine

# The Activists

## STUDENT ORGANIZING

Through the fight for abortion rights, Take Back the Night marches, the proliferation of campus women's studies classes and numerous other groups, thousands of young people have learned the power of networking with each other. Through a wave of concerted national and statewide efforts, they are putting their tremendous energy to work.

Among young feminists interviewed and others working throughout the country, actions, the stated goal is to build an inclusive movement of women, men, people of all races and backgrounds. They are seeking to secure rights that are being jeopardized, as well as those the women's movement has not yet gained.

"There is a constant drumbeat in the popular media that young people are apathetic, uninterested and aren't concerned about social issues. In fact, it is the opposite. More young people are involved in social and political causes than at any time during the Vietnam War," said Kathy Spillar, thirty-five, an organizer for the Fund for the Feminist Majority, which works nationally to organize women activists on college campuses in the fight against parental-consent laws and notification for abortion.

Spillar was referring to the twenty-fifth annual survey of college freshmen conducted by the American Council on Education and the University of California at Los Angeles, which revealed a shift in priorities for students in 1990. Those responding in the sample of 194,182 freshmen at 382 colleges and universities throughout the country indicated that student activism was on the rise, interest in pursuing business careers and making money was on the decline, and concern for the environment and better race relations was increasing.

Almost 43 percent of the freshmen, described by the survey as an all-time high number, said it was "essential" or "very important" to "influence social values." The survey also found that a record 39.4 percent of college freshmen said they took part in demonstrations in their last year in high school.

"These trends show that there is a rapidly expanding number of college students who are dissatisfied with the status quo and who want to be personally involved in bringing about change in American society," said Prof. Alexander W. Astin of UCLA's Graduate School of Education, as quoted by the Associated Press on January 29, 1991.

With all these movements involving the young, worsening social conditions seem to be providing a more fertile climate for change. Marybeth Maxwell, twenty-five, organizing director for the U.S. Student Association in Washington, D.C., said more than ever, the middle class are feeling more personally threatened by current policies.

"Things are harsher. There aren't any grants. Money is drying up for education. There is greater tolerance for racism. Our right to choose abortion is being threatened in a way that no one could ever imagine would ever happen. There is greater violence against women. There is greater tolerance of sexual harassment. It hurts more, people can feel it more," Maxwell said.

"I'm not saying that we didn't feel it in the Eighties, but it just snowballed, and the impact of the ten years of Republican rule is really coming home to people. I mean, George Bush just vetoed a civil rights bill. He's only the third president in history to veto a civil rights bill."

## Abortion-Rights Activists

More than two years after the 1989 Supreme Court's *Webster* decision, the Pandora's box continues to be opened with the states chipping away at abortion rights.

The specific target group is one with the least voice in politics: young women.

To individuals watching from the sidelines alone, this attack could look hopeless. But to the individual organizing with other individuals, each legal threat represents only Round One.

Some students, such as Nancy Bowles, twenty-one, are fighting back. In 1990, she was attending Lewis and Clark College in Portland, Oregon, when she learned about two measures on the November state ballot that would restrict abortion rights. Measure 8 would have outlawed almost all abortions in the state, and Measure 10 would have mandated parental notification for minors seeking abortion. Bowles told how she helped organize students across the state to achieve a landmark victory against parental-consent laws.

The students had the greatest impact, making up one-third of the 2,500 volunteers who stood outside polling places and held up signs to "Vote No on 8 and 10" to simplify and highlight the ballot measures. They also helped launch a massive grass-roots effort of voter-registration drives, candlelight vigils, speakouts, rallies and a speaking tour by Karen and Bill Bell, whose daughter died in 1988 from a back-alley abortion, which she sought as a result of the Indiana parental-consent law.

Every individual campus in Oregon rallied behind the effort. Students from Lewis and Clark covered twenty-five polling sites on election day. The voter turnout on campus was 67.5 percent, and 85 percent of those students voted pro-choice. Students from Reed College covered twenty-two polling places. At Oregon State University, Students for Choice also registered voters and held information drives.

On election day, the parental-consent measure was defeated in a close vote. With their voting power and vigilance at the polling places, students had clearly made a difference in pushing the close vote over the edge.

"Five percent of the people polled after the election said that the people outside the polling place affected their vote and they voted pro-choice. Because of that 5 percent, we won on Ballot 10 by four points. So young women saved the day," said Bowles.

"We're very encouraged by what happened in Oregon, and we're going on the road. We're going to stop being on the defense and work on the offense for a while."

As the challenges have mounted, the battle for reproductive freedom has become perhaps the most volatile and visible front line for young people's activism.

## NARAL: Building Coalitions

The massive efforts of pro-choice student activists are reflected in a campus newsletter for the winter of 1991 distributed by the National Abortion Rights Action League (NARAL). In those eight pages are reports from dozens of schools describing innovative efforts within their states. The newsletter also documents that in the 1990 state and national elections, pro-choice activists played a key role.

While abortion was one of many issues candidates debated, it had more of an impact in deciding an election's outcome when there was a close margin of victory. Nationwide in those elections, the pro-choice movement picked up four governors, two U.S. senators and eight members of the U.S. House of Representatives, according to NARAL. It also reports that legislative bodies in a number of states, including Arizona and Idaho, switched from anti-abortion to pro-choice majorities.

In Texas, students at a string of schools unified to help elect pro-choice candidate Ann Richards in a close race for governor. A network of fifteen campus pro-choice organizations took part in the Texas Abortion Rights Action League's Pro-Choice Student Voter Participation Project, in which students across the state registered, identified and turned out over 10,000 pro-choice voters.

One student from Ohio State University's Students for Choice, Shelli Craver, reports how Ohio students identified pro-choice voters by collecting signatures at different campuses. In the final week of the campaign for pro-choice candidate Anthony Celebrezze, they got out the pro-choice vote with a "students calling students" project to remind all 10,000 signatories of their pledge.

At a "Working Women's Breakfast" with the candidate, Craver reminded the older people of the students' power: "Many of you consider us to be future 'working women.' However, we are hard at work already, as students and as political activists."

The NARAL newsletter also lists seemingly less dramatic victories that nonetheless represented student efforts across the nation. At Fordham University in New York, a conservative Catholic campus, a newly formed pro-choice group scored a coup in just sponsoring a speaker. Other schools got involved in a wide array of issues. Along with other activists in the state, the Smith College pro-choice group helped campaign against and defeat Question 3, a voter initiative that would have rolled back taxes to 1988 levels and wiped out virtually all social services in Massachusetts.

Students I visited at the State University of New York-Albany also seemed to suffer no energy crisis. Their Students for Choice group started the semester after the *Webster* decision, and has since become a political force on campus. Organizers note that campus and New York state candidates have solicited their endorsement.

"We started as a whisper, and now we're a scream," said Gina Knarich, one of the group's leaders.

Students for Choice sponsors a table in the student union three times a week with information about reproductive rights, ranging from abortion laws to Medicaid funding and minors' access to facts about sexually transmitted diseases. It also offers a state NARAL guide to candidates, listing specific stances on abortion. Every month it holds a rally, sponsors a defense of an abortion clinic and publishes a newsletter. It also holds weekly meetings.

"It's that strange mix of being ambitious, yet we feel there is nothing less that we can do," said Laura Tarantini, another group leader.

"We just have a core of people that plug and plug and plug," said Ilyssa Wesche, who also runs the group. "There is this high peer pressure for us to come through with this information."

The group at SUNY and others listed are informally and formally united under the umbrella of NARAL's National Campus Organizing Project. It provides a network for students already organizing, involves them in NARAL's grass-roots political work, develops organizing skills for young activists and builds coalitions on a local level between the campus and community.

Ellisa McBride, twenty-four, the project's coordinator for its first two years, from 1989 to 1991, is known to college students throughout the country as their national pro-choice leader. One October morning in Washington, D.C., talking over breakfast in a café, she and Marybeth Maxwell described their unique coalition in organizing pro-choice students. I learned how their project represents the philosophies and strategies of young activists in the 1990s.

McBride said that NARAL started the national project after noticing the untapped power of college students, who had made themselves seen and heard at the April 9 march in Washington, D.C., for abortion rights. "Before that, there hadn't been any attempt to involve students on a systematic level," she said.

NARAL started on the principle of networking with already organized students, the United States Student Association's 350-member campuses, which represent two and a half million students. Typically, campuses join through their student governments or through state organizations, such as in New York, Illinois and Wisconsin. NARAL tapped into the database of 200 pro-choice activists made available by USSA's women's caucus. In 1991, the project had contacts on 500 to 600 college campuses.

McBride says the real impact of NARAL has been with legislative work. The organization provides abundant tools to these groups and others that have joined the coalition, including reports of others' activities, educational materials, guidance for voter registration and lobbying. In McBride's small corner office at NARAL headquarters, there are stacked boxes of organizing guides, rolls of stickers with the slogan, "Students—vote while you still have the choice" and piles of educational videotapes.

While NARAL's specific focus is the urgent abortion battle, McBride says the grass-roots groups such as the one at SUNY-Albany stress reproductive freedom as well as issues of access for low-income women, birth-control education, child care and sterilization abuse.

Maxwell said this shift represents a growing awareness among college activists that different "women's issues" are connected to each other, and are also related to different spheres of social justice. For example, the concept of reproductive freedom is a unifying force, with its variety of concerns for the poor, the young and people of color. The broad work of USSA, which tackles economic access to education, crime on campus, racism and discrimination against gays and lesbians, is also helping to expand the focus of women's rights.

"[Campus activists] are saying we need to expand, even when we think about our language, from the word 'choice' to 'reproductive freedom,' " said Maxwell. "That still means that we're working our butts off just to make abortion legal, because that right is not here right now. But I think students are increasingly making the connections to other issues, which is very, very exciting."

She gave an example of the concept of "educational access" to illustrate how a wide range of issues are perceived as related.

"I find among students a really sophisticated understanding of what access to education means," Maxwell said. "It really blows me away. Access means there has to be a campus climate that condemns class-related violence, that condemns racist violence and harassment, which condemns harassment of women students, which allows women students to take part in education and not be condescended to, not be violated, not be harassed. That means access to disabled students, as well as basic economic access to increase financial aid."

McBride and Maxwell, who were both activists on their college campuses as undergraduates, said the enhanced connections being made between issues is the result of student organizations growing stronger. They gave the example of lessons learned by their peers, activists of the 1980s, who mobilized to deliver sanctions against apartheid in South Africa. In general, white students slowly learned how racism abroad was related to racism in this country, and how isolated different student groups were in their efforts.

"People brought it home a little bit more. They said, 'Yes, we have to care about South Africa,' and students [had an impact in] getting sanctions against South Africa. But we also have to look in our own backyard and address the apartheid that happens in our society, in our own campus," said Maxwell, who attended Marquette University in Milwaukee.

Activism in the 1990s carries the major challenge for students to heal past divisions. For feminists, a goal is for people of color and whites to work together. McBride said one of the keys is for white people to know other groups' concerns and address them. She described some of the efforts of students organizing after *Webster*.

"[White students] said to the women of color on their campus, 'We want to work with you on this, we want to work together.' And the women of color said, 'Okay, fine, but we have to start to play a role in shaping the agenda as well.' As you start to build coalitions, you necessarily broaden the focus of your work and draw the connections to different issues."

In the pro-choice battle, McBride also noticed many men getting involved throughout the country. She and Maxwell reflected what pro-choice men had told me, that reproductive rights holds the attraction of a vital civil rights issue.

"Part of it is because it's one of the biggest acts in town," McBride said. "It's the most exciting political thing happening on campus, and people want a part of it."

At a meeting of the Reproductive Rights Coalition at the University of Wisconsin in Madison, I learned that four out of nine members of the steering committee were men. One, Charles Chen, twenty, a finance major, even keeps the group afloat with his genius fund-raising abilities, the women there told me.

Men also have felt an added pull to join the fight from their girlfriends. "I also think that young women are more assertive in their own relationships, about what they expect in terms of birth control and other issues and support," Maxwell said. "That is definitely affecting how some of the men are looking at the issue."

Pro-choice activists are also letting men know how abortion affects them personally. "One pro-choice activist at Ohio State told me that the way she attracts fraternity boys into the organization—or at least into supporting it, giving money or signing petitions or coming to rallies—is she tells them the birth-control failure rate," said McBride. "She gives them a whole page of that, and when they get all riled up and nervous, she tells them to come to the pro-choice rally, to give people a sense that this is you too, this is your life, men as well as women."

The central caution, though, in working with pro-choice men, is that they don't dominate the activist groups.

"At times, there are conflicts, actually, about whether men should be taking leadership positions in the pro-choice groups, and most of the women we have worked with feel that men should be involved and play a supportive role, especially personally, but that women should be in the leadership of pro-choice groups. It's not unanimous, and some of the men disagree with that. They want to, or feel it's appropriate for them to take leadership," said McBride.

Maxwell said one of the visible results of the pro-choice movement on student activism is that it is building young women leaders. USSA organizers have conducted regional activist trainings for five years since

1985, and in 1990 witnessed an upsurge in women attending. This is in contrast to the beginning when they had to recruit women to ensure a balance.

"More women, because of activism on issues like this, are starting to see themselves as leaders and coming to the training anyway. They are starting to see themselves as activists, as organizers," Maxwell said.

Above all, NARAL's campus project is a unique example of cooperation between the generations. Young women are taking advantage of older people's resources and established reputations to reach some of their potential as activists. Meanwhile, young organizers like McBride are free to lead on their own.

Keeping up a continuous relationship with young women shows that they are valued by older activists, not just seen as "warm bodies" to turn to when a crucial vote is happening in their state. McBride emphasized the need for young women to have their own space to look after their own needs. "I think it has to be a multigenerational movement, but students also have to have their own organization because working on campuses is different than working in communities," she said.

## Students Organizing Students

The other major national reproductive-rights network and information resource for college and high school students is organized by Students Organizing Students, based in New York City. SOS formed days after the *Webster* decision, and now works in coalition with existing groups. In 1990, it spread to become a network of 150 college and high school chapters.

Nina Chamyan, twenty-three, national student coordinator and one of the original four SOS founders, explained that the group fulfilled a strong desire young people had to take political control over their lives after *Webster*.

"It was being sparked by every young woman who was shocked by that decision. You know, there were so many people talking and crying out for something like SOS that would basically help to create the student force as a formidable, powerful voice that would help dictate policy in this country, especially policy that would directly affect us."

While abortion rights are a priority, Chamyan stressed more of a focus on reproductive freedom, which demands diversity. As part of the group's history, poor women and women of color are active at all levels, she said. SOS's founders were two white people, one Latina and one Asian/Latina.

This diversity reflects the need for self-determination on a wide spectrum of issues, she said. Abortion rights are only the beginning.

"Young people today in the Nineties will not only be fighting for a law we have always had. I mean, this is always something we have had as women, the right to choose. But we are going to be out in the streets fighting for all the things that we never had.

"And that's prenatal care. That's day care that's affordable and accessible birth control, that's AIDS awareness and activism, that's sex education," said Chamyan.

"I mean, young people are dying! High school–age children are dying from AIDS, and they are still debating whether they should use the word 'condom' when talking about AIDS prevention in the guidelines for sex education. I don't think that we can stand for that. I don't think that we can allow someone who is so removed from reality to help make those decisions that are going to help save our lives. That is something that we have never had to address."

Chamyan has been on the road for months talking to students, and was difficult to track down. When I finally talked to her months after my initial attempt, she told me about her widespread travels to help activists connect.

She told about her travels to Guam, where a battle has been waged over an abortion law that would have prohibited virtually all abortions. A federal judge struck it down in August of 1990. She helped start an SOS chapter at the University of Guam and several high schools.

"When I went there, I was able to tell them that there are young women all over this country who are watching you, and keeping you as a model, and want to make sure that you always have the right to choose. And I think that is a very strong support for them," Chamyan said.

SOS has also coordinated its membership with organized national actions. It mobilized more than sixty colleges and high schools to boycott Domino's Pizza, which gives hundreds of thousands of dollars yearly to anti-abortion organizations, and is a key supporter of Operation Rescue. SOS engineered the dumping of 10,000 potatoes in Idaho as the governor was considering signing legislation that would have severely restricted abortion rights in that state. In coalition with about thirty other regional and national women's groups, SOS also has worked on a collection of essays by young women, documenting their roles in and feelings about the reproductive-rights movement.

Like NARAL, SOS has emerged with the support of older women, who have held fund-raising drives crucial to supporting the New York office and national networking. Its advisory board includes prominent names from the American Civil Liberties Union, national women of color networks and other feminist advocate circles.

But SOS like USSA, is unique as a separate, independent entity for young people. Even the New York SOS offices are a sharp contrast to NARAL's more established corporate image. Housed in a Broadway office building, it has a more of a college grass-roots feel, with industrial-looking black walls, wide empty spaces and articles taped to the wall. Its logo of three abstract figures holding up the letters SOS, drawn by artist Keith Haring, also reflects its youthful personality.

One SOS national organizer, Andrea Rose Askowitz, twenty-two, described the need for the group's autonomy. "Eighty percent of all women who get abortions are between the ages of fifteen and twenty-nine. We're talking about us. We're talking about women who are my age. We're talking about me. That's why we're doing this together. We're doing it because no one else is going to do it for us."

## Other National Campus Networks

Another national network driven by the philosophy of multi-issue organizing is the Civil Liberties and Public Policy Program, which is housed at Hampshire College in Amherst, Massachusetts. With its primary function as an activist resource, it has held a national yearly conference, "The Fight for Reproductive Freedom," since 1987, issues a seasonal newsletter and acts as an information clearinghouse about reproductive rights.

Like other national networks, the Civil Liberties Program tries to get back to the fundamental qualities of the early women's movement. The group occasionally holds speakouts on birth control and abortion, which were held before either were legal.

Student activist coordinator Sarah Buttenwieser, twenty-seven, writes in a special October 1990 student issue of *The Guardian* that the project seeks "a collection and amplification of our voices and our personal stories of struggle. . . . These have made the oppression of women much more difficult to deny, and made it impossible to suppress our actions toward change."

Other multi-issue networks with a focus on reproductive rights are the Progressive Student Network, based in Iowa City, Iowa and Chicago, and the Democratic Socialists of America youth section, based in New York City.

## Acquaintance Rape Battles

Students are organizing on an individual campus level to combat another intensely disputed and personal issue: acquaintance rape. While acquaintance rape happens everywhere, college activists have made strides to bring it to the forefront of public debate.

Some of the most strenuous attempts are to make universities responsive with a variety of treatment and prevention measures including setting up counseling services, rape crisis hot lines and a centralized visible office; publicizing these services; conducting surveys to document the extent of the problem on campus; and more consistently, systematically and strictly prosecuting cases.

One challenge for activists is that unlike with reproductive rights, there is not as yet a well-known national network specifically for people fighting acquaintance rape, as of this writing. (Some networks fighting many types of rape with a large component on acquaintance-rape prevention are the National Coalition Against Sexual Assault in Washington, D.C., the National Network for Victims of Sexual Assault in Arlington, Virginia, and the Men's Anti-Rape Resource Center in Washington, D.C.) This can mean that they are inventing their own strategies and are isolated in their struggles. At the 1991 NOW First

Young Feminist Conference, I witnessed rape-prevention activists from dozens of campuses meeting each other and acknowledging their common experiences for the first time.

A frequent complaint was a lack of concern, commitment or funding for programs. In a speech, Susan Denevan told about her personal battles with the administration of the University of Minnesota, which was representative of other schools, and how her political career had begun. She had been a counselor on campus for the sexual violence program, which suddenly was being threatened.

"[The program] was funded in 1985 because the university was very concerned about image, because one of its high-profile basketball players had been brought up on rape charges twice, so in order to look good, the university started a program. And four years later when they thought no one was looking, they tried to take away the peer-counseling element and crisis line," she said.

"I became involved with others in a political battle to restore the sexual-violence program, and it resulted in my being arrested along with twelve other people in a series of demonstrations last February," she said, referring to 1990.

"A result of the actions is that the university has increased the budget for more people on staff and will increase the services and program development."

This was one of the few stories with a happy ending. Organizers from the University of Florida, Gainesville, told me how their two counseling programs, among the most advanced and acclaimed in the country, had been under siege. The first, the Sexual Assault Recovery Services, gives counseling to victims, and the second, the student-run Campus Organized Against Rape, delivers education.

In recent years, Dr. Claire Walsh, the founder of both programs, has become an unofficial national expert on campus organizing around this issue. Walsh and COAR representatives have appeared on at least a dozen national television talk shows and shared their knowledge with about 500 universities and media organizations.

Supporters of these programs say that administrative changes have crippled the first program and threatened the second. An Associated Press report from November 1990 lists activists' claims that administrators have harassed activists, cut financial support, fired their employees and severed the relationship between the two programs. Administrators and the student-body president countered by saying the programs have been financially mismanaged and have been guilty of political advocacy.

The controversy prompted student protest rallies, a supporting petition signed by 1,500 students and a flurry of letters to the editor of the University of Florida student newspaper. Walsh later resigned, citing differences with the administration.

Betty Campbell, twenty-seven, program coordinator for COAR, and others from the campus said that administrators are "trying to put rape back in the closet" and protect an image. She contends administrators aren't educated enough about the problem of acquaintance rape, which has only been in public dialogue for about five years. However, one more recognized incentive for all administrators is to avoid bad publicity with prevention of these crimes or to avoid a civil law suit from a victim claiming the university was negligent in not taking any preventive measures.

Campbell, who had been recently fired and rehired, explained why she has fought hard for the program.

"I think that it gives life back to folks," she said. "It gives victims a chance to feel that there is somebody in this world who cares about them. These programs give them power, whereas sexual assault, it makes people feel like they don't have power."

Campbell stressed that COAR is unique in the country because it helps shift the focus of rape prevention to men. COAR conducts programs for both male and female students, uses male peer counselors and has a male president.

But even in cases when relations with the administration are smoother, the basic education battles are universal. Rape-prevention educators are also struggling with their fellow students to change attitudes and challenge myths.

As at the University of Florida, more and more rape-prevention educators across the country have realized that the only way to really address these perceptions and stop rape is to take the message to men.

## Men Stopping Rape

One winter evening in Madison, Wisconsin, I witnessed one of the national pioneers, Joe Weinberg, thirty-eight, a rape-prevention educator, at work. He is part of a "second wave" of the anti-rape reform movement that has involved student activists, legislators, judges, athletes and celebrities.

About twenty-five members of a fraternity were gathering in the overheated, cramped, back rec room for a formal discussion. The topic of the evening was acquaintance rape—an awkward and somewhat unfamiliar issue. But Weinberg soon eased the tension by not launching into the expected attack.

"I don't go in a fraternity and say, 'Oh God, are these guys screwed up! Have you ever heard such stupid things as they were saying?' " said Weinberg, who spends much of his two-hour workshops discussing common sexist attitudes that can lead to rape. "I say, 'As screwed up as it was, unfortunately it made sense to me. Unfortunately, it's something that I have felt.' "

Weinberg, who has addressed thousands of men across the country on this subject since 1985, also has a sympathetic appearance. With his heavyset build, outrageous sense of humor and hair falling to the base of his neck, he could pass for one of the pledges.

"I'm also good at making trouble," jokes Weinberg. "I love walking into a room and saying, 'Isn't it crazy being a man? Let's talk about it.' "

Still, he does not sugarcoat his message. Weinberg cites the grim statistics about rape, stressing that it can only stop with a change in the attitudes and behavior of men—those who mostly commit rape and are ultimately responsible for their behavior.

Weinberg, who also works as a carpenter, has made a strong personal and public commitment to this issue. In his everyday life, he is never timid about talking openly about the subject, as suggested by the ever-present "Stop Rape" button on his jacket lapel, which sometimes attracted attention during his frequent business trips to a town lumberyard.

With his rape-prevention work, he has mainly been making waves among college students. In 1988, he formed a unique rape-education consulting firm, Joseph Weinberg and Associates, which has given him the chance to speak at more than forty college campuses. His audiences across the country have ranged from an athletic team and health-center staff at the University of Utah to a human sexuality class at the University of Maine. He has also broken barriers with the next generation, including a class of ninth-graders in Urbana, Illinois, and even regular sessions with juvenile prisoners and a Boy Scout troop in Madison.

When I spoke with him in 1990, he was concentrating his efforts back at the University of Wisconsin, where his Madison rape-awareness group, Men Stopping Rape, presented more than twenty fraternity workshops. Peggy Miezio, assistant dean of students, said these workshops fill a critical gap at the university.

"What's special is that the groups are led by men. And it's a very different experience than a group of women coming in to talk to a group of men," Miezio said. "We women certainly need men to say this is not a women's issue: This is a people's issue."

In his work with men, Weinberg's approach is still rare. Mainly emphasizing how to avoid rape by strangers, a great majority of rape-prevention programs at universities still almost exclusively targets women by giving out safety tips, issuing whistles or teaching self-defense. Weinberg says even the select number of programs that do address acquaintance rape put an unrealistic burden on women for prevention, with the message that she is responsible for setting his limits.

"Most of the education consists of basically telling women not to go out of the house," Weinberg says. " 'Go in the house, keep your door locked and carry a bazooka.'

"Those programs are well meaning, but they reinforce the same old stereotypes. It's something *she* is doing wrong. 'She's in the wrong neighborhood, the wrong place, she's dressed wrong, she's too drunk. She shouldn't be there with that guy.' There's all sorts of denial from men and women about rape, and most programs don't really address that."

But as public awareness of the issue and pressure from students and rape crisis workers continues to build, a handful of universities are slowly beginning to arrange and initiate such education for men. While

Weinberg said he knows of only a few other men speaking nationally with this feminist-based message, he sees his firm as "blazing a trail" for others. Based on the mushrooming number and extended lengths of his out-of-town business calls, Weinberg has become a full-time consultant.

At other universities, this movement for men is growing. At Brown University in the spring of 1989, students sponsored a conference called Men Can Stop Rape Now. Some campus efforts have spread to the communities. In 1973, a group of students at Cornell University in Ithaca, New York, started a campus service that several years later became Ithaca Rape Crisis Inc., which actively encourages male participation as speakers to educate others. In 1989, it sponsored a survey of rape crisis centers nationwide. Out of the total of 133 centers that responded, 118 worked with male volunteers.

Ironically, some of the most organized impetus to the movement comes from one specific group that few would consider radical: leaders from the national fraternity system, a visible bastion of the male establishment.

"And that seems like good news," says Robin Warshaw, author of *I Never Called It Rape,* a landmark book on acquaintance rape. "The sort of bad news is that the reason for the motivation is fear of lawsuits. The national fraternity organizations are really putting a lot of heat on the local chapters to do this kind of education in order to fend off potential liability problems."

Mandates for programming have come from all levels in the fraternity hierarchy. In January of 1991, the National Interfraternity Conference, a network of sixty-two men's national and international fraternities, issued a statement in its newsletter, *Campus Commentary,* to "strongly encourage" all undergraduate chapters to take action with several social issues. Specifically, it included a recommendation "to schedule system-wide educational programming on date rape and use the NIC-produced video, 'Fraternity Men on Date Rape: A Candid Conversation' and the NIC-endorsed video, 'Campus Rape.'"

"Women's groups across the nation already addressed [acquaintance rape]. Now this video takes it from the men's perspective," said Jeff Cufaude, education coordinator for the NIC, based in Indianapolis.

Cufaude said it is difficult to gauge response because programming is up to the discretion of individual chapters. But Greeks can often have great influence on campuses. "Because they are already organized, they can take leadership on this issue," he said.

In taking a stand on the issue, some national fraternities have put out formal statements, backing them up with posters and workshops. Other efforts are more localized, as with individual chapters bringing in campus educators such as Weinberg or with members becoming more active in rape-awareness groups.

Weinberg was lucky to find Men Stopping Rape, a group that stresses the male focus. He first discovered this need for men's education in 1985 when he joined Men Stopping Rape, one of about 100 to 150 campus and community-based men's rape-prevention and education groups active throughout the country in 1991. In the aftermath of a sudden divorce, he sought the male friendships he was lacking as well as a way to work out some lingering hostile feelings toward women.

"When I came to the group, I was newly separated from my wife," he said. "I had been married for about five years, and was extremely angry—angry at her, angry at women."

However, Weinberg was still skeptical of the group, picturing it as a stereotyped "sensitive man" touchy-feely operation, an impression he had picked up a year earlier while browsing over its first literature.

"And their brochure said something like, 'Men, if you want to understand the oppression of women, wear a dress in public, carry a purse or wear earrings.' I remembered that, and here I am about to go to my first Men Stopping Rape meeting and I thought, 'My God, a bunch of men in dresses and purses. I've got earrings, but I've got *masculine* earrings.' There was some homophobia; I thought, 'Oh God, I'll be with a bunch of homosexuals.' "

But soon, dealing with these prejudices, he realized the group was more in touch than he had supposed and he found it a refuge.

"It was really powerful that here were men who were questioning the things that I had never thought about: What does it mean to be a man? Who was I? Who am I?"

Many of these discussions about sexism overlapped with other related topics, such as violence against women. Weinberg became concerned about the acquaintance-rape issue, noticing its roots in common attitudes he had grown up with and had always accepted.

He devised his program's content with the pro-feminist perspective of Men Stopping Rape and other scholarly work. A voracious reader, he dedicated himself to hours of independent research about the dynamics of sexual violence, sexism and counseling techniques. While he has no formal college degree, the hundreds of books stacked in his apartment—on every table, in towering bookshelves, even lining the bathroom countertops—testify to his scholarship on the subject.

In his workshops, one of his central messages is redefining consent for sex, often misunderstood in the early dating situations common to college life. A man may then even unintentionally force sex upon a woman whose signals he does not understand. For example, a man might wrongly interpret a woman's revealing and sexy clothing as giving him permission to have sex with her.

To avoid such confusion, he emphasizes the necessity of communication, considering consent only as a clear, freely given "yes." In cases without this consent, and when the woman is experiencing any doubt, he labels the situation as rape. This definition sticks even when force is not used and the woman does not struggle.

While also giving specific hints for prevention, he dares men to reevaluate conditioned "cave-man" views. Weinberg says harmful sexist attitudes, including believing in men's right to dominate or blame the victim, perpetuate rape. With such introspection, he hopes that men can learn to understand the deeply rooted motivations behind the violence.

Specifically, he challenges his audience to question their membership in the "men's club," which pressures men to "score," no matter what the cost to the woman—or to his own conscience.

Men must also question the sexism around them in the media, locker-room jargon and our everyday language. "The language men use is universal. When we can start talking about the language, then we can start talking about the violence and the sexism behind the language."

Startling some, he often asks his audiences to think of a positive word for a sexually active female. There are none.

"We can call a man a 'male slut,' but it's not the same slap in the face as when you call a woman that," he says.

Then he asks to hear the same label to describe a man and is usually barraged: "Romeo, Casanova, player, stud, dude, all that stuff," he says.

Weinberg's unconventional approach often causes controversy.

Some may consider his advice of asking permission for sex as too awkward and overly cautious. Since the precautions he recommends emphasize new standards, Weinberg may be describing certain behavior as rape that just about everyone in the room has been guilty of.

Regardless of these implications, the several men I interviewed to whom Weinberg had spoken didn't describe him as an accuser. Ted Zahn, a former president of Alpha Delta Phi fraternity in Madison, which had one of the workshops in 1989, says that his house's members appreciated Weinberg's sympathetic approach. "I think that when someone comes into your fraternity wanting to talk about anything in general, you're kind of leery. You think you don't want to hear it. But I know for a fact it really captivated people."

"I think a lot of guys really didn't realize what rape actually was," Zahn says. "I think that when you get informed like that, you just kind of take on a whole new attitude toward it. You become a little more cautious, a little more aware."

## More Mainstream

This organizing at fraternities is a sign that feminist movements on campuses are becoming more mainstream.

Stefani Schwartz, twenty-one, a NARAL intern, is a member of one of six sororities at Gettysburg College, a private liberal-arts school in Pennsylvania. She reports that pro-choice issues are injecting a new activist spirit into her previously apathetic campus. The pro-choice groups are reaching out more to the Greeks, who make up 80 percent of the student population. She said she talked to four sorority presidents who expressed interest in getting their chapters involved.

"Last year we had a retreat, and we talked about the environment, drugs and alcohol, the abortion issue and racism. And everyone stood up and gave their views. And they had a little panel discussion. I think that's a great place to start," said Schwartz.

Louise Kier, chairman of the National Panhellenic Conference based in Indianapolis, which represents twenty-six national sororities, also stressed the potential for education on social issues. She said that because of the sororities' tax status, they cannot spend money for political advocacy, but, in her view, members of sororities are ideally encouraged to develop their own views.

"People have mislabeled Greeks as conservatives, supportive of establishment," Kier said. "Women who've sought affiliation have represented the outermost of the political and social spectrum. It's not a homogeneous blob of people who had nothing better to do than go Greek, which I hear from a lot of reporters. We don't impose political doctrines. We provide a nurturing atmosphere in which they can pursue their own political thoughts."

It is becoming more common for sororities and fraternities to sponsor education on less controversial social issues. For example, Chi Omega, based in Cincinnati with 175,000 members and 170 chapters, has programs on eating disorders, substance abuse, personal growth and financial growth. It also has professionally produced a series of manuals about acquaintance rape, which were sent to all chapters, according to Jill Klein, director of business operations for Chi Omega.

Another Greek leader, Fred Yoder, editor of publications for Sigma Chi based in Evanston, Illinois, with 210,000 members and 210 active chapters, also observed more social concern. "I'm a creature of the Fifties, and they are certainly more active than my generation, particularly so in the last five to ten years. Definitely."

Still, some Greeks and non-Greeks told me that they are pessimistic that sororities will be a significant source for future feminist organizing on campus. Often their interest lasts only as long as an issue is popular within the group. As I learned personally on my campus, the pressure to conform and not make waves is often mighty.

## OFF-CAMPUS ACTIVISM

Once off a college or high school campus, young feminist organizers are more difficult to track. They often lack visible support systems and access to communities of people their own age.

"I think college students have a lot of networks open to them," said Nadia Moritz, twenty-six, director of the Young Women's Project at the Institute for Women's Policy Research in Washington, D.C. "I think the problem with women after they graduate from college or graduate from high school or quit high school is: What do you do? You're all by yourself.

"There aren't many networks for you to plug into because all the established women's groups or co-ed groups are older than you and experiencing different problems than you are experiencing."

Young feminists out of school are active mainly in smaller grassroots work, such as at rape crisis centers or family-planning clinics. Some of this work doesn't necessarily involve a "women's issue." They could be working on social justice, such as North Carolinians Against Racism and Religious Violence, based in Durham, which is run by young African American women. Other young women have also taken leadership roles in housing or health-care issues. Much of the most hidden types of activist work is "survival" organizing, such as with forming unions or getting better working conditions in low-income jobs.

Moritz said that she does not know of any national young feminist groups independent from established women's organizations. But young people are still taking part in other established feminist organizations, such as NOW and NARAL, especially at local and state levels. They are vital within these groups at all levels to look after young women's needs and provide their perspectives. One major example of their need for vigilance is parental consent, which can be seen by older people as a bargaining chip to keep abortion legal, but perceived by young women as a more direct threat.

In recent years, a few national networks of young feminists have also emerged within older women's organizations. One with great national potential is NOW's Young Feminist Conference Implementation Committee (CIC), a task force of nine young women within NOW. This was probably the most significant outcome of the 1991 First Young Feminist Conference in Akron. Besides planning an annual young feminist conference, the task force, officially formed in April 1991, was established to provide an institutionalized young feminist voice at national conferences, a database of young feminists and their organizations and do outreach to get young feminists to join NOW.

Jennifer Goldberg, twenty, a member of the original planning committee for the NOW First Young Feminist Conference, was ambitious and optimistic while listing these goals. She said that the CIC would reflect the diversity of the original planning committee, which represented women on welfare, Latinas, Asians, African Americans, Jews, people of different sexual orientations and those with disabilities.

"We have such a diverse group of people that I think we'll really be able to address the needs of every community of young feminists and I think that's what's going to get people involved," said Goldberg, a student at Towson State University in Baltimore.

The first network, the Feminist Futures program, has emerged from the Center for Women Policy Studies in Washington, D.C.. In 1990 it began issuing a seasonal newsletter to provide a forum for young women and space for sharing organizing ideas.

Also in 1990, Nadia Moritz traveled through the South and East and arranged meetings of young women, most of whom were already activist through other groups.

"The most common thing was that people really wanted to feel the force of a movement they had a lot in common with. They wanted to feel the energy. There were all these isolated women coming to meetings saying, 'Who else is here?' "

Moritz said that individual leaders, especially those in the South, are often isolated without young women's networks.

"They are struggling," she said. "There are leaders, but they desperately needed support."

Her vision is to start an East Coast network that would provide resources and contacts for young feminists. It would also represent issues pertinent to young women that are not addressed by other groups.

Another function would be to get women to start a dialogue and think collectively about issues. "We just need to talk. We need to get people to talk to other people, because then they realize they are connected. They say, 'Wait, this is a women's issue,' 'This is why' and 'You're getting left out and this is why you are getting left out.' "

Some are also calling for more young women who are not presently in college to have a more autonomous national voice. Mara Verheyden-Hillard, the former director and originator of the Feminist Futures program, points out that there are no independent national networks for young feminists. Those listed above operate under the auspices of national women's groups, which exert final editorial control. She said that she has witnessed young activist women being frustrated at having their events and politics controlled by the older people in charge.

# Conferences as Barometers

The need for contact and support among young feminists on a national level has been conveyed by the success of three large conferences planned by young women for young women, held since 1989, that have each given birth to young feminist networks. The events have also provided observable groups of young feminists to act as a barometer for their movement. Although cost and travel limited attendance, scholarships and outreach were at work to promote at least some diversity. While there may have been others, these are the only major young feminist events that I have been able to track.

The first, the Feminist Futures conference, was sponsored by the Center for Women Policy Studies and attended by about 500 people in fall 1989, in Washington, D.C. The following year, in the same city, Moritz's Young Women's Project, which had been adopted by the Institute for Women's Policy Research, held a conference for East Coast feminists with a crowd of 200. The most colossal and geographically diverse event was NOW's First Young Feminist Conference, held in Akron, Ohio, which was attended by more than 700 people from forty-five states, ages eight and up.

At each, the greatest achievement seemed to be just relieving isolation of individual feminists, giving them information and prompting them to raise new questions.

"It sounds so idealistic," said Julianna Sikes, seventeen, who trekked alone to the NOW conference from Rochester, New York, where she is training as an athlete. "But I'm here to learn what I can do."

While embroiled in debates about feminism, veteran organizers also seemed invigorated. Networking was going on at a furious pace, with people exchanging cards and phone numbers like dealers at blackjack tables in Vegas. At the NOW conference, lines streamed out the door of the immense conference hall for at least two hours as people announced their ideas and activities.

But these events still had shortcomings in gauging a young feminist movement beyond a college level. Most of the people in attendance were college students. And most of the education seemed to be for the younger people, who were at a more basic level of understanding about sexism. The more advanced activists wanted more time to talk together, without hearing as many lectures from older people, and plan for the future.

"I have gone to so many of these," said Emily Coplon, twenty-four, of New York City, who attended the YWP event in 1990. "And I keep waiting for the next step, and it's always Feminism 101."

## NOW

The NOW conference effectively conveyed the national organization's potential for young women. Those in attendance had the advantage of its established and practical framework for getting things done. From the beginning, petitions were circulating throughout the audience. Soon following, organized issue hearings were held to give consideration to every point. The final session followed parliamentary procedure, with twenty-two resolutions passed and sent on their way for consideration at the summer national meeting. The highlight votes dealt with young women's issues: promoting acquaintance rape education in school districts, advocating equity in education where not enforced and working to give universal access to health care. In contrast, at the other two conferences, time did not allow for any resolutions or statements to be prepared.

The NOW conference also contradicted an image of NOW as a stodgy, older, white middle-class women's organization. While a diversity of views was expressed, many young women present were just as—if not more—outspoken as those at the most radical activist events. That weekend, Akron was as charged as meetings I attended in the most bohemian New York City or Bay Area enclaves. For example, in dealing with the abortion issue, no one voiced a willingness to compromise on abortion rights, and addressed throughout were the needs of poor women and women of color.

Many in attendance were active leaders in their communities on a local level. Some present had started campus NOW chapters, such as at the University of California at Davis and Santa Barbara, to gain a national network and support.

Like others present, Jennifer Goldberg said that she had been resistant to NOW until she attended a recent conference for abortion-clinic defenders in Washington, D.C., that NOW co-sponsored. The many NOW members present were young and of diverse backgrounds, shattering her stereotype of the group.

"There was this image going on that it's the National Organization for White Women, all older middle-class white women. I thought, 'I really don't fit into that at all. I'll never join NOW.' "

Berkeley student Janelle Rodriguez said "They have money, the resources, the know-how, the experience, the membership." But she added, "They haven't always taken the best course of action, needless to say, but if that can be turned around and used for whatever it can be used for . . . I think it's an excellent resource and want to make it happen."

She echoed the often-heard criticism that NOW is not diverse enough in regard to age, race and class. But she sees definite efforts for improvement. California is among the most progressive states, with an "affirmative action" seat on the state board, which is filled by Rodriguez. She monitors the voting action to make sure it is sensitive to diversity and not using the white middle class as a standard model.

"They need to get their shit together, but it's not to say they aren't trying. It needs to go much further, but an attempt is being made."

## Young Women's Groups

Many young women doing activist work are working in isolation from others their own age. But in writing this book, I have tracked down a smattering of young feminist groups that have come together informally throughout the country. The Feminist Futures' first fall 1990 newsletter listed a few dozen with largely a general feminist focus. The major functions listed in descriptions were a feminist support system, a focus for young women to define their own issues and a career network.

Like others listed, Nadia Moritz's Young Women's Project started with the meeting of a few friends in a large city who felt they were missing the mutual connections of the generation before. They also sensed a need for a real, collective, activist young women's voice that could be charged by their individual energies.

In 1988, they decided to form the Young Women's Project with informal discussions in Moritz's living room. Later, they presented a proposal and mission statement to the Institute for Women's Policy Research, which adopted the program. The project is publishing an organizing handbook with practical advice—everything from starting a multi-issue group to organizing around one concern, such as starting a child-care collective. In fall of 1990, it also filled a gap with the release of a thirty-page preliminary research report on issues concerning young women.

But perhaps the most booming and extensive young feminist group in the nation is WIN, the Women's Information Network, with a Washington, D.C., membership. More than any other, it reveals a strong desire for young professionals to connect socially and also reflects their unique organizing philosophies.

WIN started in 1989 when four young women working in politics came up with the idea to form a group at a political reception. They decided to start small with a dinner party.

"Well, the word really spread, and sixty people showed up for the dinner party," said Andrea LaRue, twenty-five, a founder, who works for a Texas congressman. "We thought, 'Oh, we're not the only people who feel lonely in this town.'

"It was right after the 1988 election cycle, and a lot of people were political junkies and came to Washington and needed things like jobs, health care, housing. We really had a lot in common. We started talking to these sixty people to see who they were, where they were from and where they wanted to go."

After about five months of these gatherings, they planned an agenda with the same drive that motivated them in politics. WIN also knows its constituency; the events are well-tailored to the group—young women working in the Democratic party or in progressive organizations. Nine hundred people attended WIN events in its first year, and its membership rose to 275, spanning a range of women twenty-five to thirty-five years old.

Their October 1990 newsletter reveals a mix of career networking and feminist social consciousness. The group holds receptions for, and staffs campaigns of, older women candidates; sponsors intellectual events, such as forums on issues; conducts community service projects, such as tutoring for low-income children; and coordinates social affairs, such as the dinner parties.

The newsletter lists a job bank and articles give updates on legislation relevant to women. Included are other "progressive" events, such as meetings of an El Salvador human rights group and a world hunger group. One week, a reading group focused on a selection of essays by Adrienne Rich and the book *This Bridge Called My Back.*

Vanessa Kirsch, twenty-five, who works for a D.C. pollster and is the group's chairperson, said the most successful program is Women of Achievement. It involves inviting a prominent, older woman in politics to a dinner and an informal discussion. While many older women have been receptive, they have generally been startled at WIN's aggressiveness in finding role models.

"We're not cutthroat, and we're not trying to climb the corporate ladder," Kirsch said. "We're trying to make the process more comfortable, more appealing and more supportive. One of the things that is shocking to people is how aggressive we are about finding role models and really questioning our future and really trying to plan out rather than just letting it come at us.

"And I think maybe that's a little threatening to people who say 'Why do you do that? I never did.' But with all the things we have to decide in life, we really have to plan more."

She also emphasized that some of the greatest support comes from the membership. Kirsch calls WIN "female bonding."

"Basically, it's our solution to the golf course. Men are bonding on the golf course, and we're trying to create some other kinds of bonding because it really isn't accepted that young women go out and talk professionally about their futures—whereas men do it all the time. Young men are always out there in Washington with softball teams on the Hill, and golf, or whatever. And we do it socially."

Another feminist group for young professionals with a more businesslike focus is the Young Women's Action Network in Chicago. The Monodnock Building on Dearborn Avenue is an appropriate setting for its regular meetings. It stands in the heart of the Loop, the city's central business district. Constructed in 1891, the sixteen-story building is steeped in business history as one of the earliest skyscrapers of its type.

Instead of a free-form consciousness-raising group from the Sixties, this 1990 feminist meeting more resembles a convergence of a Fortune 500 company board. The spring meeting I am attending takes place in the eighth-floor conference room, around an octagon-shaped wooden table. About half of the twelve women present came from work and are wearing suits or dresses. Mary Servatius, one of the founders, reads from an agenda to keep order and move through business efficiently.

To most of these women, this meeting resembles several they have attended for their jobs during the week. All work at nonprofit organizations that have a feminist focus, in foundations, as advocates for low-income women, advocates for reproductive rights. Their faces all look weary, and the clock is being watched to make sure that the train home is not missed.

There are job announcements, the formation of a planning committee, updates on a program to mentor teenage girls, ideas for future educational programs. The next event, its first so far, is a speech by a prominent Illinois pro-choice organizer.

Servatius, who works in the building, first started the group to support young women working in the nonprofits. After it initially failed, she and others decided to give it more of a feminist focus after she noticed a gap in young feminists coming together in professional nonprofit organizations. Older women had brought up the subject of their absence at a large national conference.

"There was this symposium in November 1988, here in Chicago," said Servatius. "Gloria Steinem was the keynote speaker. It was really interesting. There were 300 people, and probably [only] twenty-five young women under thirty."

But the group has had problems in meeting regularly, and was dormant for several months after this reproted meeting. Meetings had only gone on about once every two months, with a few outside programs a year.

"In the Sixties, a lot of that organizing went on around kitchen tables; women weren't so much in the work force," said Servatius. "Now we're trying to squeeze in organizational meetings after work, and before school. There is so much going on and there are so many more work responsibilities that women have. Something like 75 percent [of this generation] are in the work force. It's just much harder to find time. I know for myself, the commitment has lessened trying to do work and school."

Besides the time factor, with less of a social focus, people don't have a bond to keeping it going, while also burdened with their day-to-day work. Member Elise Mann, twenty-five, explained that they are lacking the personal sharing and trust-building qualities of the feminists of the 1960s.

"[Older women] strive to do more along the touchy-feely lines," said Mann, "and I think we haven't been socialized for that."

Another reason they don't have discussions about feminism is that their consciousnesses are already raised. They are working in the trenches of the movement and have a sophisticated understanding of the issues. As a result, any activist work done outside their jobs may take on the quality of work. There is little partying involved in joining this revolution.

Like other professional groups for people out of college, the Chicago organization attracts those already involved in feminist work. As a result, other people who want to get a foot in the door of the movement who are not at a college campus may find it difficult to find a peer group. While they can become active in older women's groups, consciousness-raising on their level may not be available. After being in school, people often find that they lack the exposure to others necessary to continuing to develop their ideas. It seems that after one graduates, all intellectual activity is generally expected to halt with the first paycheck and discussion of engagements, wedding plans and down payments.

## Direct Action

Unlike the Chicago network, not all young women's groups are so patient in effecting change, especially those that gather around issues of reproductive freedom. Instead of working through the system, they strive to directly confront and challenge it.

At another largely nonprofit business building, this time in New York City, there is more action going on.

At 6:30 P.M., the meeting of WHAM, the Women's Health Action and Mobilization, is called to order.

One of the young women sitting around the long tables who wears jeans and a sweatshirt makes the standard announcement: "If there is anyone present from the CIA, FBI or any other department of government, you are required by law to announce yourself.

"If there are any Right to Life people, OR [Operation Rescue] or whatever you call yourself, identify yourself now."

With that business out of the way, she looks around the table and asks if anyone wants to be co-facilitator and take the minutes. Among the twenty-five women at the four tables, which have been arranged in a square, eight people are new. About half are wearing suits, including an older leader with a blue jacket, skirt and sneakers. Others would fit into a casual student crowd. Most are in their twenties, with a few teens and older veterans. One older woman sits knitting as she listens.

The facilitator explains voting procedures and, moving to the left around the table, announcements are made relating to women's health care. "Do we always go to the left?" asks one woman as the exchange begins.

But the main order of business is regular escorting every weekend at three New York City abortion clinics. Along with activists from other local groups, the WHAM! members stand vigilant to walk with patients past the gauntlet of regular anti-abortion forces often standing at the entrances of clinics pleading with women to change their minds.

"We still have the right to health care and abortion, but we don't have access to it," explains one member.

People review past business and present a flurry of updates on planned actions or "whammies." One woman announces the trial of the Safe Sex Seven—which has recently become the Safe Sex Six— after an arrest at a protest the year before of Cardinal O'Connor's "anti-woman, anti-condom, anti-abortion and anti-gay preaching. The group also plans where it will meet for a large New York City protest against the imminent Persian Gulf War.

WHAM!, which has a total membership list of 1,200, formed after the *Webster* decision with one main premise: Women's health care is political (as its slogan goes). Since then, as with other groups in the growing clinic defense movement, it has also been driven to fight Operation Rescue, which are concerted anti-abortion actions to shut down clinics, often by lining up hundreds of bodies before a door. Instead of sharing the more legislative focus of NOW or NARAL, it takes to the streets with a direct-action approach. This is attractive especially to young people who have energy for protest and are often not satisfied with slower methods.

"The oppression against women is increasing," said WHAM! member Ann Wagoner, twenty-three, who is also an editor at *The Guardian.* "The Supreme Court is packed. There is a feeling of an inability to act, and here's a way to act and do something and not just be sitting on your ass and not participating.

"Direct action is a form of empowerment, a last resort. Because there's no other recourse. Dinkins is a pro-choice mayor and he hasn't done shit."

One clinic defender interviewed, a student at New York University, said she was frustrated after joining a major women's group that didn't satisfy her more militant needs for abortion rights. Many radical feminists criticize that NOW is too moderate and is more of a "lobby" than a grass-roots group. A group of clinic defenders from Detroit present at the NOW conference said that they were impatient with Molly Yard's long-term focuses, such as to wait until after the year 2000 to reintroduce ERA, when enough women legislators will be in place.

WHAM! seems to model itself in procedure and tactics after ACT-UP, the dynamic direct-action group that has helped make strides in funding for and awareness of HIV and AIDS. From the beginning, WHAM has had a close association with ACT-UP, with many of its founders coming from that group's women's caucus.

At this meeting, as at those held by ACT-UP, people huddle around tables picking up copies of informational newspaper articles and newsletters left in piles.

In contrast to the love-child, peace-now, hippie groups of the Sixties, ACT-UP and WHAM share the same postpunk sense of shock and anger. Wagoner explains that to get media attention, it must be theatrical. Simple arrests are "old hat."

As with early radical feminists who took to the streets WHAM! members have catchy slogans, such as "Get your rosaries off my ovaries!" and "Every ejaculation a college education!" In its newsletter, WHAM! features a "Misogynist of the Month."

Pictures of a past protest against cuts in federal funding for poor women show members veiled in black carrying a casket with the sign: "A woman dies faster from a botched abortion than a man." At an upcoming $500-a-plate Church fund-raiser, WHAM! joked it would disseminate fliers and plan a mock "counterprotest" from the Sisters of our Lady of Vengeance, or a cluster of members dressed as priests, nuns and monks.

Janice Pemberton, twenty-three, an AIDS crisis counselor and UCLA student who attended a WHAM! meeting in New York, started the second presently known chapter in Los Angeles in 1991. She said she is drawn to the group for its "militancy" and the same kind of commitment that ACT-UP is known for. For her, it fills a void in providing a model for regular escorts to clinics. The groups available to her generally only appear during large-scale hits by Operation Rescue, but she wants to provide regular protection.

As with the WHAM! members in New York, abortion is not Pemberton's only focus. She wants to provide escorting to ensure women's other health needs at the clinics as well. "I think a lot of women's health issues are tied up in the clinic. I mean, they don't know if you're going in for a Pap smear or birth control or a cervical cancer check or whatever. They don't really care.

"So if you have a mammogram and are coming back for the results, and you can't get in, to me, that's a woman's health issue."

I witnessed a strong example of the commitment of both pro-choice —and anti-abortion—forces one Saturday morning in October at an East Side Manhattan clinic.

Just a few feet from the front door, behind the blue New York Police Department barrier, are the front lines of the abortion struggle. Before the entrance, huddled in prayer, stand eight antichoice protesters. They hold posters of dead fetuses, including one that says "Freedom of Choice?" with an aborted head on a scalpel. Waiting in the wings about halfway down the block is a young man with a Bible, who approaches women he sees walking toward the clinic.

Upstairs, the teeming waiting room, with more than one hundred people sitting on the stark vinyl chairs, resembles a crowd scene from Penn Station. Only it is quiet. People sit and stare or talk quietly in twos. They are predominantly people of color, with 80 percent black and the rest Latino or white.

Outside the clinic, spread out in a larger radius around the three street corners are four escorts wearing pink jackets that read "Volunteer Escort" in English and Spanish.

I talk to one woman, Kyra, thirty-three, a New York University student, who says she rides her bicycle thirty blocks here every Saturday because of her strong beliefs for women's rights.

We look at the anti-abortion group chanting at a black woman who is approaching.

"Anyone who isn't white, they assume they're having an abortion. They will say, 'Don't kill your black baby,' " says Kyra, who doesn't know who I am and doesn't want to give me her last name.

Mike, twenty-three, a WHAM! member standing nearby, says, "They say they're messengers of God."

I ask Kyra if she ever got caught in any violence. She says the clinic was bombed a few years ago, but she personally has been in only a few "skirmishes" in which was kicked. She talks about one regular foe, an older woman living on the Upper East Side.

"If you try to block her, she will kick and punch. A few weeks ago, she punched a WHAM! member really hard."

Kyra talks about more regular verbal confrontations with the other side. "They come up to you and ask why you are worshipping the devil, killing children."

Kyra also has extended her duties beyond this block. "One girl had me take her to a hotel. She said, 'I'm really shaken up. Can you take me?' "

Suddenly, we see a small elderly lady break through two escorts in pink jackets and rush toward the door. The police stop her and she leaves reluctantly. Kyra says that was the woman she was talking about earlier.

I also learn how trained the escorts' eyes have become with their regular duty. She points ahead to a well-groomed couple with dark leather jackets walking into a coffee shop. As we were talking, she had seen them sit in their car for a half hour and then walk around the block a few times.

"You're being observant," I say, trying to write on my small notepad, my fingers numb from the cold and my pen jamming up.

"You can tell, from the body language, types of people."

"You usually get a man and a woman or a woman and woman. There's a hesitation."

Another escorter standing nearby adds: "You can tell women don't look terribly happy. There's a look."

Kyra says they usually come with a boyfriend, mother or aunt. "They spot the people on the block. They stop and look—it's that split second where you slow down and assess what is happening."

But the clientele are mainly obvious because of the clinic's low rate of $150 to $300 for abortions. It mainly attracts young people and women of color from out of the area, and often from small towns in New Jersey where discretion is not possible.

Suddenly I look up from my notebook and see a man's face. He gives the name of the clinic in a questioning tone. Kyra says, "Yes," and joins him and the young woman he is with, without skipping a beat.


## Fighting Poverty

Other young feminists have taken to the streets to promote social change following their own unique visions and philosophies. Some fight grass-roots battles against poverty that have otherwise been abandoned as hopeless or not worth the effort.

Among them, Elise Mann is innovating new partnerships and coalitions. Here, at her gritty third-floor loft office on the South Side of Chicago, is the cutting edge of feminism. Outside the building other offices have been abandoned, with their windows boarded and insides burnt out.

Mann explained that she feels the future of the women's movement is to "jump start" interested groups with its foundation of knowledge and resources. She is the executive director of Women United for a Better Chicago, founded in 1983, which has brought the strength of the women's movement into the inner city as an advocacy and organizing tool. It has specifically reached out to some of the most disempowered and stigmatized: the city's public-housing residents.

"I think that there's a real fear around poverty that permeates the society, whether it's by the feminists or archconservatives or what have you," said Mann. "I think it really boils down to recognizing people's dignity, self-respect."

Women United, a historically multiracial group, has helped public-housing residents set up their own action group CHARTA, or Chicago Housing Authority Residents Taking Action. The group, which emerged from a Women United public-housing conference in 1987, empowers women by providing information about housing and city policies, and giving them more of a voice and feeling of control in their lives.

"That's a whole area, a whole population of women, that hasn't been touched or reached out to during the women's movement," said Mann. "There are 150,000 that live in public-housing developments in Chicago. I'm talking the vast majority, 80 percent, are single heads of households. There is always the stigma around people living in public housing, and not a lot of attention paid to working together."

Mann, who is white, comes from the mixed lower and middle-class South Side neighborhood of Hyde Park and grew up with a strong role model. Her father, a state representative, was instrumental in dialogues between the Jewish and black communities in the 1960s and 1970s, and was an early ally of the late Chicago mayor Harold Washington, a progressive African American.

Now Mann has followed his lead and is further applying her feminist principles to empower others. The board of Women United hired her in 1988 right after she graduated from Northwestern University in Evanston, Illinois.

"They took a chance on someone like me who had a history of student activism but no experience in the nonprofit sector," she said.

Since, Mann and her board have helped CHARTA with the basics: acting as fiscal agent to get it grants, teaching how to prepare for and run a meeting, and sharing their office space.

Alberta McCain, fifty-five, who is black and the president of CHARTA, explained that her group's independence has determined its effectiveness in meeting its own needs. Now CHARTA is almost a completely separate entity.

"They gave suggestions," said McCain, "but [they didn't] say, 'If you don't follow my way you won't have it or it won't be right.' They gave us freedom, and I think that's a credit to them as well as to us."

One of the first organizing efforts was to make the housing developments' tenant advisory councils more accountable to residents. They had become self-serving through the years and were not responsive to the tenants. Mann says the elections were corrupt, done through petitions, to which only a privileged handful of people had access.

CHARTA started a secret ballot election, which brought some of the members to formal leadership.

"That is really participatory democracy, what I think feminism is all about," said Mann.

CHARTA has also helped make the housing developments more true to their original purpose of temporary housing. It helped implement a freeze on rent when someone gets a job, to allow them a period to save and get back on their feet.

McCain said the power comes through information. One example is a flier published that outlines the often overlooked "repair and deduct" clause in the lease that covers minor repairs. She also holds workshops about "empowerment," from developing leadership skills to holding forums for candidates to tell how they will help residents.

Mann recognizes that conflicts exist between Women United organizers and CHARTA residents, who often have different ideas of how things should be run. CHARTA is also challenged in confronting such a mammoth and entrenched system. It has a limited budget and resources, and can make only a minimal difference in the realm of the larger-scale reform that is much needed.

But Mann said one great achievement is realizing the true meaning of diversity for feminist groups. She said it comes with outreach that includes addressing the issues of those who most need empowerment.

"I think that some of the problems that I've seen with some of the groups is they are wanting to have diversity, but they are not really wanting to know what that means, in the fullest sense of the word," said Mann. "They are always wanting to invite people in, and not wanting to go out."

## Labor Organizing

Like public-housing residents, other women organizing across the country have the same motivation: survival. They are people who haven't chosen to take the life path of activists; it just happened that way. Many are struggling across the country to improve labor conditions in low-paying fields in order to improve their lives.

One effort is to institutionalize a voice and leverage for workers, or form unions, in traditional women's fields, such as the service industries. Organizing labor is one of the most recognized strategies for raising the wages of women in low-income jobs.

Chrystl Bridgeforth, twenty-six who works in the national office of the Coalition of Labor Union Women in New York, said unions provide needed security for the growing numbers of women entering the work force. "If you go to work, the employer is getting a service from you, and you are getting paid by the employer. But if you are a union member, you are getting something more. You have a relationship with the employer."

She also emphasized protection from injury, especially in nontraditional work. "We don't all have easy jobs. There's people who have to go out there and work on an assembly line, to work with things hazardous to their health. What if there isn't something to check how much lead is in there? That means anyone could bring anything in, and you have to accept it because you need the paycheck."

More than 30 percent of workers (twenty-eight million) earn a less-than-adequate or low wage, generally defined as $5.30 an hour or less. But among unionized workers, only 13 percent earn low wages. Almost half of these workers in this category live in households with children.

At each wage level, unionized workers are more likely to be covered by their employers' health insurance. They also have more leverage to negotiate benefits, such as child care and parental leave.

But union organizers are stressing a special need for women to unite in new frontiers, traditionally female careers. They want to take the battle from the automobile plant to the typing pool. The largest women's occupational category is secretarial and clerical workers, with women making up 80 percent of the 142 million full-time workers, according to 1990 statistics from Institute for Women's Policy Research.

While these workers' wages are central to family income, salaries are low. The median weekly salary for full-time nonsupervisory secretaries and clericals is $300. But full-time unionized workers in these occupations earn an additional $56 a week more than those not covered by a union contract. Only 13 percent of workers in these fields are unionized, according to the Institute.

Donene Williams, twenty-seven, the president of the Harvard University local of clerical workers, has witnessed firsthand the changes and the challenges. When she started work at Harvard in 1987 as a secretary, clericals were in the last leg of an arduous drive that had started when she was ten years old. In her basement office, rows of black-and-white pictures of different stages in organizing, leading up to the victory campaign, hang on a beam of the low ceiling.

Now the unionization of the 3,400 support-staff workers stands as a model for other clericals at both public and private universities.

Williams first got involved as an "activist" whose main job was to go out and talk to co-workers one on one. She said while it was intimidating at first, this practice was their greatest weapon. When she and about eighty others finally got to the negotiating table, they were able to document the workers' problems with story after story.

"[Administrators] really had a misconception of what our lives were like," Williams said, speaking with the same serious and straightforward tone she likely used at that table. "We said for our people, the American dream isn't to own our own home. It's to live in an apartment without roommates."

The gains were dramatic in the first three-year contract. They negotiated an average of a 32 percent increase in salaries, a pension improvement and a pool of $50,000 for child care and $25,000 for education, to be set aside each year.

Williams said organizers unwittingly innovated their own effective feminist negotiating skills, which she describes as a "less combative, a less competitive style.

"It forces the employer to work on our terms. They aren't used to this. As you can imagine, Harvard is a bastion of white maleness. They're used to fighting hard and doing things the best and coming out on top.

"And we're forcing them to work in the manner in which we want to work: 'You sit down and you figure out what are all the parts of the problem, and figure out what is the best thing to do, and do the right thing.' "

Organizers also were successful in looking after the interests of everyone in the group, not just their own. Williams, who was head of the negotiating team for health benefits, explained. "It's single-minded as a young person to say I only care about child care and education benefits. 'I won't retire for thirty years, so it's not important to me.' "

She described the end goal: "It's developing a community at

Harvard. It's finding people working in isolated parts of the campus and bringing them together and finding a sense of common ground.

Most of the people in the union fit Williams's demographic group: young women in their twenties. As a result, these clericals had difficulty in visualizing themselves as union members, who are traditionally white males in industrial fields, such as in welding or carpentry. Williams certainly does not fit the burly macho stereotype, with her small thin build and short blond hair.

"Most of us have never been in a union or don't come from a background with family members in unions," said Williams, who attended California State University and was raised in a household supported by public aid. "I knew basically that unions helped people get higher wages and that they had to go on strike sometimes. That's what I knew about unions."

She stressed why both women's image of themselves in unions and unions' reception of women have to change. "It's not a part of [women's] culture because unions have been traditionally populated by men and run by men. That's not necessarily true anymore because of the way the American work force is changing. More and more women are working, and more and more women are the sole income providers for their families."

## WOMEN OF COLOR EXPLORE IDENTITIES

### Activism Through Art

Back in Chicago, I saw another revolution improving women's lives. But like others, it wasn't visible in the newspapers or on the evening news.

This winter night, I felt as if I were going to a secret, underground event. I had the address of the Wholesome Roc Café, but the buildings in this frayed North Side neighborhood were not well marked and the streets were dark. In the shadows, I saw the white, windowless building with the correct address, parked as close to the front door as possible and rang the bell. As I stood out there shivering, I felt as if I were about to enter a speakeasy, common during the gangster days more than half a century earlier. Did I need a secret password?

But I knew I had reached the right place when a young woman answered and light poured out from the doorway. She led me through what looked like a gallery. In the hallways were vibrant paintings of black women in contemporary dress, from a Southern lady with a bonnet to a blues singer.

In a larger room, a small crowd of young black women were gathering for the upcoming performance around the few dozen seats. The small café counter was open for business, and some were drinking cider and eating burritos one of the women had prepared. On the side was a spiral staircase that led up to a loft where the owner, another young woman, lived.

After taking a while to get up their nerve, the two performers, Jamika Ajalon and Nikki Mitchell, both wearing loose and colorful cotton vests, approached the part of the floor set aside as a stage. Very carefully, Ajalon lit some incense sticks. Then she held up a ceramic bowl that held cottony white dried spores, the kind that form in a dandelion's last stages of life. She scattered them lightly around herself, and Mitchell began playing the flute lightly from the sidelines.

After setting this gentle tone, Ajalon began her reading of "The Red Season":

"It's painful. It hurts a little. Like sipping honey lemon tea, too hot and sticky. Lemon much stronger than the honey. Down an inflamed throat.

"It's living on the very edge, one foot dangling. One breath from diving over. It's the needle barely tickling the skin of an overly inflated balloon. The rough scream just behind my chapped lips, the reason for my RED SEASON. . . ."

". . . So why in the hell—an educated black girl like me got to be so angry, with that ring in her nose like a raging bull—why she got to walk around with nappy hair singin' Marley and whistlin Makeba melodies like she so sad, so angry. . . .

"Well, I'm gonna tell you right here that I have a right to every insane bone in my body and if I want to spit, it's my business. If I want to grow thick big tree branches on my head, it's my business. . . ."

While her work is entirely unique, she has had inspiration from others. Ajalon, twenty-three, a poet, who also works at a feminist and African American bookstore in the city, credits black feminist writers such as Audre Lorde and Bell Hooks for laying the groundwork for her art. Both have done landmark work to bring black women to feminism.

Since reading them and others, starting in high school, she has dedicated her life to her art. Originally from suburban St. Louis, she started out at the journalism school at the University of Missouri-Columbia. Now she has decided to be an artist and studies film and video at Columbia College in Chicago. In the past few years, her work has been published locally and in national black lesbian publications. In the future, she wants to get a master's degree in black women's studies and teach "something combining black women's studies and film" at a university.

Ajalon seems to be joining a movement of feminist women of color who are in a renaissance of art, literature and theory. The Wholesome Roc is a symbol of their increasing organization. It was founded in the late Eighties and has served as an enclave for black feminists and lesbians to gather and share ideas.

"We are becoming a lot more visible, even here in the Midwest," said Ajalon, who in person shows a softer side than her stage persona. "But there is definitely a core group of people forming across the nation."

The self-exploration seems to mirror the discovery of white middle-class women twenty-five years ago when they gathered informally in groups. They too expressed rage and formed theories and frameworks to explain the unspoken. But here issues of race are predominant and inseparable in discussion of identity and in struggles to relate to other feminists.

## Three Seeds Planted

When I was in school at the University of Illinois in Champaign in the late 1980s, I rarely heard the connections made between racism and sexism in feminist dialogue. The feminists and people of color were engaged in their own separate battles to make a more user-friendly campus.

But at the University YWCA on Wright Street, the same place where we used to go to see the late-night campus movies on weekends, a revolution of thought is taking place. In the corner wing of the YWCA, three different feminist groups of three different races have taken root simultaneously in the midst of a whirlwind of social forces. They seem to have suddenly been cultivated from the ground, as if they grew from the dandelion spores Jamika Ajalon blew out into the air.

They are the Womanist Circle, for black women, formed in 1988; La Fuerza, for Latinas, started in 1989; and the Reflecting Pool, for whites, formed in 1990. Together, these three small groups of feminists provide models of some of the most powerful organizing structures for the future of the women's movement. They are based on the most fundamental tools of the wave from twenty-five years ago, consciousness-raising groups, but are also driven with some distinctive Nineties perspectives and innovations.

All three of the YWCA groups were founded by activists working in different organizations who felt isolated and needed a space to work out their experiences and gain support from their peers. The women of color were often working in antiracism groups that were not giving them a serious voice. Unlike some white feminists at the YWCA, they were not satisfied with women's studies as a way to explain their identities.

Like the other groups, the Womanist Circle, attended regularly by about ten women, emerged to build solidarity and support among black women. It also recently started holding meetings in residence halls arranged through black student unions.

"Two black women specifically have come through this and said, 'This is great, because I never felt I could talk to women, because they're too chatty or so and so,' " said member Tiffany Ferguson, twenty, who is from Chicago and wants to be a public interest attorney. "And they have come to the Womanist Circle or come to the assertiveness-training workshops and said, 'I didn't feel I was in competition or someone was picking on me or seeing what I had on, [we were] just being with one another and sharing our experiences.' "

Along with La Fuerza, the Womanist Circle discusses the experience of living as "the other" in society. One effect is "internalized racism," or actually absorbing and even subconsciously believing negative stereotypes about themselves. Some also define it as feeling society's anger toward one's own group.

"I was raised that black people are beautiful: 'Aren't you glad you're black? Isn't it wonderful?' I have always been comfortable saying, 'I'm glad I'm black,' " Ferguson said with a laugh.

"Unfortunately, a lot of people haven't been exposed to that or haven't been raised like that, and I really feel they can't say, 'I'm glad I'm black. I'm glad I'm a black woman.' "

At La Fuerza, co-founder Hortencia Velez, 20, explains that her group also fills a gap by providing connection among Latina women of different backgrounds. She noted two disjointed parts of the group's regulars, which include about a dozen women: those from the suburbs who had little sense of tradition, and those from immigrant families from the inner city. Together, they challenge the stereotype of Latinos as a monolithic group.

One member, Susana Vasquez, twenty, who grew up in a predominantly white suburb knowing only the basic Spanish she learned in high school, said that she found the group to be a link to the Latina community. For the first time, she felt that she was embracing rather than avoiding her identity as a Latina. At a younger age, she felt the support to examine both parts of herself was not available because she was a bi-cultural child raised by a white mother.

While the suburban Latinas are trying to find connection, those from the city are trying to deal with their cultural expectations. Velez, who comes from the inner city, said that she and others feel a lack of support in their education from traditional families:

"Every single Latina from the inner city of Chicago has gotten a comment from a father or a brother who said, 'You are just going to get pregnant, and your education won't mean anything.' It's different for Latinas because you are born and raised to be a care-giver and to have a mother role at the end."

In La Fuerza, they each create their own role models. Older graduate students provide inspiration for academic success. Vasquez said her mother is white, and has not thought about these issues. Velez's mother died two years ago, and her father is questioning why she started the group. But through these discussions, she has learned how to talk to him.

"Here, you learn how to speak up, or at least we learn how to formulate our ideas so we can get in a good argument," said Velez.

But perhaps the most isolated person among those in the three groups is Sherrie Towery, twenty-one, who is white. In her past two years of college, she has been embroiled in battles against racism and knows very few white role models for this effort.

She especially found herself struggling when she made headlines on campus as the first white vice president of the Central Black Student Union. Then, after reading a passage about white antiracism activists by Malcolm X, she slowly realized that she could do the most good working in the white community.

"I realized that through being around a bunch of people who think racism is bad, I wasn't fighting the problem I claimed I wanted to fight," said Towery.

She founded the Reflecting Pool at the YWCA, where other feminists had been informally meeting and discussing these issues and attitudes toward race. She said as a white group, it fills a longstanding gap that is still present in the women's movement in addressing racism. Much has to do with internal personal work process that is required to unlearn white racism. The group also works to understand perspectives of women of color and build bridges with them.

Also significant about the group is that it is a safe, nonjudgmental place for white women to explore basic issues and feelings about racism. It also takes the burden off women of color, who are often expected to educate white women about their attitudes. This sharing helps relieve feelings of guilt that often accumulate when white feminists realize they are part of the same sexist and racist system they have been criticizing.

"That's why the Reflecting Pool is a good place. We're all learning together that you don't have to feel dumb about saying these things. The fact is that you were raised to think these things. I think the Y is a good place where we can say, 'It's the norm,' " Towery said.

The Reflecting Pool gives Towery a forum to discuss issues particular to white people fighting racism, such as those she confronts in her personal life. She has had conflict, becoming completely intolerant of racist remarks by white friends—now former friends—from her hometown, a white middle-class suburb. At home, where these issues were not widely discussed, her mother also does not understand why she is fighting these battles and worries about its effect.

"She sees it as me being this odd person in society who feels these things, and therefore life won't be as easy. She sees me as countercultural, and that's a negative thing," said Towery.

Towery had a long history with the YWCA in becoming politicized. During her freshman year, she went to a lecture sponsored by the Y about racism being fought in the 1960s to gather material for a speech class. She wondered about efforts waged since then and has continued to develop her own theories. Now she is a member of the national student council of the YWCA.

After a semester of Reflecting Pool meetings, in spring of 1991, Towery was encouraged with a list of twenty names and eight to ten regulars at her bimonthly meetings. But through her fight, she is still challenged by a lack of white peers. Also, after two years of studying racism, she said she is at an impasse. She has surpassed the knowledge of the older white feminists on campus, who are grappling with these issues, and most other white students, some of whom have told her they don't view racism as existing.

"I feel I'm educating all these other white people about it, and I want someone to teach me something for a change," she said.

Often people are intensely curious about what drives Towery. She describes a natural interest in civil rights that has been cemented into commitment with her years of study and exploration. Like feminists with a heightened awareness, she explained it would be impossible "to go back to the old stereotypes" of indifference about how white people are supposed to act. She plans a career in teaching and wants to stay involved with the YWCA for the rest of her life.

## CAREER ACTIVISM

Looking at the diversity of young women organizers it becomes clear that there is no one correct way to effect change. Many people interviewed expressed the common-sense belief that individuals can do the most good in the women's movement by choosing their own channels where they can be effective.

Jamie Lee Evans, twenty-three, who works to raise money for domestic-violence shelters and rape crisis centers in Oakland, gave advice to people wanting to become activists:

"Everyone has to reflect on their lives and see where they are dissatisfied, see what parts of America they dislike, whether it be war, violence against women, violence against animals. Take a look around and see what you're not happy with. There is probably an organization of some people who are as unhappy as you are, and then you can work to make a stand on that and work for change."

A countless number of young people are working in subtle ways, such as in voting or promoting equity in their workplaces, although they don't have feminist-oriented careers. This more mainstream approach is practical, especially at their stage of life. Many who had graduated from college told me that getting their own lives together and gaining independence was the only struggle for liberation for which they had time to spare.

But a common route for those more interested in organizing is to make a career of it. At this point, where real-life commitments are being made to feminism, the women overwhelmingly stood out. While men expressed feminist beliefs, those active after attending college were almost exclusively female.

Often a diversity of women activists find refuge working in the non-profit sector. Chrystl Bridgeforth, who is black and originally from a working-class neighborhood in the Bronx, works as a national organizer of union women in New York City. She said this fits her personality.

"I'm a political-type person. Maybe it's a losing battle, but I want to help the underdog. Pretty soon everyone is going to be the underdog if it keeps going like this."

Some are driven by personal experience. Throughout her childhood, Jamie Lee Evans is a survivor of ritualized sexual assault and abuse both in her home and on the street, and also witnessed her mother being battered for thirteen years. She is Asian American, but was raised by white parents and spent a year in a foster home.

Now she wants to protect others. Her organization, the United Communities for Human Rights in Oakland, which was founded in

1984, is made up of women who canvass homes door-to-door to raise money for battered women and also to provide them with outreach.

Evans makes a regular statement of "taking back the night five times a week" by doing her work in the evening. This "lets women know that there are women warriors out there who are going to take risks to help them, that women are courageous," said Evans.

After growing up in Gardena, a poverty-stricken neighborhood of Los Angeles, she graduated from the University of California at Santa Cruz and now feels a responsibility to put her education to good use. She was the first person in her family to graduate from high school.

"There are no voices for poor people. I feel my family didn't have the opportunity to be active, and I do. I've got an education. I've got a voice. I've got the women who have been behind me twenty years, one hundred years. And because of what I've been through, I've got the drive."

Others interviewed realized their desires to work for a feminist cause later in their careers. Mary Servatius, thirty, who is one of the founders of Young Women's Action Network and is white, from a working-class neighborhood in Chicago, started working in a corporation after earning a business degree in college.

"I found it really claustrophobic, literally. And I did it for two years and suddenly I felt completely unfulfilled. I finally realized that I needed to do work that I felt passionate about, that I cared about, that somehow related to my life, to myself—and doing financial planning for a corporation wasn't it."

To gain that fulfillment, she worked as a volunteer at a rape crisis line during the evenings. Through this work, she met the director of a women's foundation, who hired her as program officer. She said she enjoys helping provide a network for feminist activists and learning about the issues. Servatius's foundation funds feminist projects that are working for change and appeals to bigger general foundations to give money to women's organizations. The women's foundation movement is a phenomenon that emerged at a quick pace during the 1980s; in 1989, fifty were scattered around the United States, ten of them established that year alone.

"I feel there's a real direct relationship with my life. As a woman, I fear walking alone at night, because of the fear of sexual assault. Now I'm working to end some of that, or at least trying to provide services to victims of sexual assault. It feels like home. It's something I have to struggle with, [that] makes me very angry and that I can speak very passionately about," Servatius said.

Others say that finding a job in the nonprofit world is also a challenge because of a scarcity of slots and harsh competition. "It's very difficult going from working on women's issues on a campus basis, and then getting a job and doing it," said Karen Brown, twenty-four, who is white and a researcher at the Families and Work Institute in New York City. She comes from an upper-middle-class family in Westchester, New York.

Servatius also stressed that sacrifice of salary is common with nonprofits.

"Basically, it took me four years to work up to the level of salary I had when I left the corporation. If I had stayed in the corporate world, I'd probably be making $10,000 more now," Servatius said.

"I think it's more recently [since] I reached the age of thirty that those issues are more of a concern, of making more money now. It really didn't bother me early on. I knew that there was a great opportunity to learn a lot and do things that I was passionate about. It definitely has been more of a worry, more of a concern."

While she said she understands how nonprofits can't afford to pay large salaries, Servatius wants to challenge the "suffering-for-a-cause" ethic prevalent in these organizations. Often people feel as if they are being punished for living up to their ideals by being thrown crusts of bread for compensation or being expected to work strenuous hours.

"I also think that we need to change the idea that people should put up with a lot less salary because they get to do what they want," said Servatius.

While she said she would follow no other career, Jamie Lee Evans also discussed her occasional sense of resentment with her tremendous work load in feeling that she is taking on others' responsibilities.

"It's unconscionable that there is incredible violence against women and children, and that people are not acting against it. I don't have a lot of sympathy for people who aren't out there doing their part. It's hard."

## Chapter Ten

# Conclusion

THE FIRST EXPRESSLY feminist piece of writing I ever read was "Diving into the Wreck," a poem by Adrienne Rich, which has come to my mind while writing this book and thinking about the future. Freshman year of college, I first examined, in a paper, the meaning of some of the imagery, which is as relevant now as it was when the words were written in 1972.

The narrator of the poem is on a treacherous and unguided journey: "I came to explore the wreck," she says. She is bravely diving into the ocean to investigate an old and deteriorating ship. Her equipment is a knife, perhaps for fighting; a camera, for recording what she finds; and a "book of myths," as a journal.

To get a clear view, she has to struggle to get deep, deep, deep, beyond the surface of the water:

> I go down
> Rung after rung and still
> the oxygen immerses me
> the blue light
> the clear atoms
> of our human air.
> I go down.
> My flippers cripple me,
> I crawl like an insect down the ladder
> and there is no one
> to tell me when the ocean
> will begin

In my paper, I said Rich was taking the initiative to inspect the tired and unneeded parts of society, exposing its myths. A central source of the myths seemed to be sexism, which has kept women from achieving their potential.

Now younger feminists are calling for women and men to embark on another difficult mission: a continued exploration of these myths—and others—that still requires plunging way beneath the surface.

The great payoff, the still elusive treasure waiting to be plundered, is based on the original radical feminist vision of "sisterhood," which was a more popular topic of discussion at the time the poem was written. As Bell Hooks has said, sisterhood is essential for a mass-based political movement and real change and improvements to occur. Sisterhood is still possible, and also powerful. But, for too many people, the word has become as outdated as other concepts from the Seventies, joining the ranks of disco and the leisure suit.

In researching this book, it has become clear that everyone has to take different paths and shatter their own myths. But I have also observed some general patterns of thinking that could provide useful approaches for different groups.

First, for many nonactivists, a basic myth that seems yet to be overcome is the rigid stereotype of what a feminist or an activist is. As I have written, feminism is not to gender what communism is to class. It does not mean wiping out all distinctions between the sexes and dismantling all traditions. But it does mean asking questions about them.

Besides, those interviewed who call themselves feminists have themselves illustrated that there is no one way to be a feminist. They espouse no one mode of thinking, of being, of dressing, of talking, of strategizing. A diversity of opinions and ideas defining feminism keeps it fluid, vigilant, growing and responsive to people's needs.

One danger of the feminist stereotype is that it divides women instead of uniting them. It discourages them from looking beyond the surface of what feminism is and keeps them "in their place," not recognizing their own present convictions. You can't make waves if you're afraid to even dive into the water. Yet it seems that after just a little bit of thought, people overcome this block and realize that they support some of feminism's most basic principles.

The potential of those who don't consider themselves feminists is tremendous to support a mass-based political movement. They can give organizers new strength just by acting on what they believe in.

"People have to know that activists are not a rare breed," said Jamie Lee Evans. "They are just like you. They are just like me. They are just like everyone. They come from all classes, all colors, all religions."

"It's easier for people not to do anything when they see that there is a certain breed of warriors who were born that way, who are supposed to do the work, and that's not true."

Second, for older feminists and others, there seems to be a need to shatter myths about younger people being too apathetic, too young or inexperienced to be politicized, not naturally inclined to politics. To take part in the feminist movement, young women need confidence and space to express their needs and assume real leadership roles. This should not just be done to be considerate to younger women. It is a question of survival for the torch to be passed and remain burning.

Next, to men: In joining the civil rights struggle for empowerment of women, many have realized that seeing their stake in the issues and becoming aware of sexism is the first step. But it is only the beginning. More need to do an in-depth housecleaning of their own attitudes. With this effort, they can become an essential component in a mass-based women's movement and also empower themselves.

But many men do not seem to have undertaken even the most basic thinking to break down their own stereotypes of the "feminist man" as a feminine, castrated, overly sensitive doormat of women. Often, this is a more rigid stereotype than that of feminist women, and discourages men's thought and investigation into feminism.

Finally, to all women: While commited feminist men work to think about their dominance, women must also contemplate their own contribution to the current system. One of the most difficult feminist battles is internal: to fight the myths about other women. Activists have called for a new stage of consciousness-raising about race and class and homophobia and anti-Semitism—any force that makes someone feared as "the other."

With this work, differences can be transformed from barriers into launching pads.

Yet, for all, in addition to addressing myths, the greatest key to feminism in the Nineties is perhaps the neglected element of social consciousness. It involves making a commitment to women—a most basic and fundamental principle of feminism.

This transforms feminism from an exclusive, self-centered, individualist struggle to one for women. It also acts as an insurance policy for the movement to survive and develop. People know the work isn't done when their own personal goals have been realized.

But in writing this book, I have noticed a schism in social consciousness among two distinct groups: the activists and nonactivists. The nonactivists seemed mainly to name concerns of the white and middle class and did not seem to focus beyond to people of color or those with low incomes. For example, keeping abortion legal was named, while access to abortion for the poor or younger women was not.

In contrast, the activists seemed to miss the white middle class, which is a significant power and constituency. In "progressive" and bohemian circles, even the white middle class did not seem to want to associate itself with the white middle class. Radical feminists also must not forget the bread-and-butter issues of family—child care, parental leave, making the workplace more flexible, violence against women—which affect everyone. The white middle class—which is slowly, economically, becoming the white lower class—has some important and urgent issues that should not be trivialized or scorned.

The period of pronounced activism of the 1960s can still provide some powerful lessons. Then, social consciousness was a part of popular dialogue, and people seemed to cultivate more confidence in their abilities to effect change for themselves and for others.

The 1960s also seemed to encompass more of a collective vision. I agree that individual battles are essential, such as in becoming a teacher or a social worker, being philanthropic, volunteering. But while working in one's niche, the feminist must also keep an eye on the big picture. This means being a watchdog of social policy and voting according to one's beliefs.

Young women must also do their own revision of some 1960s concepts. They need to temper grand, idealistic visions with some realism and cautiousness. Those activists and feminists interviewed seemed to realize that activists in the Sixties almost collapsed under the weight of their own ambition. Social-justice activists seemed to run a long-distance race to achieve the Utopian Society with the drive and speed of sprinters. But the runners appeared spent after the first lap.

I'll paraphrase the outlook that several activists related to me. In the Nineties, feminists have to pace themselves and keep their eyes down to see barriers that must be confronted. Meanwhile, they must also always be looking far enough ahead to see the finish line.

Making this commitment is difficult because it goes against the way young people have generally been socialized. Especially for white middle-class people, it requires a special effort to look beyond one's own experience. This involves initiative in learning about others and the risk of journeying into the unknown, being awkward and hitting snags.

Obliterating all these myths and building this social consciousness and sisterhood sounds like a lot of work. Is it worth the struggle? Why don't we just call ourselves humanists and abandon the feminist critiques? Why do we want to continue the women's movement?

The reason to break all these myths? I can summarize it in one word: power.

Feminism is one model for empowering the individual and then harnessing that collective energy for change. For the movement, more people acting on their beliefs can mean new life. This common goal of power for all women can give dialogue new freshness and drive. In political terms, a result is to stop and reverse the feminization of poverty, and accelerate and transform the feminization of power.

The motivation for power was most forcefully demonstrated by Anna Padia, director of human rights for the Newspaper Guild. A thunderous speaker, she drew rapt attention at an ambitious conference in October of 1990, planned by young women and the Institute for Women's Policy Research in Washington, D.C., with the following:

> The reason for a diverse East Coast network—why? The answer is power. Both the individual power and the collective power to make the changes you want personally, professionally on the job, in the community and in every institution that you are now in or will be involved in during the future.
>
> This is not to underestimate the power of one individual, for surely we know of individuals who have accomplished great things. Nor is this view to underestimate the tremendous power that already exists and that each of you now posseses, whether you know it or not.
>
> But take your one hand, make that into a fist. Take that fist and magnify that a thousand fold and you have a very different kind of

power. If you take that single one articulate voice of yours and you add it to a choir of a million, you have power.

Send that one postcard to that president, or the Congress or the manufacturer that makes products that are not healthy to your life . . . and you will be heard.

You will persuade. You will compel the attention to effect and implement the policies, the programs, and the very important young women's perspectives that only you can define.

To get at that power, women must visualize themselves as having the right to it. Susan Denevan, twenty-three, the 1990–1991 student body president at the University of Minnesota, said that sexism—both in self-image and in how women are treated—keeps women from achieving power. In this realm, women still basically have the myth of themselves as "the second sex."

"Due to sexism, the system of power distribution has made women not want to be involved with the process of policy-making. When we include classism, sexism, ableism and heterosexism, we see how many people have been locked out of decision-making and our reluctance grows even greater," she said, speaking at NOW's First Young Feminist Conference in 1991.

Denevan also stressed that through traditional and available channels, women can invent the future and transform institutions. "What kind of power do we as women bring to traditional politics? We bring an emphasis on community and interdependence. And not on hierarchy or self-promotion. What does this mean? It means that we see how our survival is linked with the survival of others and of our environment."

But, she added, survival is not enough, and the real source of power must be self-determination, a basic feminist goal.

"Self-determination for all peoples will only be achieved when our current system of power distribution is overthrown. Overthrown does not necessarily mean violent revolution, but it does mean directly confronting the assumptions and actions that disenfranchise all but those conforming to the white male model of leadership."

This myth-breaking of all types of sexism and stereotypes is a weighty, unsettling challenge. It involves unraveling countless assumptions about oneself and about others. It involves confrontation, feeling uncomfortable, taking risks.

But these tremendous challenges also make feminism thrilling. This is groundbreaking work! Nothing could be more revolutionary than breaking down these barriers and empowering ourselves and others. In this country, in a growing multicultural society, looking at issues of diversity is the road to future success in every area: economic, social, in personal relationships. Now feminists are at the forefront of this struggle and are pioneering concepts of understanding and overcoming and celebrating difference.

The waters seem to be at just the right temperature for entry. In traveling across the country, I have noticed a phenomenon of people becoming more aware and concerned about women's rights and other social issues. In unison, people are telling me the same ideas, using almost the same language to describe how they are feeling. Different professors of women's studies across the country have told me that they sense the pendulum swinging back slightly from the right and students becoming more committed to working for others.

Everyone's help is needed to turn any current trends into serious dialogue to propel a movement. These feelings have the potential to result in more than just influencing the looks of the new spring fashions. Instead of continuing to look back to the beat of the Sixties with nostalgia, young people can take their energies and build on past work and make something they can be proud of. The innovative work of the activists profiled gives proof that young people can bring about change.

This work can also teach outsiders a lesson in defining a feminist. In building solidarity, feminists can transcend the popular myth that they are part of a fringe group.

The issue is not just who opens the door for women.

The issue is opening the doors of opportunity and empowering all people—certainly not a trivial matter.

# Resources and Networks

## Young Feminist Networks

NATIONAL ORGANIZATION FOR WOMEN
YOUNG FEMINIST CONFERENCE IMPLEMENTATION COMMITTEE
Plans national young feminist conference and provides national network.

1000 16th Street, Suite 700
Washington, D.C. 20036
(202) 331-0066
Contact: Jennifer Goldberg at (301) 830-2666

NATIONAL ABORTION RIGHTS ACTION LEAGUE
CAMPUS ORGANIZING PROJECT
Serves as a network, helps develop organizing skills, and involves students in
NARAL's legislative work.

1101 14th Street, N.W., fifth floor
Washington, D.C. 20005
(202) 408-4600

STUDENTS ORGANIZING STUDENTS
National reproductive rights organization geared toward empowering young
women and men through education and activism on high school and college
campuses.

1600 Broadway, Suite 905
New York, New York 10019
(212) 977-6710

FEMINIST FUTURES
First national young feminist network, publishes seasonal newsletter, "Sisterline," that acts as forum for sharing organizing ideas and experiences.

Center for Women Policy Studies
2000 P Street, N.W., Suite 508
Washington, D.C. 20036
(202) 872-1770

YOUNG WOMEN'S PROJECT
East Coast grassroots organizing and education effort planned around issues of work, health and violence. Also released unique report about the status of young women in 1990, and activist handbook in 1991.

Institute for Women's Policy Research
1400 20th Street, N.W., Suite 104
Washington, D.C. 20036
(202) 785-5100

WOMEN'S INFORMATION NETWORK
Feminist-oriented social and career-networking group for Democratic professionals working in politics in D.C. area.

319 7th Street
Washington, D.C. 20005
(202) 543-9007

## Resources

YOUNG WOMEN'S HANDBOOK
1991 anthology and resource guide by and for young women. Available from the Young Women's Project at Institute for Women's Policy Research (listed above).

YOUNG WOMEN'S VOICES
1991 anthology of young women's writings about reproductive rights movement; a collaborative effort among several young women's groups.

Available from the NARAL Campus Organizing Project (listed above). Include $3 for postage and handling.

FUND FOR THE FEMINIST MAJORITY AND FEMINIST MAJORITY FOUNDATION
Direct action group with Becky Bell-Rosie Jimenez campaign against restrictions on access to abortion, and Feminization of Power Campus project to advance feminists to leadership positions on campus.

Also offers video, "Abortion Denied: Shattering Young Women's Lives," about parental consent laws; student organizing kits and Bell/Jimenez memorial bracelets.

1600 Wilson Blvd., 704
Arlington, Virginia 22209
(703) 522-2214

8105 West Third, suite 1
Los Angeles, California 90048
(213) 651-0495

CIVIL LIBERTIES AND PUBLIC POLICY PROGRAM
Information clearinghouse and resource for reproductive rights activists; holds annual conference, publishes seasonal newsletter. Has two videotapes for sale about illegal abortion experiences and young activists of speak-outs on reproductive freedom.

Hampshire College
Civil Liberties and Public Policy Program
Amherst, Massachusetts 01002
(413) 549-4600, ext. 645

MEN'S ANTI-RAPE RESOURCE CENTER
Provides clearinghouse for written information, field organizing and technical assistance and public speakers and trainings of educators. MARC works with national and local groups in other countries, making it the only "transnational" men's organization working with men to stop men from sexual violence.

P.O. Box 73559
Washington, D.C. 20056
(301) 386-2737
Contact: Rus Ervin Funk, coordinator

WOMEN OF COLOR RESOURCE CENTER
Provides information and analysis to people organizing around women of color issues. Putting together a directory of women of color organizations.

310 Eighth Street, Suite 307
Oakland, California 94607
(415) 465-1448

TAKE BACK THE NIGHT! VIDEO
A documentary by a 1989 University of California-Santa Cruz graduate and filmmaker.

Write: Jenai Lane
3134 S. Cherry Circle
Mesa, Arizona 85202
Send $15 plus $2.25 for postage.

## Other

NATIONAL WOMEN'S STUDIES ASSOCIATION
Has available guide to women's studies in country.

University of Maryland
College Park, Maryland 20742-1325
(301) 405-5573

YOUNG WOMEN'S CHRISTIAN ASSOCIATION OF THE UNITED STATES
With a twofold mission of empowering women and eliminating racism, the YWCA has student and community chapters in all 50 states and 88 countries.

National headquarters:
726 Broadway
New York, New York 10003
(212) 614-2700

GIRLS INCORPORATED
Provides sports, education and health care programs for girls 8 to 18 with 125 local affiliates in 33 states.

National headquarters:
30 E. 33rd Street
New York, New York 10016
(212) 689-3700

NATIONAL BLACK WOMEN'S HEALTH PROJECT
Provides health education and self-help

1237 Gordon Street, S.W.
Atlanta, Georgia 30310
1-800-ASK-BWHP

CHALLENGING MEDIA IMAGES OF WOMEN

P.O. Box 902
Framingham, MA 01701

MEDIA WATCH
Nonprofit organization dedicated to improving the image of women in the media. Takes pro-education, anticensorship focus. Offers half-hour video.

P.O. Box 618
Santa Cruz, California 95061
(408) 423-6355

WOMEN EXPRESS, INC.
Young feminist company that publishes "Teen Voices," a national magazine by, for and about teenage girls to provide a forum and affirm their self-worth. Seeking submissions and accepting page sponsorships by teens or other groups of women to design a page that expresses their message.

(subscription $25 a year and special teen rates)
P.O. Box 6009
JFK Post Office
Boston, Massachusetts 02114

DEMOCRATIC SOCIALISTS OF AMERICA-YOUTH SECTION
Radical multi-issue national network with chapters on 40 college campuses, holds two annual conferences for activists, offers comprehensive reproductive rights organizing manuals for students.

15 Dutch Street, Suite 500
New York, New York 10038
Contact: Dinah Leventhal at (212) 962-0390

UNITED STATES STUDENT ASSOCIATION
National multi-racial student association that works for access to higher education. Women's and women of color caucuses address issues of reproductive freedom.

1012 14th Street, N.W., Suite 207
Washington, D.C. 20005
(202) 347-USSA

## Feminist Press (for the real scoop on the women's movement)

Ms. MAGAZINE (bimonthly "magabook")

Subscription correspondence:
P.O. Box 57131
Boulder, Colorado 80322-7131

NEW DIRECTIONS FOR WOMEN (bimonthly newspaper)
Political and progressive feminist advocacy journalism.

108 West Palisade Avenue
Englewood, New Jersey 07631
(201) 568-0226

SOJOURNER: THE WOMEN'S FORUM (monthly newspaper)
Feminist newsjournal.

42 Seaverns Avenue
Jamaica Plain, Massachusetts 02130
(617) 524-0415

OFF OUR BACKS (monthly newspaper)
Radical feminist newsjournal run by a collective of women.

2423 18th Street, N.W.
Washington, D.C. 20009
(202) 234-8072

ON THE ISSUES: THE JOURNAL OF SUBSTANCE FOR THE PROGRESSIVE WOMAN
(seasonal magazine)
Feminist, humanist publication.

97-77 Queens Boulevard
Forest Hills, New York 11374

CHANGING MEN: ISSUES IN GENDER, SEX AND POLITICS (twice yearly magazine)
Feminist Men's Publications, Inc.

306 N. Brooks Street
Madison, Wisconsin 53715
(608) 256-2565

BRIDGES: A JOURNAL FOR JEWISH FEMINISTS AND OUR FRIENDS
Literary magazine, published twice annually.

P.O. Box 18437
Seattle, Washington 98118

LILITH (quarterly Jewish magazine)

250 West 57th Street, Suite 2432
New York, New York 10107

# Recommended Reading (not requiring a Ph.D. in women's studies to comprehend):

Just a start, according to sources used for this book and referrals by young feminists interviewed.

*From Abortion to Reproductive Freedom: Transforming a Movement.* Edited by Marilyn Gerber Freid. Boston: South End Press, 1990. A decades-overdue anthology that is ground-breaking in its visions for broadening the definition of reproductive health. Includes essays by Angela Davis, Byllye Avery and other luminaries of the movement.

*Feminist Theory From Margin to Center.* By Bell Hooks. Boston: South End Press, 1984. This book is revolutionary in providing an accessible and relevant feminist theory to build an inclusive mass-based political movement. Also check out her several other insightful books, including *Talking Back: Thinking Feminist, Thinking Black,* which has a more personal point of view.

*Sisterhood Is Powerful: An Anthology of Writings from the Women's Liberation Movement.* Edited by Robin Morgan. New York: Vintage Books, 1970. "First comprensive collection of writings from the Women's Liberation Movement, including articles, poems, photographs and manifestos," says the back cover. Effectively conveys the early revolutionary spirit and fundamental principles of the radical feminist movement.

*On Her Own: Growing up in the Shadow of the American Dream.* By Ruth Sidel. New York: Viking Penguin, 1990. The only recent popular book located exclusively devoted to the study of young women. Sidel, a sociologist at Hunter College who has studied the feminization of poverty (author of *Women and Children Last),* examines the conflict between young women's expectations and current social and economic realities.

*This Bridge Called my Back.* Edited by Cherrie Moraga and Gloria Anzaldua.

New York: Kitchen Table: Women of Color Press, 1981. A classic anthology presenting a fresh and inclusive definition of feminism. Also provides personal critiques of racism within the women's movement. Also see the 1990 anthology going deeper into the same themes, *Making Face, Making Soul (Haciando Caras)*, edited by Anzaldua.

*The Black Women's Health Book: Speaking for Ourselves.* Edited by Evelyn C. White. Seattle: Seal Press, 1990. An anthology of timely essays featuring work by Faye Wattleton, Alice Walker and Marian Wright Edelman, which helps define the future of the women's movement.

*The New Our Bodies, Our Selves: A Book by and for Women.* By the Boston Women's Health Collective. This comprehensive and essential health book achieves one of the greatest goals of the women's movement: helping women gain control of their bodies. This is a must-buy gift for older siblings to give to the younger sister at her next birthday.

*The Sisterhood.* By Marcia Cohen. New York: Fawcett Columbine, 1988. A narrative account of the popular leaders of the women's movement of the 1960s and 1970s. Vividly written in a television miniseries-like style.

*Outrageous Acts and Everyday Rebellions.* By Gloria Steinem. New York: Signet, 1983. A witty and inspiring anthology by the feminist media star, author and speaker. Includes the classic "I Was a Playboy Bunny" exposé.

*Shock Treatment.* By Karen Finley. San Francisco: City Lights Books, 1990. Performance monologues, essays and poetry by the controversial artist who will never make Jesse Helms's reading list. Read for its cathartic ability to express feminist rage: "One day, I hope to God, Bush/Cardinal O'Connor and the Right-to-Lifers each/returns to life as an unwanted pregnant thirteen-year-old girl working at McDonald's at minimum wage."

*Sister Outsider.* By Audre Lorde. Freedom, California: The Crossing Press, 1984. Essays and speeches by a poet laureate of modern feminism. She uniquely and evocatively explores the concepts of difference in writing about the identities of her life as a black woman, lesbian, feminist, mother, cancer survivor and activist.

*Blood, Bread and Poetry: Select Prose 1979–1985.* By Adrienne Rich. New York: W. W. Norton & Company, 1986. An anthology by another muse of the women's movement. This volume includes the influential "Compulsory Heterosexuality and Lesbian Existence" and lectures addressed to the next generation of students.

*I Never Called it Rape.* By Robin Warshaw. New York: Harper and Row, 1988. Landmark book on understanding acquaintance rape, includes Ms. Foundation study. A must-read for anyone in the media to gain more than a superficial understanding of this crime.

*The Second Sex.* By Simone de Beauvoir. Alfred A. Knopf, 1952. As the cover says, "the classic manifesto of the liberated woman." Topping syllabi of women's-studies classes everywhere.

*Century of Struggle.* By Eleanor Flexner. The Belknap Press of Harvard University Press, 1959. A history of the women's movement in the United States that reveals the deep roots of current struggles.

*Feminist Theory: The Intellectual Traditions of American Feminism.* By Josephine Donovan. New York: Frederick Ungar Publishing Company, 1990. A comprensive study of the roots and analyses of the varieties of contemporary feminism.

*A Feminist Dictionary.* By Cheris Kramarae and Paula A. Treichler. London: Pandora Press, 1985. A unique guide that defines language in women's terms and uses a wealth of historic and contemporary feminist quotes from a variety of sources.

Note:

Here is my own unpatented hint to beginners for the ultimate feminist reading resource: Purchase a reader for an introductory women's-studies class at a campus copy shop, such as Kinko's. These are the huge bound packets of copied parts of books and articles, usually costing from $15 to $30.

A reader provides a comprehensive, systematic and quality selection—with the good parts conveniently highlighted for you. This is economical because buying the originals of works copied would probably cost a fortune and take years of study.

# Bibliography

"Abortion Denied: Shattering Young Women's Lives" Fund for the Feminist Majority. (data sheet and video). Washington, D.C., 1990.

Alexander, Keith L. "Minority Women Feel Racism, Sexism Are Blocking the Path to Management." *Wall Street Journal.* July 25, 1990: pp. B1, B2.

*The American Woman 1990–91: A Status Report.* Sara E. Rix, ed., for the Women's Research and Education Institute. New York: W. W. Norton & Company, 1990.

*America's Best Colleges: 1991 College Guide.* U.S. News and World Report Publications. Washington, D.C., June 3, 1991.

"America's Income Gap: The Closer You Look, The Worse It Gets." *Business Week.* April 17, 1989: pp. 78, 79.

Anderson, Lisa. "Medium Cold: Why Women Readers Are Leaving Their Newspapers Behind." *Chicago Tribune.* November 4, 1990: Section 6, p. 4.

Bair, Deirdre. "Biographer Defends de Beauvoir's Choices." *Chicago Tribune.* December 9, 1990: Section 6, p. 5.

Barringer, Felicity. "What IS Youth Coming To?" *New York Times. August 9, 1990:* The Living Arts Section. pp. 1, 5.

Barth, Ilene. "Consent Law Can Condemn a Teenager to Death." *Newsday.* October 14, 1990: p. 8.

Belkin, Lisa. "Bars to Equality of Sexes Seen as Eroding, Slowly." *New York Times.* August 20, 1989: pp. A1, A16.

*The Black Women's Health Book: Speaking for Ourselves.* Evelyn C. White, ed. Seattle: The Seal Press, 1990.

Boston Women's Health Collective. *The New Our Bodies, Ourselves: A Book By and For Women.* 2nd ed. New York: Touchstone/Simon and Schuster, 1984.

Bowles, Nancy. "Students CAN Make a Difference." *National Abortion Rights Action League Campus Newsletter.* Winter 1991: pp. 1, 7.

Breathed, Berke. *Classics of Western Literature: Bloom County 1986–1989.* New York: Little, Brown & Company, 1990.

*This Bridge Called My Back: Writings by Radical Women of Color.* Gloria

Anzaldua and Cherrie Moraga, eds. New York: Kitchen Table: Women of Color Press, 1981.

Brody, Jane. "Personal Health: Bulimia and Anorexia, Insidious Eating Disorders That Are Best Treated When Detected Early." *New York Times.* February 22, 1990: p. B9.

Brotman, Barbara. "Feminists, but Abortion Opponents, too." *Chicago Tribune.* November 12, 1989: Section 2, p. 1, 2.

Buhl, Maria. "The Feminist Mystique: Why College Women Don't Like the Feminist Label." *In View.* September/October 1989: p. 16.

*But Some of Us Are Brave: Black Women's Studies.* Gloria T. Hull, Patricia Bell Scott and Barbara Smith, eds. New York: The Feminist Press at the City University of New York, 1982.

Buttenwieser, Sarah. "Young Women's Voices Speak Out in Struggle." *The Guardian.* October 17, 1990 (Special Student Issue): p. 9.

Cadden, Vivian and Sheila Kamerman. "Where In the World Is Child Care Better?" *Working Mother.* September 1990: pp. 63–68.

Campbell, Linda P. "Senate Study: Rape an 'Epidemic.'" *Chicago Tribune.* March 22, 1991: section 1, p. 11.

"Campus Reports," *NARAL Campus Newsletter.* Winter 1991: pp. 3–6.

Carter, Hodding III. "Housing Costs Create a New Privileged Class: Home Buyer." *Wall Street Journal.* December 13, 1990: p. A11.

Castro, Janice. "Get Set: Here They Come!" *Time* special fall 1990 women's issue: p. 50.

Celis, William III. "Growing Talk of Date Rape Separates Sex From Assault." *New York Times.* January 2, 1991: pp. A1, B7.

Chapman, Stephen. "Feminism, Children and the Assault on Motherhood." *Chicago Tribune.* January 21, 1990: Section 4, page 3.

Child Care Action Campaign. "Commonly Asked Questions" (data sheet, December 6, 1990), "CCAC Labor Force Predictions" (January/February newsletter), New York.

Children's Defense Fund. "Children 1990: A Report Card, Briefing Book, and Action Primer" (annual report), "Child Care Legislation Within Reach" (data sheet). Washington, D.C., 1990.

Cohen, Marcia. *The Sisterhood: The Inside Story of the Women's Movement and the Leaders Who Made It Happen.* New York: Fawcett Columbine/Ballantine, 1988.

Cohen, Toby. "Women Should 'Act Up' Over Breast Cancer." *Newsday.* October 21, 1990: p. 5.

Cowley, Geoffrey. "A Birth-Control Breakthrough: The FDA Finally Approves a Long-Awaited Implant." *Newsweek.* December 24, 1990: p. 68.

Craver, Shelli. "Students Vote—While You Still Have the Choice." *NARAL Campus Newsletter.* Winter 1991, p. 8.

Crittendon, Danielle. "Sex and the Lonely Girl." *Wall Street Journal.* December 6, 1989: p. A16

Daley, Suzanne. "Girls' Self-Esteem Is Lost On Way to Adolescence, New Study Finds." *New York Times.* January 9, 1991: p. B1.

de Beauvoir, Simone. *The Second Sex.* Original Knopf ed. 1952. New York: Alfred A. Knopf, 1974.

Denworth, Lydia. "Heirs of Uncertainty: The Class of '88." *Ms.* December 1988: pp. 56, 57.

DeParle, Jason, with Peter Applebome. "Ideas to Aid Poor Abound, But Consensus Is Wanting." *New York Times.* January 29, 1991: pp. A1, A12.

DeParle, Jason. "Suffering in the Cities Persists as U.S. Fights Other Battles." *New York Times.* January 27, 1991: p. A1, A15.

Diamond, Deborah Beroset. "Babies in Jeopardy: Mothers and Infants Are Falling Through the Cracks of an Unfriendly System." *Chicago Tribune.* November 4, 1990: section 6, pp. 1, 6.

Dickinson, Eleanor. "Gender Discrimination In the Art Field." Sponsored and distributed by the National Artists Equity Association (Washington, D.C.), Woman's Caucus for Art (Philadelphia), the Coalition of Women's Art Organizations (Port Washington, Wisconsin), and California Lawyers for the Arts (San Francisco) 1990.

"Domestic Abuse Leading Cause of Female Injuries." (Associated Press report) *Chicago Tribune.* August 22, 1990: section 1, pp. 1, 2.

Donovan, Josephine. *Feminist Theory: The Intellectual Traditions of American Feminism.* New York: Frederick Ungar Publishing Company, 1990.

Douglas, Susan J. "The Representation of Women in the News Media." *Extra!* March/April 1991: pp. 2, 3.

Douglas, Susan J. "Twenty Years of Media Strikes Against Feminism." *In These Times.* August 29–September 11, 1989: pp. 18, 19.

Echols, Alice. *Daring to Be Bad: Radical Feminism in America 1967–1975.* Minneapolis: University of Minnesota Press, 1989.

Ehrenreich, Barbara and Deirdre English. "Blowing the Whistle on the 'Mommy Track.'" *Ms.* July/August 1989: p. 56.

Ehrenreich, Barbara. "The Next Act: Torch Passing May Be the Biggest Challenge We've Faced In the Last 20 Years." *Ms.* December 1988: p. 32.

Ehrenreich, Barbara. "Sorry, Sisters, This Is Not the Revolution." *Time* special fall 1990 women's issue: p. 15.

Ehrenreich, Barbara. *The Worst Years of Our Lives.* New York: Pantheon, 1990.

Ferrari, Christina. "Men Who Are Joining the Fight Against Rape." *McCall's*. December 1990: pp. 71–74, 142, 143.

Fields, Suzanne. "Certain Feminists Need to Lighten Up." *Chicago Sun-Times*. May 18, 1990: p. 21.

Fierman, Jackie. "Why Women Still Don't Hit the Top." *Fortune*. July 30, 1990: p. 42.

Finley, Karen. *Shock Treatment*. San Francisco: City Lights Books, 1990.

Firestone, Shulamith. *The Dialectic of Sex: The Case For Feminist Revolution*. New York: Bantam, 1971. (1st ed. William Morrow And Company, 1970.)

Friedan, Betty. *The Second Stage*. New York: Simon and Schuster, 1981.

Friedan, Betty. "It's Time to Mobilize a New Generation Of Daughters." *Chicago Tribune*. November 12, 1989: Section 4, p. 3.

*From Abortion to Reproductive Freedom: Transforming a Movement*. Marilyn Gerber Freid, ed. Boston: South End Press, 1990.

"From First Lady's Husband." *New York Times:* May 4, 1990.

*Fund for the Feminist Majority*. "Abortion Denied: Shattering Young Women's Lives" (data sheet and video). Washington, D.C., 1990.

Garb, Maggie. "Information Is Power Chicago Women Know." *New Directions for Women*. March/April 1990: p. 12.

Gelernter, Carey Quan. "Another Choice: New Contraceptive Holds Promise." *Chicago Tribune*. Section 6, p. 7.

*Gender and Stress*. Rosalind C. Barnett, Lois Biener and Grace K. Baruch, eds. New York: The Free Press, 1987.

Gilden, Dave. "Different Stories: Women with AIDS." *San Francisco Bay Guardian*. November 19, 1990: p. 17.

Goodman, Ellen. "A Proper Match For Commencement Day." *Boston Globe* April 22, 1991: p. A27.

Goodman, Ellen. "The Wellesley Controversy as the Story That Would Not Die." (syndicated from the *Boston Globe) The Kenosha News*. June 8, 1990: p. 10.

Gordon, Lynn. *Gender and Higher Education in the Progressive Era*. New Haven, Connecticut: Yale University Press, 1990.

Gordon, Margaret T. and Stephanie Riger. *The Female Fear*. New York: The Free Press, 1989.

Gross, David M. and Sophronia Scott. "Proceeding With Caution (the twentysomething generation)." *Time*. July 16, 1990: pp. 58–62.

Gross, Jane. "Turning Disease Into a Cause: Breast Cancer Follows AIDS." *New York Times*. January 6, 1991: pp. A1, A10.

Hartmann, Mary S. "Mills Students Provided Eloquent Testimony to the Value of Women's Colleges." *The Chronicle of Higher Education*. July 5, 1990: p. A50.

Hewlett, Sylvia Ann. "Running Hard Just to Keep Up." *Time* special fall 1990 women's issue: p. 54.

Hochschild, Arlie with Anne Machtung. *The Second Shift*. New York: Viking, 1989.

Hooks, Bell. *Feminist Theory From Margin to Center*. Boston: South End Press, 1984.

Hooks, Bell. *Talking Back: Thinking Feminist. Thinking Black*. Boston: South End Press, 1989.

Humphreys, Debra. "Under Attack from the Right. *NWSAction (National Women's Studies Association)*. Winter, 1990: p. 7

Illick, Hilary. "Calling All Students: S.O.S. Organizes Pro-Choice Actions." *New Directions for Women*. January/February 1990: p. 4.

Institute for Women's Policy Research: "Raises and Recognition: Secretaries, Clerical Workers and the Union Wage Premium," "Low-Wage Work, Health Benefits and Family Well-Being." (data sheets) Washington, D.C., 1990.

Ivins, Molly. "Where the Real Sexism Lives: in the Media." *San Francisco Examiner*. May 21, 1990: p. A15.

Katz, Montana and Veronica Vieland. *Get Smart: A Woman's Guide to Equality on Campus*. New York: The Feminist Press at the City University of New York, 1988.

Kessler, Lauren. *After All These Years: Sixties Ideals in a Different World*. New York: Thunder's Mouth Press, 1990.

Kornbluh, Felicia. "Feminism: Still Hazy After All These Years." *Tikkun*. January/February 1991: pp. 23–26, 94–95.

Kot, Greg. "Rock Turns Mean and Ugly." *Chicago Tribune*. Arts Section. November 18, 1990: pp. 4, 5, 17.

Kramarae, Cheris and Paula A. Treichler. *A Feminist Dictionary*. London: Pandora Press, 1985.

Lane, Jenai. *Take Back the Night!* video documentary. Los Angeles, California. Independently produced, 1990.

Larsen, Elizabeth. "Teen Magazines: Selling Lip Gloss, Sex and Anorexia." *Extra!* March/April 1991: p. 11.

Leary, Warren E. "Inquiry Sought on Drug Tests that Exclude Women." *New York Times*. February 28, 1991: p. A20.

Lederer, Laura. *Take Back The Night*. New York: W. Morrow, 1980.

Lee, Martin A., and Normon Solomon. *Unreliable Sources: A Guide to Detecting Bias in News Media*. New York: Lyle Stewart, 1990.

Lessing, Doris. *A Man And Two Women: Stories*. New York: Popular Library, 1963.

Levine, James A. "Fathers and the Corporation." *Across the Board.* March 1986: p. 8.

Levine, Jonathan and Elaine Wishner. "Ignorance and Insensitivity Can Feed Campus Bigotry." *Chicago Tribune.* December 27, 1990: p. 19.

Lewin, Tamar. "Women Found to be Frequent Victims of Assaults By Intimates." *New York Times.* January 17, 1991: p. A12.

Lewis, Neil A. "Guam to Appeal Abortion Ruling." *New York Times.* September 22, 1990: pp. A1, A8.

Lewis, Robert. "College Grads Facing Degree of Frustration." *Chicago Sun-Times.* July 22, 1990: p. 5.

"A Little Publicity Can't Hurt." (Faye Wattleton profile) *Business Week.* March 26, 1990: p. 69.

Lorde, Audre. *Sister Outsider.* Freedom, California: The Crossing Press, 1984.

*Making Face, Making Soul (Hacienda Caras): Creative and Critical Perspectives by Women of Color.* Anzaldua, Gloria, ed. San Francisco: Aunt Lute Foundation Books, 1990.

Mann, Judy. *Mann for All Seasons.* New York: MasterMedia, 1990.

Mansbridge, Jane J. *Why We Lost the ERA.* Chicago: University of Chicago Press, 1986

McBride, Elisa. "Students Organize to Elect Pro-Choice Legislators." *NARAL Campus Newsletter.* Winter 1991: pp. 1, 2.

McClelland, Kent. *"Report on an April 1988 Survey of Controversial Issues at Grinnell College."* (unpublished study.) Grinnell, Iowa: 1989.

Miller, Andrea. "Students Rally 'Round Reproductive Rights." *The Guardian.* October 17, 1990 (Special Student Issue): p. 9.

"Mistletoe Banned As Risky to Women." (Associated Press) *Chicago Sun-Times.* December 17, 1989: p. 26.

Morgan, Robin. *Sisterhood Is Powerful: An Anthology of Writings From the Women's Liberation Movement.* New York: Vintage Books, 1970.

Moskowitz, Milton and Carol Townsend. "The 75 Best Companies for Working Mothers." *Working Mother.* October 1990: p. 31.

"Must Parents Be Told?" (editorial on parental consent laws) *Washington Post.* December 1, 1990: p. A18.

National Commission on Working Women of Wider Opportunities For Women. "Women, Work and Age," "Women and Work," "Women and Nontraditional Work," "Women, Work and the Future." (data sheets). Washington, D.C., 1990.

*National Committee on Pay Equity Newsnotes.* Washington, D.C., October 1990: p. 3.

*National Women's Studies Directory of Women's Studies Programs, Women's Centers, and Women's Research Centers.* 1990 Edition.

Neimark, Jill. "They've Got To Have It: The Twentysomethings Take Over." *Mademoiselle.* December 1991: p. 160.

Neuharth, Al. "Single-Sex Schools: Tunnel-Vision Grads." *USA Today.* May 25, 1990: p. 13A.

"Newspaper Apologizes for Editorial," *Chicago Tribune,* December 22. 1990: Section 1, p. 16.

Nicholas, Susan Cary, Alice M. Price and Rachel Rubin. *Wrights and Wrongs: Women's Struggle for Legal Equality.* 2nd ed. The Feminist Press at the City University of New York, 1986.

Nichols, Bill. "Furor Over Feminism: Wellesley 150 Question First Lady's 'Choices.'" *USA Today.* May 3, 1990: pp. 1, 2.

*Now Hear This: A Collage of Women's Voices.* Robyn Chapel, Farnaz Fatemi and Sarah K. Edelstein, eds. Santa Cruz, California: Girlie Mag Press, 1990.

"NOW May Hurt Itself By Anti-Souter Effort." *Kenosha News* (syndicated from Newsday). September 24, 1990: p. 7.

O'Neil, Kathleen and Bickley Townsend. "American Women Get Mad." *American Demographics.* August 1990: p. 26–29.

Orenstein, Peggy. "Ms. Fights For Its Life." *Mother Jones.* December 1990: p. 83.

Orenstein, Peggy. "The Politics of Birth Control." *Glamour.* October 1990: pp. 264–67, 308, 309.

Outlook 2000, United States Bureau of Labor Statistics, 1989.

Palmer, Louise. "Workers Demand Rights." *New Directions for Women.* January/February 1991: p. 1.

"Panel Decries Lack of Knowledge on Female Biology." (Associated Press) *Chicago Tribune.* December 9, 1990: section 1, p. 20.

Parrent, Joanne. "Looking for Love." *Ms.* January/February 1991: p. 80.

Parsons, Christi. "Abuse of Women More Than Meets the Eye." *Chicago Tribune.* August 26, 1990: Section 2, p. 5.

Pear, Robert. "Bush's Infant Care Proposal Draws Fire in Both Parties." *New York Times.* March 6, 199: p. A11.

Pear, Robert. "Bush Plan to Fight Infant Deaths Would Use Money Going to Poor." *New York Times.* February 7, 1991: pp. A1, A12.

Pinkney, Deborah S. "Visionary: Byllye Avery's Healthy Example Serves to Inspire Others." *Chicago Tribune.* September 7, 1990: Section 6, pp. 1, 8.

"Rape Programs at War With UF." (Associated Press) *Florida Times-Union* (Jacksonville). November 27, 1990: p. B8.

Reid, Peggy. "We Didn't Criticize Mrs. Bush." *New York Times.* May 16, 1990: p. 27.

*Rethinking the Family.* Barrie Thorne, ed. New York: Longman, 1982.

Rich, Adrienne. *Blood, Bread and Poetry: Selected Prose 1979–1985.* New York: W. W. Norton & Company, 1986.

Rich, Adrienne. *The Fact of A Doorframe: Poems Selected Old and New 1950 to 1984.* New York: W. W. Norton & Company, 1984.

Roman, Monica. "Women, Beware: An MBA Doesn't Mean Equal Pay." *Business Week.* October 29, 1990: p. 57.

Royko, Mike. "Man, oh man, let's all loosen up a bit." *Chicago Tribune.* May 22, 1990: section 1, p. 3.

Russell, Diana. *The Secret Trauma: Incest in the Lives of Girls and Women.* New York: Basic Books, 1986.

Salaholz, Eloise. "Teenagers and Abortion." *Newsweek.* January 8, 1990. pp. 32–36.

Sandroff, Ronni. "Sexual Harassment in the Fortune 500." *Working Woman.* December 1988: pp. 69–71.

Schreiber, Le Anne. "Teenage and Pregnant." *Glamour.* March 1991: pp. 236–239, 302–305.

Schifrin, Matthew, with Peter Newcomb. "A Brain for Sin and a Bod for Business." (Madonna profile) *Forbes.* October 1, 1990: pp. 162–166.

Schuessler, Nancy. "Abortion. A Right in Question." *Seventeen.* May 1989: p. 207.

Schwartz, Karin. "Lesbian Invisiblity In the Media." *Extra!* March/April 1991: p. 6.

Sidel, Ruth. *On Her Own: Growing Up in the Shadow of the American Dream.* New York: Viking Penguin, 1990.

Smith, Dinita. "Rule Breaker: 'Ladies First' Is More Than a Song for Queen Latifah." *Chicago Tribune.* December 30, 1990: section 6, p. 3.

Stein, Sharman. "Study Targets Stereotypes of Poverty." *Chicago Tribune.* January 30, 1991: pp. 1, 11.

Steinem, Gloria. *Outrageous Acts and Everyday Rebellions.* New York: Signet, 1983.

Steinem, Gloria. "Sex, Lies & Advertising. *Ms.* July/August 1990: pp. 18–28.

Stevens, Darlene Gavron. "Destination Check: A Look at Our Progress Finds Some Rough Spots Remain." *Chicago Tribune.* April 22, 1990: Section 6, p. 1.

Stiehm, Jamie. "Strong Theme: Madonna Never Sings the Song of a Victim." *Chicago Tribune.* September 22, 1990: Section 6, p. 5.

Stipp, Horst H. "What Is a Working Woman?" *American Demographics.* July 1988.

"Student Creates Teacher Corps." *Chicago Tribune (New York Times News Service Reports).* July 22, 1990: Section 6, p. 2.

"Students Organize Campaign to Build A Women's Center." *New York Times.* June 10, 1990: p. 44.

"Survey of College Freshmen Finds a Shift in Priorities." (Associated Press Report) *New York Times.* January 29, 1991: p. A18.

Swoboda, Frank. "Congress Passes $22 Billion Child-Care Package." *Washington Post.* October 28, 1990: p. A19.

"Tears of a College Crowd." (photo caption for Mills story, Associated Press photo) *The Kenosha News.* May 4, 1990: p. 1.

Templeton, Robin. "Duke Lures Students With Racist Code Words." *The Guardian.* October 17, 1990 (Special Student Issue): p. 4.

"The 35 Million: A Preliminary Report on the Status of Young Women." *Institute For Women's Policy Research,* Washington, D.C. Released October 13, 1990. Conducted by Celia Star Gody, Linda Andrews, and Christine Harter for the Young Women's Project of IWPR. Conclusions are based on data compiled by the U.S. Bureau of the Census in its Current Population Survey; the U.S. Bureau of Labor Statistics; the U.S. Department of Education; Child Trends, Inc.; and the Statistical Abstract of the United States.

Urbanska, Wanda. *The Singular Generation.* New York: Doubleday, 1986.

Tifft, Susan. "On Dollars, Scholars and Gender." *Time.* May 21, 1990: p. 85.

Uchitelle, Louis. "Women's Push Into Work Force Seems to Have Peaked, For Now." *New York Times.* November 24, 1990: pp. A1, A28.

"U.S. Women Run 1-in-9 Risk of Developing Breast Cancer, Group Says." (Associated Press Report) *Chicago Tribune.* p. 11.

Wallis, Claudia. "Onward Women!" *Time.* December 4, 1989: p. 82.

Wattleton, Faye. "Teen-age Pregnancy: The Case for National Action." *The Nation.* July 24/31, 1989: pp. 138–141.

Wiener, Jon. "Racial Hatred Rocks Campuses." *The Nation.* February 27, 1989. (Excerpted in *Utne Reader,* pp. 62–68.)

"Women of the Year." *Glamour.* December 1990: pp. 96–101.

"The Winds of Webster, the Storm of S.O.S." *The S.O.S. Alert!* August 1990, pp. 1, 4.

*Women's Realities, Women's Choices: An Introduction to Women's Studies.* Hunter College Women's Studies Collective, eds. New York: Oxford University Press, 1983.

# Index